WAR MAPS

CAMPAIGNS & BATTLES OF WORLD WAR II

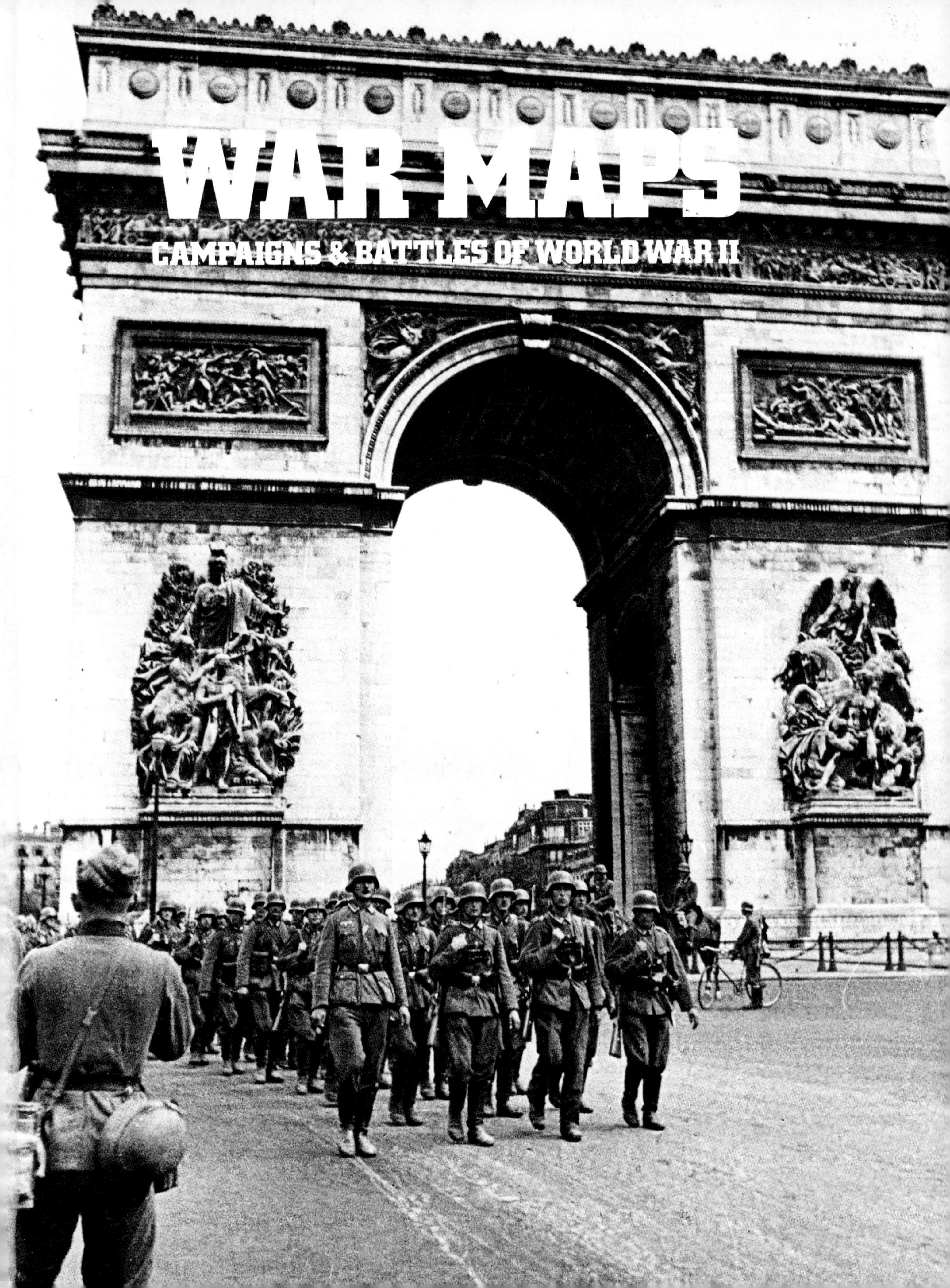

WAR MAPS

CAMPAIGNS & BATTLES OF WORLD WAR II

RICHARD NATKIEL

TEXT BY ROBIN L SOMMER

INTRODUCTION BY S L MAYER

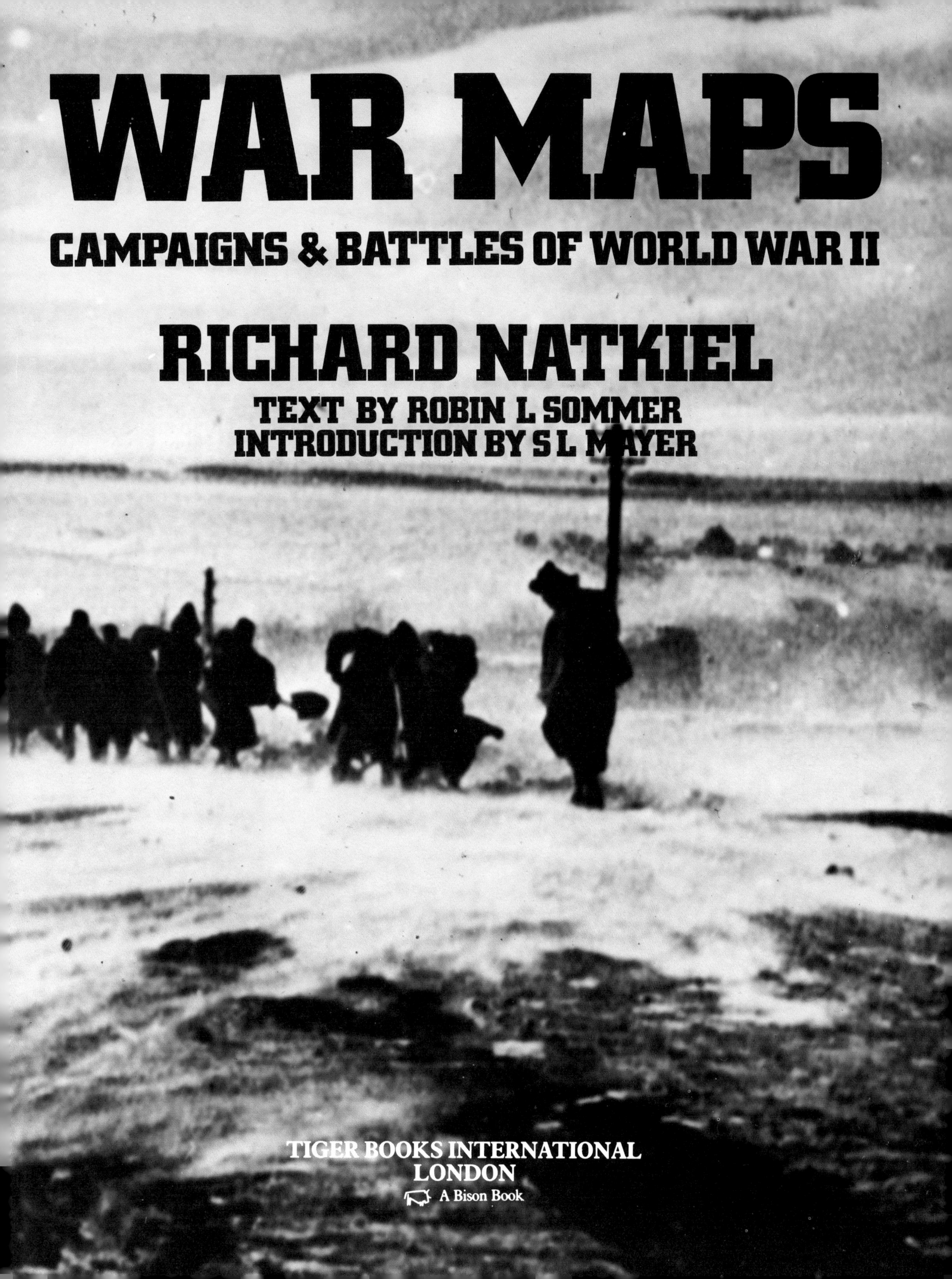

TIGER BOOKS INTERNATIONAL

LONDON

A Bison Book

This edition published by
Tiger Books International Ltd.
London.

Produced by
Bison Books Ltd.
176 Old Brompton Road
London, SW 5
England.

ISBN 1-870461-10-X

Printed in Hong Kong.

Reprinted 1988

Page 1: Occupying German troops march past the Arc de Triomphe, Paris, 1940.
Page 2-3: Italian troops on the Eastern Front, 1942.
This page: US Marines at Iwo Jima plot the position of a Japanese machine gun post, February 1945.

Contents

Introduction

It has often been stated that World War II was part of a European Civil War that began in 1914 at the start of World War I. This is partly true. In Europe, at least, the two world wars were the two hideous halves of the Anglo-German controversy that was at the heart of both conflicts. The question posed was: would Britain be able, or willing, to maintain her vast Empire in the face of German hegemony on the continent of Europe? The answer to that question never came. Britain, in seeking to thwart German interests on the Continent, eventually lost her whole Empire in the attempt –an empire that between the wars encompassed a quarter of the earth's surface and an equal proportion of its population. Put into that context, both world wars were dangerous for Britain to fight, jeopardizing the very existence of the Empire and inevitably weakening the mother country to the point that she could not maintain her world position at the end of the conflicts.

From Germany's point of view, the wars were not only dangerous in that they finally ruined virtually every town and city, devastated the countryside and dismembered the nation; they were irrelevant. In 1890 Germany was in a position from which, within a generation, she would economically dominate the whole of Europe. Inevitably, with that economic hegemony, political hegemony would soon follow, if not even precede. By 1910 the process was well in train; had no one done anything to stop her, Germany would have achieved the Kaiser's dreams without war by the mid 1920s. The collapse of Imperial Germany in 1918, followed by temporary occupation, inflation and national humiliation, set Germany back only a few years. Despite the disasters of World War I and its aftermath, Germany was quickly recovering her old position – roughly that of 1910 – by the time Hitler took power in 1933. By 1938 German power in Europe was greater than ever before, and Britain had to face the old question once again. Could she condone German political dominance of the Continent?

In 1938 some Conservatives, like Chamberlain and Halifax, recognized the threat and were tacitly willing to maintain the Imperial status quo and condone Hitler. Other Tories, like Churchill and the Labour and Liberal Parties, wanted to challenge Germany again. Had Hitler been a bit more discreet and less hurried, perhaps a bit less flamboyant and

Below: Dunkirk, scene of an ignominious retreat by Allied forces that signaled the Fall of France.

virulently anti-Semitic, Chamberlain's policy might have succeeded. Germany would have extended her power in Europe and the Empire would have been maintained. But that was to ask the impossible, to wish that Hitler were someone other than Hitler. The result – humiliation of Britain's policy when Czechoslovakia was overrun in March 1939 – forced even Chamberlain's hand, and the stage was set for round two of the European Civil War.

World War II in Europe was very like a Greek tragedy, wherein the elements of disaster are present before the play begins, and the tragedy is writ all the larger because of the disaster's inevitability. The story of the war, told through the maps of Richard Natkiel in this volume, are signposts for the historian of human folly. In the end, Germany and Italy were destroyed, along with much of Europe. With the devastation came the inevitable collapse of both the impoverished British Empire and centuries of European hegemony in the world. A broader look from the perspective of the 1980s would indicate a further irony. Despite Germany's loss of part of its Polish and Russian territory and its division into two countries, not to mention the separation of Austria from the Reich and the semi-permanent occupation of Berlin, the German economic advance was only delayed, not permanently stopped. The Federal Republic is clearly the strongest economy in Western Europe today and the fourth strongest in the world. The German Democratic Republic rates twelfth on this basis. Together their economies are roughly as strong as that of the Soviet Union, and their political reunification is now less of a dream, more of a reality toward which Germans on both sides of the Iron Curtain are striving. One day, probably within the next two decades, a form of unification may take place, and when it does, German power on the Continent will be greater than ever before. No wonder the Soviets and many Western Europeans view this prospect with fear and cynicism. What had the world wars been for? For what ideals had the blood of tens of millions been spilt?

The irony of World War II becomes even clearer when one views briefly its second half, the struggle between Japan and the United States for control of the Pacific. The question facing American Presidents from Theodore Roosevelt to Franklin Roosevelt had been: could the

Left: The successful Russian defense of Stalingrad was a major setback to German war plans.
Below: Japanese tanks pass a wrecked British ambulance in Burma, 1942.

United States maintain its security and trade routes in the Pacific in the face of an increasingly powerful Japanese Navy and economy? For decades the question was begged, until the Japanese took matters into their own hands at Pearl Harbor, the Philippines, Vietnam and Malaya in 1941. The ensuing tragedy, as inevitable in the Pacific as was its counterpart in Europe, became obvious almost from the outset. Millions died in vain; Japan itself was devastated by fire and atomic bombs, and eventually conceded defeat.

From a forty-year perspective, what was the point of the Pacific War? Japan has the third largest economy in the world and by far the largest in Asia. In recent years the United States has actually encouraged Japan to flex its political muscles, increase its armed forces and help the United States police the Western Pacific. It would seem that this conflict was as tragically futile as the European Civil War.

The greatest disaster in the history of mankind to date was World War II. This atlas is a valuable reference work for those who feel it bears remembering. Clearly, this is the case, but the lessons of the war have been less clearly spelled out – to those who fought in it, who remember it, or who suffered from it, as well as to subsequent generations who were shaped by it and fascinated by its horrific drama. The exceptional maps of Richard Natkiel of *The Economist*, which punctuate this volume, can give only the outlines of the tragedy; they do not seek to give, nor can they give, the lessons to be learned.

It would seem that if anything useful is to be derived from studying World War II, it is this: avoid such conflicts at all costs. No nation can profit from them. This is certainly truer today than if these words had been written in 1945. The advances of science have made a future world conflict even less appetizing to those who are still mad enough to contemplate such a thing. Perhaps the balance of the 20th century and the early years of the 21st will be very like the past 40 years: small conflicts, limited wars, brinkmanship, arms races and world tension – yes; general war, no. If our future takes this course, the period following World War II may be seen by historians of the 21st century as a time similar to the century following the Napoleonic Wars – one of growing world prosperity, which has indeed been apparent for some nations since 1945, many crises, but no all-out war. If that is our future, as it has been our recent past, the study of World War II will have been more than useful. It will have prepared the world psychologically to avoid world conflict at all cost. In that event, for the sake of a relatively stable, increasingly prosperous 'cold peace,' the 1939-45 conflict will not have been in vain. If war is the price for a bloodstained peace, those who will benefit are ourselves and future generations.

S L Mayer

Blitzkrieg

The Swastika Ascendant

The German humiliation at Versailles was skillfully exploited by Adolf Hitler and his Nazis, who rode to power in 1933 on a tide of national resentment that they had channeled to their purpose. The territorial losses, economic hardships and affronts to German pride embodied in the Treaty of Versailles virtually guaranteed the conflict that escalated into World War II. As Marshal Foch had prophesied when the treaty was forced upon a prostrate Germany: 'This is not Peace. It is an Armistice for twenty years.'

Hitler's stormy career seemed to reach its zenith when he seized control of the German Government in March of 1933. In fact, it was only beginning. Hitler implemented a military build-up in defiance of the Versailles Treaty, which had limited German armed forces to an army of 100,000 and a small navy without armor or air force support. Groundwork was laid for a much larger army to be built up by conscription upon a highly trained professional base organized by General Hans von Seeckt. The prohibited tanks and planes were developed secretly, many in the Soviet Union, and future pilots were trained. Meanwhile, the Nazis continued to scapegoat the Jews and other minorities for the nation's problems; they established the first concentration camp at Dachau in the same year they came to power.

Germany withdrew from the League of

German expansion in Europe

Previous page: German blitzkrieg (lightning war) tactics were expertly executed by their highly trained troops.
Below left: Germany's expansion by August 1939.
Bottom left: Detail showing the recently annexed Rhineland and Sudetenland.
Below: The Nuremberg Rally in 1934, with Adolf Hitler (center).

Nations, and by 1935 Hitler could announce repudiation of the Treaty of Versailles. He told the world that the German Air Force had been re-created, and that the army would be strengthened to 300,000 through compulsory military service. The Western democracies, France and Britain, failed to make any meaningful protest, a weakness that encouraged Hitler's ambition to restore Germany to her 'rightful place' as Europe's most powerful nation.

Nazi Germany's first overt move beyond her borders was into the Rhineland, which was reoccupied in 1936. This coup was achieved more through bravado than by superior force. Hitler's generals had counseled against it on account of the relative size of France's army, but the reoccupation was uncontested. The next step was to bring all Germans living outside the Reich into the 'Greater Germany.' Austria was annexed in March 1938, with only token protests from Britain and France. Even more ominous was Hitler's demand that Czechoslovakia turn over its western border – the Sudetenland – on ground that its three million German-speaking inhabitants were oppressed. The Nazis orchestrated a demand for annexation among the Sudeten Germans, and the Czechoslovakian Government prepared to muster its strong armed forces for resistance. Then British Prime Minister Neville Chamberlain flew to Munich to confer with Hitler.

Chamberlain rationalized that the problem was one affecting Central Europe alone, and expressed reluctance to risk war on behalf of 'a far-off country of which we know little.' France had to stand by its alliance with Britain, and the Czechoslovakian democracy was isolated in a rising sea of German expansionism. The Sudetenland, with its vital frontier defenses, was handed over. Far from securing 'peace in our time,' as Neville Chamberlain had promised after Munich, this concession opened the door to Nazi occupation of all Czechoslovakia in March 1939.

Only at this point did the Western democracies grasp the true scope of Hitler's ambitions. Belatedly, they began to rearm after years of war-weary stasis. By now Hitler's forces were more than equal to theirs, and the Führer was looking eastward, where Poland's Danzig Corridor stood between him and East Prussia, the birthplace of German militarism.

The Partition of Poland

France and Britain tried to forestall the Nazi assault on Poland by issuing a joint guarantee to the threatened nation. This was supposed to provide leverage whereby the democracies could persuade the Poles to make concessions similar to those made by the Czechs. But Hitler's aggressiveness grew more apparent throughout the spring and summer of 1939. In April he revoked both the German-Polish Non-Aggression Pact and the Anglo-German Naval Agreement of 1935. Then he sent emissaries to the Soviet Union, where Joachim von Ribbentrop concluded both an economic agreement and a Non-Aggression Pact with Josef Stalin. By 1 September 1939, the Germans were ready to invade Poland on two fronts in their first demonstration of blitzkrieg – lightning war – a strategy that combined surprise, speed and terror. It took German forces just 18 days to conquer Poland, which had no chance to complete its mobilization. The Poles had a bare dozen cavalry brigades and a few light tanks to send against nine armored divisions. A total of five German armies took part in the assault, and German superiority in artillery and infantry was at least three to one. The Polish Air Force was almost entirely destroyed on the ground by the Luftwaffe offensive supporting Army Groups North and South.

Above right: The Nazi thrust into Poland, early September.
Right: Russia counterattacks, mid to late September.
Below: The partition of Poland as agreed by Germany and Russia.

Below: German troops enter Warsaw. The city finally surrendered on 27 September after 56 hours of resistance against air and artillery attack.

Thinly spread Polish troops staggered back from their border, and German forces were approaching Warsaw a week later. The Poles made a last-ditch effort along the Bzura River to halt the German advance against their capital, but they could not withstand the forces pitted against them. The Polish Government fled to Rumania, and on 27 September Warsaw finally capitulated.

Meanwhile, Britain and France had declared war on Germany 48 hours after the invasion of Poland. Australia, New Zealand and South Africa soon joined them. Since the Western Allies had failed in their diplomatic efforts to enlist Soviet support, they faced a united totalitarian front of Hitler's Germany and Stalin's Russia (which could be counted upon to take full advantage of Poland's impotence). Stalin had made it clear that he wanted a free hand in Eastern Europe when he cast his lot with Germany. Before the month of September was out, it became obvious that Russia and Germany had reached a secret agreement on the partition of Poland during the summer months. On 17 September Soviet troops crossed the eastern frontier to take Vilnyas; a German-Soviet Treaty of Friendship was announced two days later. On 28 September, after Warsaw's surrender, Russia annexed 77,000 square miles of eastern Poland. The other 73,000 square miles, bordering on Germany, were declared a Reich protectorate.

Blitzkrieg – North

German expansion in Europe

Hitler counted on Allied reluctance to assume an active role in the war, and he was not disappointed. The six-month hiatus known as the Phony War lasted from September 1939 until April 1940, when Germany invaded Norway and Denmark. In the interim, Britain and France made plans that could only fail, because they were based on a negative concept: avoidance of the costly direct attacks that had characterized World War I. New Anglo-French strategy focused on naval blockade and encirclement – indirect methods that were no match for the new blitzkrieg tactics of Nazi Germany.

Early in 1940 Hitler turned his attention to Scandinavia, where he had a vested interest in Swedish iron ore imports that reached Germany via the Norwegian port of Narvik. Norway had a small Nazi Party, headed by Vidkun Quisling, that could be counted upon for fifth-column support. February brought evidence that the Allies would resist a German incursion into Norway when the *Altmark*, carrying British prisoners, was boarded in Norwegian waters by a British party. Both sides began to make plans for a Northern confrontation.

On 9 April the Germans launched their invasion of Norway and Denmark, based on a bold strategy that called for naval landings at six points in Norway, supported by waves of paratroops. The naval escort for the Narvik landing suffered heavy losses, and the defenders of Oslo sank the cruiser *Blücher* and damaged the pocket battleship *Lützow*. Even so, the Germans seized vital airfields, which allowed them to reinforce their assault units and deploy their warplanes against the Royal Navy ships along the coast.

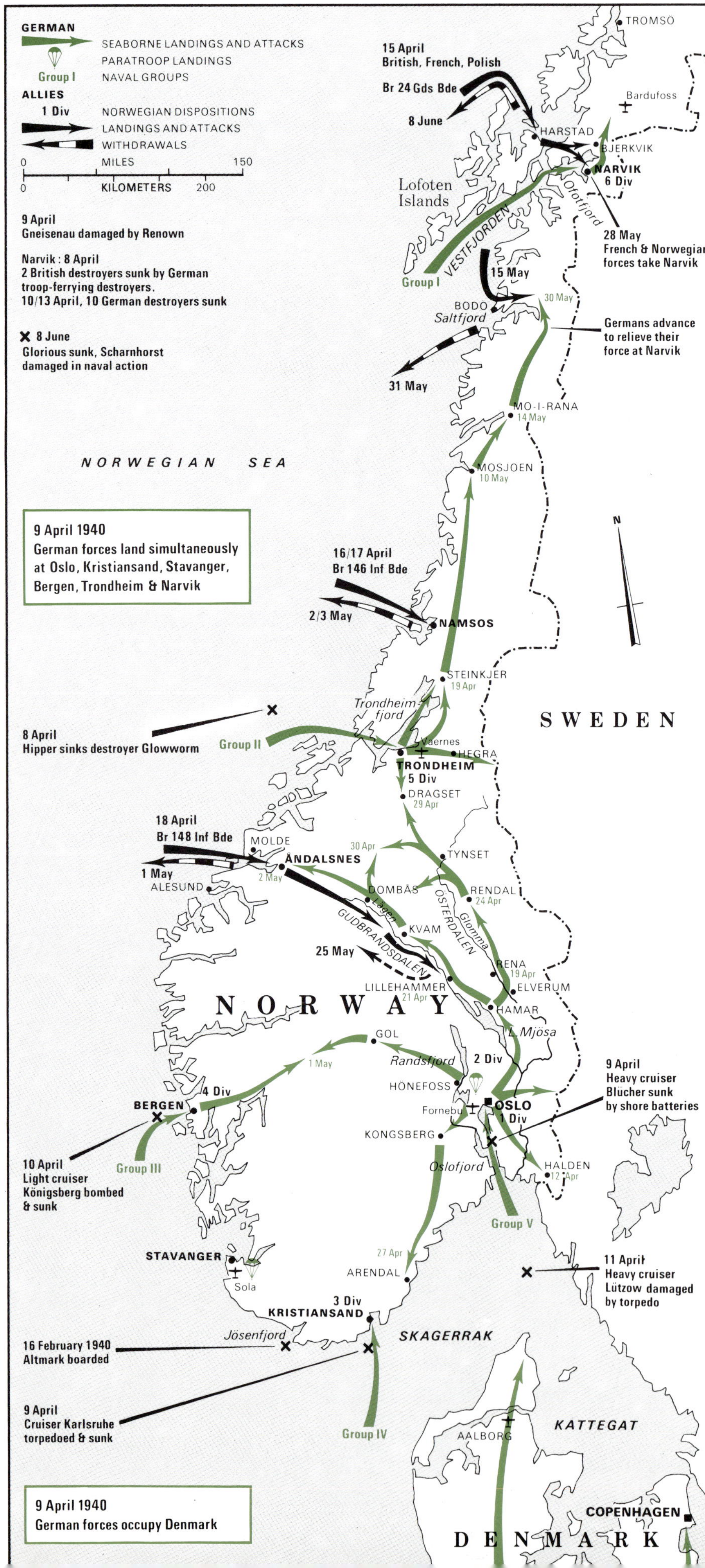

Denmark had already been overrun and posed no threat to German designs.

Norwegian defense forces were weak, and the Germans captured numerous arms depots at the outset, leaving hastily mobilized reservists without any weapons. Allied planning proved wholly inadequate to German professionalism and air superiority. Kristiansand, Stavanger, Bergen, Trondheim and Narvik were all lost to the Germans, along with the country's capital, Oslo. Few Allied troops were trained for landing, and those who did get ashore were poorly supplied.

In May, British, French and Polish forces attempted to recapture two important cities, but their brief success at Narvik was offset by the bungled effort at Trondheim to the south. Troops in that area had to be evacuated within two weeks, and soon after Narvik was abandoned to the Germans when events in France drew off Allied troops.

Norway and Denmark would remain under German occupation throughout the war, and it seemed that Hitler's Scandinavian triumph was complete. However, German naval losses there would hamper plans for the invasion of Britain, and the occupation would tie up numerous German troops for the duration. The Allies were not much consoled by these reflections at the time. The Northern blitzkrieg had been a heavy blow to their morale, and the Germans had gained valuable Atlantic bases for subsequent operations.

Opposite top left: The Reich expands to the north and east.
Opposite: German forces forge through Denmark and make six simultaneous landings in Norway.
Above: A Norwegian port burns as the Germans follow through their surprise attack.

Military Balance in the West

On the Western Front, both Allied and German armies scarcely stirred for six months after the declaration of war. The Allies had an ill-founded faith in their Maginot Line – still incomplete – which stretched only to the Belgian border. The threat of a German attack through Belgium, comparable to the Schlieffen Plan of 1914, was to be met through the Dyle Plan. This strategy called for blocking any advance between the Ardennes and Calais by a swift deployment of troops into Belgium from the vicinity of Sedan.

German General Erich von Manstein anticipated this plan, whose weak link was the hilly Ardennes region – widely believed to be impassable to an advancing army. Manstein prepared for an attack on the Low Countries to draw the Allies forward, followed by a swift surprise breakthrough in the Ardennes that would aim for Calais. This would cut off any Allied troops that had moved into Belgium to implement the Dyle Plan.

The Allies, discounting the possibility of a large-scale German advance through the Ardennes, garrisoned the Maginot Line and deployed their remaining forces along the Franco-Belgian border. There troops stood ready to advance to the River Dyle should the Belgians need assistance. Experienced French and British units were designated for this advance, which left the sector opposite the Ardennes as the most vulnerable part of the Allied line.

On paper, the opposing forces were almost equally matched. The Allies had a total of 149 divisions as against 136 German divisions, with some 3000 armored vehicles to the Germans' 2700. But the Germans had several advantages, not the least of which was superiority in the air – some 6000 fighters and bombers to the Allies' 3300. Less tangible, but no less important, was their innovative and flexible approach to modern warfare. The Allies still clung to outmoded ideas of positional warfare, and wasted their armor in scattered deployments among their infantry divisions. The Germans massed their armor in powerful Panzer groups that could cut a swath through the most determined resistance. Where necessary, dive-bombing Stukas could support German tanks that had outstripped their artillery support in the field. It was a lethal combination.

In organization, too, the Allies lagged far behind the German war machine. Their training, communications and leadership were not comparable to those of Hitler's army, which was characterized

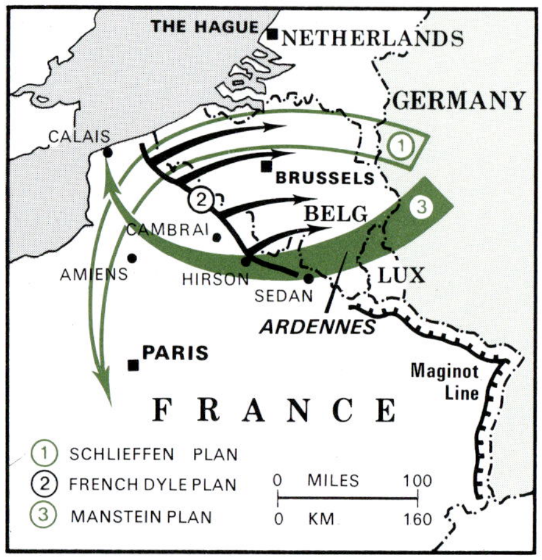

by dynamic co-ordination of every detail. General Maurice Gamelin, Allied Commander in Chief, now in his late sixties, was in far from vigorous health. Considerable friction developed between the British and French commands. The Allies also counted too much upon co-operation from the Belgians and the Dutch, who were slow to commit themselves for fear of provoking a German attack. German leadership, by contrast, was unified and aggressive – provided Hitler did not take a direct hand in military affairs.

Below left: Thrust and counterthrust at the Belgian border.
Bottom left: German soldiers fire at attacking aircraft from the remains of a demolished bridge, Holland, 1940.
Below: The forces of the Reich mass at the Siegfried Line.

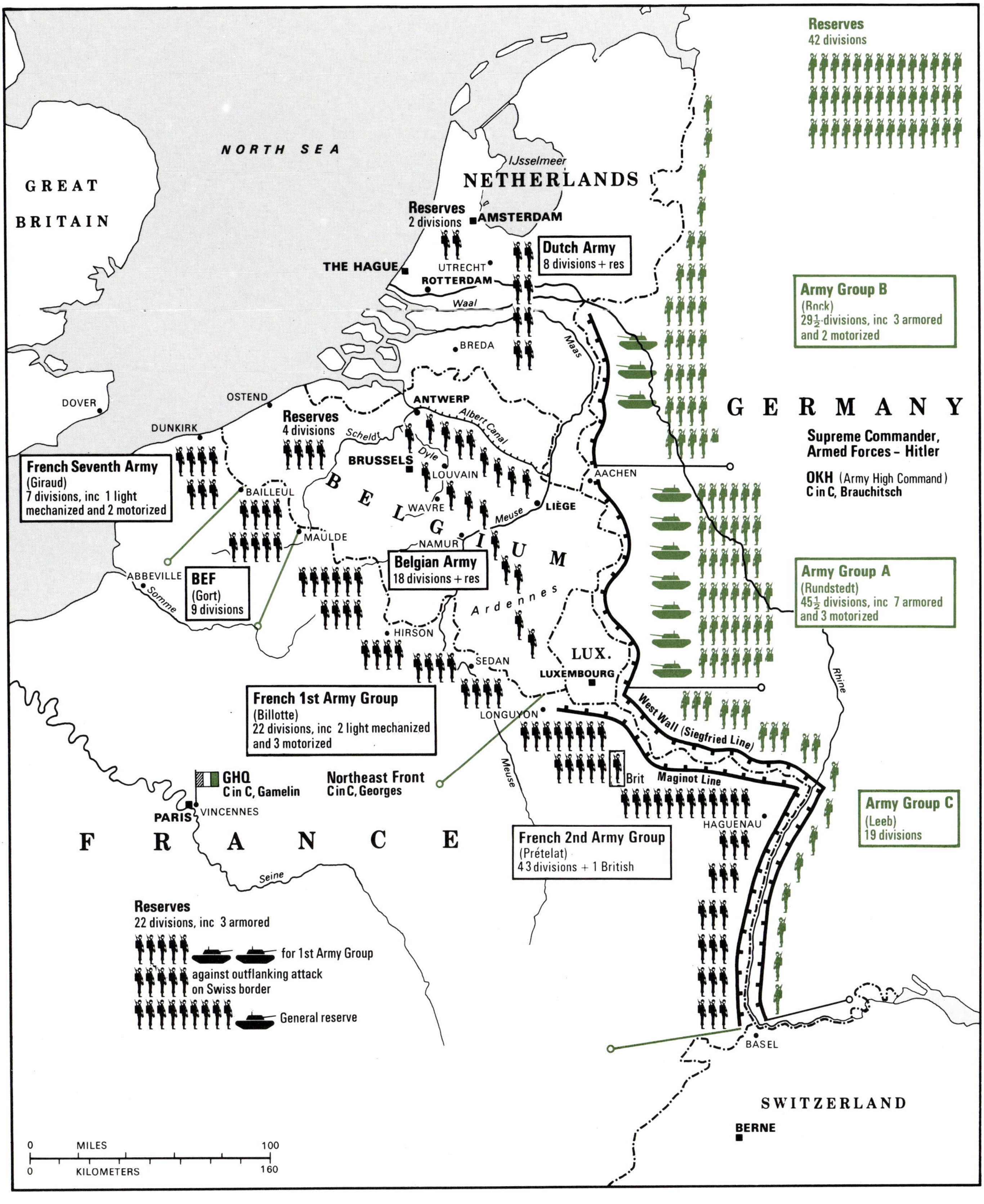

Blitzkrieg – West

The German assault on the West was launched on 10 May 1940, when aerial bombardments and paratroop landings rained down on the Low Countries at daylight. Dutch airfields and bridges were captured, and German troops poured into Holland and Belgium. Both countries called for help from France and Britain, as the Dutch retreated from their borders, flooding their lands and demolishing strategic objectives in an attempt to halt the invasion. Their demoralization was completed by a savage air attack on Rotterdam (14 May), after which Dutch forces surrendered. Queen Wilhelmina and her government were evacuated to England.

The French Seventh Army had tried to intervene in Holland, but it was repulsed. In Belgium, the German capture of Eben Emael, a key fortress, and the accomplishment of Manstein's plan to traverse the Ardennes with his Panzer divisions, gave access to the Meuse. Three bridgeheads were secured by 14 May, and the Allied line had been breached from Sedan to Dinant. The Panzer divisions then made for the sea, forcing back the British Expeditionary Force and two French armies in Belgium. Allied forces were split, and their attempt to link up near Arras (21 May) was a failure. German

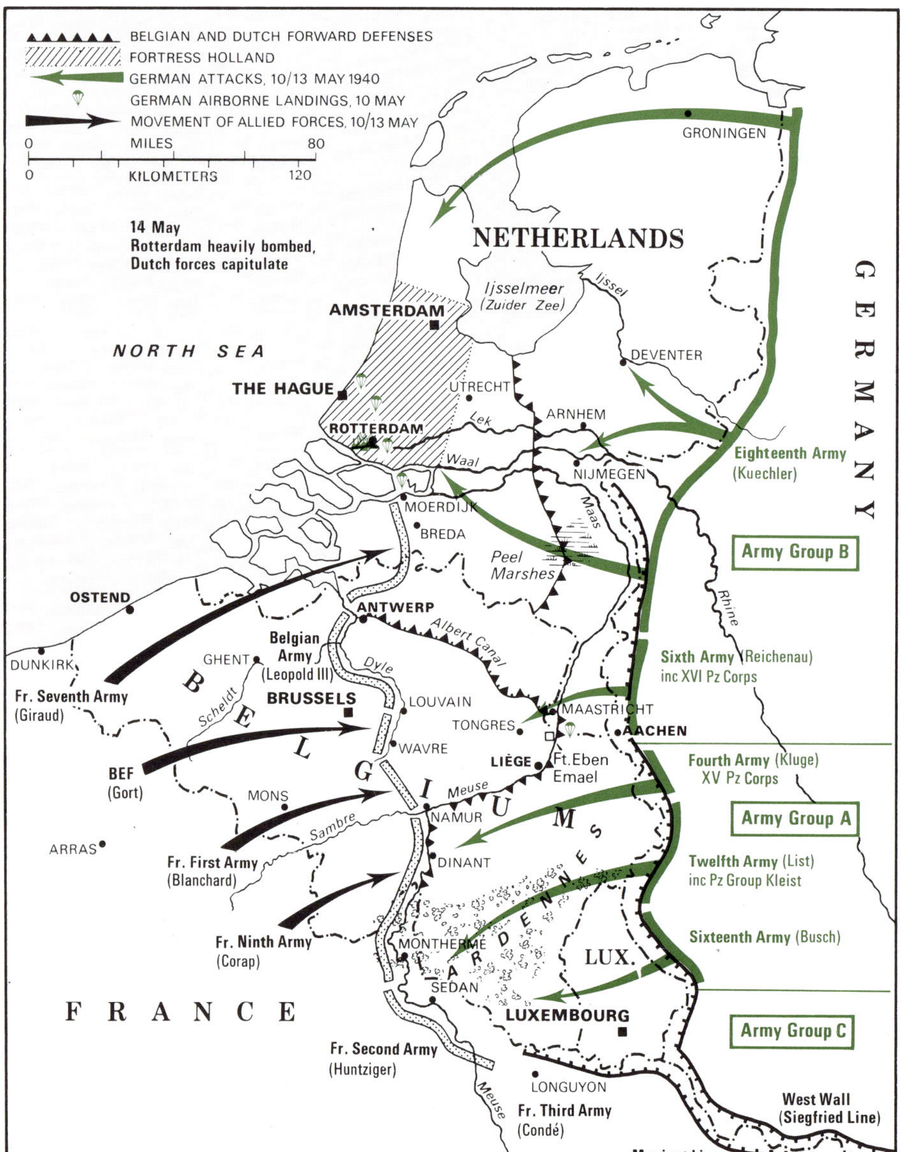

Opposite below: German forces pour into the Low Countries.
Left: Motorized Dutch soldiers are pictured traversing a dyke.
Below: The Panzer thrust to the Meuse.

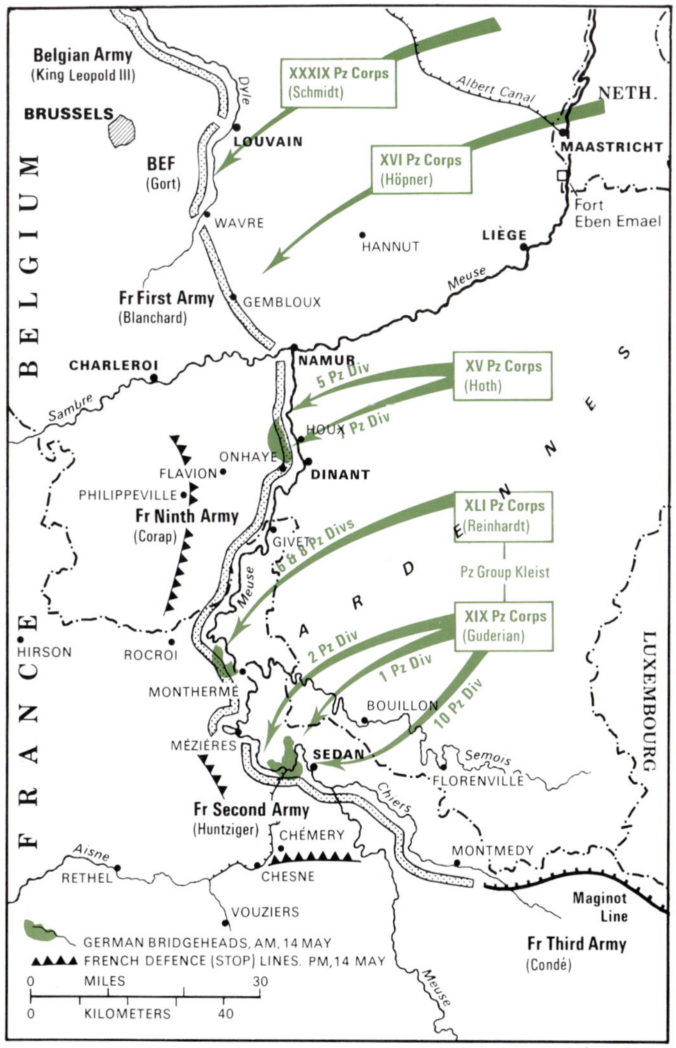

tanks had already reached the sea at Noyelles and were turning north toward the Channel ports.

Only the unwarranted caution of German commanders prevented wholesale destruction of Allied forces in Belgium. On 23 May orders to halt came down from Hitler and Field Marshal Gerd von Rundstedt. The German advance did not resume until 26 May, and the beleaguered Allies were able to fall back around Dunkirk.

Dunkirk and the Fall of France

A determined defense at Calais, and German failure to capitalize on the chance of seizing the Channel ports, enabled the Royal Navy to begin evacuating British troops from Dunkirk. Between 27 May, when Allied resistance at Calais ended, and 4 June, 338,226 men of the British Expeditionary Force left Dunkirk along with 120,000 French soldiers. The Germans tried to prevent the rescue operation with attacks by the Luftwaffe, but the Royal Air Force distinguished itself in safeguarding the exodus. With the loss of only 29 planes, RAF pilots accounted for 179 German aircraft in the four-day period beginning 27 May. Royal Navy losses totaled six destroyers sunk and 19 badly damaged, plus many smaller craft. The toll in lives and matériel would have been much higher had chance not favored the Allies in the form of Germany's inexplicable pause at Noyelles.

To the south, General Maxime Weygand tried to rally remaining French forces for defense of the Somme Line. The Germans began to attack south on 5 June, and the line gave way despite courageous fighting by many French units. By 10 June the Germans had crossed the Seine, and Mussolini took advantage of the situation by declaring war on France. Italian troops moved in and encountered stiff resistance, but overall French morale and confidence were at a low ebb. The government removed to Bordeaux and rejected Prime Minister Winston Churchill's offer of a union between Britain and France. By 16 June Premier Reynaud was resigning in favor of Marshal Henri Pétain, who announced the next day that France was seeking an armistice.

The conquered nation was divided into occupied and unoccupied zones. The Pétain Government would rule the unoccupied zone from Vichy and collaborate closely with the Germans, to the revulsion of most Frenchmen. The 'Free French,' led by Charles de Gaulle, a young army officer and politician, repudiated the Vichy régime and departed for England, where de Gaulle announced that France would ultimately throw off the German oppressors.

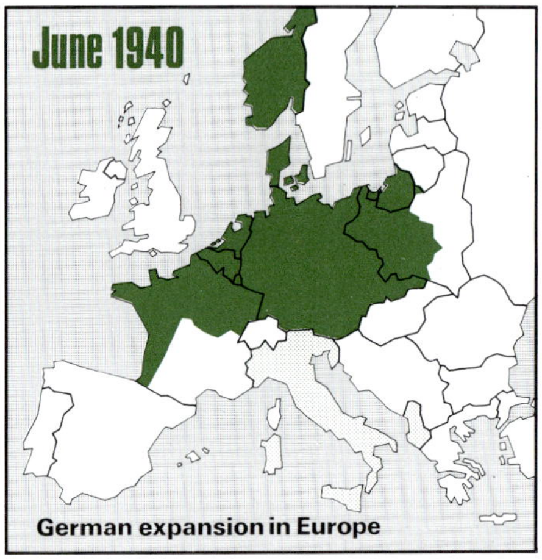

Above: Germany expands westwards to the Channel coast.
Below: The Allied front line contracts as France and Belgium are overrun.

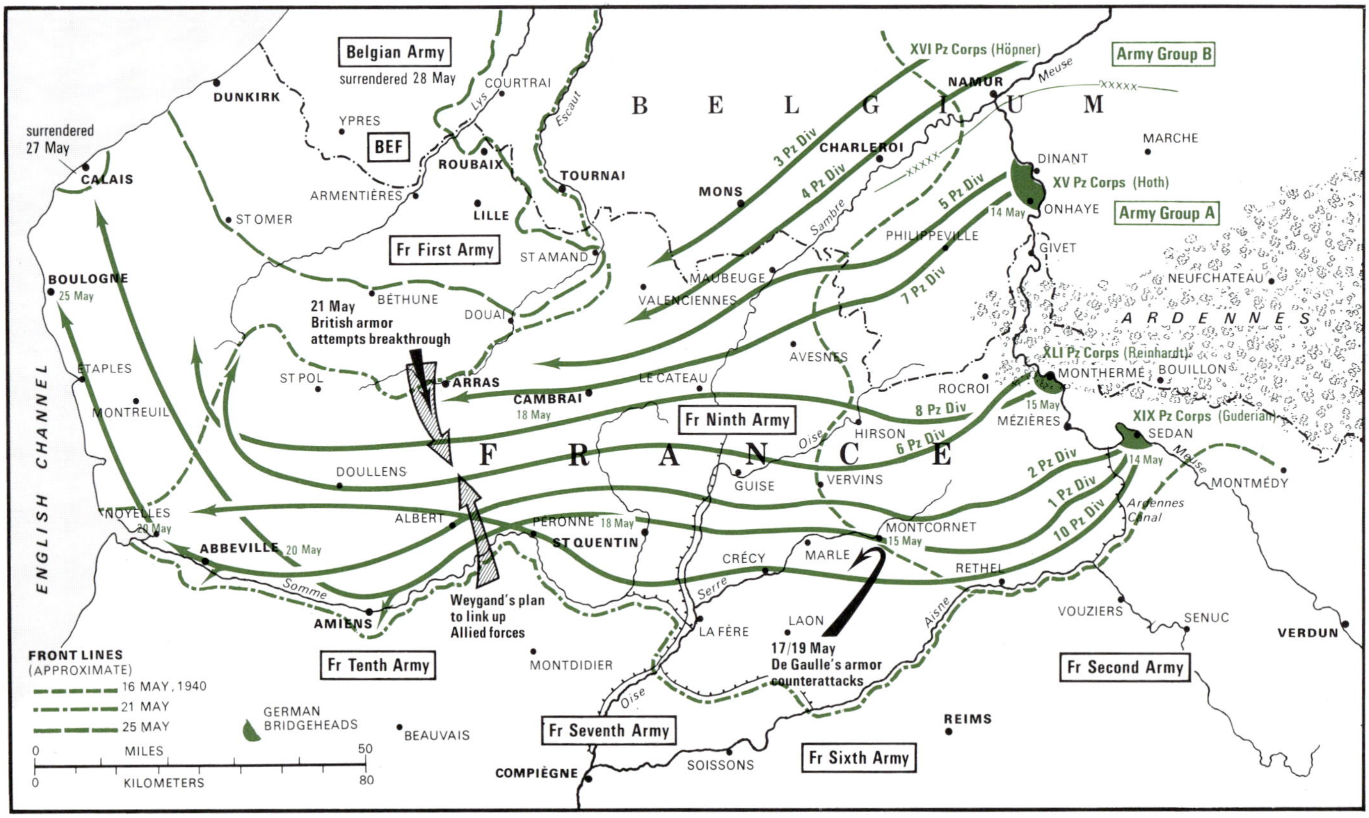

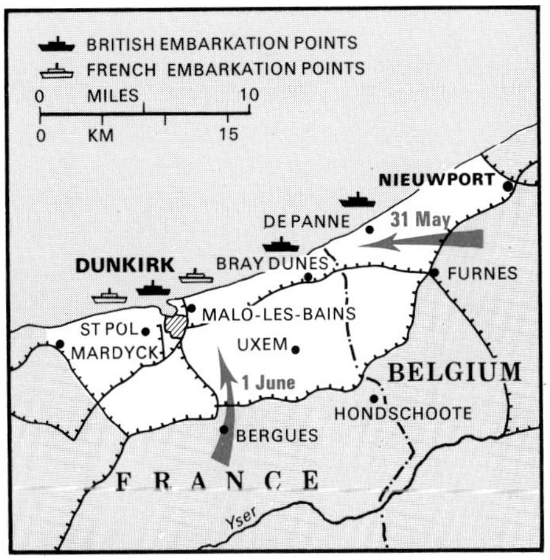

Far left: The Allies prepare to evacuate as the Germans advance.
Left: France divided under Nazi and Vichy rule.
Below: The occupying forces move into Paris in June.

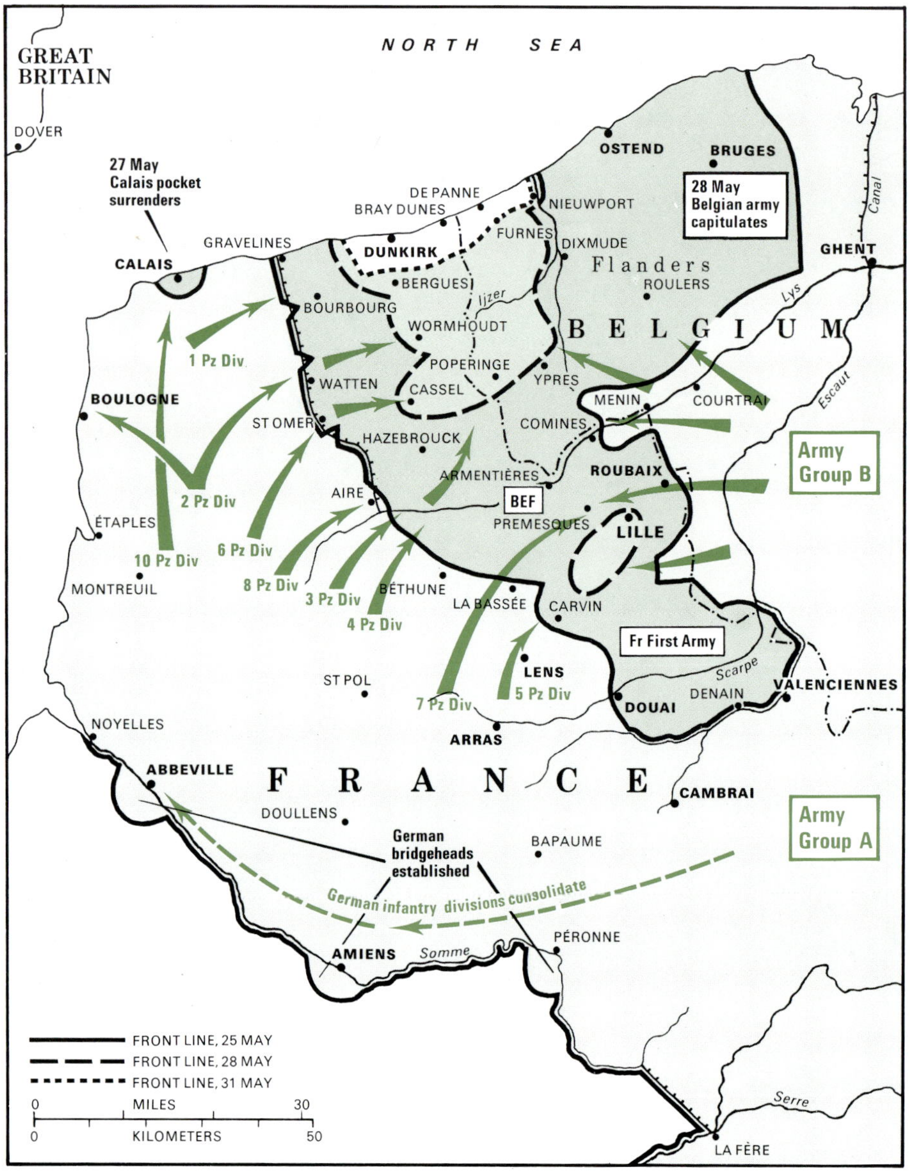

Left: German vacillation and the spirited defense of Calais gave the Allies time to evacuate from Dunkirk.
Below: A British soldier is hit by strafing Luftwaffe aircraft on the Dunkirk beach.
Bottom: The British Expeditionary Force and their French allies await departure.
Right: The aftermath of evacuation.
Below right: The German sweep southwards through France that resulted in the 22 June armistice. Note Italian incursions from the southeast.

L 181940

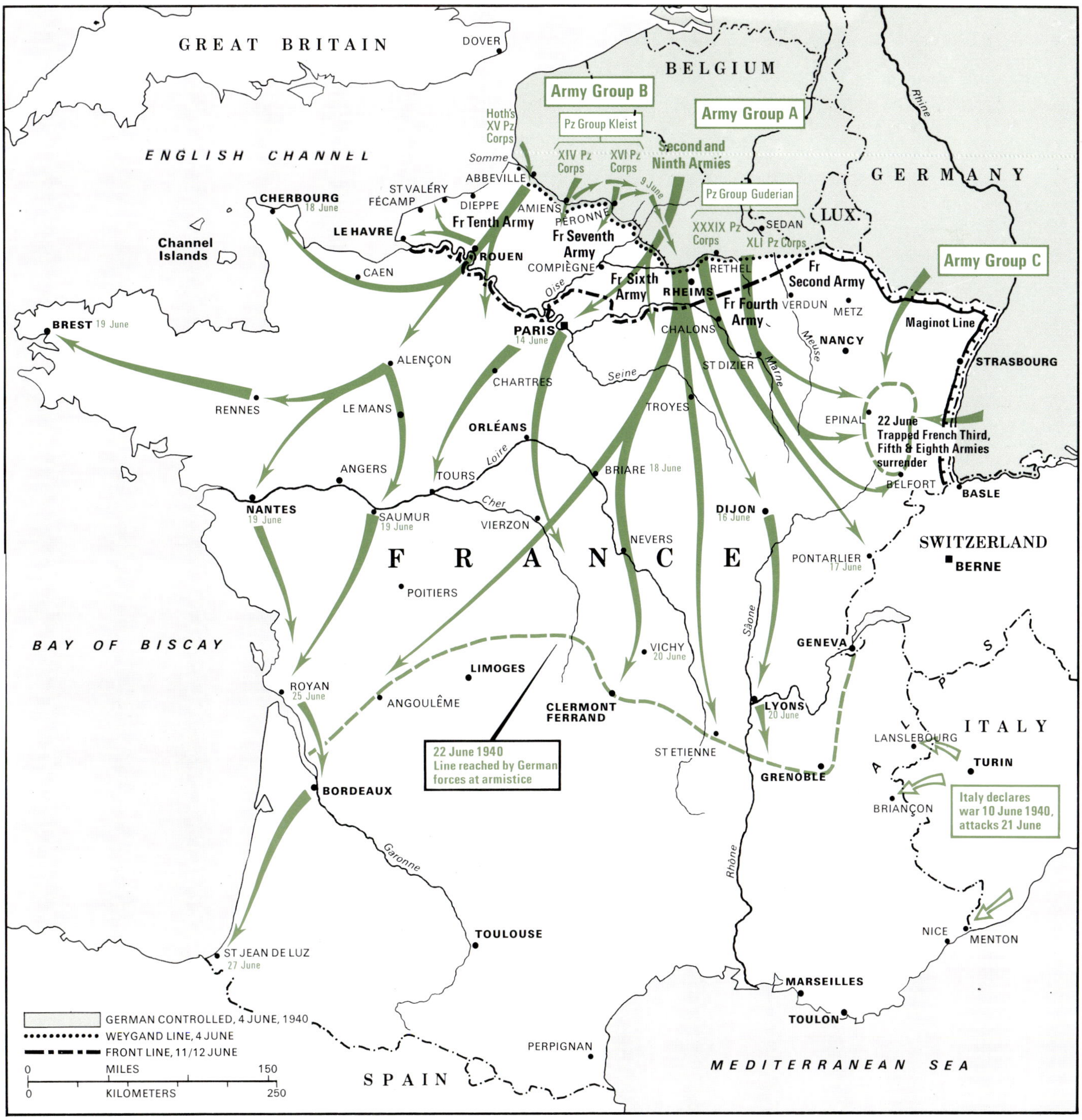
GREAT BRITAIN
DOVER
BELGIUM
Army Group B
Army Group A
Hoth's XV Pz Corps
Pz Group Kleist
XIV Pz Corps
XVI Pz Corps
Second and Ninth Armies
9 June
ENGLISH CHANNEL
Somme
ABBEVILLE
ST VALÉRY
FÉCAMP
DIEPPE
AMIENS
PERONNE
CHERBOURG 18 June
LE HAVRE
Fr Tenth Army
Fr Seventh Army
Pz Group Guderian
XXXIX Pz Corps
XLI Pz Corps
SEDAN
LUX.
GERMANY
Rhine
Channel Islands
ROUEN
CAEN
COMPIÈGNE
RETHEL
Fr Second Army
Army Group C
Oise
Fr Sixth Army
RHEIMS
Fr Fourth Army
VERDUN
METZ
BREST 19 June
PARIS 14 June
CHALONS
Maginot Line
NANCY
Meuse
ALENÇON
ST DIZIER
Marne
STRASBOURG
CHARTRES
Seine
RENNES
LE MANS
TROYES
EPINAL
22 June Trapped French Third, Fifth & Eighth Armies surrender
ORLÉANS
Loire
ANGERS
TOURS
BRIARE 18 June
BELFORT
BASLE
NANTES 19 June
SAUMUR 19 June
Cher
VIERZON
DIJON 16 June
NEVERS
SWITZERLAND
FRANCE
PONTARLIER 17 June
BERNE
POITIERS
Saône
BAY OF BISCAY
GENEVA
VICHY 20 June
ALPS
LIMOGES
ROYAN 25 June
ANGOULÊME
CLERMONT FERRAND
LYONS 20 June
ITALY
LANSLEBOURG
TURIN
22 June 1940 Line reached by German forces at armistice
ST ETIENNE
GRENOBLE
BORDEAUX
BRIANÇON
Italy declares war 10 June 1940, attacks 21 June
Garonne
Rhône
TOULOUSE
NICE
MENTON
ST JEAN DE LUZ 27 June
MARSEILLES
TOULON
GERMAN CONTROLLED, 4 JUNE, 1940
WEYGAND LINE, 4 JUNE
FRONT LINE, 11/12 JUNE
0 MILES 150
0 KILOMETERS 250
PERPIGNAN
SPAIN
MEDITERRANEAN SEA

The Attack on Britain

Right: The stage is set for the Battle of Britain, 1940.
Below: London's dockland burns after one of the first major bombing raids on the capital, 7 September 1940.

The Battle of Britain was fought in the air to prevent a seaborne invasion of the British Isles. The German invasion plan, code-named Operation Sealion, took shape when Britain failed to sue for peace, as Hitler had expected, after the fall of France. On 16 July 1940, German Armed Forces were advised that the Luftwaffe must defeat the RAF, so that Royal Navy ships would be unprotected if they tried to prevent a cross-Channel invasion. It was an ambitious project for the relatively small German Navy, but success would hinge upon air power, not sea power.

There were only some 25 divisions on British home ground, widely scattered and ill supplied with equipment and transport. The RAF alone could gain the time necessary for the army to re-equip after Dunkirk, and hold off the Germans until stormy fall weather made it impossible to launch Operation Sealion. The air arm was well led by Air Chief Marshal Hugh Dowding, who made the most of his relatively small but skillful force. The RAF had the advantage of a good radar system, which the Germans unwisely neglected to destroy, and profited also from the German High Command's decision to concentrate on the cities rather than airfields.

All-out Luftwaffe attacks did not begin until 13 August, which gave Britain time to make good some of the losses incurred at Dunkirk and to train additional pilots. On 7 September London became the main German target, relieving pressure on British airfields which had suffered in earlier bombings. RAF pilots who were shot down unwounded could, and often did, return to combat on the same day, while German pilots were captured. The short-range Messerschmitt Bf 109 could stay over England only briefly if it were

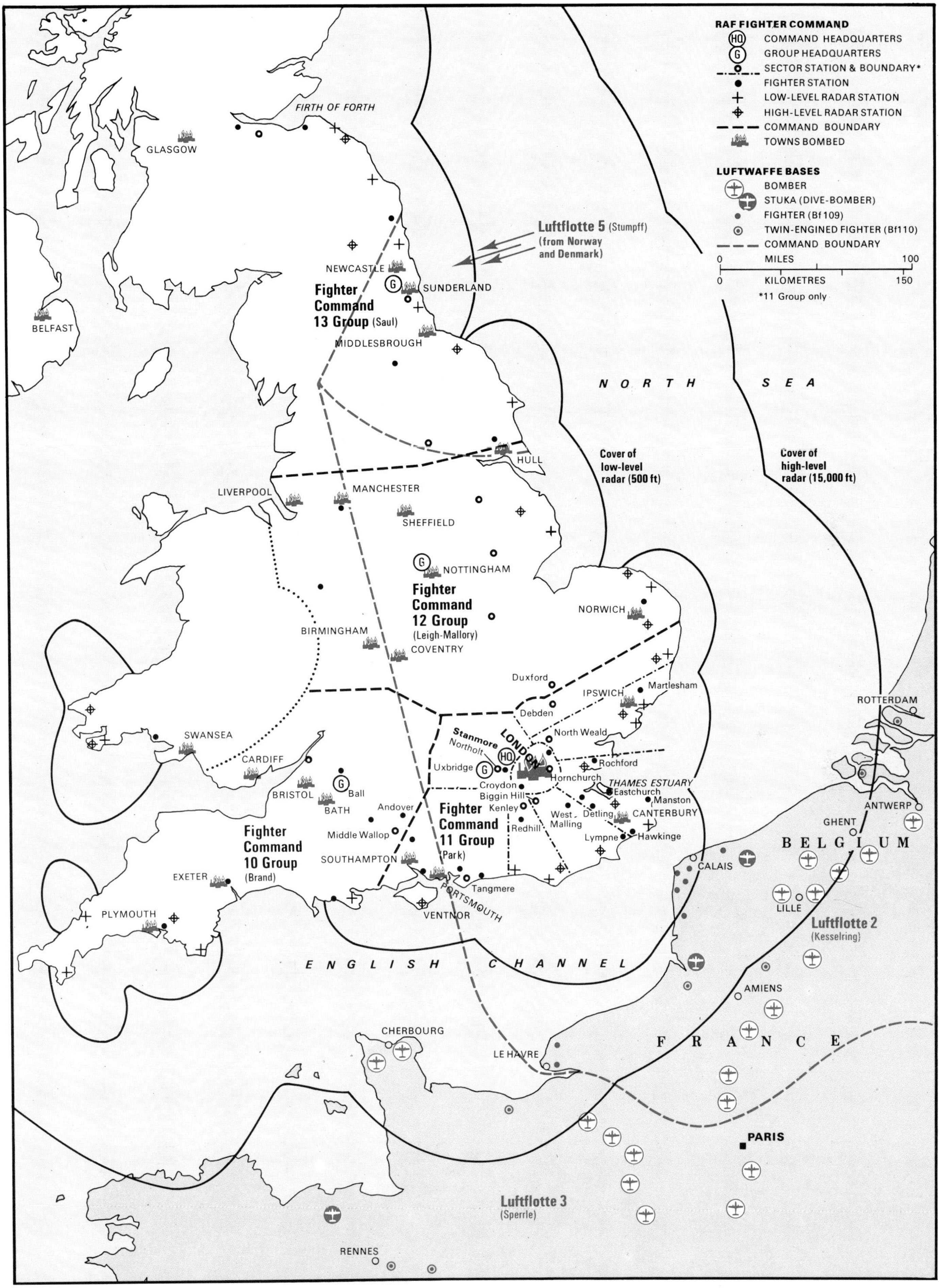
RAF FIGHTER COMMAND
COMMAND HEADQUARTERS
GROUP HEADQUARTERS
SECTOR STATION & BOUNDARY*
FIGHTER STATION
LOW-LEVEL RADAR STATION
HIGH-LEVEL RADAR STATION
COMMAND BOUNDARY
TOWNS BOMBED
LUFTWAFFE BASES
BOMBER
STUKA (DIVE-BOMBER)
FIGHTER (Bf 109)
TWIN-ENGINED FIGHTER (Bf110)
COMMAND BOUNDARY
0 MILES 100
0 KILOMETRES 150
*11 Group only
FIRTH OF FORTH
GLASGOW
BELFAST
NEWCASTLE
SUNDERLAND
MIDDLESBROUGH
Fighter Command 13 Group (Saul)
Luftflotte 5 (Stumpff) (from Norway and Denmark)
NORTH SEA
HULL
Cover of low-level radar (500 ft)
Cover of high-level radar (15,000 ft)
LIVERPOOL
MANCHESTER
SHEFFIELD
NOTTINGHAM
Fighter Command 12 Group (Leigh-Mallory)
NORWICH
BIRMINGHAM
COVENTRY
Duxford
IPSWICH
Martlesham
Debden
North Weald
Stanmore
Northolt
LONDON
Rochford
Uxbridge
Hornchurch
THAMES ESTUARY
Eastchurch
Manston
Croydon
Biggin Hill
Kenley
West Malling
Detling
CANTERBURY
Redhill
Lympne
Hawkinge
Fighter Command 11 Group (Park)
SWANSEA
CARDIFF
BRISTOL
BATH
Ball
Andover
Middle Wallop
SOUTHAMPTON
Fighter Command 10 Group (Brand)
EXETER
PLYMOUTH
Tangmere
PORTSMOUTH
VENTNOR
ENGLISH CHANNEL
ROTTERDAM
ANTWERP
GHENT
BELGIUM
CALAIS
LILLE
Luftflotte 2 (Kesselring)
AMIENS
CHERBOURG
LE HAVRE
FRANCE
PARIS
Luftflotte 3 (Sperrle)
RENNES

Bottom: Two Luftwaffe Dornier Do 17 bombers over the River Thames, September 1940.
Right: Aftermath of heavy night bombing in the Midlands city of Coventry two months later.

to return to its base in France, which helped cancel out the German superiority in numbers of planes and pilots.

The Battle of Britain raged in the skies for almost two months, while a German fleet of barges and steamers awaited the signal to depart the Channel ports for the British coast. By mid September, the invasion date had already been put off three times, and Hitler had to concede that the Luftwaffe had failed in its mission. Sporadic German bombing would continue until well into 1941, but Operation Sealion was 'postponed' indefinitely.

The Invasion of Yugoslavia

On 6 April 1941, the Germans moved to extend their influence in the Balkans by an attack on Yugoslavia, whose Regent, Prince Paul, had been coerced into signing the Tripartite Pact on 25 March. As a result, he was deposed by a Serbian coalition that placed King Peter on the throne in a government that would last only a matter of days. Hitler ordered 33 divisions into Yugoslavia, and heavy air raids struck Belgrade in a new display of blitzkrieg. At the same time, the Yugoslav Air Force was knocked out before it could come to the nation's defense.

The German plan called for an incursion from Bulgaria by the Twelfth Army, which would aim south toward Skopje and Monastir to prevent Greek assistance to the Yugoslavs. Thence they would move into Greece itself, for the invasion that had been planned since the previous year. Two days later, General Paul von Kleist would lead his First Panzer Group toward Nis and Belgrade, where it would be joined by the Second Army and other units that included Italians, Hungarians and Germans.

The plan worked smoothly, and there was little resistance to any of the attacks mounted between 6 and 17 April, when an armistice was agreed after King Peter left the country. Internal dissension among the various Yugoslavian states was a help to the Germans, who lost fewer than 200 men in the entire campaign. Another factor in their favor was the defenders' use of an ineffectual cordon deployment that was no match for the strength and numbers thrown against them. German air superiority completed the case against Yugoslavian autonomy.

Below: Yugoslavia falls in the face of pressure from Germany, Hungary and Italy, April 1941.

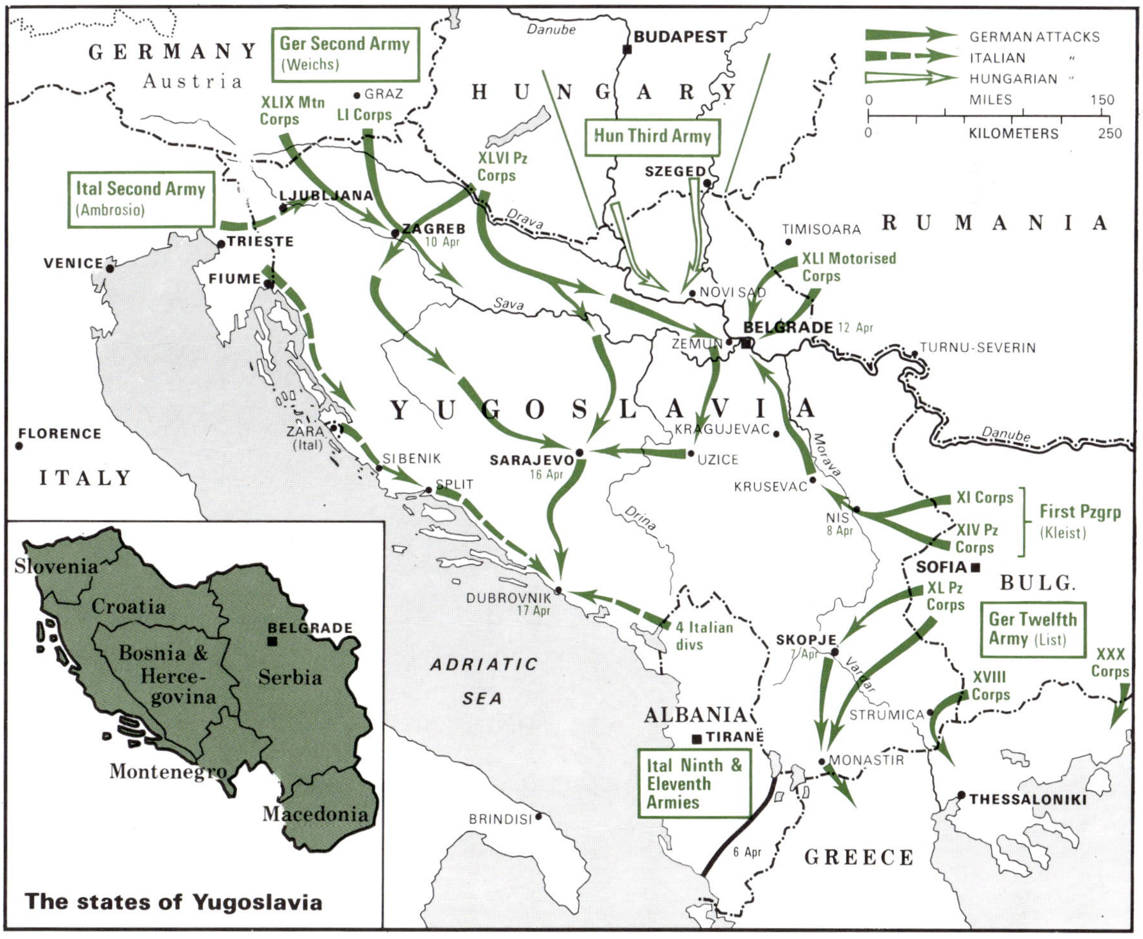

The Battle for Greece

Below: Italian attacks and Greek counteroffensives, winter 1940-41. Right: The British evacuate the Greek mainland as Axis forces thrust southwards.

The overthrow of Yugoslavia's Regency Government on 27 March 1941 changed Hitler's scenario for southeastern Europe. Prior to that, he had planned to assist his Italian allies in their ill-starred Greek campaign by persuading Bulgaria and Yugoslavia to allow his troops free passage into Greece. Now he would have to invade both Yugoslavia and Greece, where the British were landing over 50,000 men in an attempt to enforce their 1939 guarantee of Greek independence.

Mussolini's forces had crossed the Greek frontier into Albania on 28 October 1940, but their fortunes had been going downhill since November. The Greeks mobilized rapidly and pushed the Italians back until half of Albania was recovered, with British assistance, by March of 1941. The prospect of his ally's defeat, coupled with British proximity to the oil fields of Rumania, motivated Hitler to send three full army corps, with a strong armor component, into Greece. The attack was launched on 6 April, simultaneously with the invasion of Yugoslavia.

Allied forces in Greece included seven Greek divisions – none of them strong – less than two divisions from Australia and New Zealand, and a British armored brigade, as well as the forces deployed in Albania. British leaders wanted to base their defense on the Aliakmon Line, where topography favored them, with sufficient forces to close the Monastir Gap. But the Greek Commander in Chief held out for a futile attempt to protect Greek Macedonia, which drew off much-needed troops to the less-defensible Metaxas Line. The Germans seized their chance to destroy this line in direct attacks and push other troops through the Monastir Gap to outflank the Allied defense lines.

By 10 April the German offensive was in high gear and rolling over the Aliakmon Line, which had to be evacuated. A week later, General Archibald Wavell declined to send any more British reinforcements from Egypt – a sure sign that the fight for Greece was being abandoned. Some 43,000 men were evacuated to Crete before the Germans closed the last Peloponnesian port at Kalamata; 11,000 others were left behind.

Right: German mountain infantry march through the township of Lamia in April 1941.

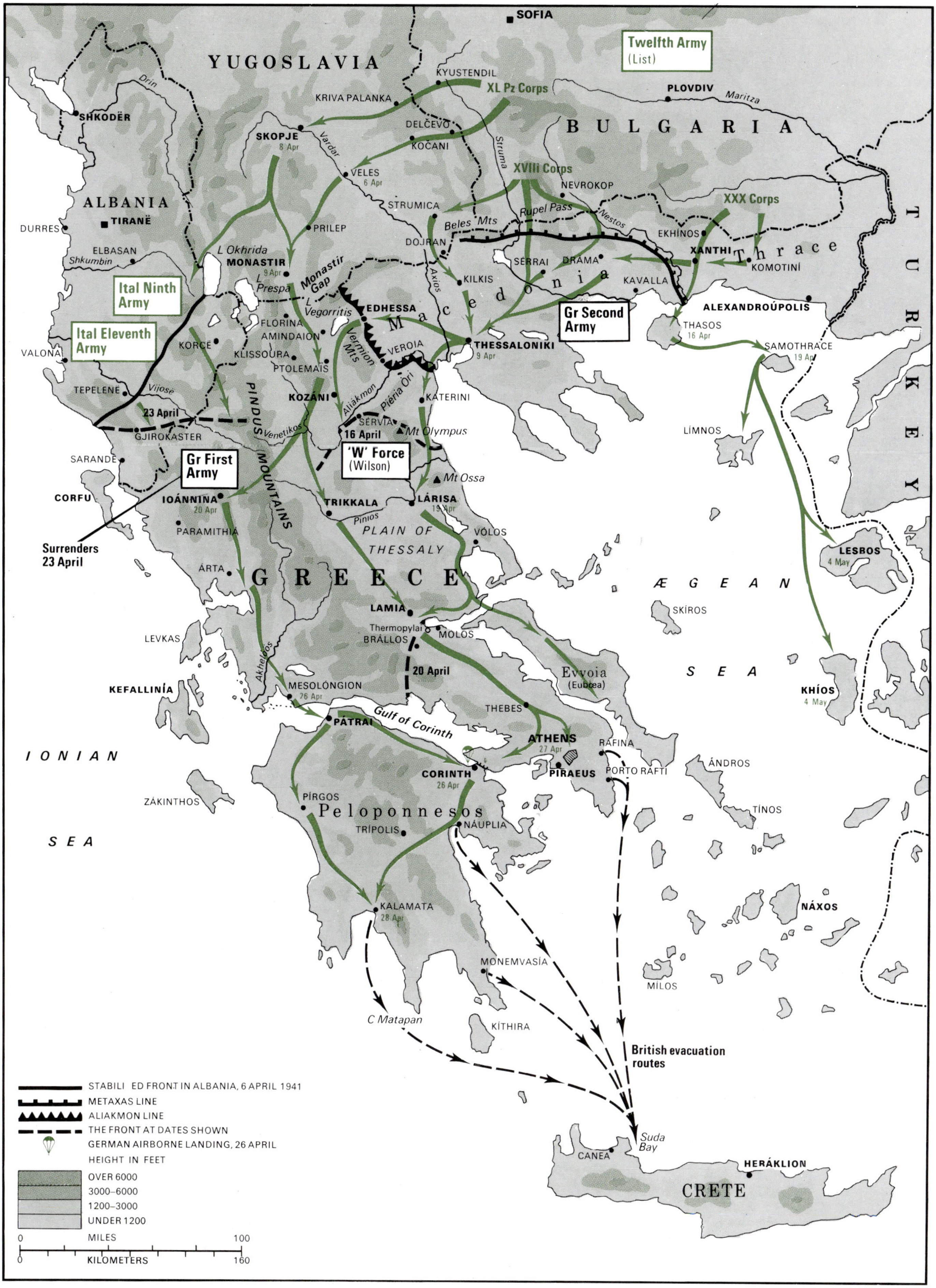
SOFIA
Twelfth Army
(List)
YUGOSLAVIA
KYUSTENDIL
XL Pz Corps
KRIVA PALANKA
PLOVDIV
Maritza
Drin
SHKODËR
DELČEVO
SKOPJE
8 Apr
KOČANI
BULGARIA
Vardar
Struma
VELES
6 Apr
XVIII Corps
NEVROKOP
ALBANIA
TIRANË
STRUMICA
Rupel Pass
XXX Corps
DURRES
PRILEP
Beles Mts
Nestos
EKHÍNOS
TURKEY
L Okhrida
DOJRAN
XANTHI
Thrace
ELBASAN
Shkumbin
MONASTIR
9 Apr
SERRAI
DRAMA
KOMOTINÍ
Monastir Gap
L Prespa
KILKIS
Axios
Macedonia
KAVALLA
Ital Ninth Army
L Vegorritis
EDHESSA
Gr Second Army
ALEXANDROÚPOLIS
FLORINA
THASOS
16 Apr
Ital Eleventh Army
AMINDAION
Vermion Mts
THESSALONIKI
9 Apr
SAMOTHRACE
19 Apr
VALONA
KORCË
KLISSOURA
VEROIA
PTOLEMAÏS
TEPELENE
Vijose
KOZÁNI
Aliákmon
Piéria Ori
KATERINI
PINDUS MOUNTAINS
23 April
SERVIA
Mt Olympus
LÍMNOS
GJIROKASTER
Venetikos
16 April
SARANDË
'W' Force
(Wilson)
Gr First Army
Mt Ossa
CORFU
IOÁNNINA
20 Apr
TRIKKALA
LÁRISA
19 Apr
Pinios
PARAMITHIÁ
PLAIN OF THESSALY
VÓLOS
Surrenders
23 April
LESBOS
4 May
ÁRTA
GREECE
ÆGEAN
LAMIA
SKÍROS
Thermopylai
BRÁLLOS
MOLOS
LEVKAS
20 April
Evvoia
(Eubœa)
SEA
Akhelóos
KEFALLINÍA
MESOLÓNGION
26 Apr
KHÍOS
4 May
THEBES
PÁTRAI
Gulf of Corinth
ATHENS
27 Apr
RAFINA
IONIAN
CORINTH
26 Apr
PIRAEUS
PORTO RAFTI
ÁNDROS
ZÁKINTHOS
PÍRGOS
Peloponnesos
TÍNOS
NÁUPLIA
TRÍPOLIS
SEA
KALAMATA
28 Apr
NÁXOS
MONEMVASÍA
MILOS
C Matapan
KÍTHIRA
British evacuation routes
Suda Bay
CANEA
HERÁKLION
CRETE
STABILIZED FRONT IN ALBANIA, 6 APRIL 1941
METAXAS LINE
ALIAKMON LINE
THE FRONT AT DATES SHOWN
GERMAN AIRBORNE LANDING, 26 APRIL
HEIGHT IN FEET
OVER 6000
3000–6000
1200–3000
UNDER 1200
0 MILES 100
0 KILOMETERS 160

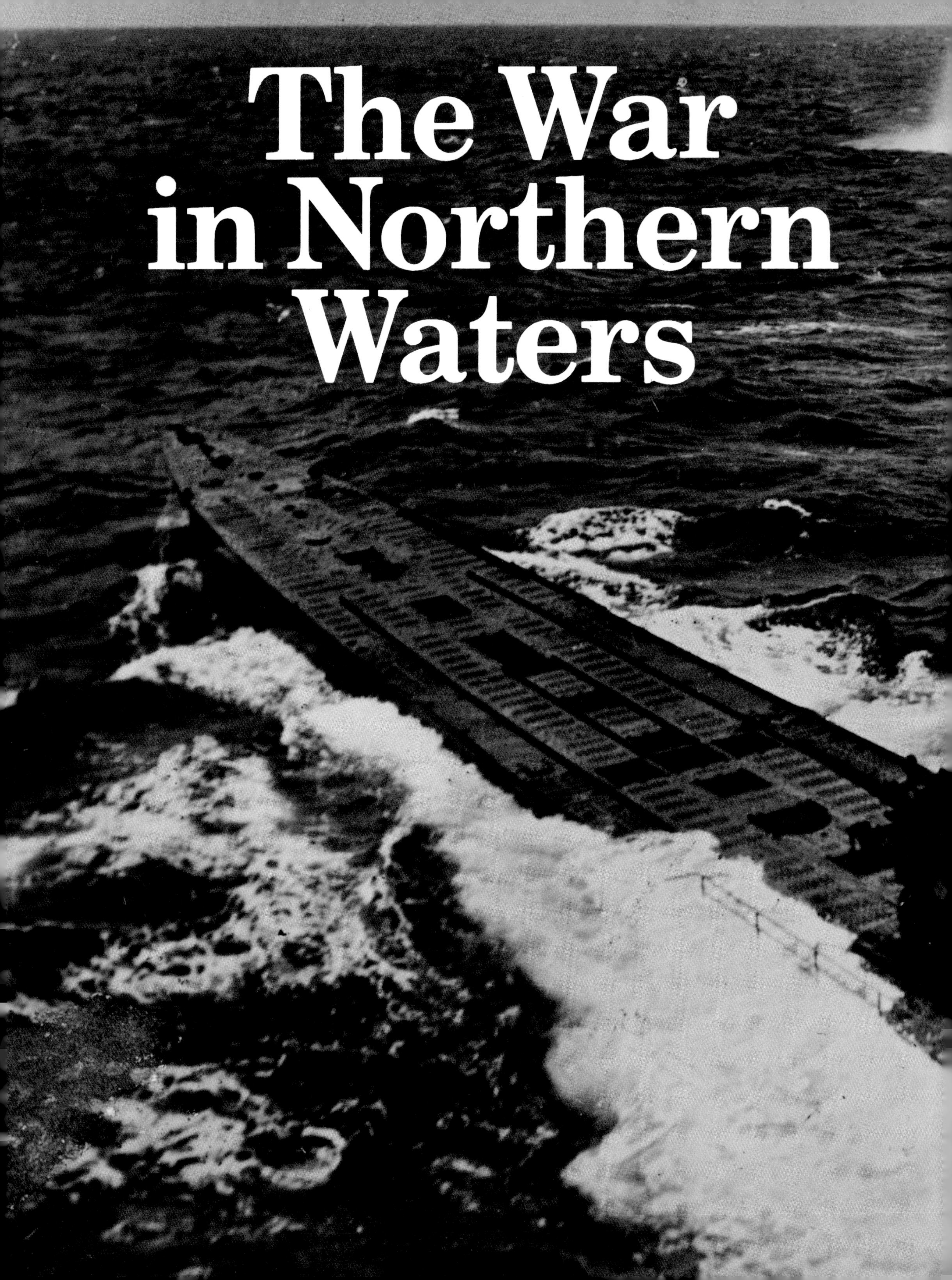
The War
in Northern
Waters

Battle of the Atlantic 1939-42

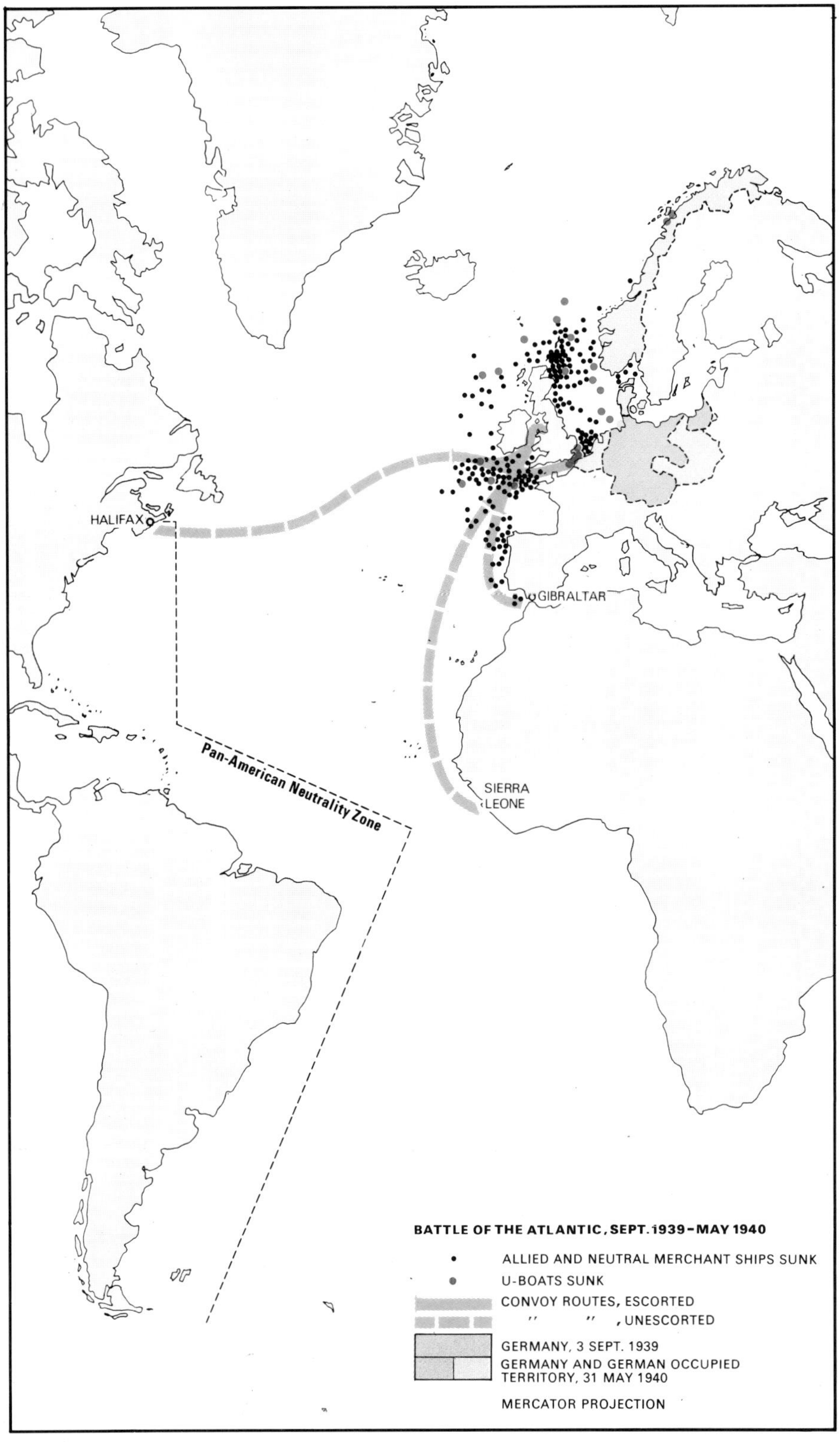

The memory of German submarine success in World War I led the British to introduce a convoy system as soon as hostilities began. The immediate threat was less than British leaders imagined, because submarine construction had not been given high priority in the German rearmament program, and Hitler was reluctant to antagonize neutral nations by unrestricted submarine warfare. This was fortunate for the British in the early months of the war, because they lacked sufficient escort vessels. Many ships sailed independently, and others were convoyed only partway on their voyages.

In June 1940 the U-boat threat became more pressing. The fall of France entailed the loss of support from the French Fleet even as British naval responsibility increased with Italian participation in the war. Germany's position was strengthened by the acquisition of bases in western France and Norway for their long-range reconnaissance support planes

Previous pages: A surfaced German U-boat immediately prior to its sinking by US Navy bombers southwest of Ascension Island, November 1943.
Opposite and below right: Early developments in the Battle of the Atlantic.
Below: USS Spencer *closes on a U-boat off the east coast of America.*

and U-boats. And German submarines, if relatively few in number, had several technical advantages. Their intelligence was superior to that of the British due to effective code-breaking by the German signals service. British Asdic equipment could detect only submerged submarines; those on the surface were easily overlooked at night or until they approached within striking distance of a convoy. Radar was not sophisticated, and British patrol aircraft were in very short supply.

As a result, the Battle of the Atlantic was not one of ships alone. It involved technology, tactics, intelligence, air power and industrial competition. The Germans made full use of their advantages in the second half of 1940 (known to German submariners as 'the happy time'). U-boat 'wolf-packs' made concerted attacks on convoys to swamp their escorts, and numerous commanders won renown for the speed and success of their missions.

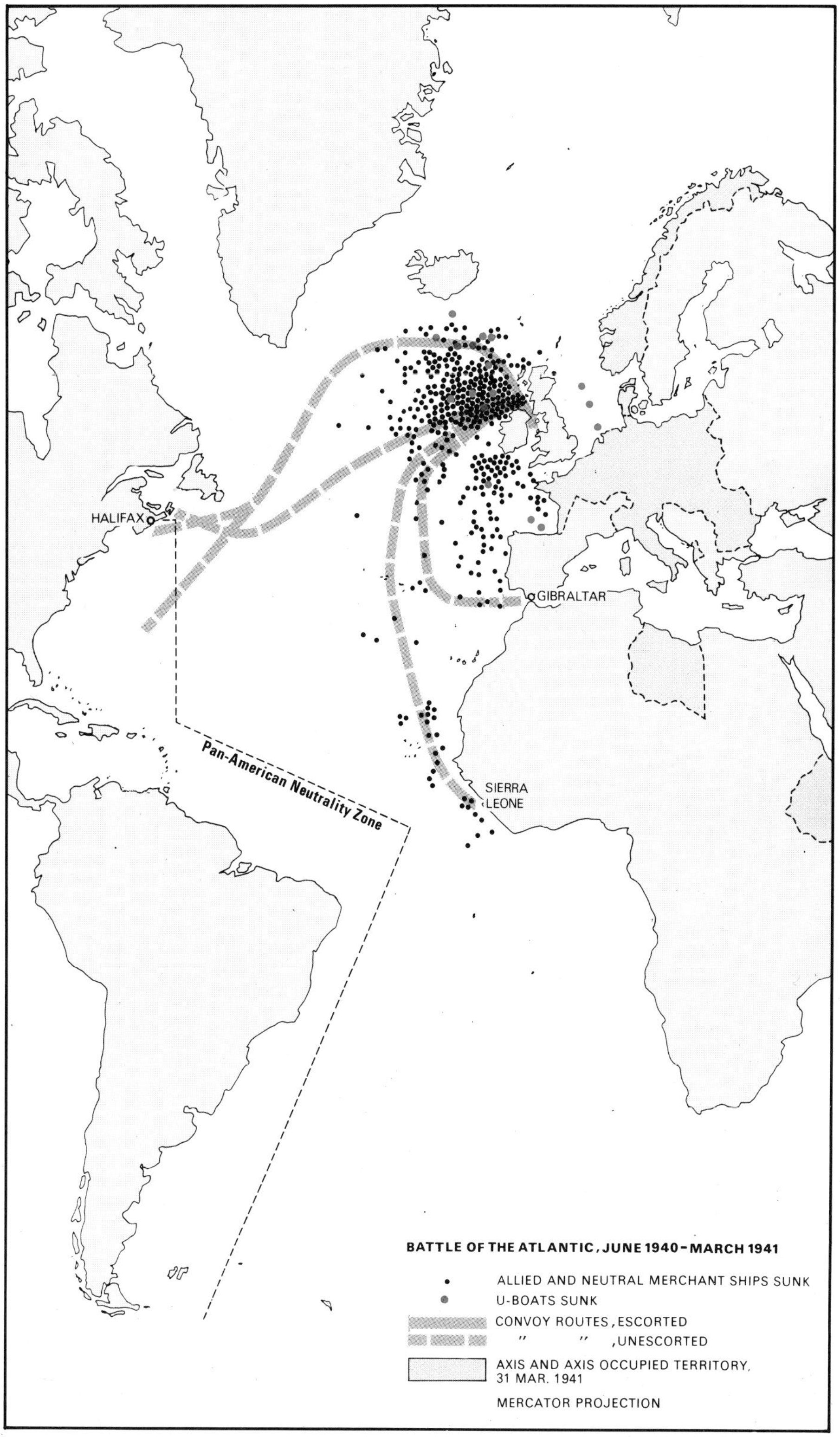

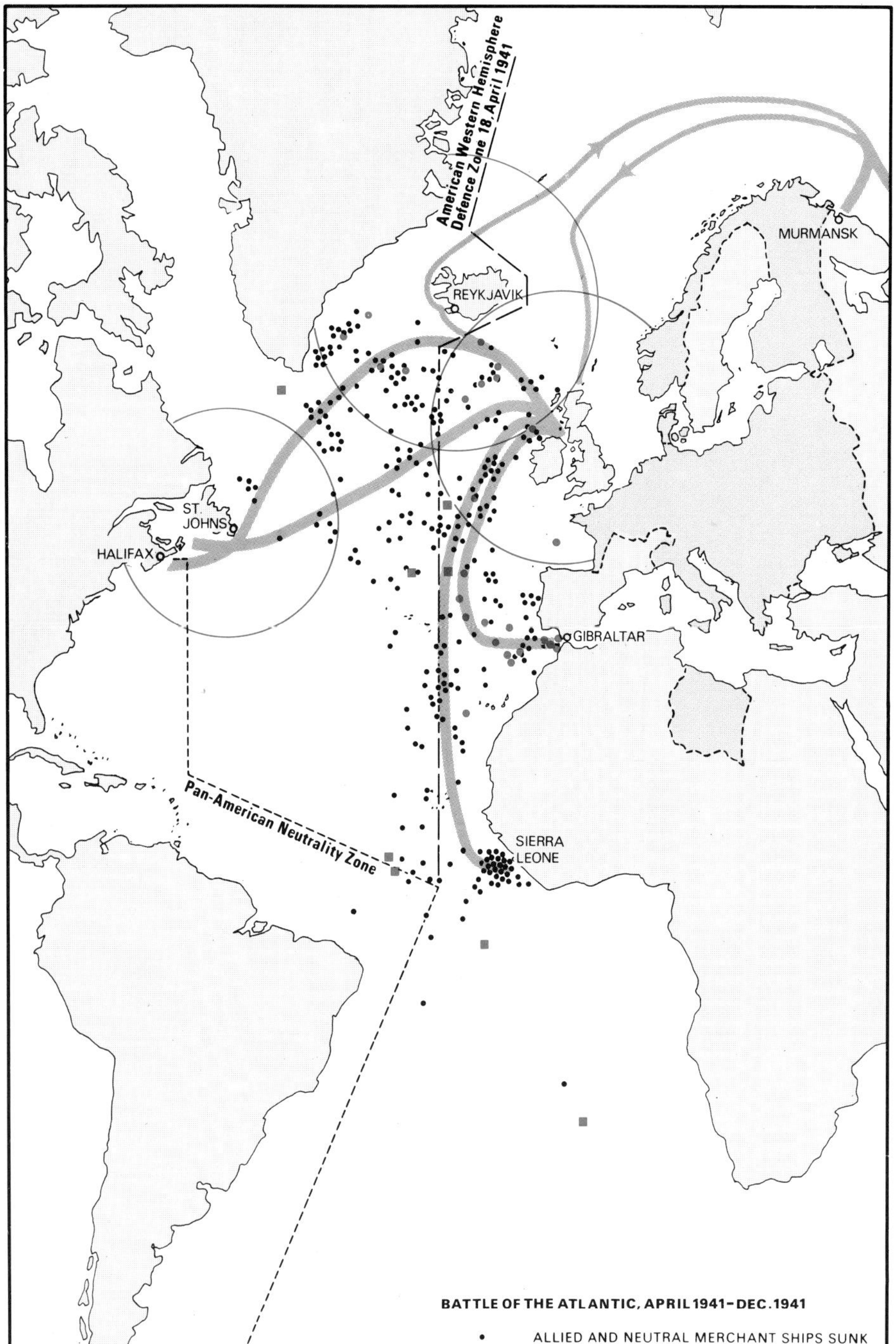

By March 1941 this picture was changing. Many U-boats had been destroyed, and replacement construction was not keeping pace. The British provided stronger escorts and made use of rapidly developing radar capabilities to frustrate German plans. Three of the best German U-boat commanders were killed that March, and Churchill formed the effective Battle of the Atlantic Committee to co-ordinate British efforts in every sphere of the struggle. The remainder of 1941 proved that a balance had been struck: German U-boats tripled in number between March and November, but shipping losses in November were the lowest of the war to that date. US assistance in both convoy duty and supplies helped improve the British position, as did intelligence breakthroughs.

When the United States formally en-

Opposite and below right: The Battle of the Atlantic continues, with Allied air cover now apparent.
Below: US troops disembark in Iceland. Air cover from Reykjavik drastically reduced U-boat strikes in the area from 1941 onwards.

tered the war at the end of 1941, the situation changed again. The US Navy was preoccupied with the Japanese threat in the Pacific, and the East Coast was left vulnerable to German submarine operations. For the first half of 1942, the US ships sailed without escorts, showed lights at night and communicated without codes – afflicted by the same peacetime mentality that had proved so disastrous at Pearl Harbor. Sparse anti-submarine patrols along the East Coast were easily evaded by the experienced Germans. It was months before an effective convoy system was established and extended as far south as the Caribbean. But by late summer of 1942 the US coastline was no longer a happy hunting ground, and the U-boats turned their attention back to the main North Atlantic routes.

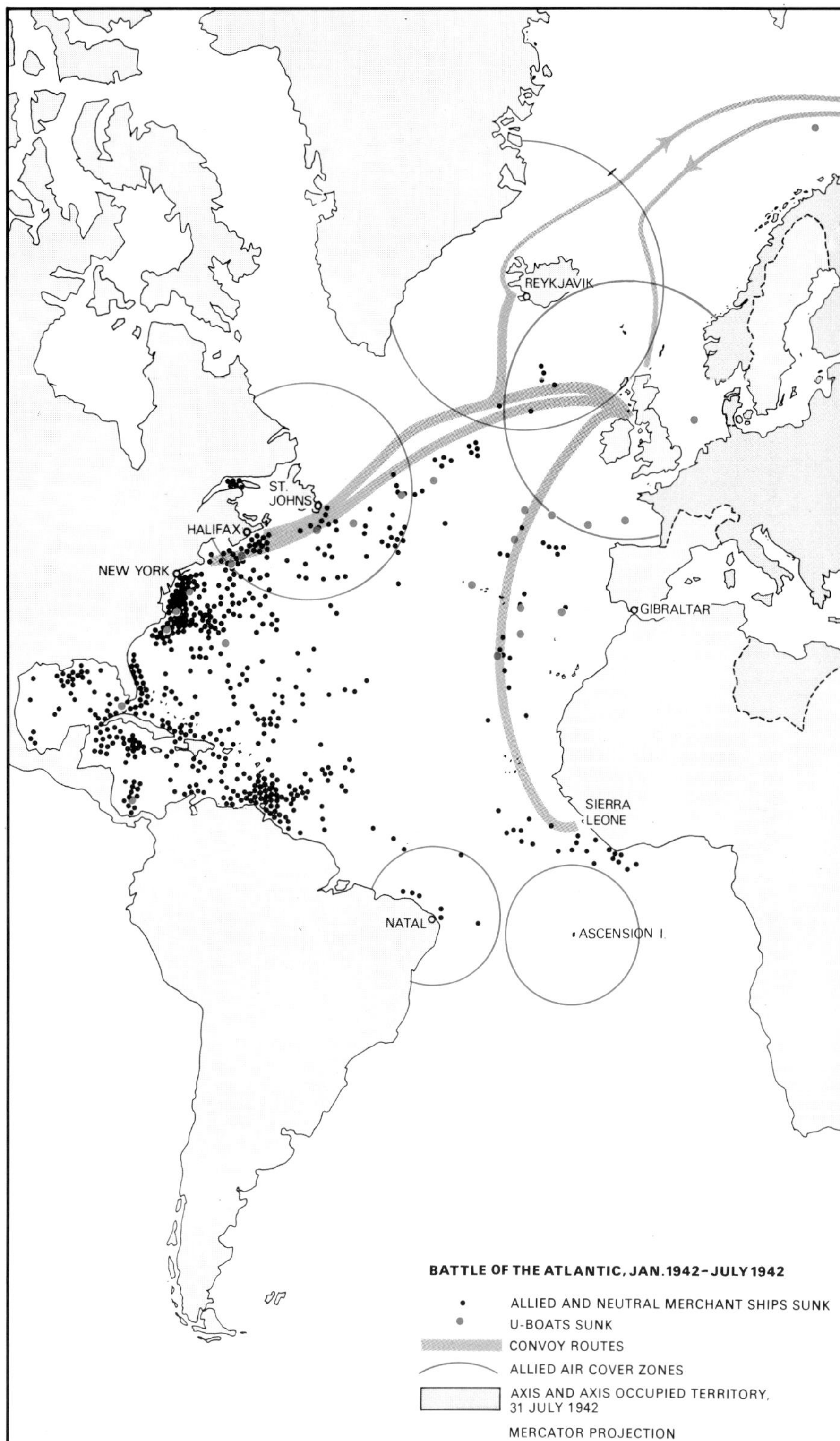

Stalking the *Bismarck*

The formidable German battleship *Bismarck* was ready for action in the spring of 1941. Armed with 15-inch guns and protected by massive armor plate, she was an ocean raider to reckon with, accompanied on her first foray by the heavy cruiser *Prinz Eugen*, which had finished her trials at the same time. On 18 May the two warships left Gdynia for Bergen, where RAF reconnaissance planes spotted them two days later. Their presence in Norwegian waters could only mean a foray into the Atlantic, and Royal Navy vessels in and around Britain were warned of the coming confrontation. Meanwhile, the German ships put to sea in foggy weather, bound for the Denmark Strait under command of Vice-Admiral Günther Lütjens. Not until late on 23 May were they spotted in the Strait by the cruisers *Suffolk* and *Norfolk*.

British Vice-Admiral Lancelot Holland, commanding the *Hood* and the new battleship *Prince of Wales*, altered course to intercept the raiders. *Prince of Wales* still had workmen aboard and was by no means fully prepared to fight. *Hood* was a veteran, but she took a German shell in one of her aft magazines just as she closed with *Bismarck* and blew up. Only three crew members of 1500 survived. *Bismarck* then scored several direct hits on *Prince of Wales*, ending the engagement. Leaking fuel from a ruptured tank, *Bismarck* left the scene, shadowed by *Prince of Wales* and two cruisers. *Prinz Eugen* broke away and returned to Brest, and the Royal Navy lost contact with the damaged German battleship. On 26 May she was spotted by an RAF Catalina north of Gibraltar.

Force H, heading northeast from Gibraltar, included the carrier *Ark Royal*, which launched her Swordfish against the disabled *Bismarck*. A torpedo strike jammed *Bismarck*'s rudder and left her an easy prey to the battleships *Rodney* and *King George V*, which arrived that night (26-27 May) to pour heavy-caliber shells into the German warship. A torpedo from the cruiser *Dorsetshire* completed the *Bismarck*'s destruction. She sank with all but 110 men of her crew, which numbered 2300.

Below: Charting the Bismarck*'s course to destruction, May 1941.*
Right: The loss of Allied convoy PQ-17 in July 1942 proved a grievous blow to morale. Almost two-thirds of the ships involved failed to reach their destination, Archangel, and thousands of tons of urgently needed matériel were lost.

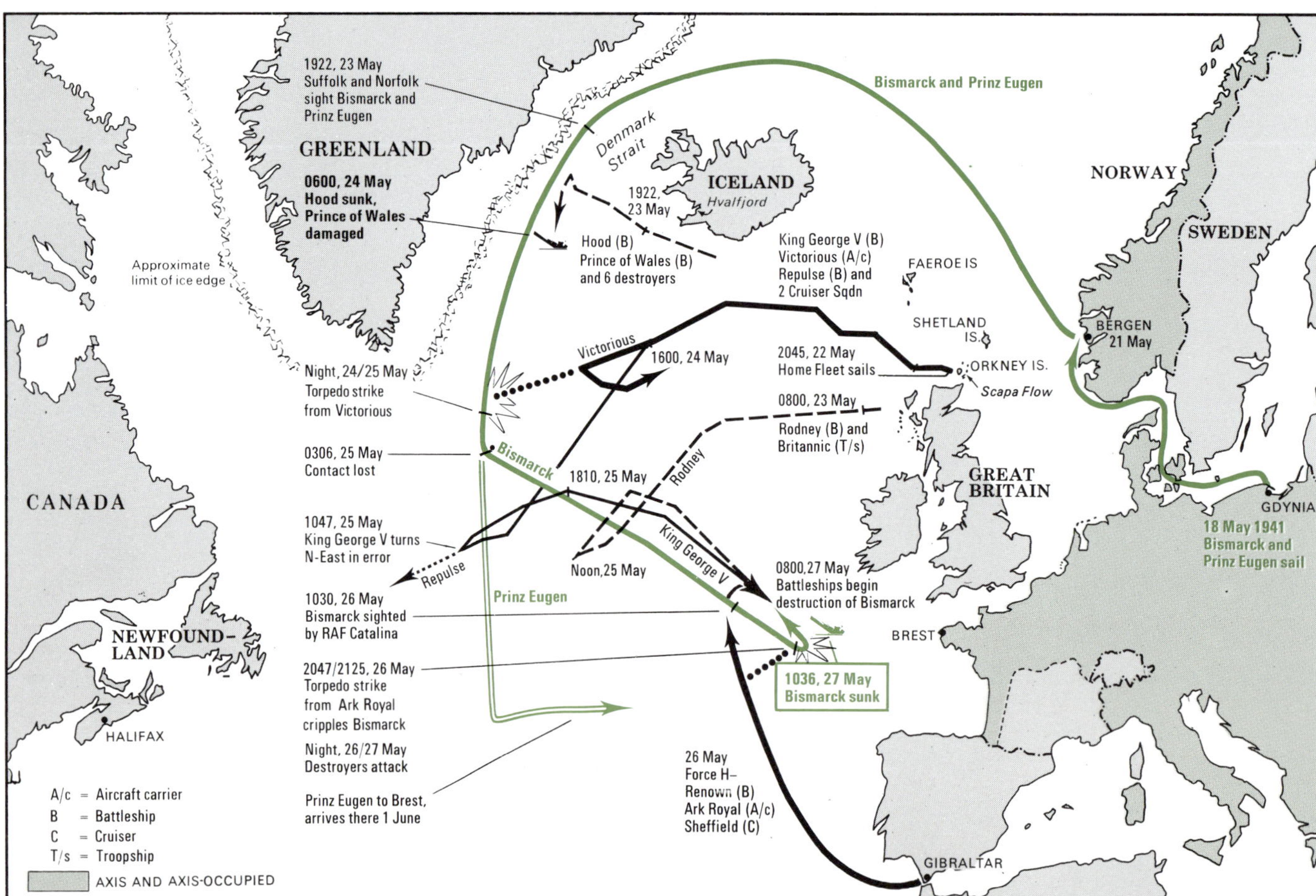

The Arctic Convoys

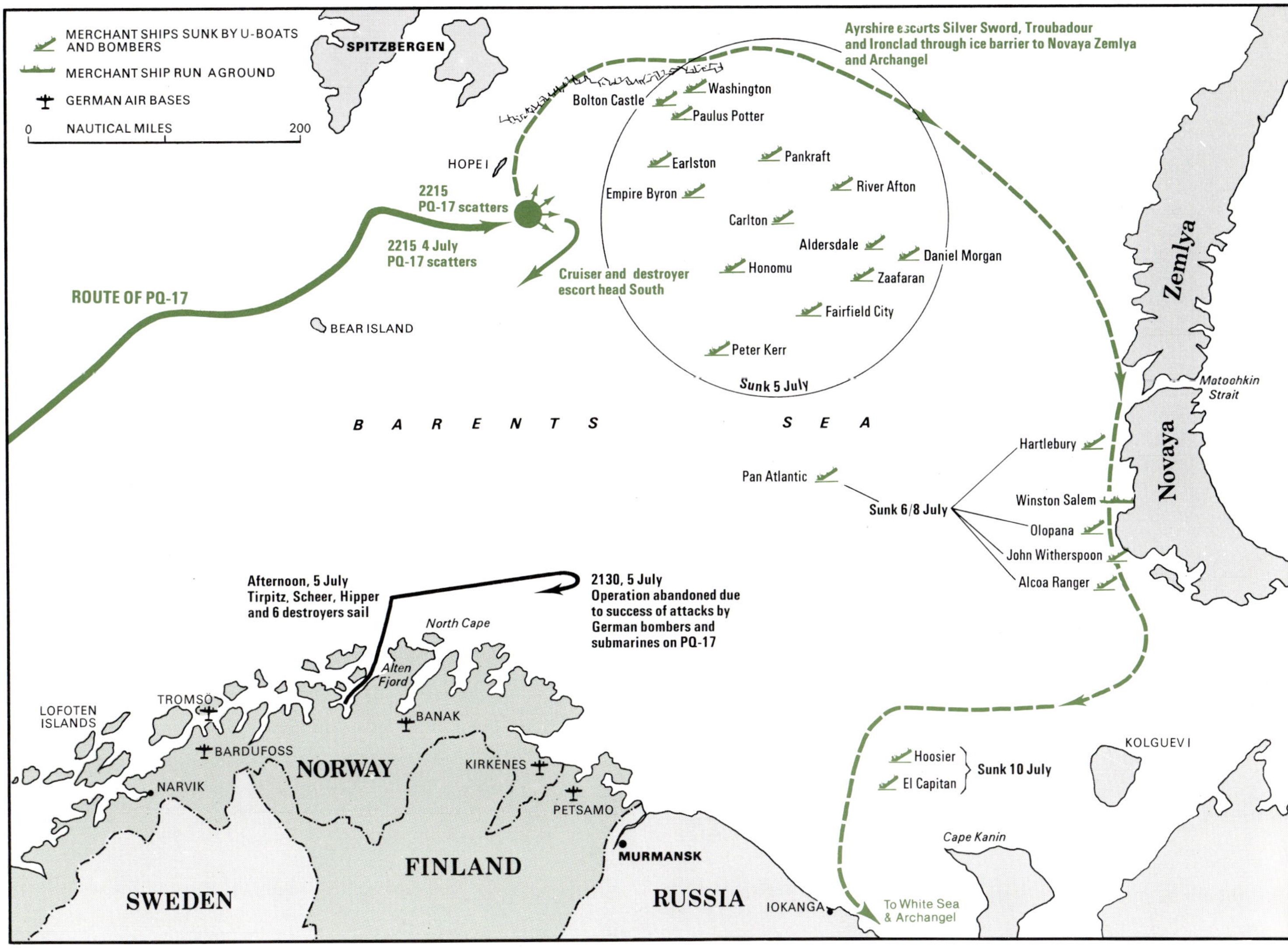

Hazardous duty fell to the men who convoyed supplies to Russia after the German invasion of June 1941. The forces of nature on the arctic run posed a threat equal to that of the Germans. Savage storms and shifting ice packs were a constant menace. In the summer months, the pack ice retreated north, and convoys could give a wider berth to enemy airfields on the Norwegian and Finnish coasts, but the long summer daylight made them vulnerable to U-boats. When the ice edge moved south again, the U-boat threat lessened with the hours of daylight, but it was more difficult to stand clear of the airfields.

Many Allied seamen lost their lives on the arctic run, including most of the members of PQ-17, which sailed for Russia on 27 June 1942. Thirty-six merchant ships were heavily escorted by Allied destroyers, battleships, submarines, a carrier and various smaller craft. Near Bear Island in the Barents Sea, the convoy lost its shadowing aircraft in heavy fog. At the same time, word came that German surface ships *Tirpitz*, *Scheer* and *Hipper* had left their southern bases.

Early on 4 July, German planes torpedoed a merchantman and sank two ships of the convoy. The German ships arrived at Altenfjord, Norway, and operations control in London expected an imminent sailing to intercept the convoy, whose distant cover had been withdrawn per previous plans. Sir Dudley Pound, First Sea Lord, saw a chance for the convoy's ships to evade the German raiders by scattering; orders to this effect were issued on 4 July. The long-range escort, except for the submarines, left the convoy to rendezvous with the close cover, leaving PQ-17 scattered and defenseless. German U-boats and aircraft began to pick off the hapless ships, and the surface-ship mission that set sail from Altenfjord on 5 July was canceled as unnecessary late that day.

Between 5 and 8 July, almost two-thirds of the convoy was sunk in icy waters hundreds of miles from its destination of Archangel. The armed trawler *Ayrshire* succeeded in leading three merchantmen up into the ice, where they camouflaged themselves with white paint and rode out the crisis. These three were among the eleven merchant ships that finally reached Russia with desperately needed supplies. The other 25 went down with their crews and thousands of tons of matériel destined for the Soviet war effort.

The Sea Roads Secured, 1943-45

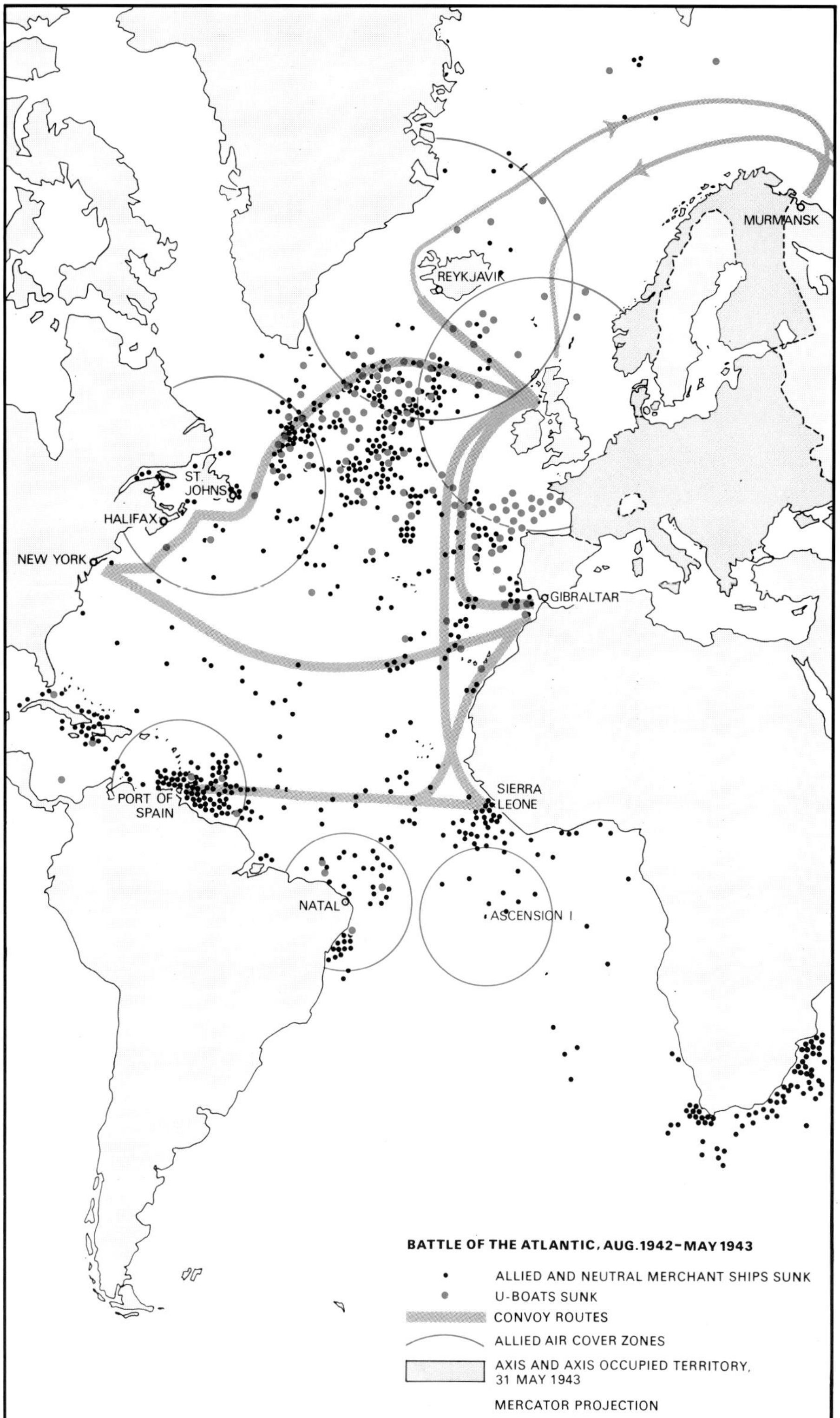

By mid 1942 the Battle of the Atlantic had shifted away from the US East Coast to more distant areas, where German U-boats continued to make successful raids on Allied shipping. Many oil tankers and other vessels were lost south of the Caribbean, off the Brazilian coast and around the Cape of Good Hope. Before the year was out, the Allies had augmented the convoy system by specially trained Support Groups – escort vessels that would help endangered convoys or seek out U-boats in areas where they had been detected. These groups usually included a small aircraft carrier and an escort carrier, along with surface forces. They were free of normal escort duties and could therefore hunt the U-boats to destruction.

A cryptographic breakthrough at the end of 1942 increased Allied intelligence on German deployments, and changes in the code system (June 1943) made it more difficult for the Germans to anticipate Allied movements. Even so, late 1942 and early 1943 brought great difficulties. Allied commitments were increased by the invasion of North Africa, which drew off North Atlantic escort forces, with

Opposite: Continuation and (below right) conclusion of the Battle of the Atlantic. Below: A U-boat victim burns in mid-Atlantic. By the summer of 1943 the worst Allied shipping losses were over.

corresponding shipping losses. In March 1943, the climax of the Battle of the Atlantic, 120 Allied ships were sunk. Then the support groups returned from North African waters, and the US industrial effort paid dividends in accelerated production of escort carriers and other needed equipment. Improvements in radar and long-range scout planes, years in the making, came to the fore, and Allied crews began to capitalize on their hard-won experience. In April 1943, shipping losses declined, and the following month 41 U-boats were destroyed. On 22 May the German submarines were ordered to withdraw from the North Atlantic.

After the summer of 1943, the U-boats were never again the threat that they had been. The 'wolf-pack' tactic was abandoned in 1944, and the remaining submarines prowled singly in an area increasingly focused around the British Isles. At the war's end, fewer than 200 were still operational. Allied victory in the Atlantic was largely a function of superior co-ordination of effort, which ultimately offset the initial German advantage in submarine technology.

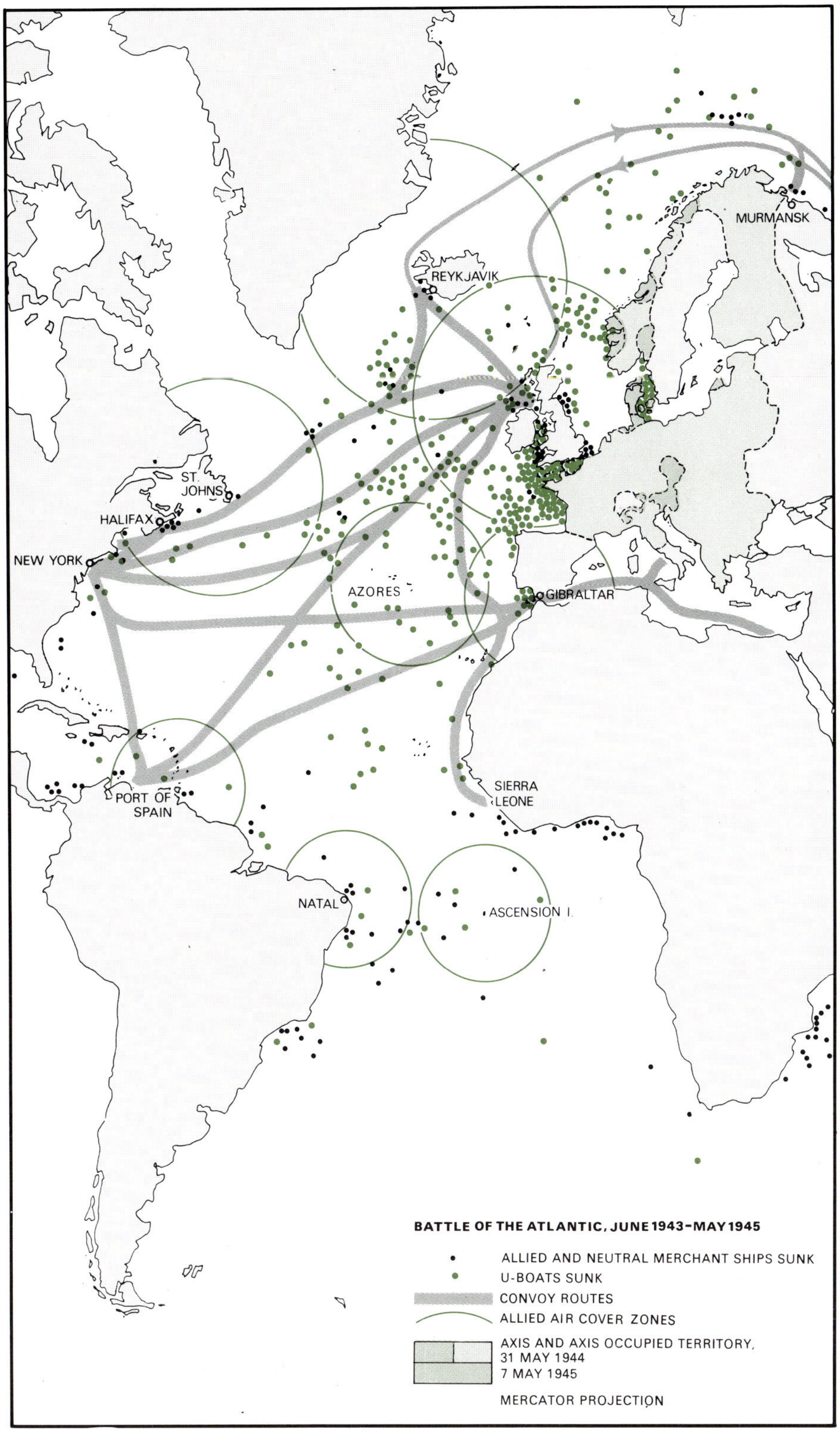

The Desert War and the Mediterranean

Rommel's First Offensive

Previous pages: The German retreat from El Alamein, November 1942.
Right: The Germans press eastwards through Libya into Egypt.
Below: Rommel enters Egypt.
Bottom left: Rommel and his officers inspect a captured British tank.
Bottom: The Allies isolated at Tobruk.
Below right: Rommel directs operations.

The first German troops began landing in North Africa on February 1941, under command of General Erwin Rommel, who would earn the nickname 'Desert Fox.' His leadership abilities were acknowledged by comrades and enemies alike. Rommel soon saw that British forces in Africa were weak, and that no reinforcements would be forthcoming. On 24 March German forces took El Agheila easily, and the 5 Light Division went on to attack the British 2 Armored Division at Mersa Brega. There they encountered stiff resistance, but the British failed to counterattack and lost their advantage.

Instead of choosing among three alternative courses of attack, Rommel moved boldly on all three fronts: north to Benghazi, northeast to Msus and Mechili and east to Tengeder, to threaten British supply lines. Field Marshal Archibald Wavell, in overall command of British forces, lacked the men to counter this multiple attack, launched on 5 April. His single armored division fell back and was reduced to a remnant by mechanical failure. The defense at Mechili, 3 Indian Brigade, was soon overwhelmed, with what remained of the 2 Armored Division. The 8 Australian Division retreated from Benghazi to Derna, thence toward Tobruk, which was being reinforced with the 7 Australian Division.

On 14 April the German 5 Light Division penetrated the Tobruk perimeter a short distance, but was driven back. Italian troops were now coming up to replace the German units making ready to cross the Egyptian frontier. The British garrison at Tobruk was isolated in the midst of Axis forces, and on 25 April the Germans broke through the Halfaya Pass into Egypt. Rommel was dissatisfied with the failure to capture Tobruk, and another full-scale attack struck the British there on 30 April. Axis troops pushed a salient into the western sector, but it was contained after four days of fighting.

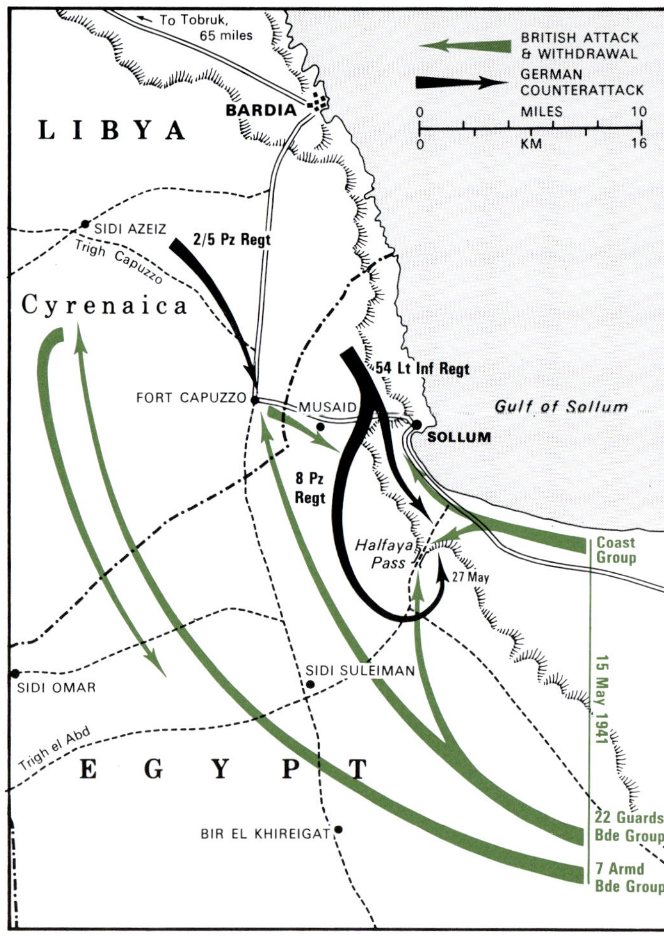

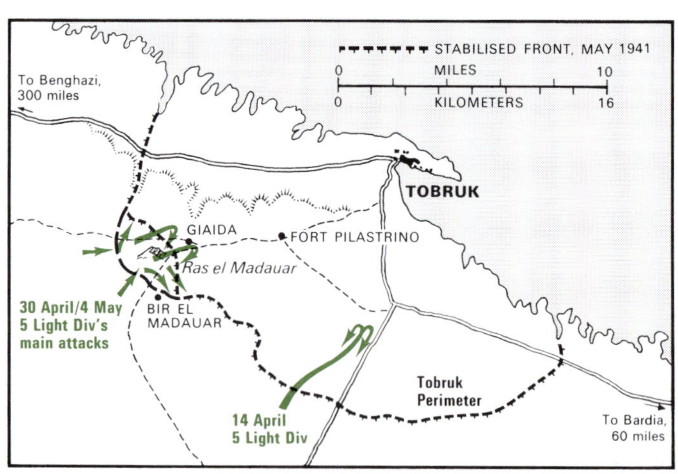

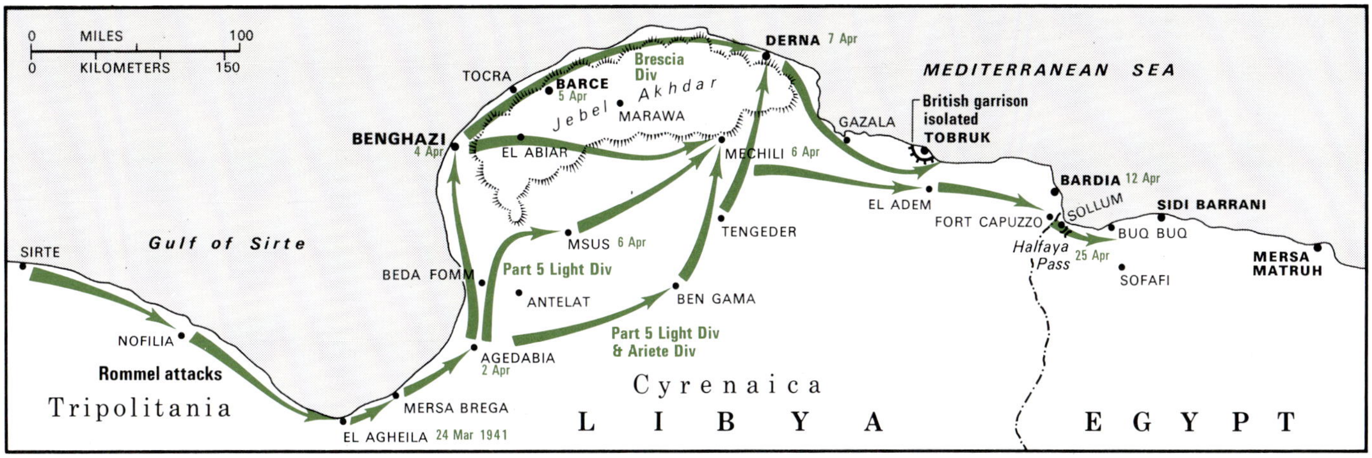

0 MILES 100
0 KILOMETERS 150
MEDITERRANEAN SEA
DERNA 7 Apr
TOCRA
BARCE 5 Apr
Brescia Div
Jebel Akhdar
MARAWA
BENGHAZI 4 Apr
EL ABIAR
MECHILI 6 Apr
GAZALA
British garrison isolated TOBRUK
BARDIA 12 Apr
EL ADEM
SOLLUM
SIDI BARRANI
FORT CAPUZZO
BUQ BUQ
Halfaya Pass 25 Apr
SOFAFI
MERSA MATRUH
TENGEDER
MSUS 6 Apr
SIRTE
Gulf of Sirte
BEDA FOMM
Part 5 Light Div
ANTELAT
BEN GAMA
NOFILIA
Part 5 Light Div & Ariete Div
AGEDABIA 2 Apr
Rommel attacks
Cyrenaica
Tripolitania
MERSA BREGA
EL AGHEILA 24 Mar 1941
LIBYA
EGYPT

The German Drive on Gazala

Rommel's German units, the *Deutsches Afrika Korps* (DAK), and their allies suffered a setback in the Crusader Battles with the British Eighth Army late in 1941. Tobruk was relieved, and Rommel had to pull back to El Agheila, having suffered 38,000 Axis casualties as against 18,000 for the British. His men were exhausted, supplies were running out and 300 German tanks had been destroyed in the Libyan desert.

British forces pursued Rommel to El Agheila, believing that his shattered units would be unable to react. However, successful air raids on Malta had restored the German supply line across the Mediterranean, and Rommel's forces were quickly rebuilt to fighting strength. On 21 January 1942 they made an unexpected advance that pushed Eighth Army

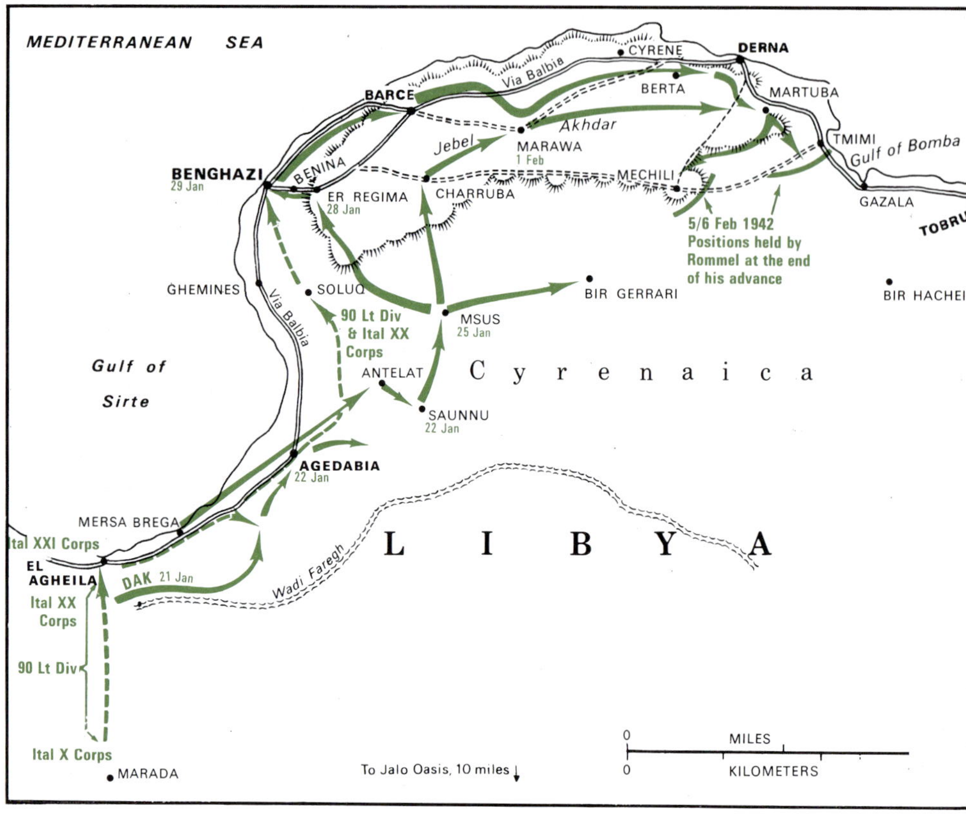

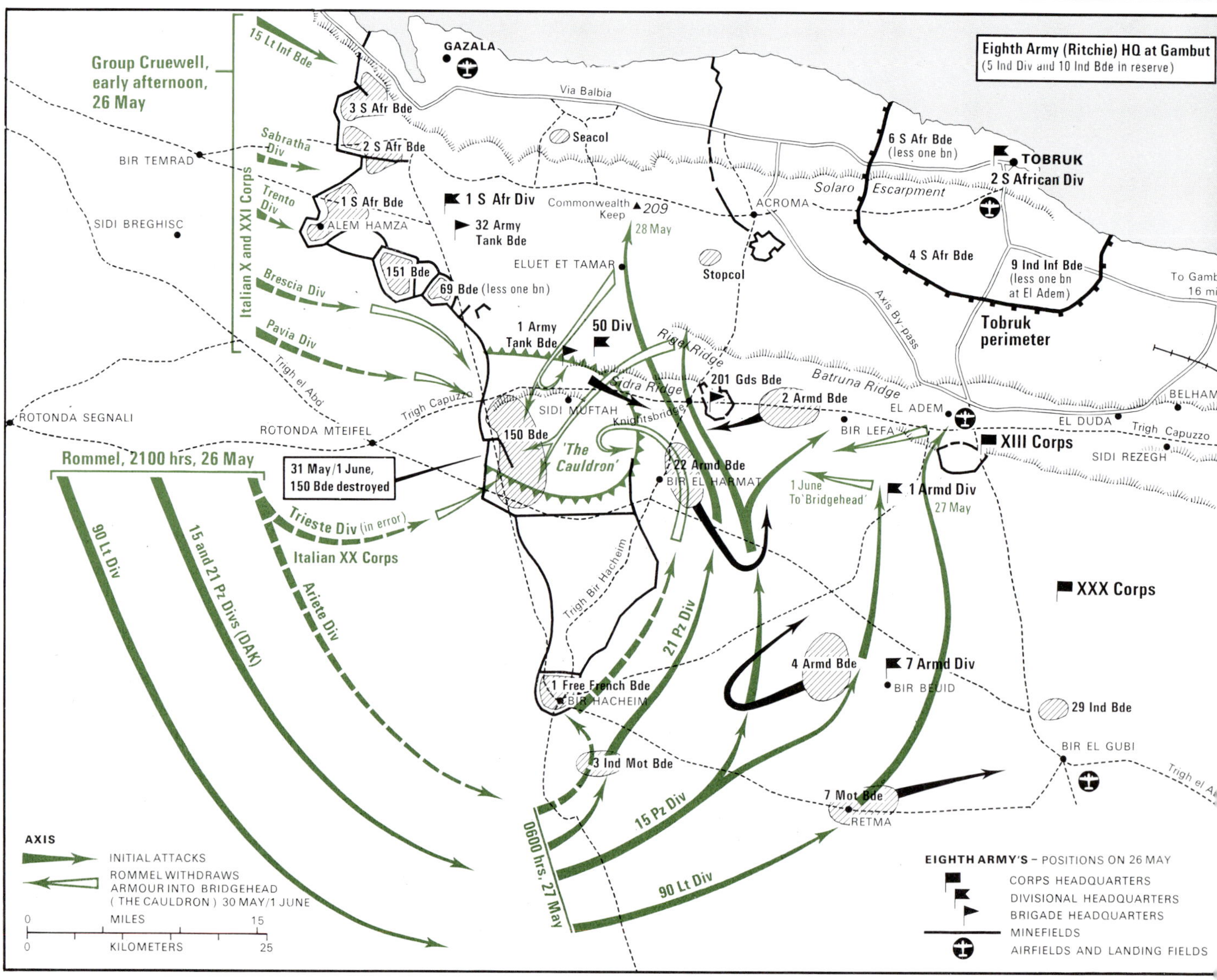

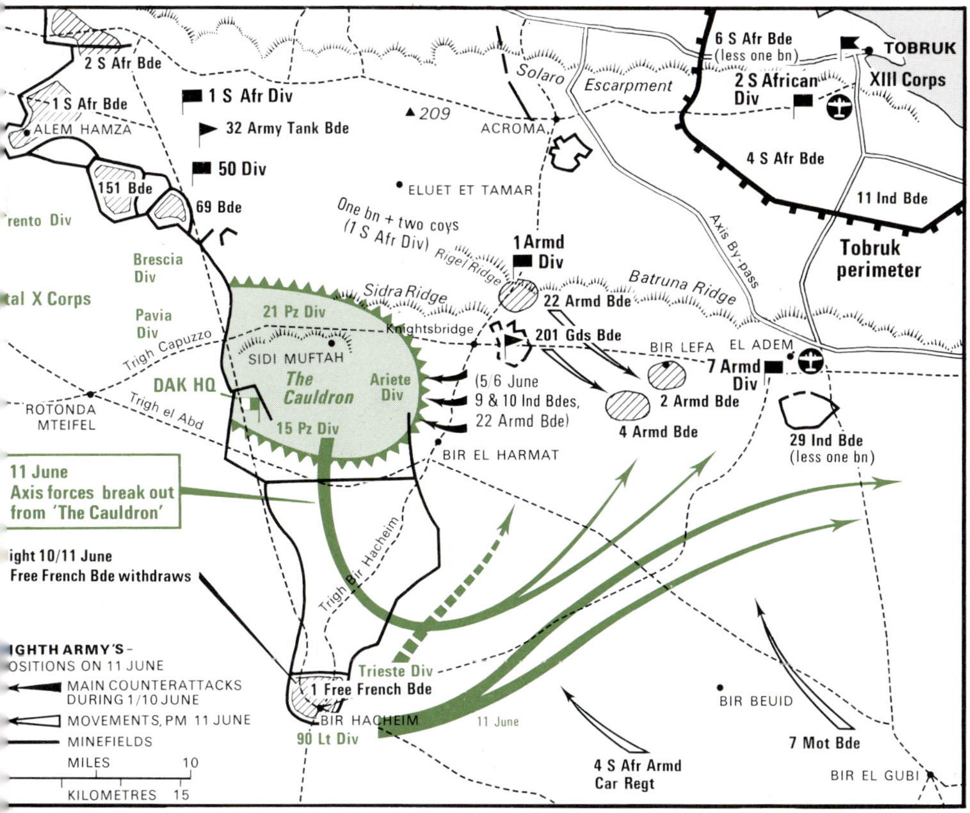

back toward Agedabia. In a matter of days the British faced encirclement at Benghazi and were forced to retreat to the defensive position at Gazala. The line there consisted of minefields running south to Bir Hacheim and a series of fortified keeps that were manned by XIII Corps brigades.

DAK forces under Cruewell swung around Bir Hacheim on 26 May to outflank the Gazala Line, but they were attacked from both sides on Sidra Ridge and stopped short with loss of a third of their armor. Their water and fuel were running out, and Rommel tried to push a supply line through the British minefields without success. He then moved all his remaining armor into 'the Cauldron' to await the impending British counterattack.

Cruewell's isolated forces were finally supplied on 4 June, and Eighth Army failed to counterattack until 5/6 June, when it was beaten off with heavy losses. The defense at Bir Hacheim crumbled and DAK broke out of the Cauldron to force the British back from the Gazala Line even beyond Tobruk. Axis forces had surrounded the British garrison there by 18 June.

Opposite above: Rommel advances eastwards, pushing the Eighth Army back toward Gazala and Tobruk.

Opposite: The Allied stand on 26 May, with fortified keeps (shaded) scattered along the minefield (bold line).

Above left: Breakout from the Cauldron.
Below: An Afrika Korps Panzer III advances.

The Fall of Tobruk

Eighth Army was severely demoralized by the German triumph at Gazala, which contributed to the distrust between infantry and tank units that had surfaced during the Crusader Battles. British leadership had failed to capitalize on several advantages, including a numerical superiority in armor, the DAK containment in the Cauldron and the well-prepared defense line at Gazala.

Rommel launched his drive on Tobruk from the southeastern sector on 20 June 1942. Heavy dive-bomber attacks displayed German air superiority to devastating effect, after which DAK pushed through the perimeter defenses. By mid-morning German troops had reached the minefields, and the airfields were overrun soon after. At 1900 hours 21 Panzer Division moved into Tobruk.

There was sporadic fighting within the perimeter through the night, but the Germans had overcome almost all resistance by the morning of 21 June. General Klopper, the South African in command of the garrison, surrendered, and the road to Egypt was open.

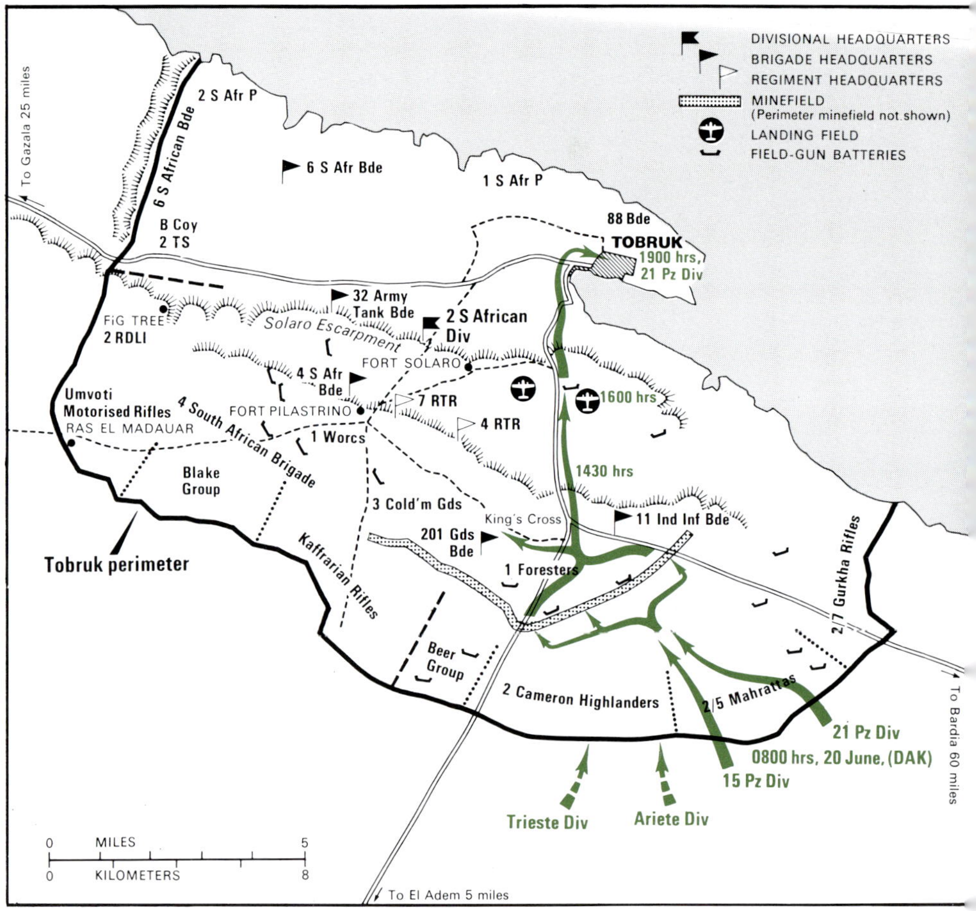

Right: The perimeter defenses are breached, and the fall of Tobruk is less than 12 hours away.
Below: British troops surrender to their Axis adversaries. Rommel's victory, completed on 21 June, cleared the way for an advance into Egypt.

The Naval War in the Mediterranean

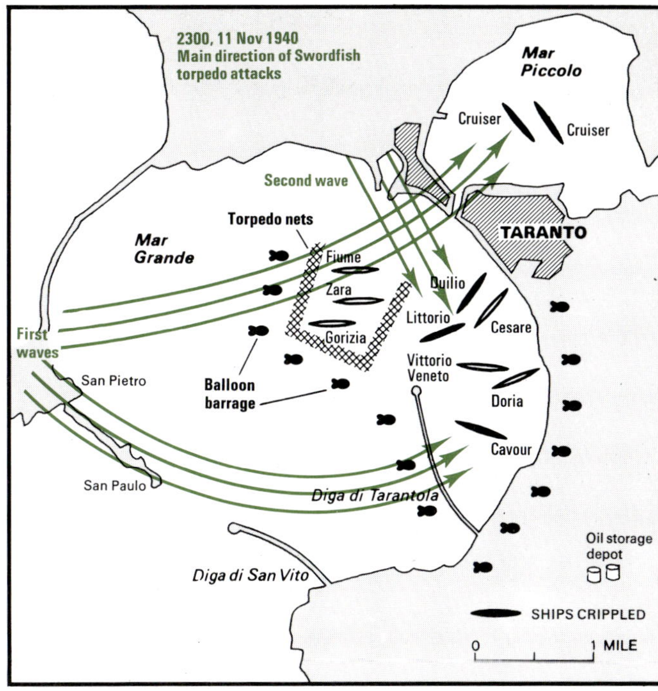

The Royal Navy faced a difficult task in the Mediterranean, where the well-equipped and modern Italian Navy enjoyed a position from which it could strike at will. British forces were split between Gibraltar (Force H) and Alexandria, with Malta at the center – a key position, but highly vulnerable. Only light and submarine naval forces were based on Malta, and Mediterranean Fleet commander Sir Andrew Cunningham was constantly seeking ways to enhance the British position in the Mediterranean through flexible use of his surface ships, including a limited number of carriers.

Cunningham's forces scored several successes against the Italian Navy in chance encounters during July 1940, and plans were laid to attack the Italian fleet in harbor at Taranto. On the night of 11 November, 21 Swordfish torpedo-bombers were launched from the carrier *Illustrious*: all but two returned, having sunk the new battleship *Littorio* and two modernized battleships and inflicted heavy damage on other craft. It was a major coup for the British, and soon followed by another successful strike at Cape Matapan, Greece.

Italian naval forces moved toward Greece in late March 1941, to interdict convoys carrying British troops to assist the Greeks during the Axis invasion of the Balkans, then imminent. On 27 March, RAF scouts reported three Italian cruisers heading east, and Admiral Cunningham put to sea from Alexandria. Three battleships, an aircraft carrier and destroyer escorts comprised his force, which was to rendezvous south of Crete with Vice-Admiral H D Pridham-Wippell commanding a force of four cruisers and four destroyers.

The principal target among the Italian force converging south of Crete was the battleship *Vittorio Veneto*, the pride of Mussolini's fleet. Air strikes were launched against her, but only one torpedo found its mark. Then the Italian cruiser *Pola* was heavily damaged, and the heavy cruisers *Zara* and *Fiume* were sent back to help; all three were destroyed.

The remainder of the Italian force fled back to its bases, including the *Vittorio Veneto*, which found safe harbor at Taranto to the disappointment of Admiral Cunningham and his men.

Above: The successful night attack on the Italian fleet in Taranto on 11 November 1940 mounted by 21 Swordfish torpedo-bombers from HMS Illustrious.
Below: A second blow was dealt to Italian naval might at Cape Matapan on 28 March 1941.
Following pages: HMS Barham, *a battleship of the Allied Mediterranean fleet, at Gibraltar.*

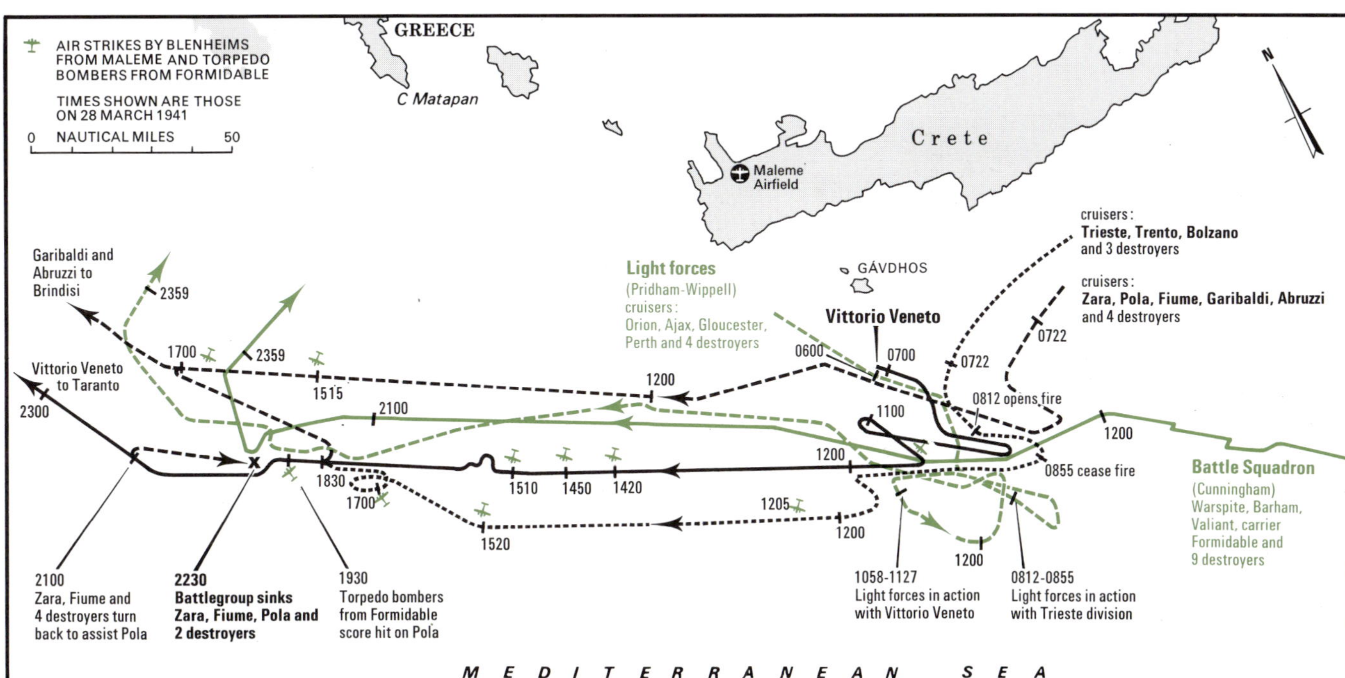

The Malta Convoys

The British island fortress of Malta was in serious straits by mid 1942. Its location astride Axis supply lines made it the target of incessant air attack, and its own supply lines were increasingly tenuous. Convoys to Malta had to be suspended in July due to their heavy losses. It was clear that Malta could not hold out against both the Luftwaffe and the Italian Regia Aeronautica without food or fuel, and Operation Pedestal was mounted as a desperate effort to convoy supplies from England.

Twenty warships under command of Vice-Admiral E N Syfret left the Clyde on 3 August with 14 merchantmen, 32 destroyers and various smaller craft. The aircraft carrier *Furious* accompanied the group with a cargo of fighter planes for Malta's RAF squadron. On 10 September, when the convoy passed through the Strait of Gibraltar in fog, a dummy convoy was dispatched from Port Said toward Malta as a diversion. Next day it returned to port, having failed to distract Axis leaders from the main operation, which was shadowed by reconnaissance aircraft from the morning of 11 September. That afternoon *Furious* flew her planes off to Malta and turned back, and the Axis made its first overt move in the form of a U-boat attack on the carrier *Eagle*, which was sunk.

The next day brought heavy Allied losses to Axis planes and submarines. The freighter *Deucalion* went down, the destroyer *Foresight* was so badly damaged that she had to be sunk and the *Indomitable*'s flight deck was bombed out of operation. At this point Syfret turned back according to plan, leaving Rear Admiral H M Burrough to escort the convoy the rest of the way with four cruisers and four destroyers. Two of the cruisers were disabled in the next few hours, *Cairo* so badly that she had to be sunk. At dusk, two of the merchantmen were destroyed and one damaged. The American tanker *Ohio* was hit but stayed with the convoy, as did the damaged cruiser *Kenya*.

Early on the morning of 13 September, five more merchantmen and the cruiser *Manchester* were lost to torpedoes, and renewed air attacks sank *Wairanama* and did additional damage to *Ohio*, with its irreplaceable fuel cargo. By the time light forces from Malta met the convoy, all but five of the merchantmen had been sunk, along with one aircraft carrier, two cruisers and a destroyer. But the fuel and other supplies that got through enabled Malta to hold on.

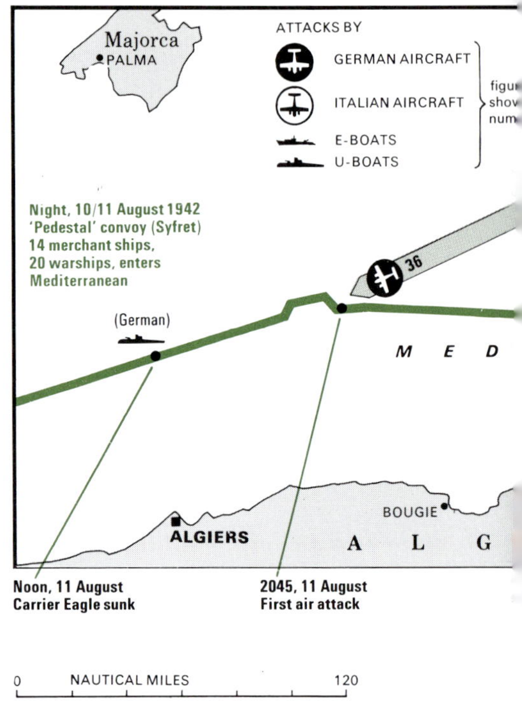

Above: The hazardous passage to Malta.
Below: The damaged tanker HMS Ohio *limps toward port with destroyer escort.*
Right: General Eisenhower (left) on Malta with Viscount Gort, the island's governor.

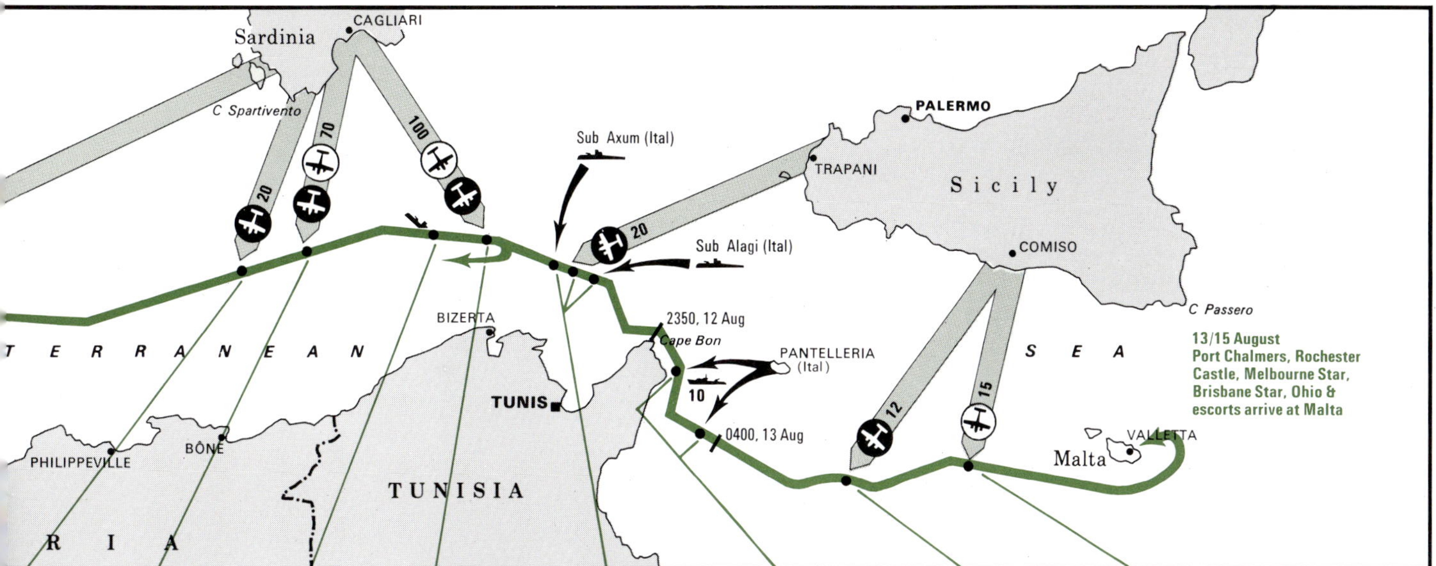

15, 12 August cond air attack

1215, 12 August Deucalion damaged, sunk later

1600, 12 August U-boat sunk

1840, 12 August Foresight sunk, carrier Indomitable damaged. Main covering force ('X') withdraws as planned

2000, 12 August Cairo, Clan Ferguson & Empire Hope sunk. Nigeria, Brisbane Star, Kenya & Ohio damaged

Night, 12/13 August Santa Eliza, Wairangi, Almeria, Lykes & Glenorchy sunk. Manchester damaged. sunk later. Rochester Castle damaged

0800, 13 August Waimarama sunk, Ohio damaged

1125, 13 August Rochester Castle & Ohio damaged. Dorset damaged, sunk later

1900, 13 August Merchant ship straggler sunk by German aircraft

El Alamein: The First Battle

Below: The German tanks advance, with Italian support.
Right: The first Battle of El Alamein.
Below right: General Grant tanks of the Allied 22nd Armored Brigade advance south of El Alamein.

After the fall of Tobruk, Rommel was promoted to Field Marshal, a status that strengthened his argument for advancing to Egypt at once. (The original Axis plan called for a halt while naval and air forces massed to invade Malta.) Using the supplies newly captured at Tobruk, Rommel crossed the Egyptian frontier and attacked the British at Mersa Matruh (26-27 June), where Eighth Army was now under tactical command of General Claude Auchinleck, Commander in Chief, Middle East. The British could not contain the German advance and retreated to the next defensible position – a line south from the small rail station of El Alamein.

Auchinleck had few reserve units with which to prepare his position from El Alamein, near the coast, to the Qattara Depression, an area of wilderness that was considered almost impassable. His depleted forces took their positions along this line to bar the way to the Nile. Meanwhile, Rommel's forces had also been much reduced in recent battles – to some 2000 German infantry and 65 tanks – while fuel and other supplies were dwindling (these had consisted largely of booty captured at Tobruk and Mersa Matruh).

Eighth Army's artillery units were instrumental in repelling the first German and Italian attacks on 2-4 July; their coordination was much better than it had been under General N M Ritchie from whom Auchinleck had assumed command. The British Commander in Chief was now in a position to essay some limited counterattacks, whose targets were Italian rather than German divisions. This choice was deliberate, as it compelled Rommel to waste fuel in widespread efforts to assist his Italian cohorts.

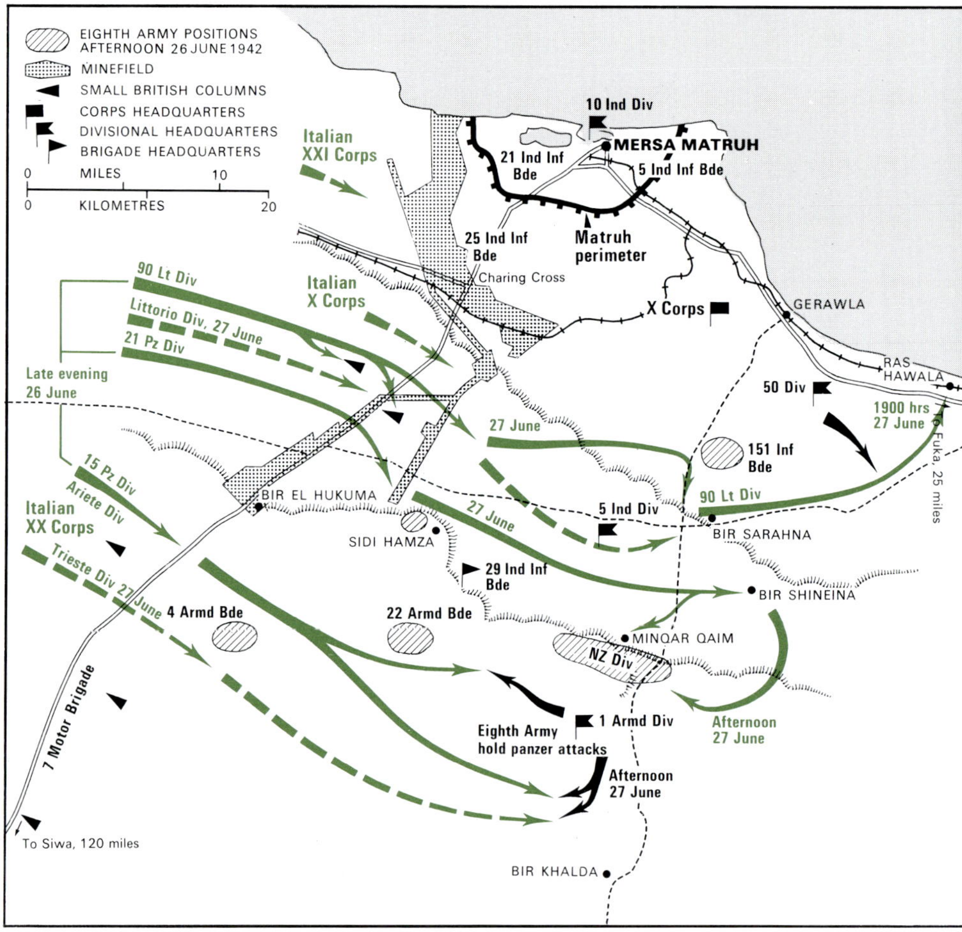

The *Sabratha* unit fell to the 9 Australian Division on 10-11 July, and the British recovered Tell el Eisa as a result.

Larger Allied efforts were mounted in the Ruweisat Ridge area, where opposing forces grappled to an exhausted standstill. Both sides were simply worn out, and Auchinleck's refusal to continue the attacks known collectively as the First Battle of El Alamein was to cost him his command.

Below: The Allied retreat along the Mediterranean coast to El Alamein.

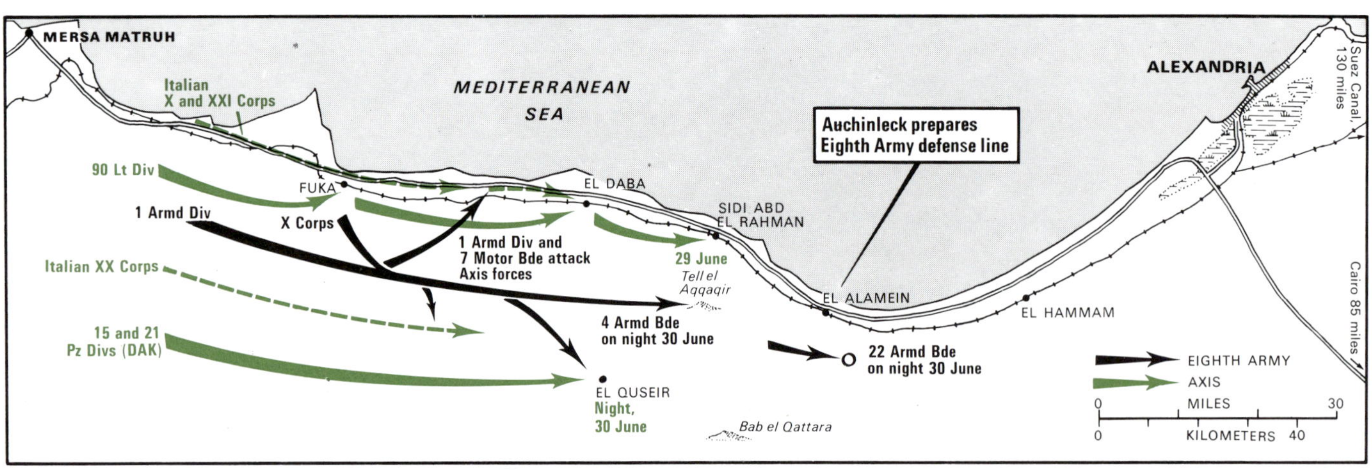

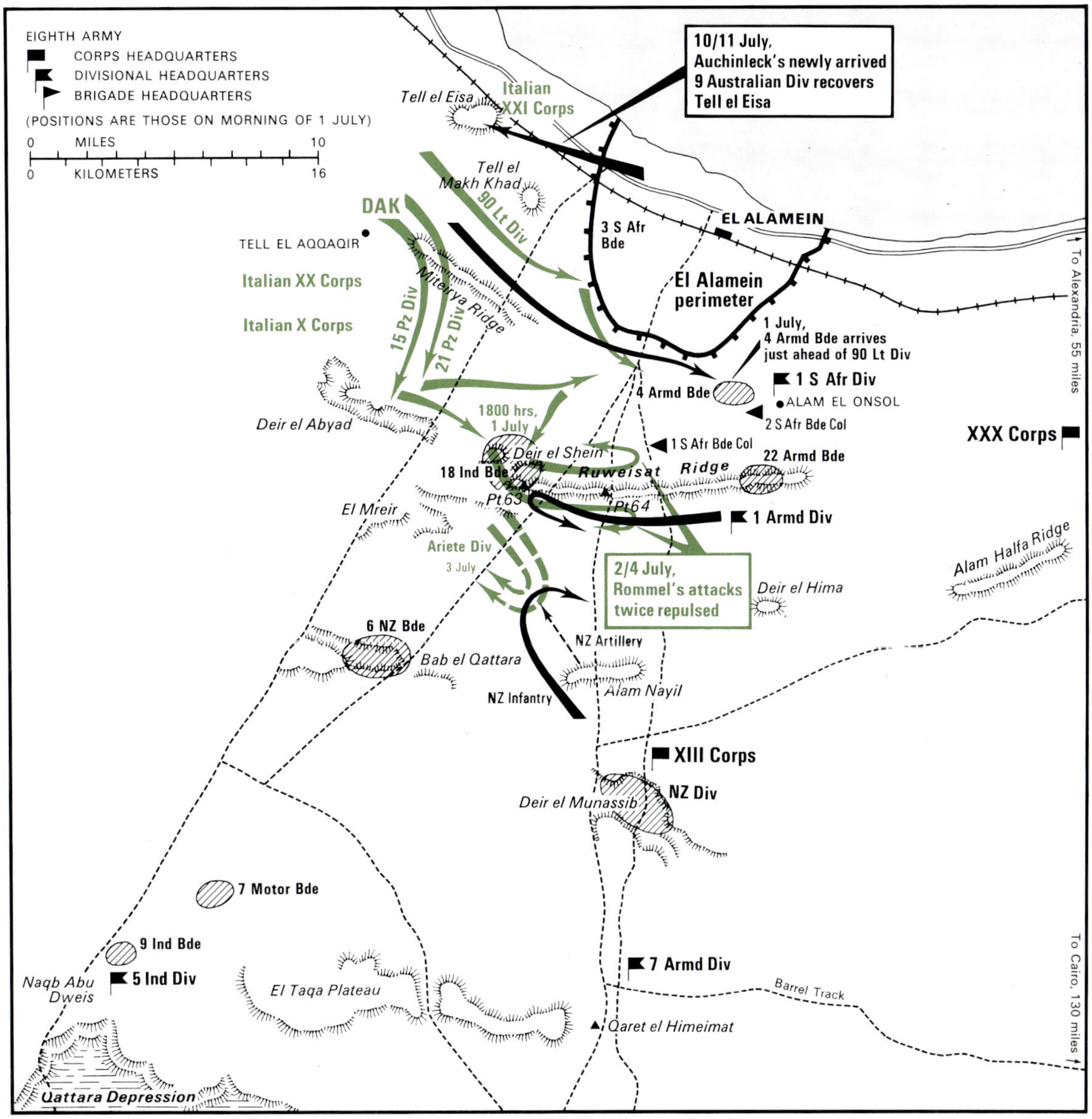
EIGHTH ARMY
CORPS HEADQUARTERS
DIVISIONAL HEADQUARTERS
BRIGADE HEADQUARTERS
(POSITIONS ARE THOSE ON MORNING OF 1 JULY)
0 MILES 10
0 KILOMETERS 16
10/11 July, Auchinleck's newly arrived 9 Australian Div recovers Tell el Eisa
Tell el Eisa
Italian XXI Corps
Tell el Makh Khad
90 Lt Div
DAK
TELL EL AQQAQIR
Italian XX Corps
Italian X Corps
15 Pz Div
21 Pz Div
Miteirya Ridge
EL ALAMEIN
3 S Afr Bde
El Alamein perimeter
1 July, 4 Armd Bde arrives just ahead of 90 Lt Div
4 Armd Bde
1 S Afr Div
ALAM EL ONSOL
2 S Afr Bde Col
1 S Afr Bde Col
XXX Corps
Deir el Abyad
1800 hrs, 1 July
Deir el Shein
18 Ind Bde
Ruweisat Ridge
22 Armd Bde
Pt63
Pt64
El Mreir
1 Armd Div
Ariete Div
3 July
2/4 July, Rommel's attacks twice repulsed
Deir el Hima
Alam Halfa Ridge
To Alexandria, 55 miles
6 NZ Bde
Bab el Qattara
NZ Artillery
NZ Infantry
Alam Nayil
XIII Corps
Deir el Munassib
NZ Div
7 Motor Bde
9 Ind Bde
Naqb Abu Dweis
5 Ind Div
El Taqa Plateau
7 Armd Div
Barrel Track
Qaret el Himeimat
Qattara Depression
To Cairo, 130 miles

The Battle of Alam Halfa

In August 1942 Churchill arrived in the Middle East to make changes. General Harold Alexander replaced Auchinleck as Commander in Chief, and General Bernard Montgomery took charge of Eighth Army. Less than three weeks later, he would face Rommel's last attempt to break through the position at El Alamein.

Montgomery's defensive plan was based loosely upon Auchinleck's: to hold the Alam Halfa Ridge and counter a German threat in the South with 7 Armored Division. Rommel used the tactic this plan had anticipated when, on 30 August, his main attacks swung south of the British positions with the object of turning north again beyond Alam Halfa to surround Eighth Army. The presence of 7 Armored Division on the right flank forced him to turn north earlier than he had intended, with the result that DAK failed to break through the Alam Halfa position. Harassing air attacks and a shortage of fuel compounded Rommel's difficulties. His 15 Panzer Division tried to outflank 22 Armored Brigade on 1 September, but this effort was stymied by an improved British antitank system. Axis forces pulled back to prepare a deep

Below: A Vickers gun noses over the barricades.
Right: The Axis attack on Alam Halfa failed to achieve its objectives.
Below right: Rommel's staff confer as the Allied defense turns into counterattack.

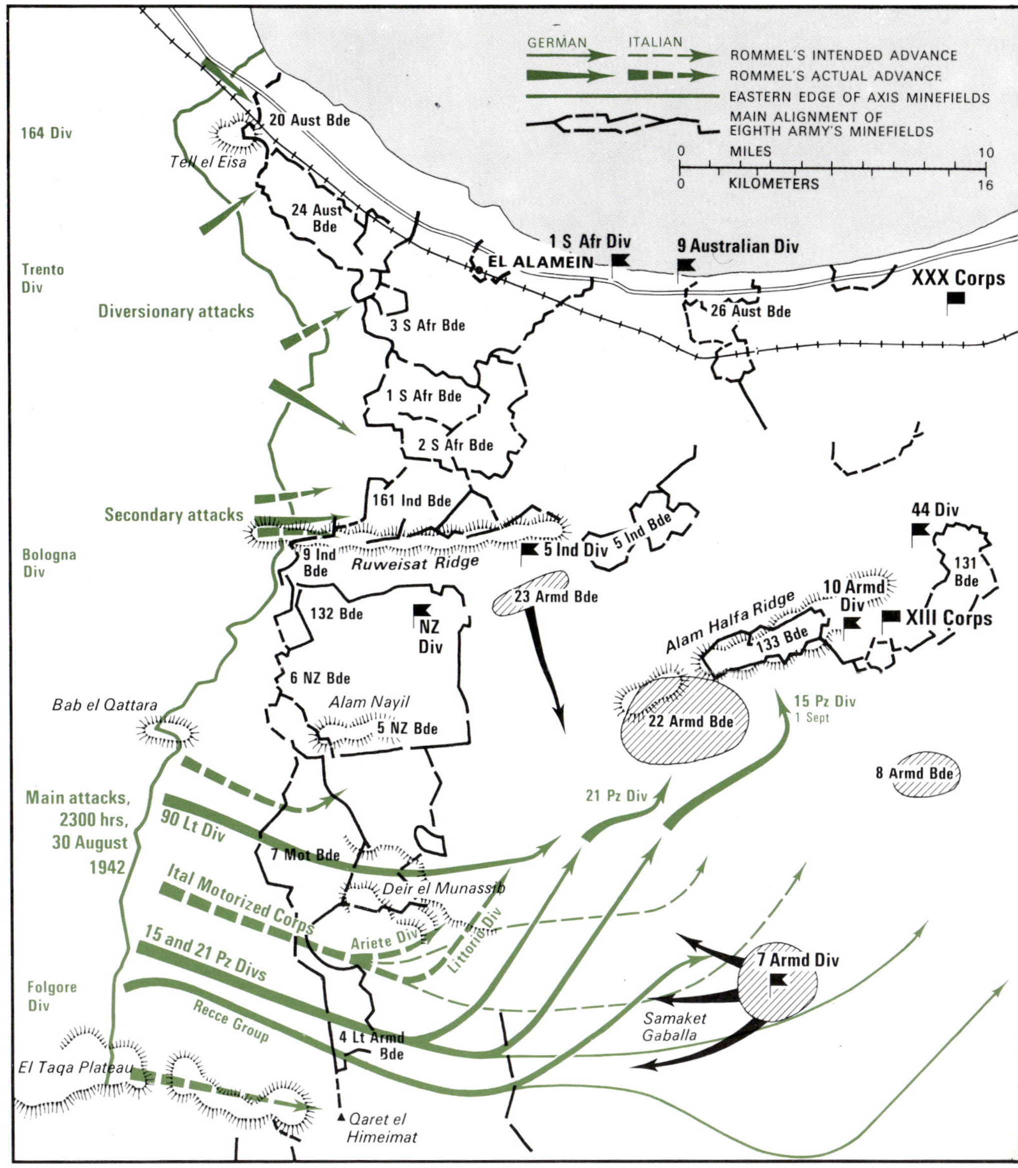

defensive position between the Qattara Depression and the sea.

Rommel had to hold the new line of defense or be overwhelmed – he lacked both the vehicles and the fuel for a mobile battle. By the same token he could not retreat. On 6 September, Axis forces were back where they had started, committed to an immediate counterattack for every foot of disputed ground.

El Alamein: The Second Battle

In his new command, General Montgomery lived up to his reputation as a careful planner who emphasized both training and morale. Eighth Army had suffered many changes of fortune and command in the North African Theater, and morale had eroded to a serious degree. Failures of co-operation and confidence had resulted in faulty operations, and Montgomery addressed himself to rebuilding Eighth Army into an optimum fighting unit. At the same time, he was amassing a force superior to the Germans' in every respect: troops, tanks, guns and aircraft.

The Germans were well dug in along a line between the sea and the Qattara Depression, and Montgomery's plan was to attack north of the Miteirya Ridge. The infantry of XXX Corps was to push forward to the Oxalic Line and open corridors through the minefields for passage of the X Corps' Sherman tanks, which were finally proving a match for the German Mark IV. Axis forward defenses were manned largely by Italian troops, and Rommel was hospitalized in Germany; he did not arrive until 25 October, when the battle was underway. General Stumme commanded in his absence.

The British infantry made a good start toward its objectives on 24 October, but it proved impossible to move the tanks forward as planned. The German 21st Panzer Division was kept out of the main battle for several days by diversionary efforts from XIII Corps, and the German defense suffered as a result of General Stumme's death from a heart attack during the first day of fighting. The Axis fuel shortage had become critical with the sinking of two tankers in Tobruk Harbor.

When Rommel returned to North Africa, he launched a series of unsuccessful counterattacks that ended on 3 November, when the British armor began to break through into open ground. Hitler at first forbade a withdrawal, but by 4 November Axis losses had made it inevitable. Rommel and his remaining forces made good their retreat.

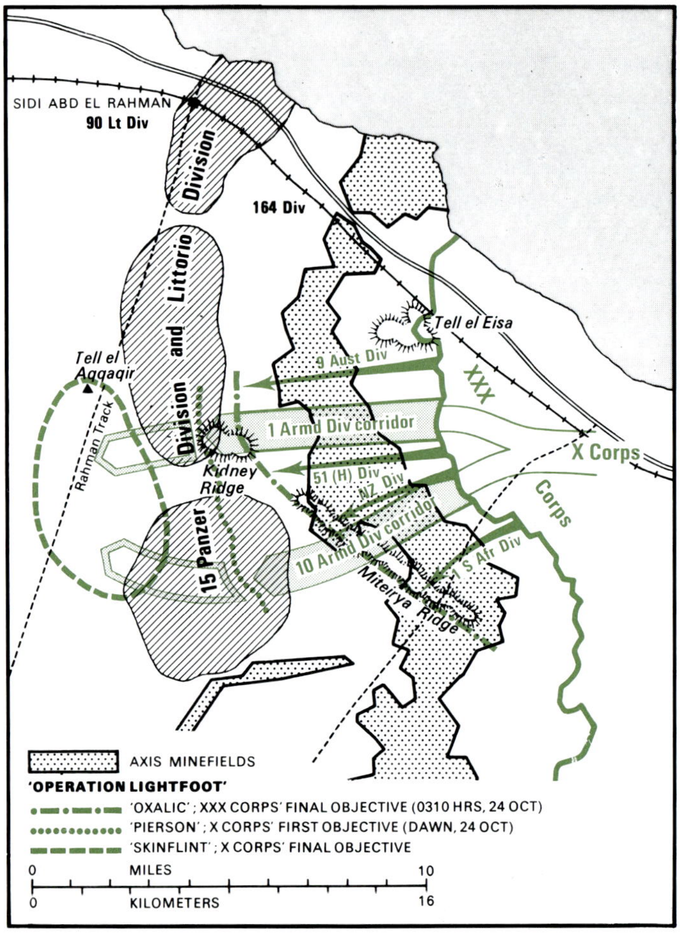

Above right: The attack plan for corridors to be driven through Axis minefields to provide safe passage for Allied tanks. Right: General Montgomery directs operations at El Alamein. On his right is General Sir Brian Horrocks.

Above: Italian infantrymen in the field at El Alamein.
Right: The second battle saw the Eighth Army repel Axis attacks.

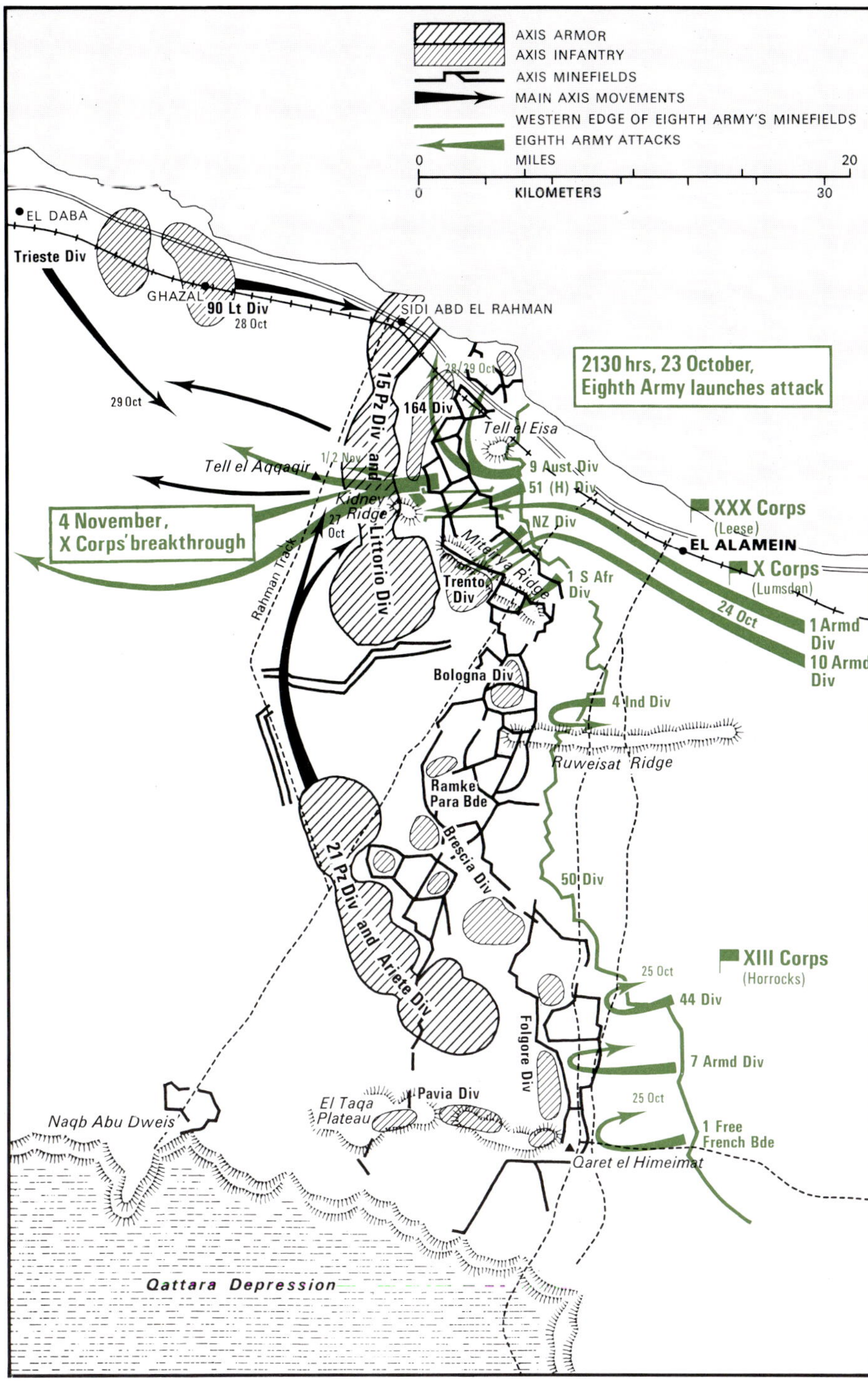

Operation Torch

On 8 November 1942, four days after Rommel began to retreat from El Alamein, American and British forces made a series of landings in French North Africa. This operation, code-named Torch, was the first real Allied effort of the war. It was hoped that the numerous Vichy French forces in North Africa would not resist the landings, and the US had undertaken diplomatic missions to local French leaders with this object in view. (Anglo-French relations were still embittered by the events of 1940.) Despite these efforts, sporadic French opposition delayed planned Allied attacks on Casablanca and Mehdia, and two destroyers were lost off Algiers. However, the weakest point of the Allied plan was its failure to occupy Tunisia in the first landings. German troops began to arrive there on 9 November to cover Rommel's retreat and formed a defensive perimeter.

The Allied capture of Vichy leader Admiral Darlan at Algiers helped diminish resistance from French forces; fewer than 2000 casualties were incurred in the three main landing areas. The largest difficulty was pushing the considerable Allied force the 400 miles to Tunis before the Germans could pour in troops and aircraft from Sicily. This they did with great speed, on instructions from Hitler and Commander in Chief Mediterranean Field Marshal Kesselring. Allied forces under General Dwight D Eisenhower, American Commander in Chief of the Torch operation, were stopped short in Tunisia by early December.

Below: US troops march on Algiers' Maison Blanche airfield.
Bottom: The Operation Torch landings.
Right: The Allied push into Tunisia.
Below right: The Germans reinforce.

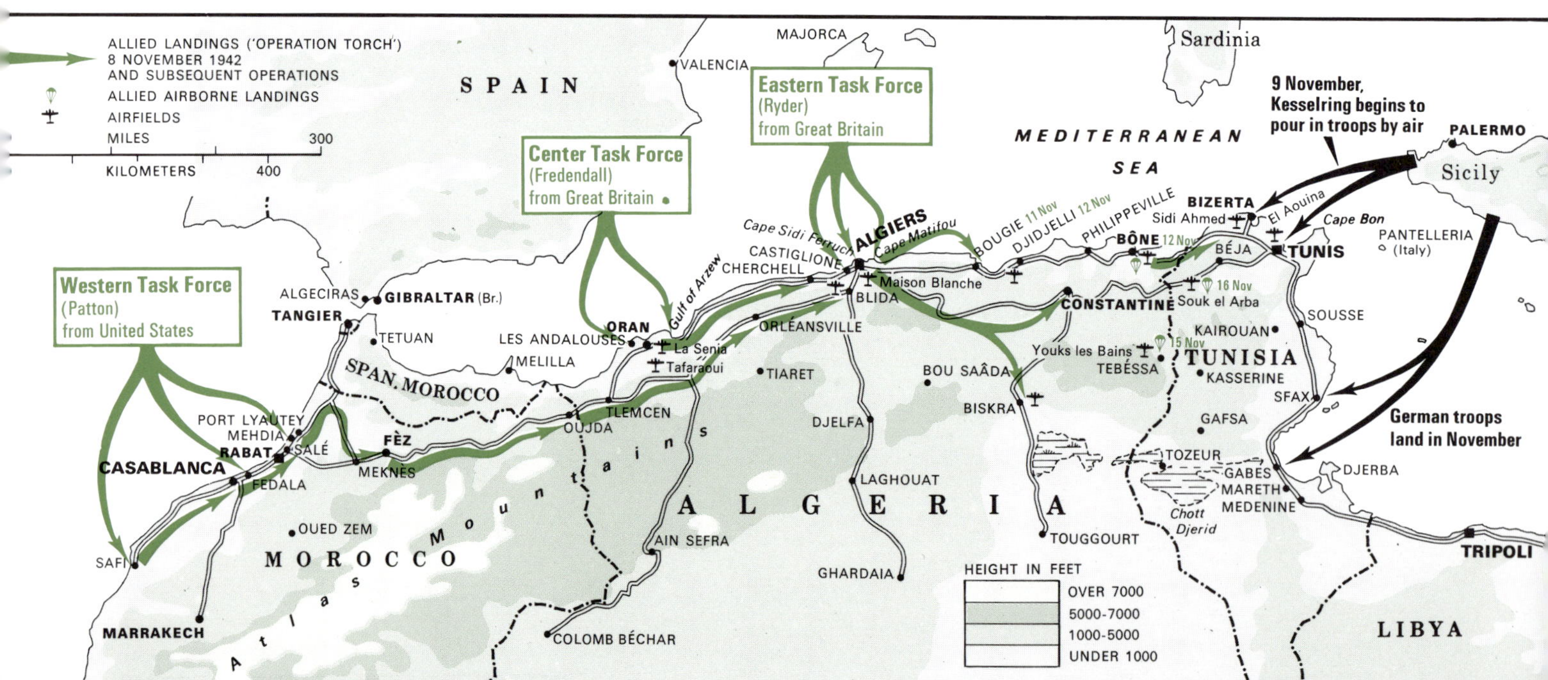

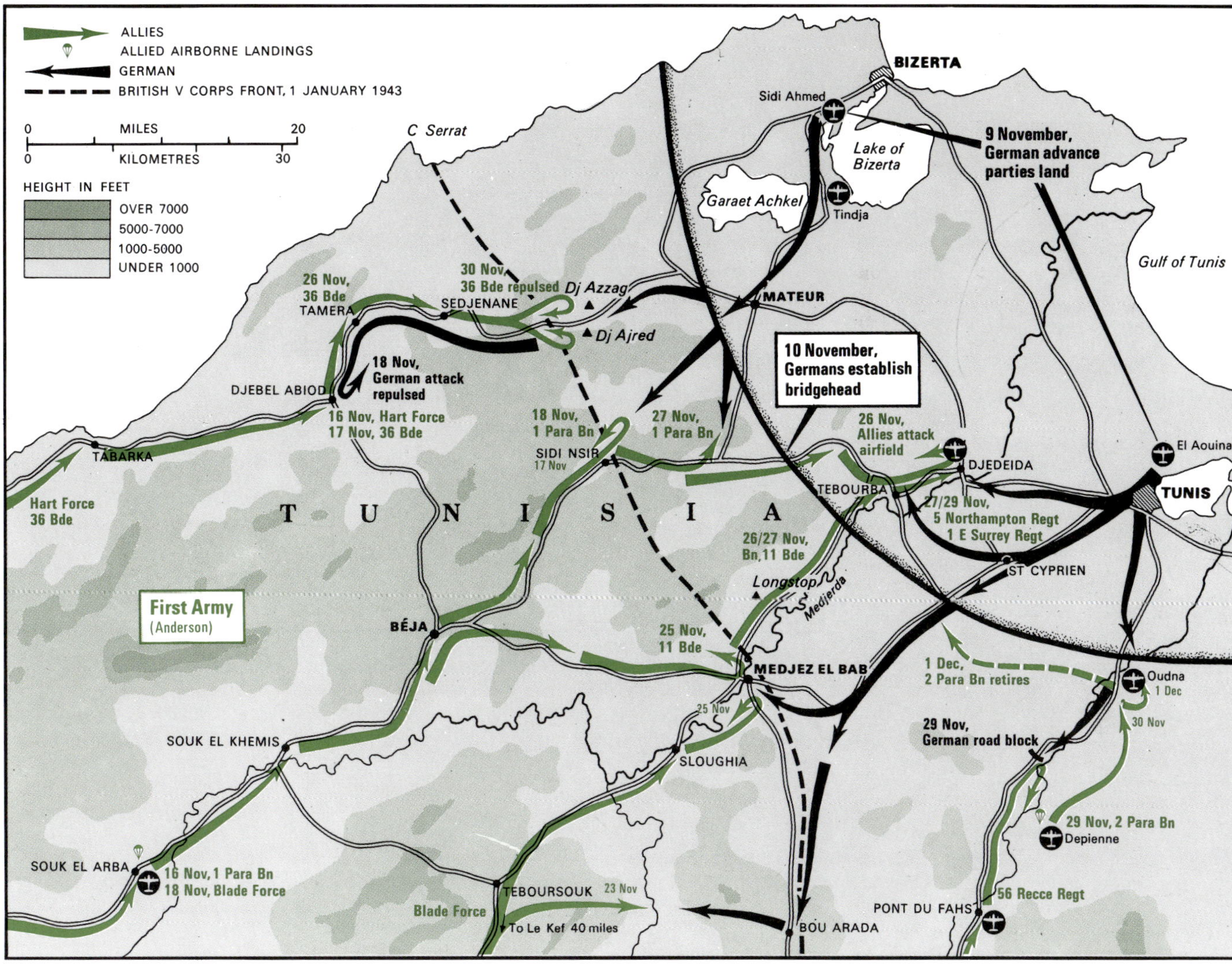
ALLIES
ALLIED AIRBORNE LANDINGS
GERMAN
BRITISH V CORPS FRONT, 1 JANUARY 1943
0 MILES 20
0 KILOMETRES 30
HEIGHT IN FEET
OVER 7000
5000-7000
1000-5000
UNDER 1000
BIZERTA
Sidi Ahmed
C Serrat
Lake of Bizerta
9 November, German advance parties land
Garaet Achkel
Tindja
Gulf of Tunis
30 Nov, 36 Bde repulsed
26 Nov, 36 Bde
TAMERA
SEDJENANE
Dj Azzag
Dj Ajred
MATEUR
10 November, Germans establish bridgehead
18 Nov, German attack repulsed
DJEBEL ABIOD
16 Nov, Hart Force
17 Nov, 36 Bde
18 Nov, 1 Para Bn
27 Nov, 1 Para Bn
26 Nov, Allies attack airfield
TABARKA
SIDI NSIR
17 Nov
DJEDEIDA
El Aouina
TUNIS
Hart Force 36 Bde
TEBOURBA
27/29 Nov, 5 Northampton Regt 1 E Surrey Regt
T U N I S I A
26/27 Nov, Bn,11 Bde
ST CYPRIEN
Longstop
Medjerda
First Army (Anderson)
BÉJA
25 Nov, 11 Bde
MEDJEZ EL BAB
1 Dec, 2 Para Bn retires
Oudna
1 Dec
30 Nov
25 Nov
29 Nov, German road block
SOUK EL KHEMIS
SLOUGHIA
29 Nov, 2 Para Bn
Depienne
SOUK EL ARBA
16 Nov, 1 Para Bn
18 Nov, Blade Force
TEBOURSOUK
23 Nov
56 Recce Regt
PONT DU FAHS
Blade Force
To Le Kef 40 miles
BOU ARADA

From Tripoli to Tunis

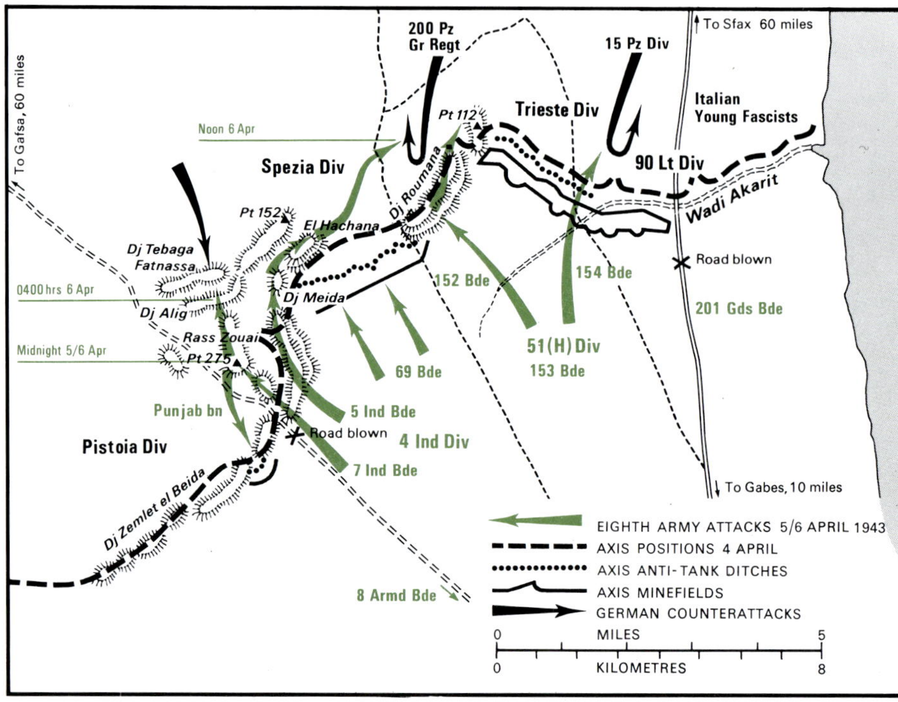

Eighth Army's pursuit of Rommel's forces was hampered by weather and supply problems. It took Montgomery almost three weeks to reach Agedabia (23 November 1942), and he had to halt there until he was resupplied. Soon after, the short-lived German position at El Agheila was outflanked and the race toward Tunisia resumed.

The port of Tripoli offered the British hope of alleviating their supply problems, but the Germans got there first and did as much damage as they could to port installations before pushing on to Tunisia. The British reached Tripoli on 23 January 1943, and it was not until mid-March that the port began to function effectively as a pipeline for British supplies. Meanwhile, Axis forces had consolidated behind the Mareth Line after inflicting 10,000 casualties on Allied troops from the Torch landings at the Battle of Kasserine. Rommel now faced Montgomery's Eighth Army in his last battle in Africa – a bitter fight that raged from 6 to 27 March. Axis forces were outflanked, and by mid-April had retreated up the coast to form a tight perimeter on the hills around Bizerta and Tunis.

Rommel urged evacuation of German and Italian forces from Africa when he returned to Germany, but his counsel was ignored. Thirteen understrength Axis divisions sought to defend Tunisia against 19 Allied divisions that had recovered from their earlier reverses to take on an overwhelming superiority in air power and armor. The Allies had 1200 tanks to the Axis' 130, 1500 guns to the Axis' 500.

Hill 609 was hotly contested by American forces seeking access to the so-called Mousetrap Valley leading to the coastal plain. British troops made some progress at Longstop Hill and Peter's Corner, which commanded the Medjerda Valley. Then General Alexander switched experienced units from Eighth Army to V Corps, which made possible a decisive victory. Allied troops broke through in early May. Tunis fell on the 7th, and five days later Italy's Marshal Messe and Germany's General von Arnim surrendered with some quarter of a million troops. These forces would be sorely missed by Hitler when the Allies launched their invasion of Italy.

Above: The Eighth Army's attempt to progress up Tunisia's east coast was delayed at Wadi Akarit.
Right: The Allied conquest of Tunisia. Bizerta and Tunis fell on 7 May.
Below: The Eighth Army's progress in the wake of El Alamein.

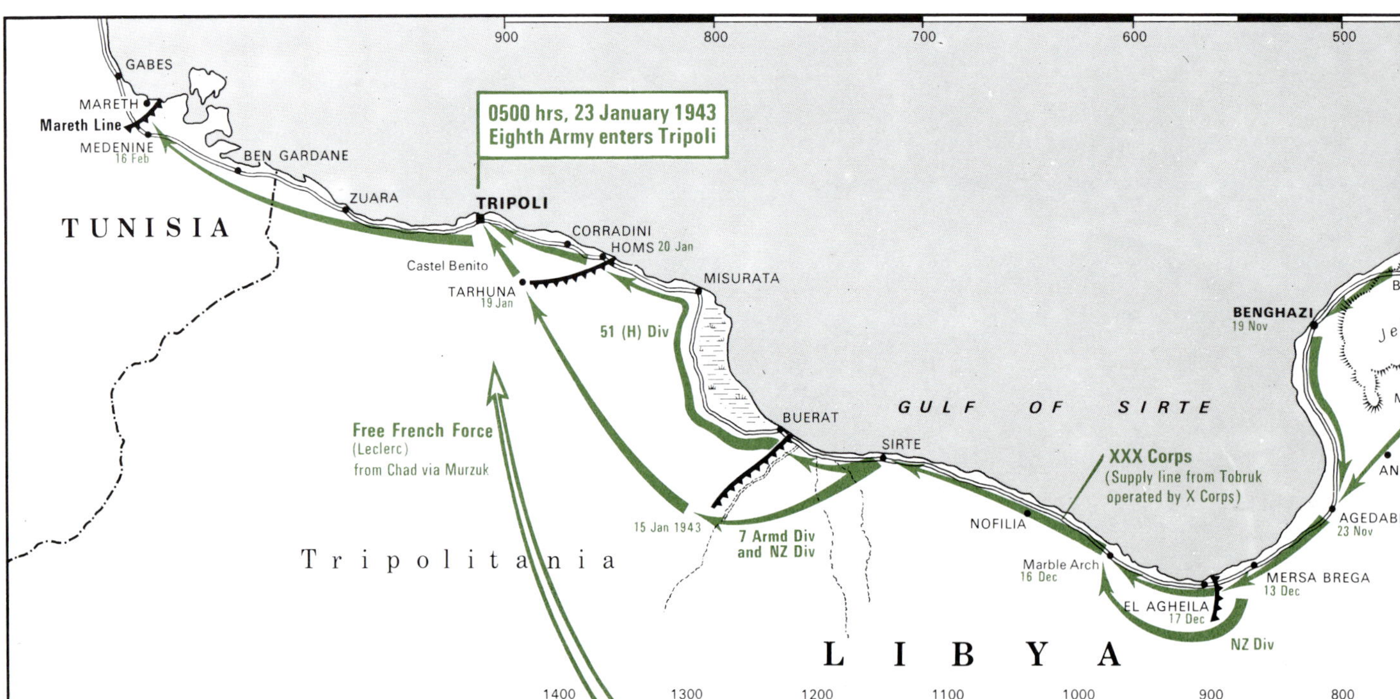

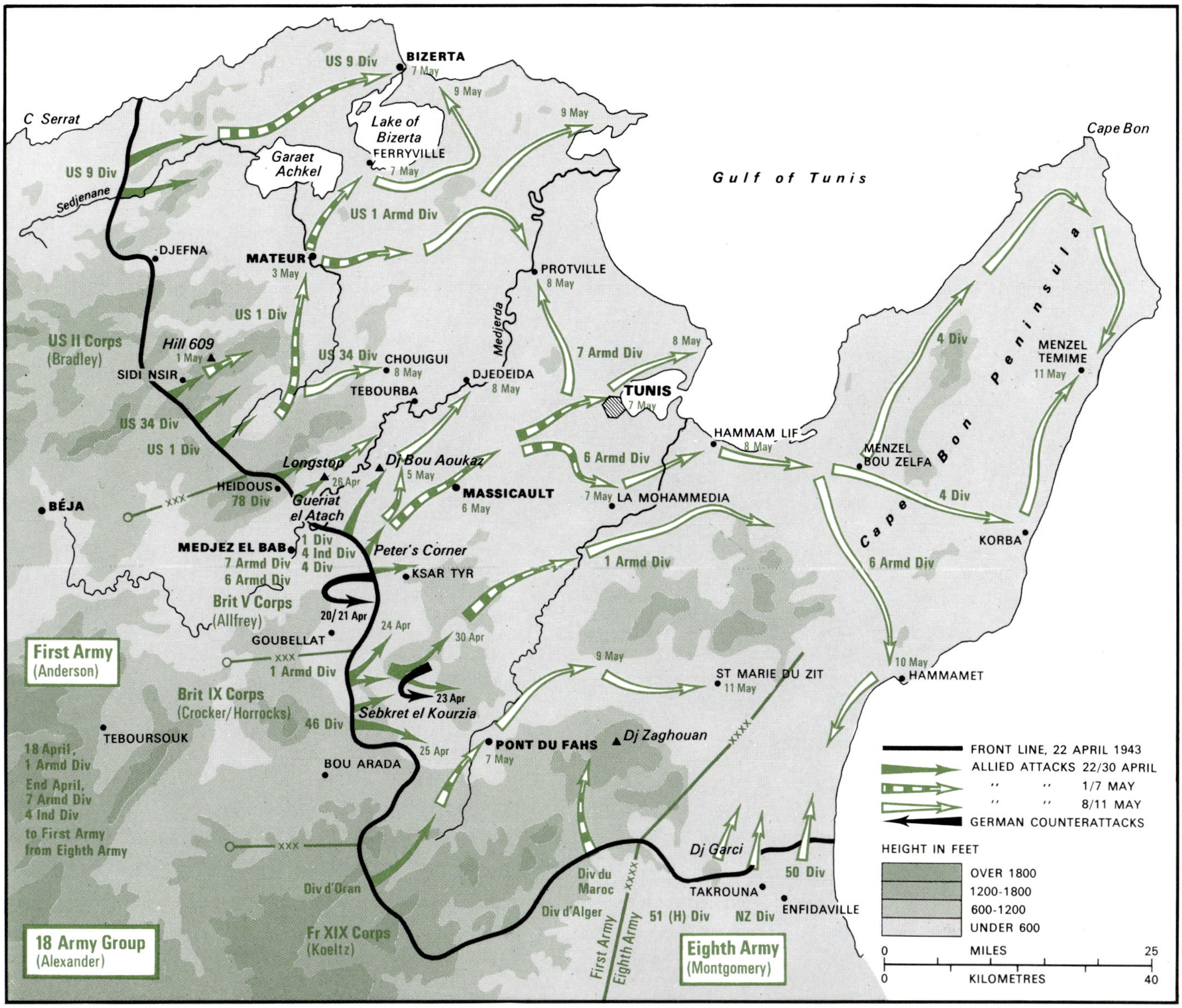

BIZERTA
7 May
US 9 Div
9 May
C Serrat
Lake of Bizerta
FERRYVILLE
7 May
Garaet Achkel
US 9 Div
Sedjenane
Gulf of Tunis
Cape Bon
US 1 Armd Div
DJEFNA
MATEUR
3 May
PROTVILLE
8 May
Medjerda
US 1 Div
US II Corps
(Bradley)
Hill 609
1 May
US 34 Div
CHOUIGUI
8 May
DJEDEIDA
8 May
7 Armd Div
8 May
4 Div
MENZEL TEMIME
11 May
Cape Bon Peninsula
SIDI NSIR
TEBOURBA
TUNIS
7 May
US 34 Div
US 1 Div
HAMMAM LIF
8 May
Longstop
26 Apr
Dj Bou Aoukaz
5 May
6 Armd Div
MENZEL BOU ZELFA
HEIDOUS
78 Div
BÉJA
Gueriat el Atach
MASSICAULT
6 May
7 May
LA MOHAMMEDIA
4 Div
KORBA
MEDJEZ EL BAB
1 Div
4 Ind Div
4 Div
7 Armd Div
6 Armd Div
Peter's Corner
KSAR TYR
1 Armd Div
6 Armd Div
Brit V Corps
(Allfrey)
20/21 Apr
24 Apr
GOUBELLAT
30 Apr
First Army
(Anderson)
1 Armd Div
9 May
ST MARIE DU ZIT
11 May
10 May
HAMMAMET
23 Apr
Brit IX Corps
(Crocker/Horrocks)
Sebkret el Kourzia
46 Div
TEBOURSOUK
25 Apr
PONT DU FAHS
7 May
Dj Zaghouan
18 April, 1 Armd Div
End April, 7 Armd Div
4 Ind Div
to First Army from Eighth Army
BOU ARADA
FRONT LINE, 22 APRIL 1943
ALLIED ATTACKS 22/30 APRIL
" " 1/7 MAY
" " 8/11 MAY
GERMAN COUNTERATTACKS
HEIGHT IN FEET
OVER 1800
1200-1800
600-1200
UNDER 600
Dj Garci
Div d'Oran
Div du Maroc
TAKROUNA
50 Div
ENFIDAVILLE
Div d'Alger
51 (H) Div
NZ Div
18 Army Group
(Alexander)
Fr XIX Corps
(Koeltz)
First Army
Eighth Army
Eighth Army
(Montgomery)
0 MILES 25
0 KILOMETRES 40

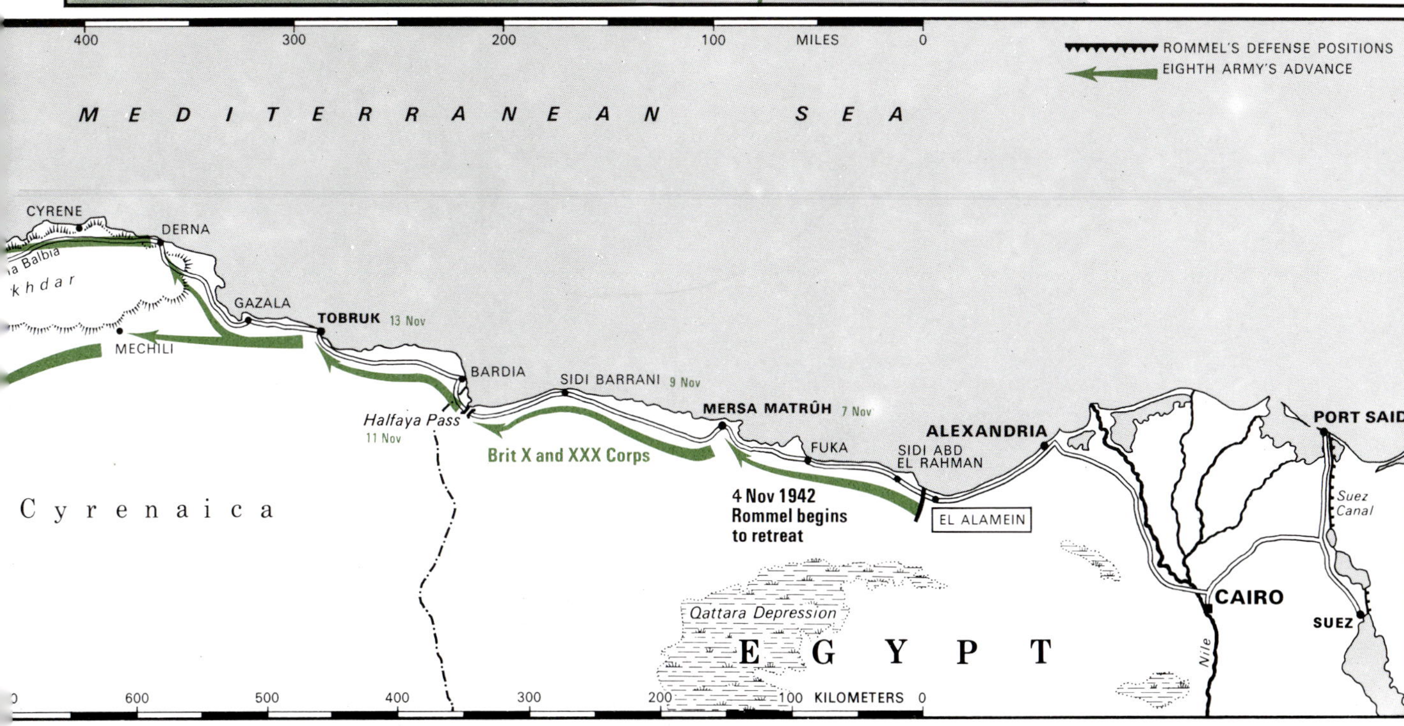

400
300
200
100
MILES
0
ROMMEL'S DEFENSE POSITIONS
EIGHTH ARMY'S ADVANCE
MEDITERRANEAN SEA
CYRENE
DERNA
GAZALA
TOBRUK 13 Nov
MECHILI
BARDIA
SIDI BARRANI 9 Nov
MERSA MATRÛH 7 Nov
Halfaya Pass
11 Nov
Brit X and XXX Corps
ALEXANDRIA
FUKA
SIDI ABD EL RAHMAN
PORT SAID
4 Nov 1942
Rommel begins to retreat
EL ALAMEIN
Suez Canal
Cyrenaica
Qattara Depression
CAIRO
SUEZ
EGYPT
Nile
600
500
400
300
200
100
KILOMETERS
0

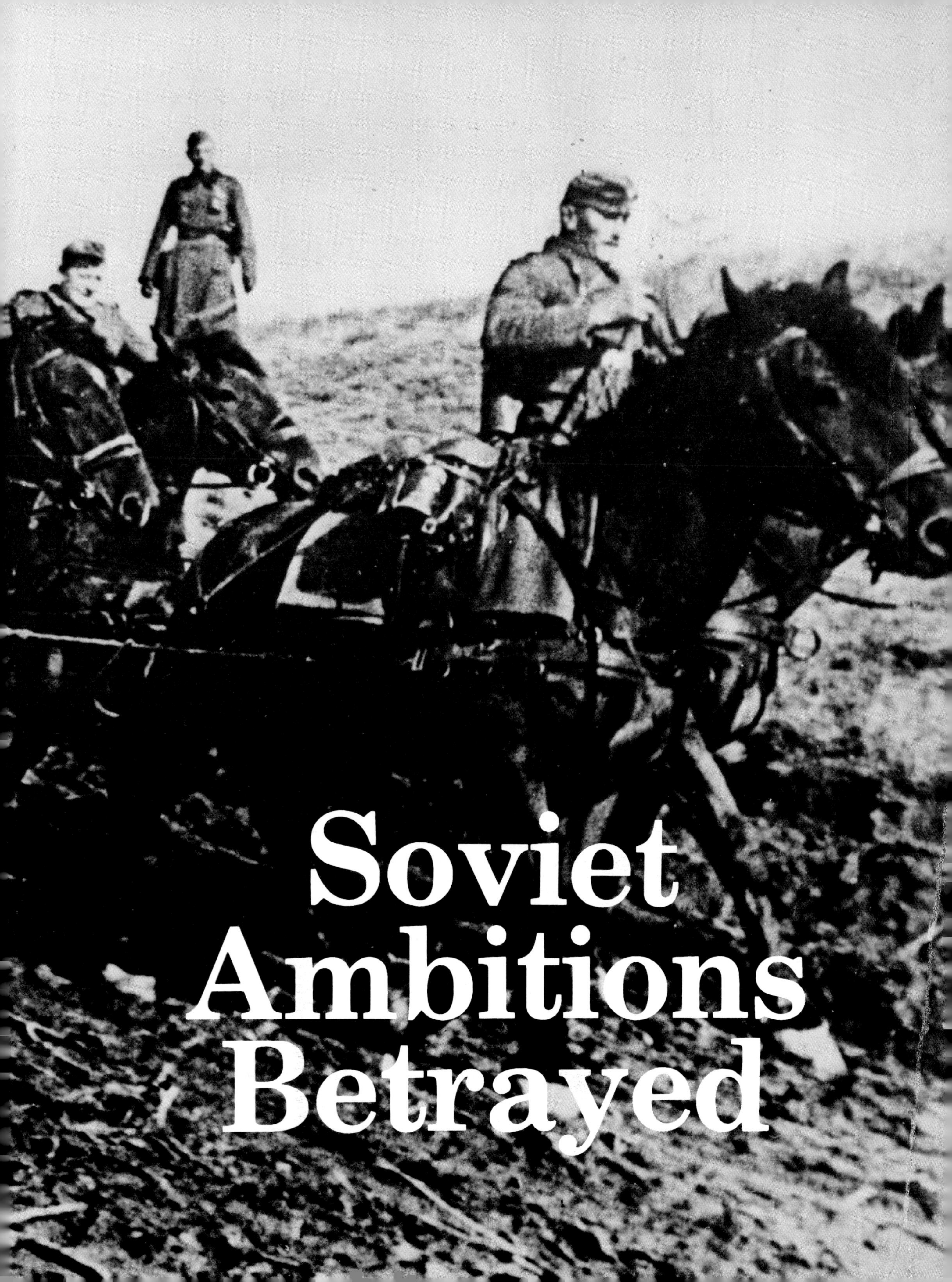

Soviet Ambitions Betrayed

The Winter War: Finland, 1939-40

On 30 November 1939, the Soviet Union invaded Finland, after failing to obtain territorial concessions demanded in early October. Five different Soviet armies crossed the Russo-Finnish frontier on four major fronts, but the conquest of this small neighboring nation proved much more difficult than had been foreseen. Deep snow and heavy forest forced Russian tanks and transports to stay on the roads, where they were easy targets for the mobile, well-trained Finnish ski troops. Russian convoys were shot up and separated, and formations were isolated and defeated in detail. The Finns never had more than nine divisions in the field, with few guns and almost no tanks. But their confidence was high, and they had the advantage of fighting on familiar ground with tactics suited to the terrain.

By 31 January 1940, the Russians had made deep penetrations in the north by dint of superior numbers, but the Mannerheim Line, on the Karelian Isthmus, was holding on. The Seventh and Thirteenth Soviet Armies assaulted this line from 1 through 13 February with forces that included six tank brigades and 21 infantry divisions. A massive bombardment preceded these attacks, which achieved a breakthrough in mid-February. The Finns were forced to surrender, and to cede the Karelian Isthmus and considerable territory in the north. They would seek to make good these losses the following year in an alliance with Nazi Germany.

The Finnish fight was solitary and ultimately hopeless, because the British and French Governments feared to arouse Soviet hostility by involving themselves. Nevertheless, the Russo-Finnish War had far-reaching consequences in the international community. As a result of it, the French Government fell due to dissension about helping the Finns, and the League of Nations was thoroughly discredited. Hitler formed a false impression of Soviet inefficiency that probably influenced his decision to turn on his Russian ally. And the Red Army was awakened to deep-seated internal problems that became subject to reform in the months that followed.

Previous pages: The Wehrmacht advance with difficulty along a muddy Russian road, 1941.
Below: The Russians breach Finland's Mannerheim Line in February.
Right: Soviet soldiers dismantle Finnish anti-tank obstacles.

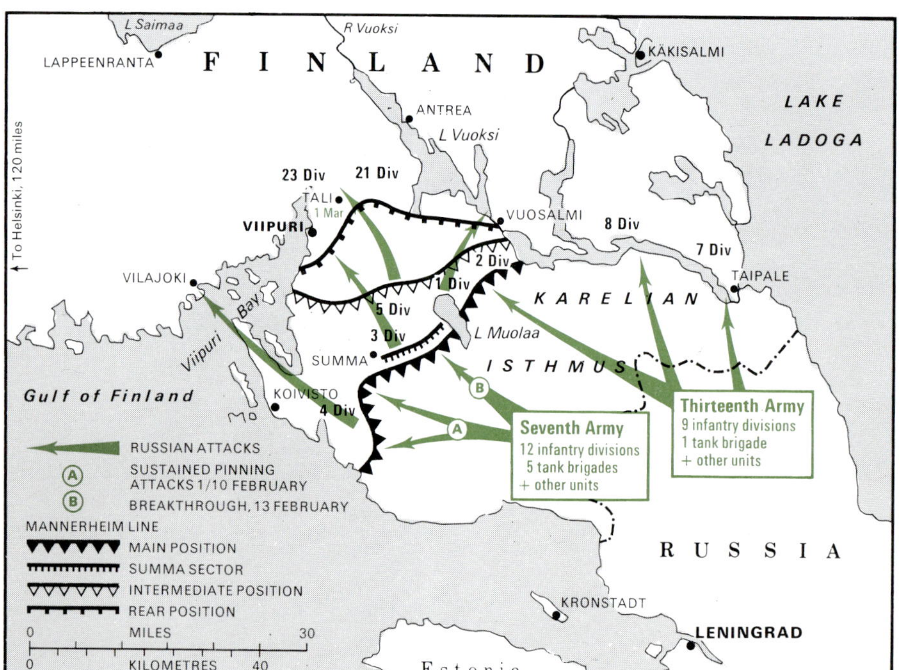

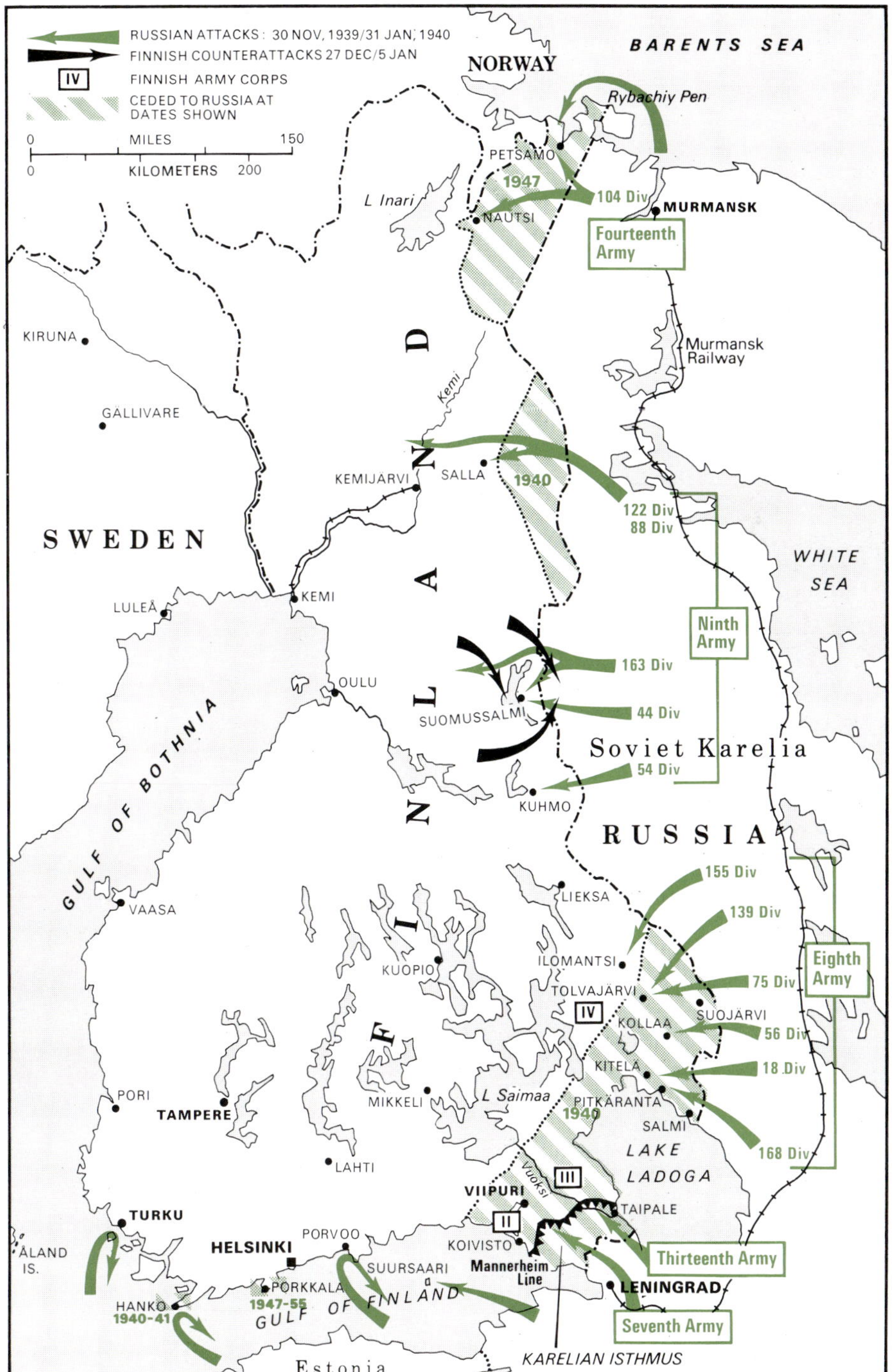

Above: Earlier Soviet penetration in the north and east from November 1939 had met effective Finnish resistance.

Military Balance on the Eastern Front

The German High Command spent almost a year planning the invasion of Russia, code-named Operation Barbarossa. Three different plans were devised, of which the one giving priority to the capture of Leningrad was chosen. German leaders estimated Red Army strength along the frontier at some 155 divisions (in fact, there were 170 within operational distance.) The front was divided in half by the Pripet Marshes. In the north, von Leeb's Army Group North was to aim itself against Leningrad, where it faced an almost equal number of Russian divisions. However, these were deployed so far forward that they were vulnerable to being pushed back against the coast. Von Bock's Army Group Centre, with two Panzer armies, was the strongest German force in the field; facing it was the comparatively weak Red Army West Front. Most Soviet troops were south of the Pripet Marshes, positioned to defend the agricultural and industrial wealth of the Ukraine. Von Rundstedt's Army Group South was to thrust southeast against these forces.

The German plan called for swift penetration deep into Russia in June, to destroy the Red Army long before winter. A massive German buildup began, but Stalin and his advisors were so determined not to give Hitler any excuse to attack that they ignored all the warning signs. In fact, the Red Army was still on a peacetime footing when the invasion began on 22 June. Most units were widely scattered for summer training; others were too close to the western frontier. The reforms that followed upon the Russo-Finnish War were far from complete, and there was almost no Russian reserve to deal with deep incursions. The Germans had good reason to be optimistic about the invasion of Russia.

Below: Soviet cavalrymen on the march, 1941. Horse-mounted troops were more mobile than tanks in the severe Russian winter conditions, and were thus more effective than appearances suggested.

Above left: The initial German thrusts to Moscow and Kiev.
Far left: A northern attack was later added to the original two-pronged assault plan.
Left: Hitler finally identified Leningrad as the prime target, and it was this plan of attack that was selected.
Right: The Eastern Front from the Baltic to the Black Sea, showing the relative strengths and dispositions of the two protagonists.

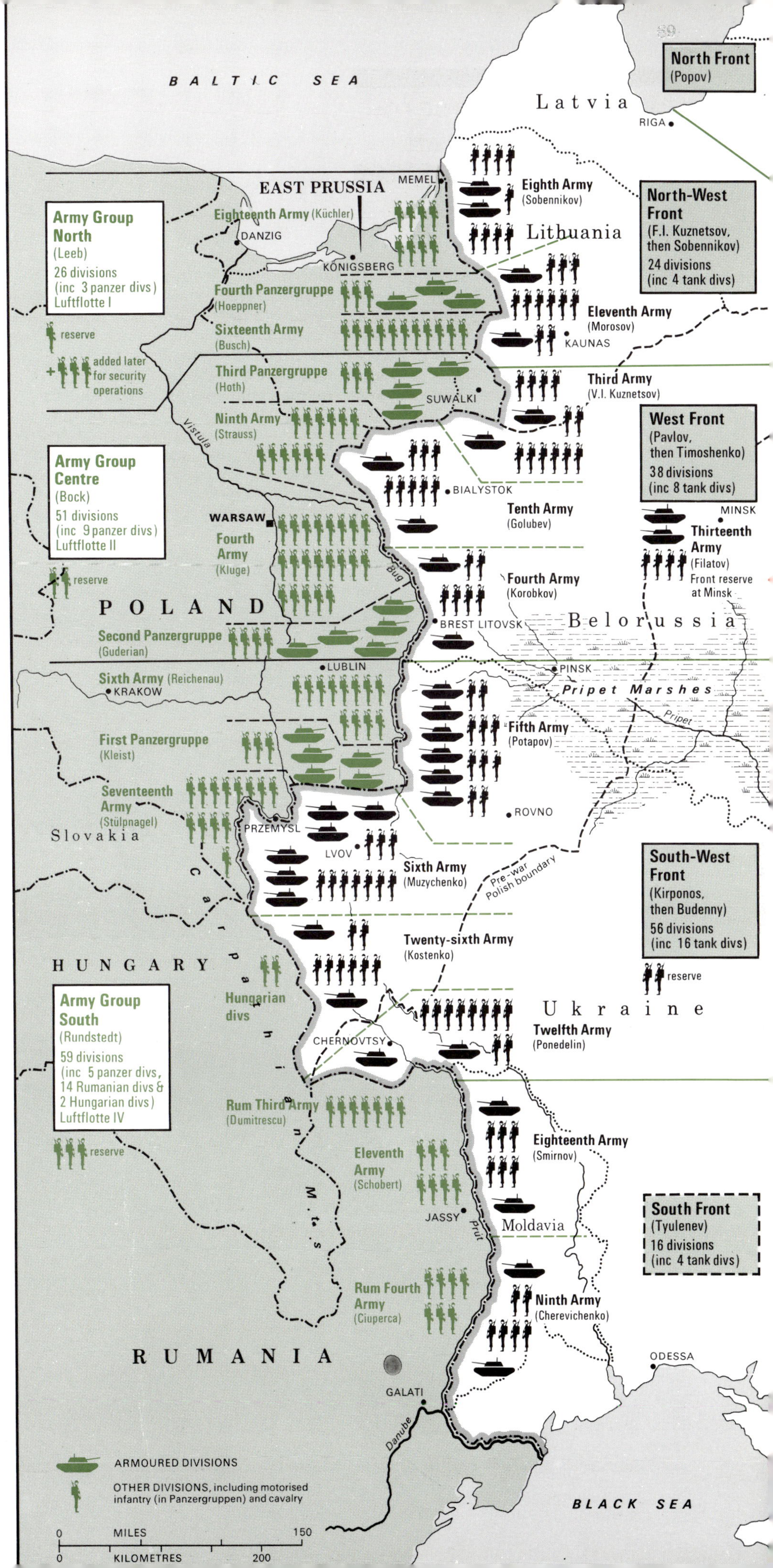

Operation Barbarossa: 1941

Below: The crew of a German Panzer attempt to free their tank from frozen mud by lighting a fire.
Right: The front line moves progressively eastwards as German pressure forces Russia to yield.

German forces achieved almost total surprise in their 22 June invasion of Soviet territory, which was preceded by a devastating air attack that all but wiped out the Red Air Force. Fourth Panzer Group took a series of northern objectives that brought it to the Luga by 14 July. Army Group Centre sealed off Russian forces at Bialystok and Gorodische, taking 300,000 prisoners and 2500 tanks in a week's operations. Army Group South faced the greatest resistance in the Ukraine, where the Russian Fifth Army counterattacked on 10 July to prevent an assault on Kiev.

This development incited Hitler to divert Army Group Centre from its attack on Moscow via Smolensk into the Ukraine offensive. Second Army and Heinz Guderian's Second Panzer Group were ordered south to destroy the Soviet Fifth Army and surround Kiev. Guderian was radically opposed to abandoning the Moscow offensive, but he turned south on 23 August as ordered. An unsuccessful Russian counteroffensive failed to halt the German advance north of Gomel, and the Soviet South-West Front suffered heavy losses every time it gave battle. Many divisions were trapped in pockets and destroyed piecemeal, while at Kiev alone, half a million Red soldiers were captured.

By mid November the Germans had seized Rostov and the Perekop Isthmus, which commanded the Crimea. In the center, their victories at Smolensk and Bryansk had enabled them to capture Orel, Tula and Vyazma. The Baltic States had been occupied, and the Finnish alliance had helped open the way to Leningrad.

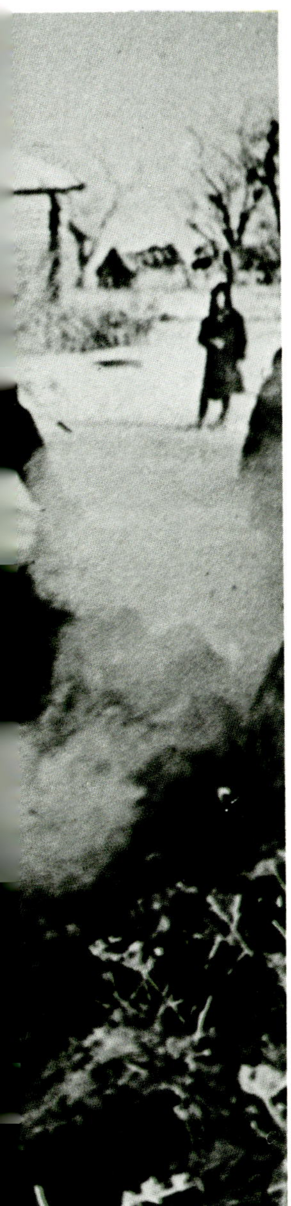

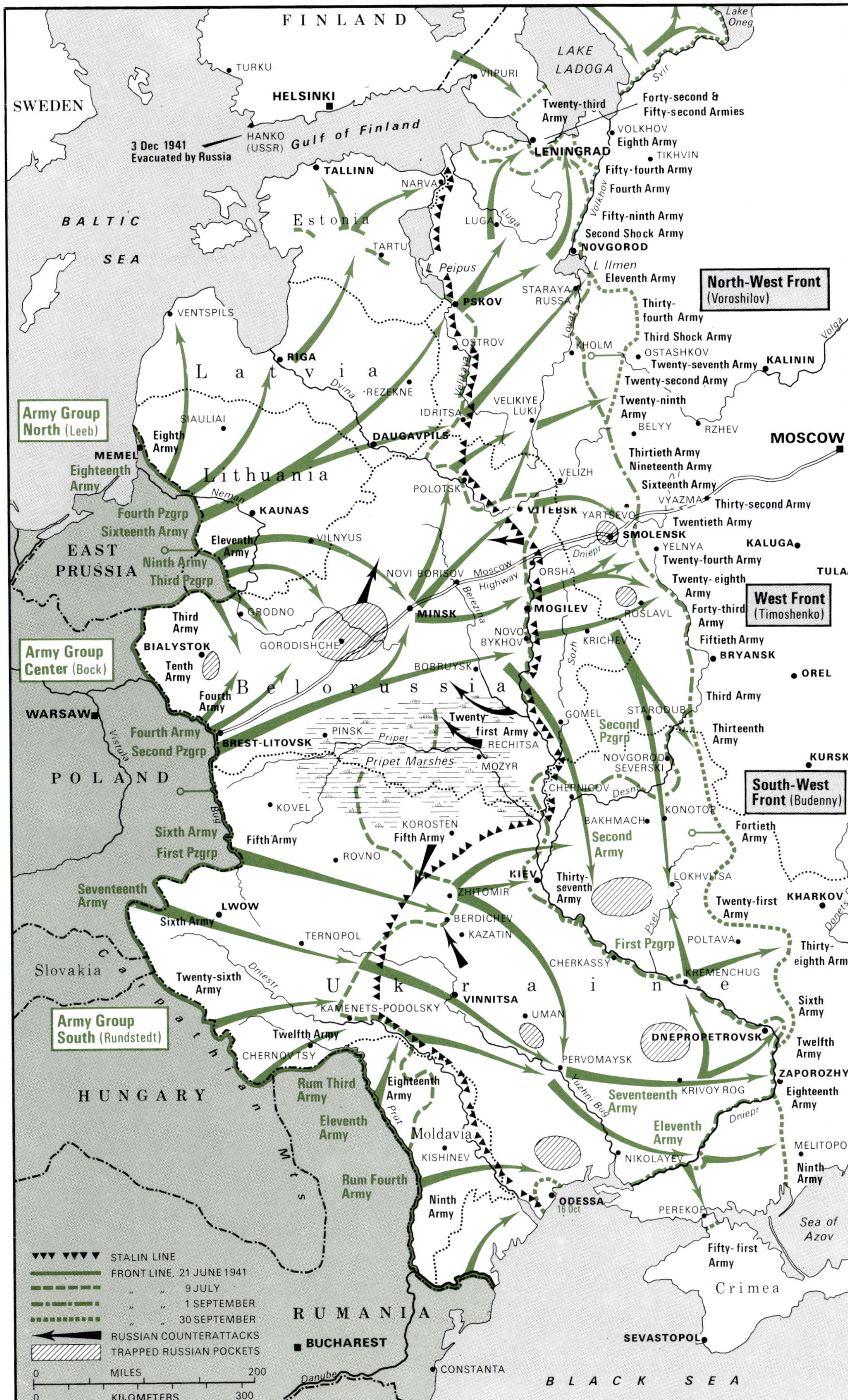
FINLAND
SWEDEN
TURKU
HELSINKI
HANKO (USSR)
3 Dec 1941 Evacuated by Russia
Gulf of Finland
VIIPURI
LAKE LADOGA
Lake Oneg
Svir
Twenty-third Army
Forty-second & Fifty-second Armies
VOLKHOV
Eighth Army
LENINGRAD
TIKHVIN
Fifty-fourth Army
Fourth Army
Volkhov
TALLINN
NARVA
Estonia
LUGA
Luga
Fifty-ninth Army
Second Shock Army
NOVGOROD
BALTIC SEA
TARTU
L Peipus
L Ilmen
Eleventh Army
North-West Front (Voroshilov)
STARAYA RUSSA
PSKOV
Thirty-fourth Army
VENTSPILS
Third Shock Army
OSTROV
Lovat
KHOLM
OSTASHKOV
Twenty-seventh Army
KALININ
Volga
RIGA
Latvia
Dvina
REZEKNE
Velikaya
Twenty-second Army
Twenty-ninth Army
IDRITSA
VELIKIYE LUKI
Army Group North (Leeb)
SIAULIAI
BELYY
RZHEV
MOSCOW
MEMEL
Eighth Army
DAUGAVPILS
Eighteenth Army
Thirtieth Army
Nineteenth Army
Lithuania
VELIZH
Sixteenth Army
Neman
POLOTSK
VYAZMA
Thirty-second Army
Fourth Pzgrp
KAUNAS
VITEBSK
YARTSEVO
Twentieth Army
Sixteenth Army
EAST PRUSSIA
Eleventh Army
VILNYUS
SMOLENSK
Dniepr
YELNYA
KALUGA
Ninth Army
Third Pzgrp
NOVI BORISOV
Moscow Highway
ORSHA
Twenty-fourth Army
TULA
Twenty-eighth Army
Third Army
GRODNO
MINSK
Berezina
MOGILEV
ROSLAVL
West Front (Timoshenko)
Forty-third Army
Army Group Center (Bock)
BIALYSTOK
GORODISHCHE
NOVO BYKHOV
Sozh
KRICHEV
Fiftieth Army
BRYANSK
Tenth Army
BOBRUYSK
OREL
Belorussia
Fourth Army
WARSAW
Vistula
GOMEL
STARODUB
Third Army
Fourth Army
Twenty-first Army
Second Pzgrp
PINSK
Pripet
RECHITSA
Second Pzgrp
Thirteenth Army
BREST-LITOVSK
Pripet Marshes
MOZYR
NOVGOROD SEVERSKI
KURSK
POLAND
Bug
CHERNIGOV
Desna
South-West Front (Budenny)
KOVEL
KOROSTEN
BAKHMACH
KONOTOP
Sixth Army
First Pzgrp
Fifth Army
Fifth Army
Second Army
Fortieth Army
ROVNO
KIEV
Thirty-seventh Army
LOKHVITSA
Seventeenth Army
ZHITOMIR
KHARKOV
LWOW
Twenty-first Army
Sixth Army
BERDICHEV
KAZATIN
Psel
Donets
TERNOPOL
POLTAVA
Thirty-eighth Army
First Pzgrp
Slovakia
Carpathian Mts
Dniestr
CHERKASSY
Twenty-sixth Army
Ukraine
KREMENCHUG
VINNITSA
KAMENETS-PODOLSKY
UMAN
Sixth Army
Army Group South (Rundstedt)
Twelfth Army
DNEPROPETROVSK
Twelfth Army
CHERNOVTSY
PERVOMAYSK
ZAPOROZHYE
Rum Third Army
Eighteenth Army
KRIVOY ROG
Eighteenth Army
HUNGARY
Yuzhni Bug
Seventeenth Army
Prut
Eleventh Army
Eleventh Army
Dniepr
Moldavia
MELITOPOL
KISHINEV
NIKOLAYEV
Ninth Army
Rum Fourth Army
ODESSA
16 Oct
Ninth Army
PEREKOP
Sea of Azov
Fifty-first Army
Crimea
STALIN LINE
FRONT LINE, 21 JUNE 1941
" " 9 JULY
" " 1 SEPTEMBER
" " 30 SEPTEMBER
RUSSIAN COUNTERATTACKS
TRAPPED RUSSIAN POCKETS
MILES 0 200
KILOMETERS 0 300
RUMANIA
BUCHAREST
SEVASTOPOL
CONSTANTA
Danube
BLACK SEA

The Finnish Front

The 1941 alliance with Germany brought significant improvements in Finland's forces. Mobilization and training systems were revamped, as the Finns prepared to regain the territory lost to Russia the previous year by expediting the German assault in the north. Marshal Carl von Mannerheim, hero of the Russo-Finnish War, would lead first the army and then the state for the balance of World War II.

Joint German-Finnish attacks began on 19 June 1941, with early successes around Lake Ladoga. The Russians were outflanked there and began to withdraw by water, until the Finns had pursued to a point near their former frontier (1 September). On the Karelian Isthmus, another attack reached Vuosalmi on 16 August, but was stopped short of Leningrad by a second Russian retreat. At this point Mannerheim called a halt: having regained the territory lost in the previous year, he was reluctant to become more deeply involved in the attack on Russia.

Offensives did not resume until several days later, when attacks north of Lake Ladoga and against the Murmansk railway achieved their objectives. Then the Russian resistance grew increasingly stronger, and by early December the Finns were on the defensive. The front line stabilized along an axis east of the 1939 Russo-Finnish boundary.

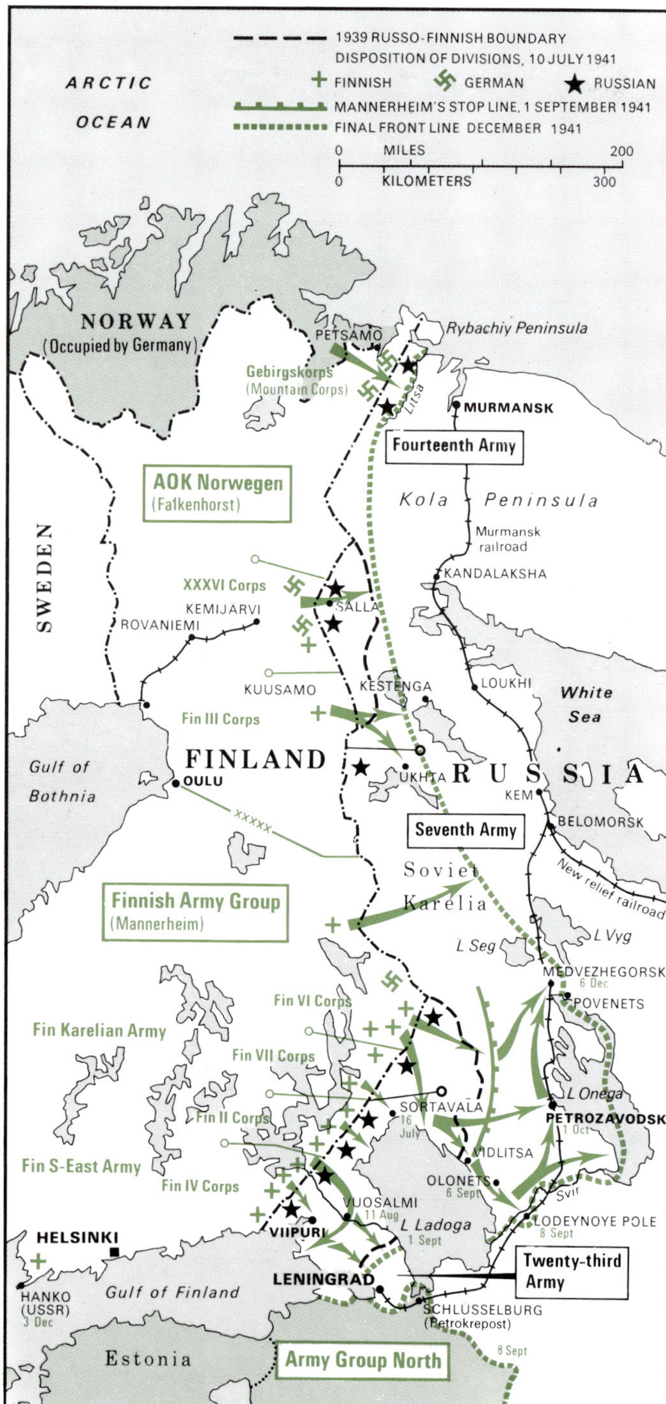

Below left: With German assistance, the Finns established a front line to the east of their 1939 border.
Below: Finnish infantry adopt defensive positions on the Mannerheim Line as Russian pressure increased.

The Attack on Leningrad

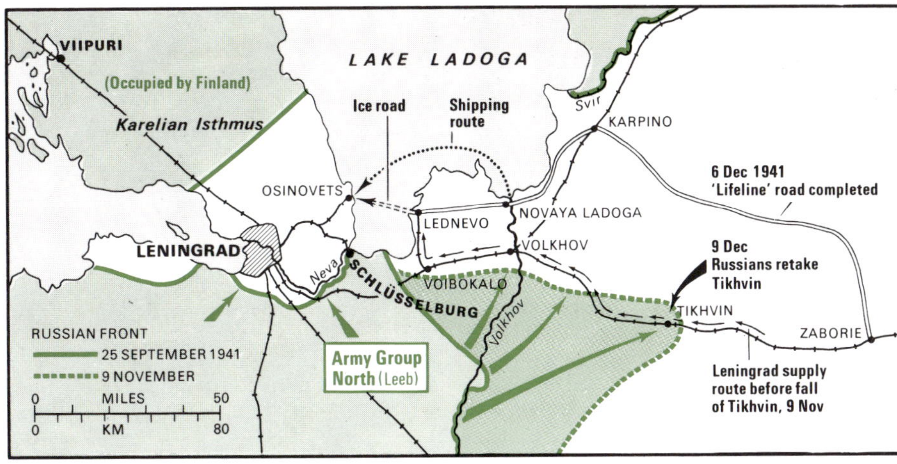

German Army Group North, commanded by General Wilhelm von Leeb, arrived near Leningrad on 1 September 1941. The Germans had decided not to storm the city, but to isolate it and starve out its defenders. Artillery bombardments began immediately, and within two weeks Leningrad had been cut off entirely from overland communication with the rest of Russia.

The city had only a month's supply of food – heavily rationed – and starvation set in by October. The following month, 11,000 died of hunger. Meager supplies continued to come in by barge across Lake Ladoga in the early fall, but on 9 November the Germans took Tikhvin, the point of origin, and ice on the lake made navigation impossible. Four weeks later, the Russians opened a new 'Lifeline' road from Zaborie to Lednevo, but winter weather and difficult terrain slowed supply trucks to a crawl.

Thousands more had succumbed to starvation in Leningrad by early December, when the Red Army's counteroffensive began to make itself felt. Tikhvin was recaptured, and the Germans were pushed back to the Volkhov River. The Russians repaired the railroad and opened an ice road across the lake, which was now frozen solidly enough to bear the weight of trucks. By Christmas Day, it was possible to increase the bread ration in Leningrad. But relief came too late for many: on that same day, almost 4000 died of starvation.

Above: Supply routes to the besieged city of Leningrad.
Below: Finnish members of the Waffen-SS in action.

Moscow – Strike and Counterstrike

Below: The German Army Group South pushes to capture the Ukraine, but is forced to withdraw to the Mius River.
Bottom: Muscovites dig defense lines around the capital, 1941.
Right: The German assault on Moscow.

After capturing Kiev, the Germans redeployed their forces for the assault on Moscow. They had a superiority of two to one in men and tanks, three to one in the air. Fourteen Panzer divisions were involved in the attacks that converged on Russia's capital beginning 30 September.

By 7 October large pockets of Soviet troops had been cut off around Vyazma and Bryansk. They were systematically destroyed in the next two weeks, after which heavy rains put a serious check on German mobility. The Mozhaisk defense line offered increasing resistance, and by 30 October German forces had bogged down miles from Moscow. Many men and tanks were lost in the frustrating advance through a sea of mud.

When the weather changed, it did little to help the German cause. The freeze that set in hardened the roads, but German soldiers found it difficult to adapt to the extreme cold, which also created new problems with their vehicles. By 27 November, units of the Third Panzer

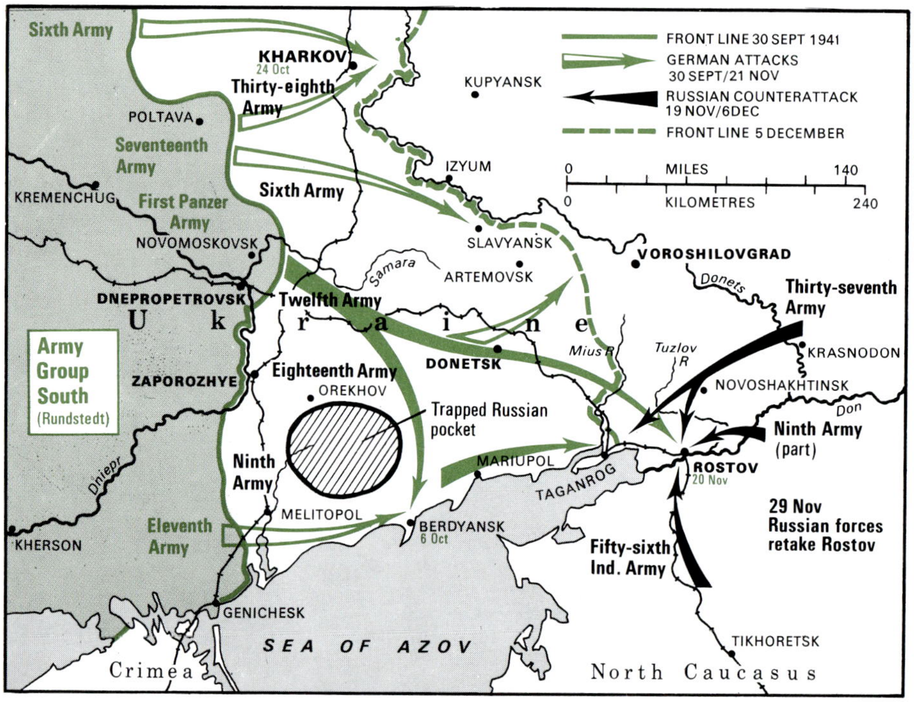

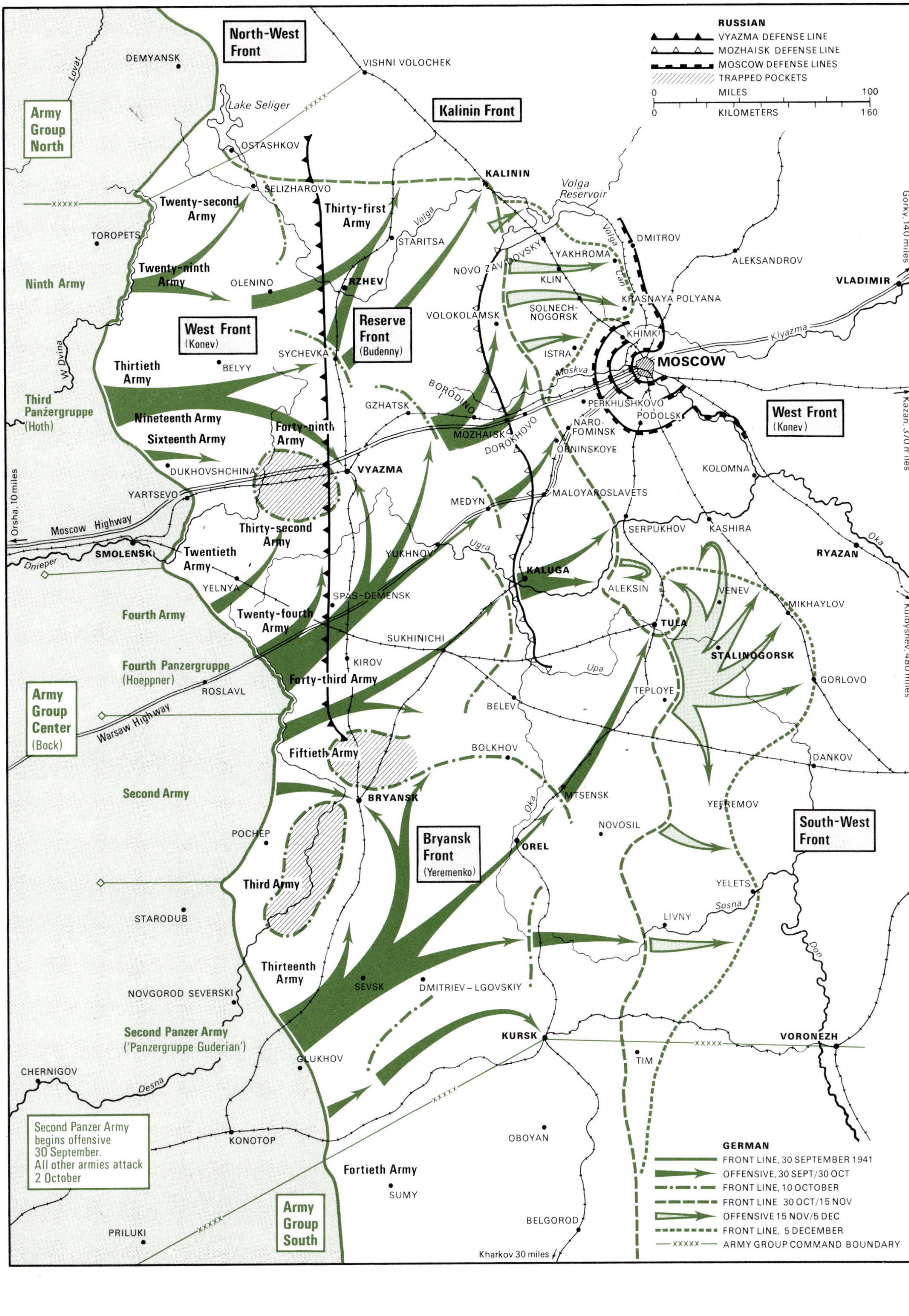
North-West Front
Kalinin Front
RUSSIAN
VYAZMA DEFENSE LINE
MOZHAISK DEFENSE LINE
MOSCOW DEFENSE LINES
TRAPPED POCKETS
0 MILES 100
0 KILOMETERS 160
Army Group North
Ninth Army
Third Panzergruppe (Hoth)
Fourth Army
Fourth Panzergruppe (Hoeppner)
Army Group Center (Bock)
Second Army
Second Panzer Army ('Panzergruppe Guderian')
Army Group South
Twenty-second Army
Twenty-ninth Army
Thirty-first Army
West Front (Konev)
Reserve Front (Budenny)
Thirtieth Army
Nineteenth Army
Sixteenth Army
Forty-ninth Army
Thirty-second Army
Twentieth Army
Twenty-fourth Army
Forty-third Army
Fiftieth Army
Third Army
Thirteenth Army
Fortieth Army
Bryansk Front (Yeremenko)
West Front (Konev)
South-West Front
DEMYANSK
Lovat
Lake Seliger
VISHNI VOLOCHEK
OSTASHKOV
SELIZHAROVO
KALININ
Volga Reservoir
Volga
Gorky, 140 miles
TOROPETS
STARITSA
DMITROV
YAKHROMA
NOVO ZAVIDOVSKY
ALEKSANDROV
OLENINO
RZHEV
KLIN
Can
VLADIMIR
KRASNAYA POLYANA
SOLNECH-NOGORSK
VOLOKOLAMSK
KHIMKI
Klyazma
SYCHEVKA
ISTRA
MOSCOW
W. Dvina
BELYY
Moskva
BORODINO
GZHATSK
PERKHUSHKOVO
PODOLSK
Kazan, 370 miles
MOZHAISK
DOROKHOVO
NARO-FOMINSK
OBNINSKOYE
DUKHOVSHCHINA
VYAZMA
KOLOMNA
YARTSEVO
MALOYAROSLAVETS
MEDYN
Orsha, 10 miles
Moscow Highway
SERPUKHOV
KASHIRA
SMOLENSK
Dnieper
YUKHNOV
Ugra
Oka
RYAZAN
KALUGA
YELNYA
SPAS-DEMENSK
ALEKSIN
VENEV
MIKHAYLOV
TULA
SUKHINICHI
STALINOGORSK
Kuibyshev, 480 miles
KIROV
Upa
ROSLAVL
TEPLOYE
GORLOVO
BELEV
Warsaw Highway
BOLKHOV
DANKOV
MTSENSK
BRYANSK
YEFREMOV
NOVOSIL
POCHEP
OREL
YELETS
Sosna
STARODUB
LIVNY
Don
SEVSK
DMITRIEV – LGOVSKIY
NOVGOROD SEVERSKI
KURSK
VORONEZH
GLUKHOV
TIM
CHERNIGOV
Desna
KONOTOP
OBOYAN
Second Panzer Army begins offensive 30 September. All other armies attack 2 October
SUMY
PRILUKI
BELGOROD
Kharkov 30 miles
GERMAN
FRONT LINE, 30 SEPTEMBER 1941
OFFENSIVE, 30 SEPT/30 OCT
FRONT LINE, 10 OCTOBER
FRONT LINE, 30 OCT/15 NOV
OFFENSIVE 15 NOV/5 DEC
FRONT LINE, 5 DECEMBER
ARMY GROUP COMMAND BOUNDARY

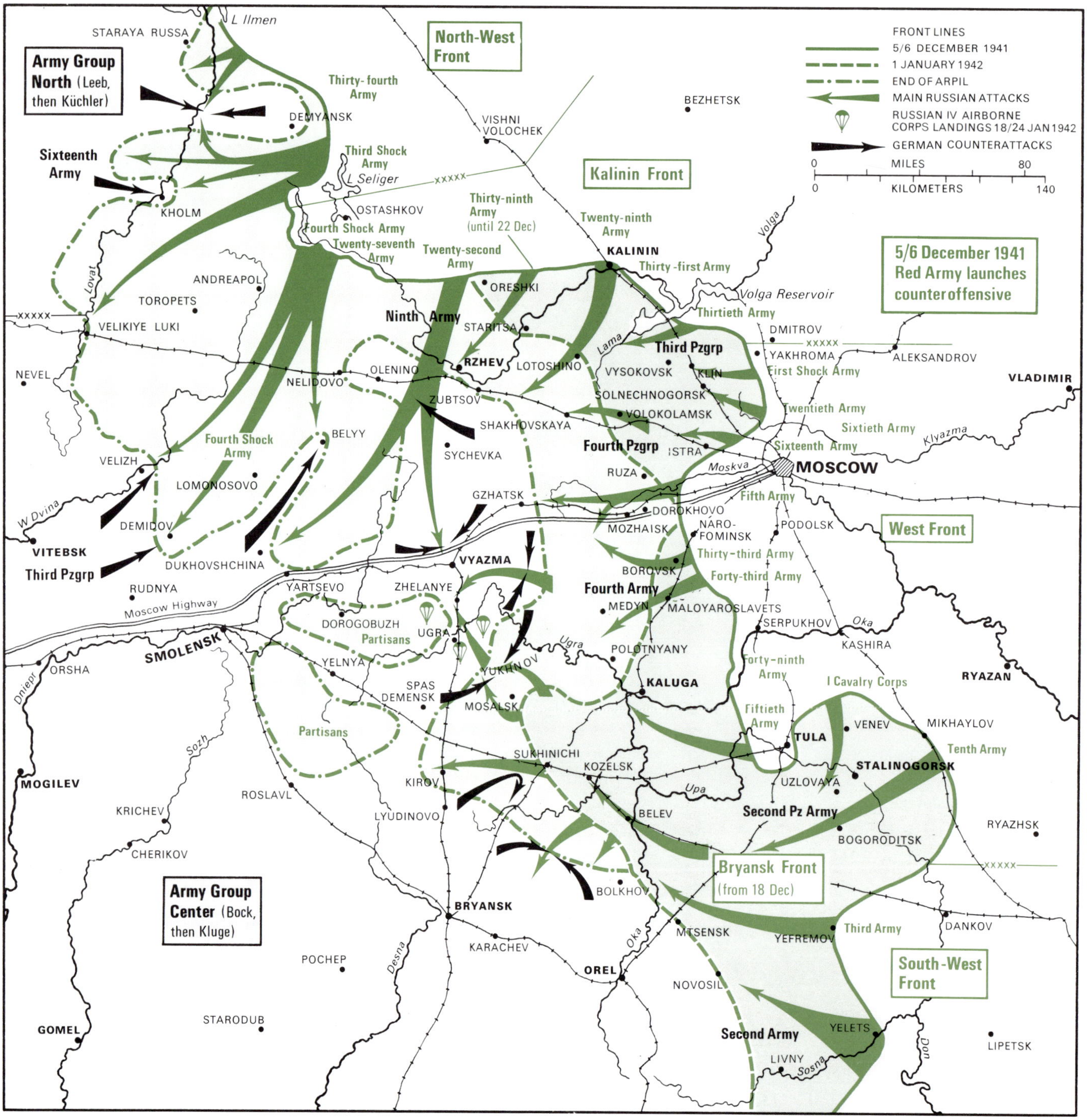

Group finally reached the Volga Canal, 19 miles from Moscow center, but they lacked the support for a frontal assault on the city. Elements of the Second Panzer Army had gotten as far as Kashira, but they had to fall back for the same reason.

By 5 December the Germans realized that they could go no farther for the time being. Valuable time has been lost in the capture of Smolensk, whose courageous defenders had helped delay the German advance on Moscow until the dreaded onset of winter. Now the capital could not be completely encircled, and heavy bombing did not offset the failure to close Moscow's window on the east. Fresh Soviet troops began to arrive from Siberia even as the Germans faced temperatures that plummeted to 40 degrees below zero.

On 8 December Hitler announced a suspension of operations outside Moscow, but the Soviet High Command was not listening. Employing the reserves it had gathered in previous weeks, the Red Army launched a great counteroffensive that recalled the winter of 1812, when Napoleon's forces came to grief on the same ground. Avoiding German strongpoints, the Soviets advanced by infiltration – passing over fields instead of roads, making skillful use of Cossack cavalry, ski troops and guerrilla forces. The Germans were harried from flank and rear, forced from one position after another. Tanks and planes became inoperable in the extreme cold, and supply lines were tenuous or nonexistent.

With the recapture of Kalinin and Tula, the Russians removed the immediate threat to Moscow. Their offensive drove on into late February, and German troops took refuge in strongly fortified defensive positions (called hedgehogs) in hope of holding out until fresh troops could arrive. Hitler had ordered 'No retreat,' and airborne supplies kept many enclaves going through the winter. But Operation Barbarossa had foundered in the snowfields of Russia. The Soviets were regaining ground from Leningrad to the Crimea.

The Red Army Fights Back

During the fall of 1941, the Russians were able to evacuate much of their factory equipment and many key workers to the east, where they began to rebuild their industrial machine. Railroad equipment was also evacuated, giving the Soviets an edge in the number of locomotives and freight cars per mile of track. The transportation breakdown foreseen by Hitler did not materialize, and Russian troop reserves were built up in Siberia to replace the great losses incurred on the Eastern Front. At the same time, war matériel from the West began to reach Russia via Archangel, Murmansk, Vladivostok and Persia.

Since Operation Barbarossa had been designed to achieve a quick victory during the summer months, German troops had never been equipped for winter warfare. Soviet troops by contrast, were routinely equipped with clothing and vehicles appropriate to the theater of operations. The Soviet Supreme Command (*Stavka*) had rallied from the shock of invasion to make effective use of the huge army that had been so wastefully deployed in June of 1941.

The Russian counteroffensive that began on 5-6 December saw immediate and dramatic gains on many fronts. The siege of Moscow was broken by the Kalinin, West and South-West Fronts (army groups). Supplies began to reach Leningrad in time to avert universal starvation in the besieged city. In the south, the Kerch Isthmus was retaken and the Crimea re-entered with help from the Red Navy. The Russians had gone all the way back to Velikiye Luki and Mozhaisk before they had to rest and regroup in late February 1942.

Opposite: The Red Army launches its counteroffensive.
Right: Russian territory regained by the end of April 1942.
Below: A political meeting of the Russian Twentieth Army near Smolensk.

The Course of Global Conflict: 1939-45

The Treaty of Versailles: Blueprint for Hostilities

Germany had had no part in the negotiations that resulted in the Treaty of Versailles; it was entirely the work of the 32 nations that had been leagued against her in World War I. The 80,000-word draft of the proposed peace treaty was approved by the Allied Peace Congress on 6 May 1919, and German representatives did not even see the document until the following day. They protested bitterly against its terms, and there were demonstrations all over Germany and a change of government before it was signed.

By the treaty's terms, Germany ceded Alsace-Lorraine to France, the towns of Eupen and Malmédy to Belgium, the city of Memel to Lithuania, and the province of Posen and a 'corridor' through West Prussia to Poland. German Austria, Poland and Czechoslovakia were declared independent. The port city of Danzig was internationalized as a 'free city,' and the valuable coal region of the Saar passed under League of Nations administration and the economic control of France.

In addition, Germany lost all of its overseas empire, most of its armed forces and control of the Rhineland – which was to be occupied at Germany's expense until the Treaty of Versailles was fully executed. A clause that even some of the victors disputed forced Germany to claim

full responsibility for the war and to promise financial reparation 'for all damage done to the civilian population of the Allies and their property.' The initial payment was set at five billion dollars; subsequent reparations were limited only by 'the utmost of [Germany's] ability' to pay. Disarmed, dishonored and heavily mortgaged, the conquered nation embarked upon years of distress and resentment that would culminate in the conflict that was to eclipse even the Great War itself.

Previous page: USS Arizona *explodes at Pearl Harbor, 7 December 1941.*
Opposite: Admiral Chester W Nimitz points the way to Tokyo. Seated (left to right) are General MacArthur, President Roosevelt and Admiral Leahy.
Left: European boundaries before and after Versailles.
Below: The Allied premiers convene in Paris for the Peace Conference in 1919.

German Expansion, 1939-40

The German Army that went to war in 1939 was armed and organized much like that of 1918, but there had been important developments in the interwar years. The Stuka dive bomber now served as a form of mobile artillery at need. Submachine guns offered an advantage in portability over the Vickers and Bren machine guns used by the British. Allied forces had more tanks, but the Germans were much better at using them tactically. German generals knew how to fight the war of movement, while the French were still fixated on their Maginot Line - a static and incomplete system that anticipated a second Verdun. The Germans had no intention of fighting another such action.

The new blitzkrieg style of German warfare rolled over Poland, Norway, Denmark and France in a matter of months. The British Army was shattered by the French campaign, but the evacuation from Dunkirk and the crucial weeks bought by the Battle of Britain staved off invasion of the British Isles. Mussolini took advantage of Allied defeats to enter the war on the German side, but Italian

armies in both Greece and North Africa were struggling before the end of 1940. By that time, German U-boats were taking a heavy toll of Allied shipping on the convoy routes.

Above left: Saluting the Swastika.
Left: Axis expansion in the late 1930s.
Above: German and Italian territorial gains in 1939 and 1940.
Right: The dreaded Ju 87 Stuka dive bomber, whose success in Europe became legendary.

German Conquest at Its Height

Below: 1942 saw the high tidemark of German expansion. Allied landings in North Africa combined with the Soviet counteroffensive on the Eastern Front were to turn the tide and sound the death-knell for Hitler's territorial aspirations.

Having been balked in his plan to invade the British Isles, Hitler directed his attention to the east, where he gained control of the Balkans in the spring of 1941. He shored up the tenuous Italian position in North Africa, then ordered the implementation of Operation Barbarossa – the invasion of the Soviet Union. Operations beginning 22 June 1941 inflicted great losses on the Red Army, but the expected quick and easy victory was not forthcoming. German confidence and supplies began to erode with the onset of an early winter that found troops unequipped for freezing conditions. The Russian Bear shook off its tormentors in a counteroffensive that prevented the capture of Moscow, then Stalingrad, in 1942. Russian civilians proved able defenders of their embattled homeland, and the Germans went onto the defensive in Russia. An ill-advised declaration of war on the United States after Pearl Harbor guaranteed open and active American involvement, with all the industrial and military strength that this implied. Hitler's Germany had overreached itself.

The Propaganda War

Below: Two examples of war propaganda from German (left) and Soviet artists; their respective messages are clear.
Right: Anti-Semitic feelings found expression in such German posters as 'The Eternal Jew'.

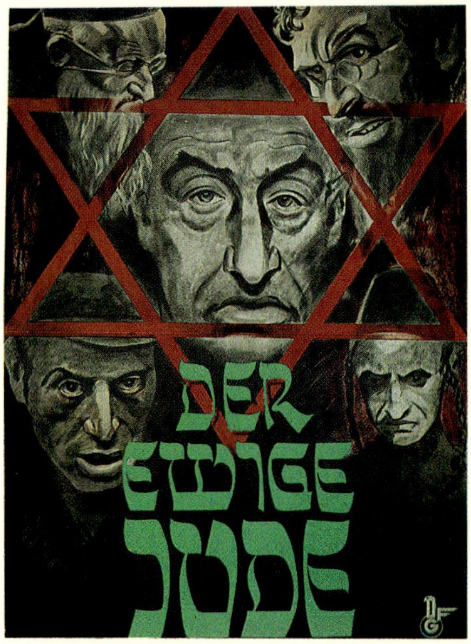

Propaganda was used by all of the belligerents in World War II to incite patriotism and inflame popular feeling against 'the enemy,' both outside and within the country. Luridly illustrated Soviet posters trumpeted 'Kill the German Beasts!' and 'Destroy the Hitlerite Army – It can and must be done!' Soviet leaders did not feel fully confident of their peoples' loyalty in every phase of the war, in which they lost more soldiers and civilians than any other single belligerent.

Germany produced comparable war art from 1943 on, after the office of National Socialist Leadership was created. Psychological warfare played a major role in the German war effort, with the production of films, posters, magazines and other media that fostered unquestioning loyalty and hatred of minorities, who were accused of subverting the war effort. During World War I, propaganda had been so falsified by all parties involved that genuine atrocities like 'The Final Solution to the Jewish Problem' were widely disbelieved – until Allied liberation of concentration camp survivors in 1945 revealed the incredible truth.

The US propaganda effort was less obvious, but not necessarily less effective. Marine recruitment posters bore the legend: 'We're looking for a few good men,' emphasizing the Marines' reputation as an élite force. 'War Bonds' and 'Victory Gardens' abounded to foster wholehearted co-operation on the home front. 'Remember Pearl Harbor' was taken up as a powerful rallying cry in the war against Japan. Thus dictatorships and democracies alike waged the propaganda war with deep intensity and unshakeable conviction of the rightness of their cause.

Below: Japan's sphere of influence and activity, December 1941.
Below right: Soldiers return to Japan from Manchuria to a hero's welcome.

Japan Asserts Its Power

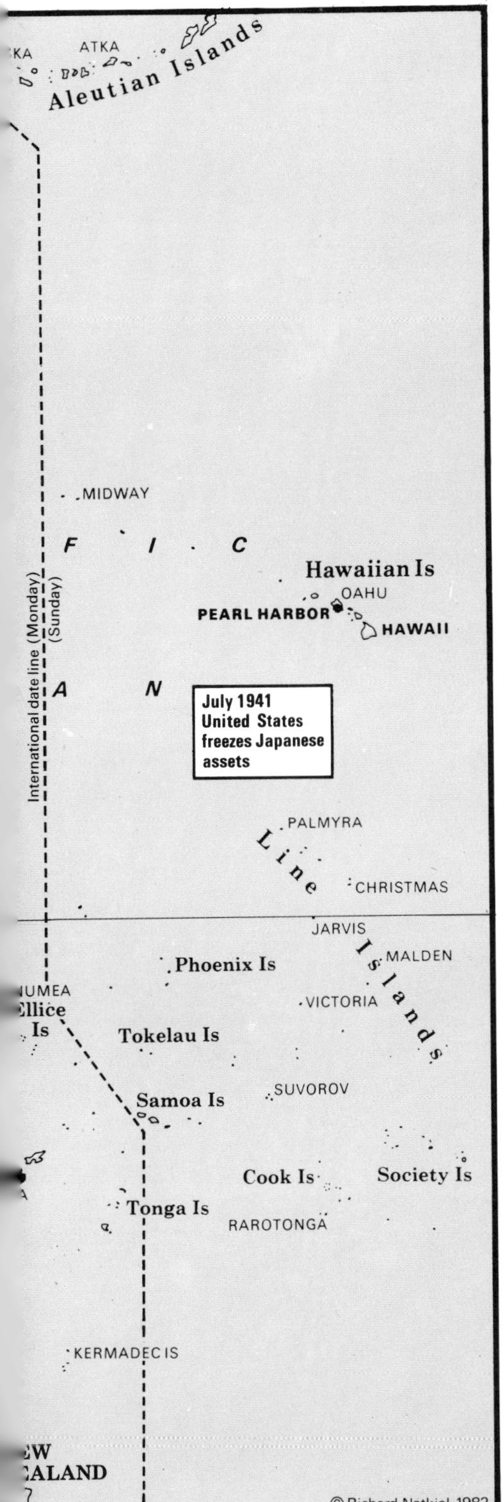

Japanese resentment at the Pacific settlement following World War I gathered strength through the 1920s. 'Patriotic Societies' agitated for an aggressive foreign policy, and the Japanese constitution gave the military a disproportionate voice in national affairs. The rise of Chinese Nationalism posed a threat to Japan's position as the leading Asian power, and the West was widely distrusted as racist in its attitudes – not without cause.

All these factors were involved in the Japanese seizure of Manchuria (1931), which was made by the so-called Japanese Manchurian Army acting independently of the government. Two years later, Japan withdrew from the League of Nations and accelerated her arms production. Serious fighting with China broke out in 1937 and resulted in Japanese occupation of most major Chinese ports and extensive areas of their territory.

To prevent the Chinese from being supplied through French Indochina, the Japanese put pressure on the area and ended by occupying it in 1941. This brought open opposition from the US in the form of an export embargo. Japan's recent pacts with the Axis Powers and the USSR had imperiled Allied interests in the Pacific, and stringent sanctions against Japanese trade and oil imports were decisive. Faced with the loss of 75 percent of her trade and 90 percent of her oil supplies, Japan sent her aircraft carrier force into the Pacific on 26 November 1941. On 2 December General Tojo, now militant Prime Minister of Japan, ordered it to attack the US Pacific Fleet at Pearl Harbor, Hawaii.

Below right: Japan's surprise attack at Pearl Harbor, Hawaii, on 7 December 1941 (below) raised the curtain on nine months of feverish expansion in the Pacific – yet the scale of this empire-building was destined to sap her strength.

The Japanese Sweep the Pacific

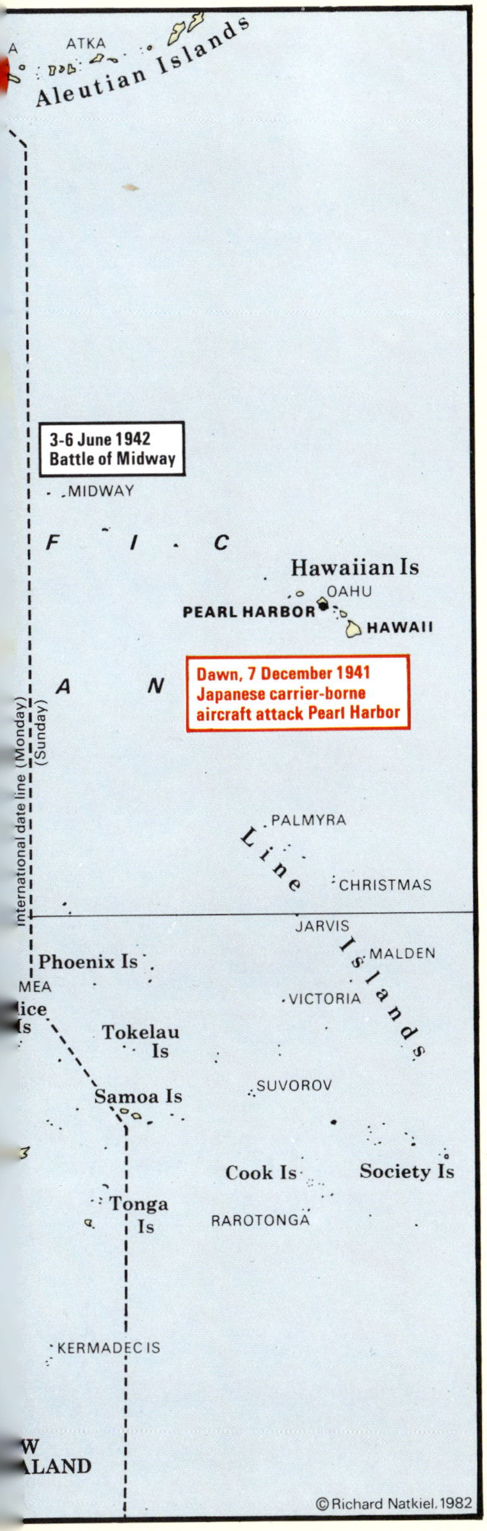

When the Japanese aimed their stunning strike at Pearl Harbor, their strategists expected – and achieved – a series of rapid victories in the Pacific. They had no real choice: without access to oil, their war machine would grind to a halt even as US industry geared up for new feats of production under wartime conditions. The oil-rich East Indies were an inevitable target, as were the Allied colonies astride the sea routes.

Available forces were relatively modest – some 80 percent of the 51 Japanese divisions were tied up in China and Manchuria. On the plus side, the outnumbered Japanese troops had good air support, jungle-warfare training and an impressive fleet that included 10 carriers and 8 modern battleships. (The US Pacific Fleet had nine battleships of World War I vintage and four carriers that – fortunately – were absent from Pearl Harbor when the initial attack was launched.) Japanese Imperial Headquarters believed it was possible to achieve their objectives within six months if they moved decisively, and for the first four months they effectively had the Pacific War to themselves.

At a cost of only 23 warships (none larger than a destroyer), the Japanese overran the Philippines, Malaya, Burma, the Dutch East Indies and a number of British islands between December 1941 and May 1942. Then the Doolittle Raid on Tokyo (18 April) awakened them to the danger of bombing on the home islands, and inflamed the Japanese 'Victory Disease' (as one of their leaders would call it). The Japanese resolved to extend their defense perimeter despite their diminishing resources – and thereby ensured that they would lose the war.

Below: Japan's empire-building was finally curtailed as a two-pronged Allied offensive from the east and southwest forced a retreat.
Below right: US and British combined chiefs of staff discuss Allied strategy.

The Allies Strike Back at Japan

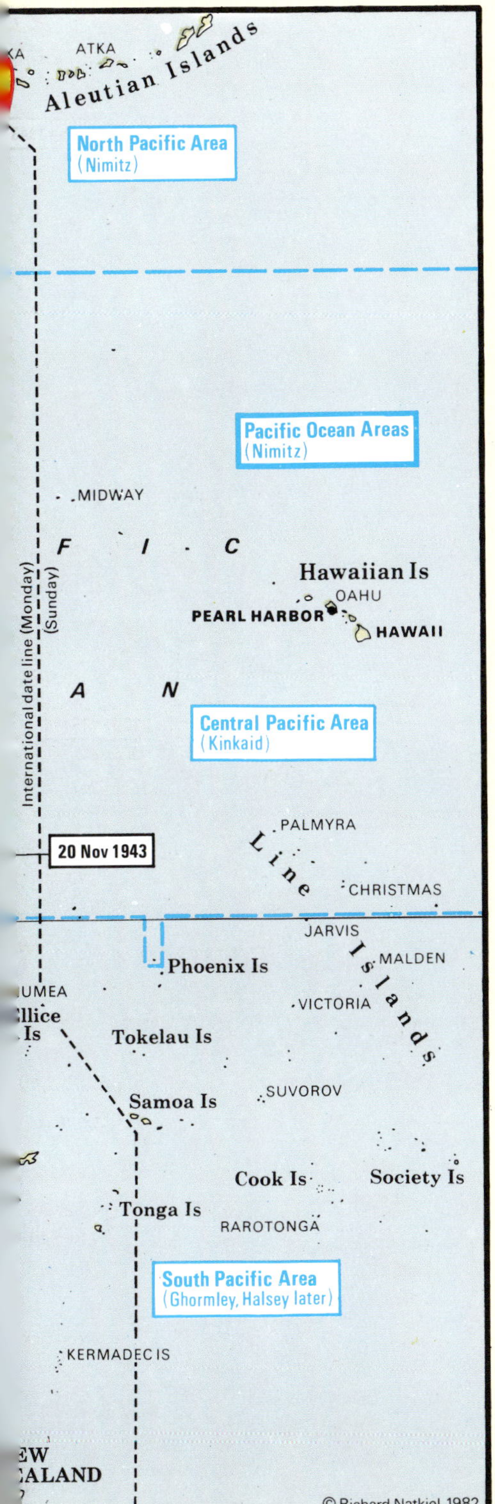

As US forces gained experience in the challenging Pacific Theater, their leaders saw the necessity for mounting two major lines of advance against Japan. US Navy carrier forces were strengthened for their essential role, amphibious assault capability was increased and a fleet train was created to supply the fighting ships hundreds of miles from their bases. These units were to advance toward Japan via the central Pacific islands.Test case for the 'island-hopping' strategy was Tarawa, where US forces fought one of the costliest battles in their history in proportion to the numbers engaged in November 1943. Three thousand US Marines were casualties, and only 17 of the 4000 Japanese defenders were captured. An intensive study of this campaign helped the Americans to avoid their mistakes on Tarawa in subsequent operations. They accepted the fact that the Japanese would have to be flushed out of their caves and bunkers one by one, using grenades, flamethrowers and anything else that came to hand.

The other half of the Allied offensive was in the southwest Pacific, where American and Australian forces under General Douglas MacArthur made slow but certain progress with massive support from land-based aircraft. Australian forces had a strong vested interest in defeating the Japanese, who were sure to attack their homeland if they could isolate it from American support.

The Defeat of Nazi Germany

Germany's long retreat began in 1943; the Battle of Kursk in July of that year was the death knell for hopes of victory in the east. Two months before, Italy had been knocked out of the war, and it was only a matter of time before the Allies would try to break into Fortress Europe. The German threat to the Atlantic supply routes was effectively nullified, and before the year was out, US and British bombers were attacking both industrial targets and population centers within the Reich.

By the middle of 1944, after successful massive Allied landings in Normandy and breakthroughs aimed at the Rhine, the combined might of US and Soviet industry and armies had become overwhelming. British resources were strained, but not to the breaking point. In fact, Allied organization and equipment were at their peak. The Germans, by contrast, were drained in every area: men, money, armaments and leadership. By the time Allied forces converged on the Elbe to link up with the Russians (April-May 1945), most German units were prepared to show the white flag. Town after town surrendered eagerly to the Allies in preference to the feared Russians.

Below left: The contraction and (below) final defeat of Hitler's Germany.
Right: Berlin lies in ruins, the target of round-the-clock raids by British and US bomber aircraft.

Below: The reversal of Japanese supremacy in the Pacific was confirmed by the Allies' recapture of the Philippines in early 1945. Defeat was then only a matter of months away.
Below right: A postwar view of the business district of Kobe, showing the damage caused by incendiary attack.

Dissolution of the Japanese Empire

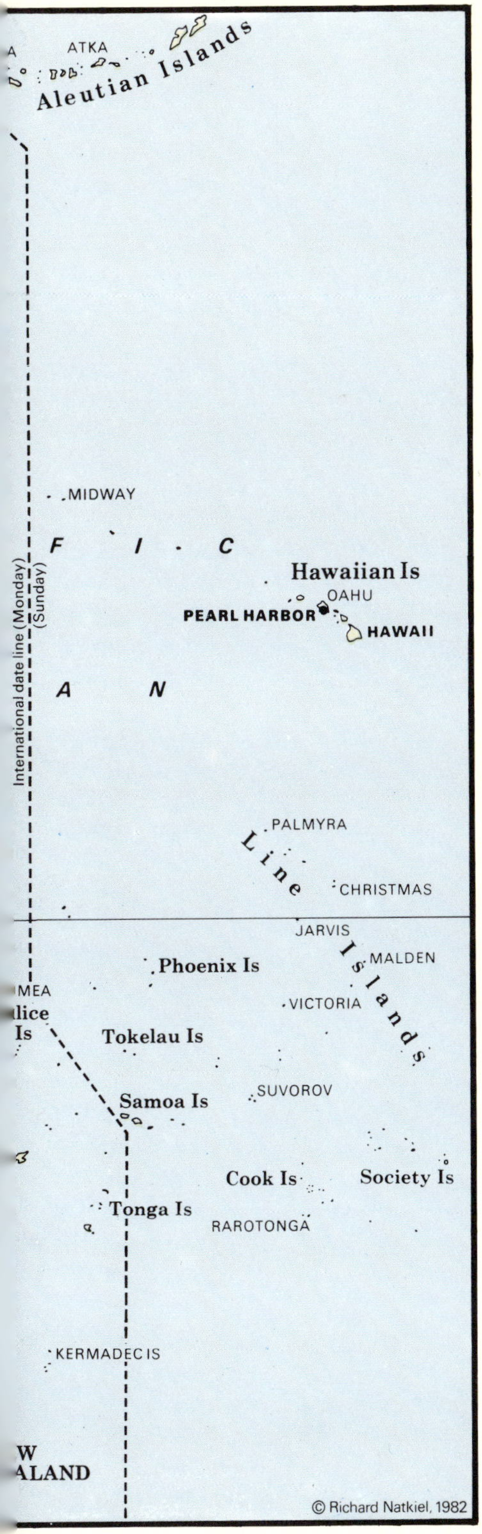

The first real check to the Japanese came with the Battle of the Coral Sea, six months after Pearl Harbor. There US carriers commanded by Rear Admiral Frank 'Black-Jack' Fletcher dashed Japanese hopes of capturing Port Moresby, the key to New Guinea. The battle made history as the first naval engagement in which opposing ships never sighted each other – all fighting was done by carrier-based planes. Both sides made serious errors in this new form of warfare, but many of these were corrected by US forces in the subsequent Battle of Midway.

In this action, the island of Midway served as an 'unsinkable aircraft carrier' for Admiral Chester W Nimitz. Bungled Japanese intelligence contributed to a disaster from which the Japanese Navy would not recover – the loss of every carrier commanded by Admiral Chuichi Nagumo. After Midway, the Japanese would be incapable of supporting the far-flung conquests so rapidly made in preceding months.

To preclude a second Japanese attempt on Port Moresby, the Americans determined to seize Tulagi and Guadalcanal in the Solomon Islands. It was a six-month struggle in which US forces gained additional skills from day to day despite heavy losses, and it set the tone for the duration of the Pacific War – a campaign that moved steadily toward Japan by avoiding heavily garrisoned enemy strongholds and seizing weaker positions to use as a springboard to the next American objective.

General Matsuichi Ino summarized after the war: 'The Americans attacked and seized, with minimum losses, a relatively weak area, constructed airfields, and then proceeded to cut supply lines . . . Our strongpoints were gradually starved out.' It was a brilliant improvisation on the theme of the indirect approach.

The Japanese Juggernaut

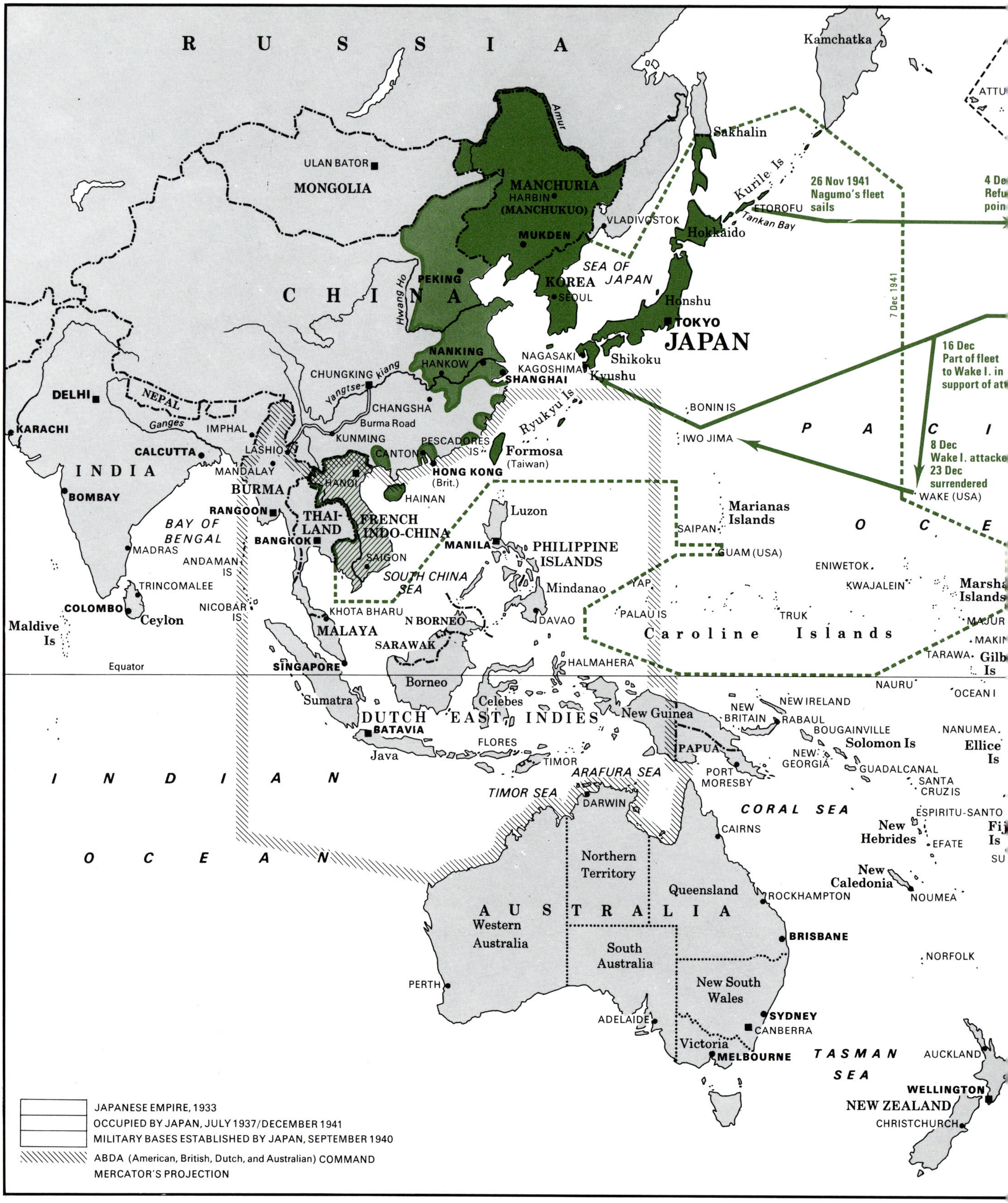

Previous page: The battleship Yamato *fitting out at Kure, Japan, in 1941.*
Above: Japan's occupied territories.
Right and far right: The Pearl Harbor attacks in detail.
Above right: The magazine of the US destroyer Shaw *explodes during the raids.*

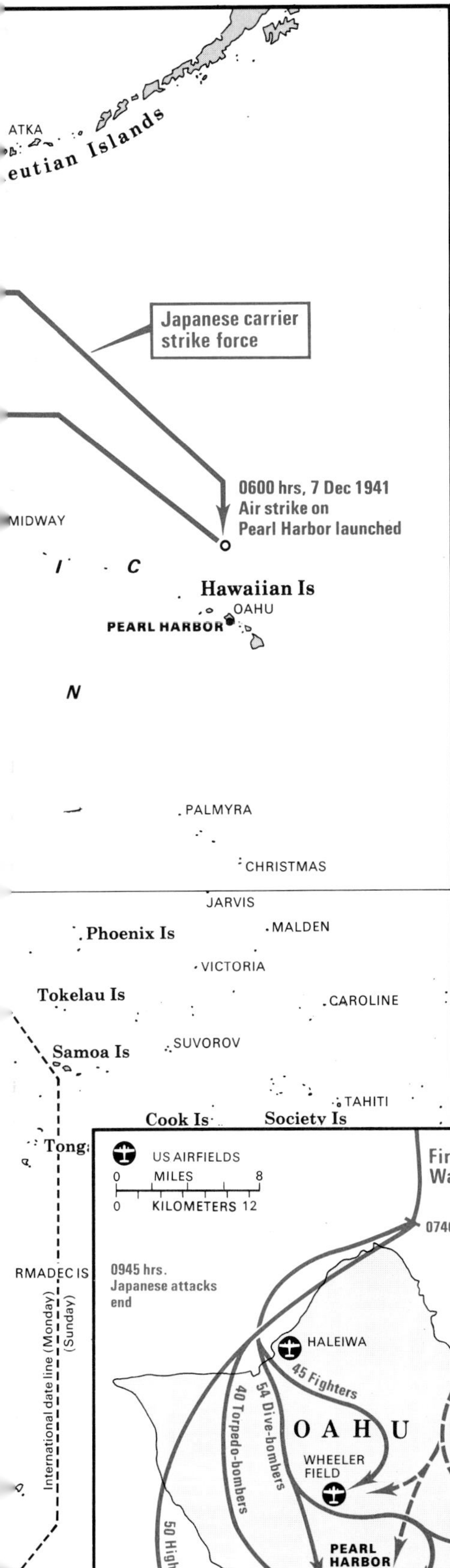

Pearl Harbor

The Japanese strike force that approached Pearl Harbor on 6 December consisted of six fleet carriers escorted by two battleships and two heavy cruisers. Anchored in Pearl Harbor were eight battleships of the US Pacific Fleet, numerous destroyers and tenders, and submarines and minesweepers. The carriers *Lexington* and *Saratoga* were away on a supply mission to Wake Island, which was fortunate for the future course of the war on the Allied side.

Radio monitoring of increased Japanese radio traffic in the several days preceding the attack made it clear that an operation was underway. All Pacific forces had been alerted, but those at Pearl Harbor remained on a peacetime footing despite the danger. Aircraft on the several Oahu airfields were undispersed, and ships were anchored in line with many members of their crews ashore. Reconnaissance flights had not been increased above the average.

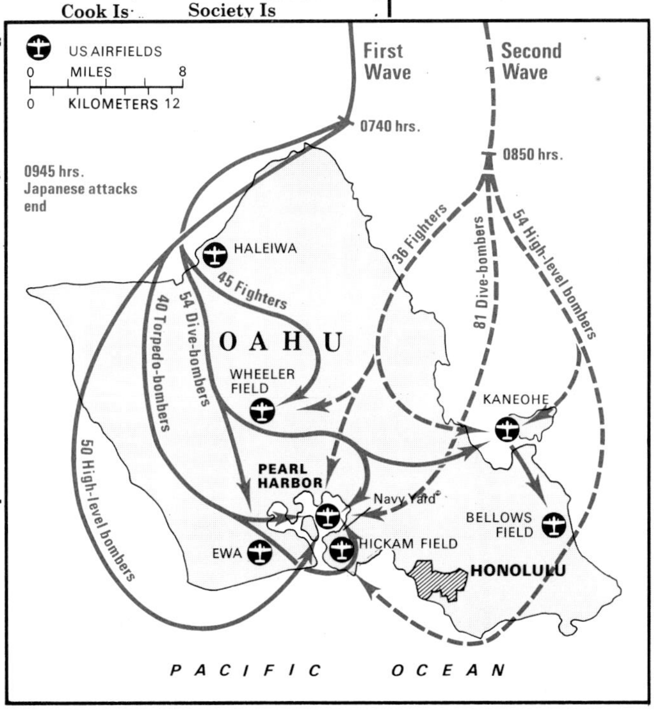

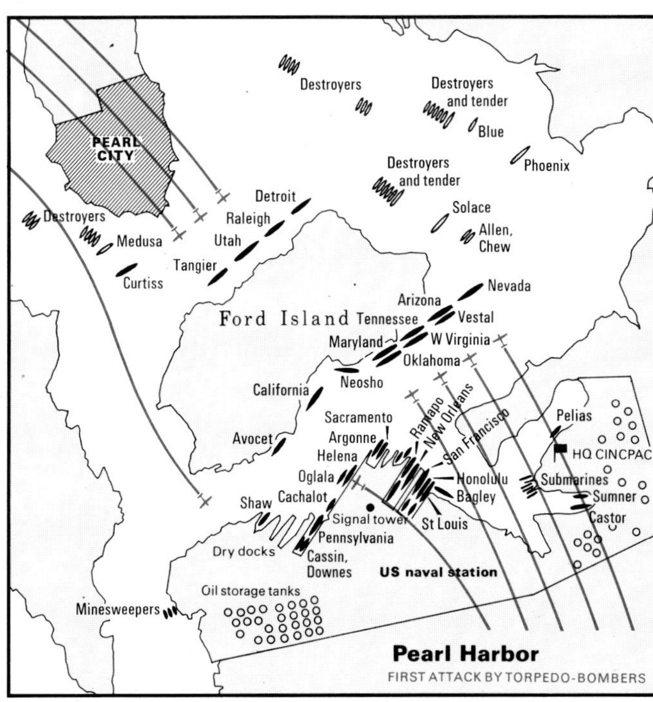

The Japanese launched the first wave of their two-part air attack at 6:00 AM on 7 December. A radar station reported incoming planes at 7:00 AM, but this report was unaccountably ignored. An hour later, torpedo bombers came in to attack the harbor as fighters began to strafe the airfields. Virtually all the US aircraft were destroyed on the ground. In the harbor, five of the eight battleships were hit immediately; minutes later, *West Virginia* was in flames and sinking, *Oklahoma* had capsized and *California* was badly damaged. *Arizona* had exploded and *Nevada* had to beach herself as she made for the harbor entrance under fire from the second wave of the Japanese attack. Dive bombers and high-level bombers had joined the first aircraft contingent to create additional devastation.

By the time the second wave struck, US forces had rallied from the initial shock to offer a more effective defense. At 9:45 AM, Vice-Admiral Nagumo's aircraft returned to their carriers with loss of nine fighters, fifteen dive bombers and five torpedo bombers.

Had Admiral Nagumo launched an additional attack against the harbor, he might have destroyed the port facilities entirely and accounted for the absent aircraft carriers as well. Instead, he chose to withdraw the strike force, from which he dispatched several units to attack Wake Island (8 December). US Marines garrisoned there sank two Japanese destroyers and held the island against steady air and sea bombardment for two weeks, until they were overwhelmed by a Japanese landing.

Malaya

Lieutenant General Tomoyuki Yamashita commanded the Japanese Twenty-fifth Army in its whirlwind invasion of Malaya (December 1941). In this campaign, which drove all the way to Singapore and was described by Winston Churchill as the worst disaster in British military history, Yamashita earned the nickname 'Tiger of Malaya.' His force consisted of three divisions supported by 600 aircraft, as against Lieutenant General A E Percival's two divisions with some 150 aircraft.

Northern landings met little opposition except at Kota Bharu, where Takumi Force, a regimental group, had to fight its way ashore. Meanwhile, air attacks wiped out all but some 50 British planes.

A double advance south was led by the Japanese 5 Division, which grappled with 11 Indian Division around Jitra on 11 December. The defenders were pushed back steadily, as the Japanese Guards Division moved down the coast and 5 and 18 Divisions progressed inland. Within 70 days, Yamashita's troops had overrun all of Malaya through a combination of superior force, speed and surprise. General Percival was tricked by skillful jungle-warfare tactics into believing that the Japanese force was vastly superior in size, and on 15 February 1942 he and his men surrendered.

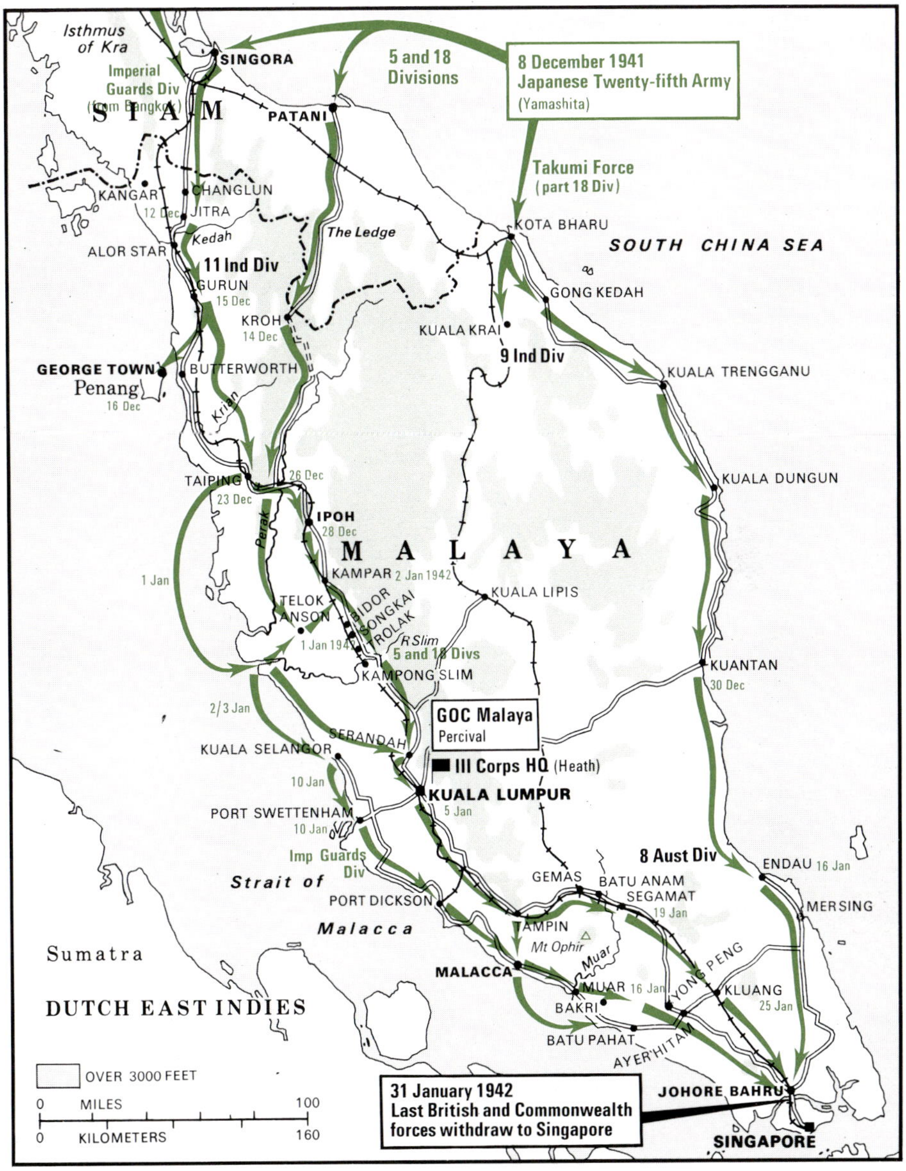

Above left: Aftermath of Pearl Harbor, with USS Downes *at left, USS* Cassin *at right and USS* Pennsylvania *at rear.*
Left: The garrison flag flies as Hickam Field burns.
Right: The Japanese conquest of Malaya, completed in January 1942.
Below right: Singapore falls in February.
Below: General Yamashita (foreground) surveys newly-conquered territory.

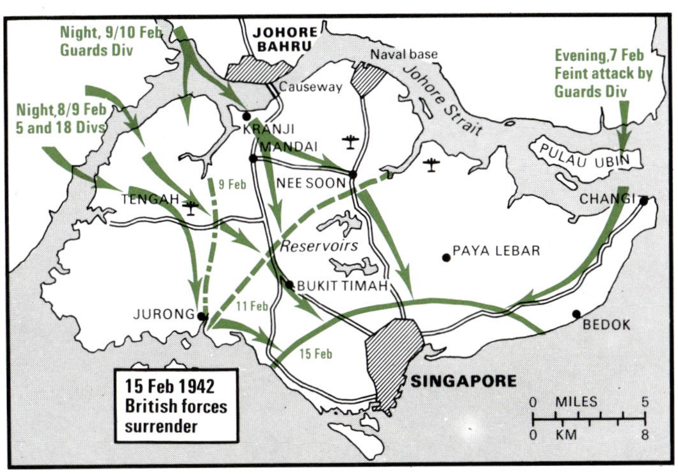

The Fall of Hong Kong

Simultaneous with the Japanese invasion of the Malay Peninsula on 8 December 1941 came the invasion of Hong Kong, whose defenders were hopelessly outnumbered. Within 24 hours they had been pushed back to the Gindrinkers Line, which was breached by the capture of Shing Mun Redoubt. The mainland then had to be evacuated, an operation which was completed on 13 December. Five days later the Japanese crossed Kowloon Bay on a wide front and captured more than half of Hong Kong Island. Fierce resistance continued until several days before Christmas, but after most of the reservoirs were captured, the garrison was forced to surrender on 25 December.

Above: British soldiers face captivity after the fall of Hong Kong.
Right: Hong Kong and the surrounding area.

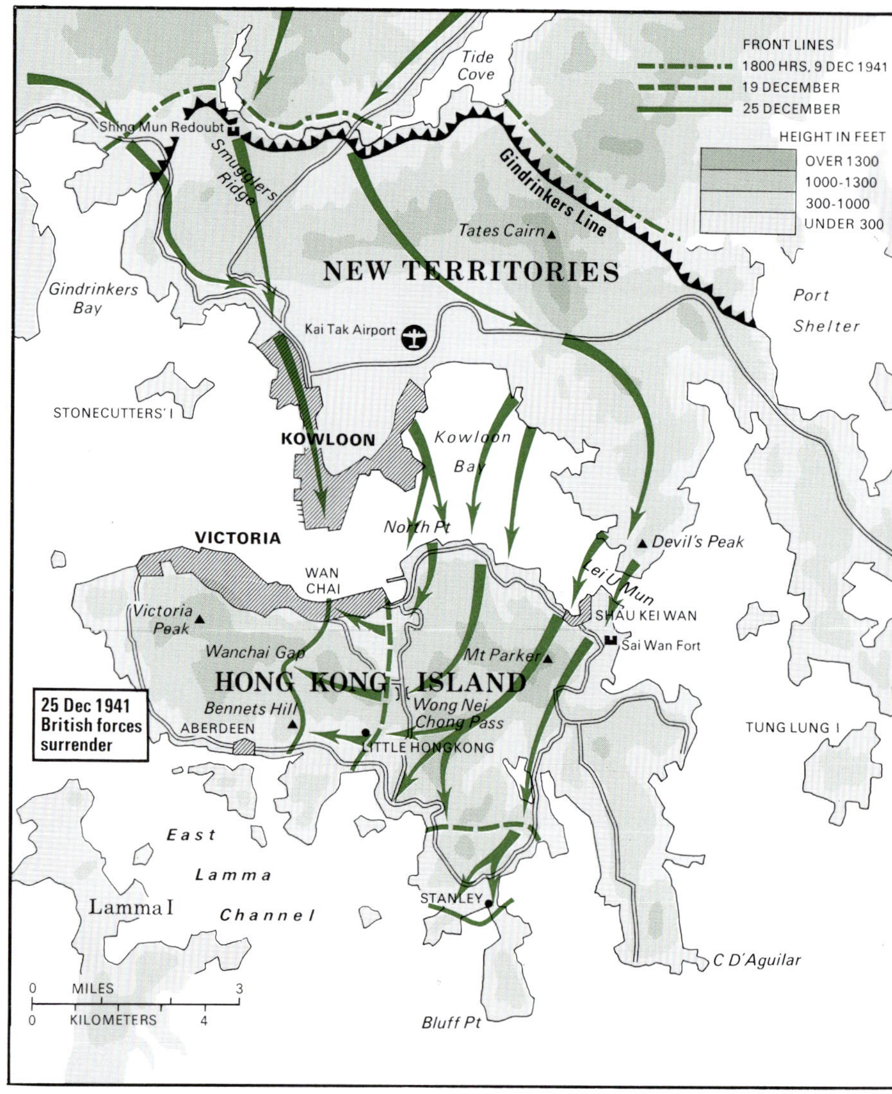

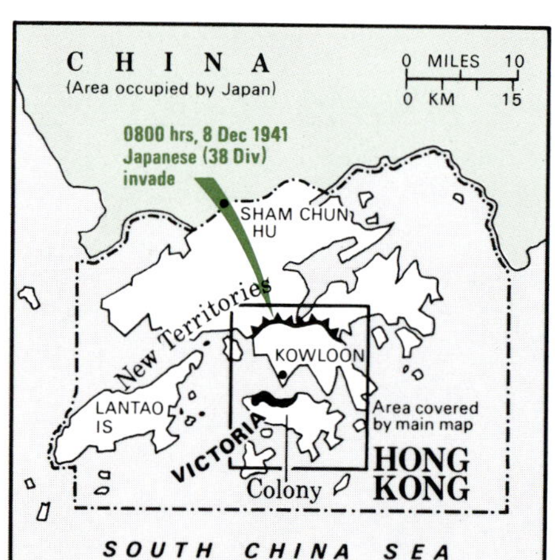

Above: The Japanese take Hong Kong on Christmas Day 1941.
Opposite top: The Japanese conquest of Bataan, completed in April 1942.
Opposite: The last US forces to hold out on Corregidor Island, south of Bataan, were finally neutralized on the morning of 6 May.

Victory in the Philippines

In July 1941, when the Philippine Army joined forces with the United States, General Douglas MacArthur was made commander of US Forces in the Far East (USAFFE). His ten divisions included some 19,000 American troops and 160,000 Filipinos – most of them ill equipped and undertrained. There were also 200 aircraft at his disposal. The Japanese believed, with some justification, that their Fourteenth Army of two divisions supported by 500 aircraft could conquer the Philippine Islands.

Heavy air attacks struck US air bases on 8 December (the same day as Pearl Harbor, but dated a day later by the International Date Line). Word of the Pearl Harbor disaster had impelled USAFFE to fly its bombers off Clark Field in the morning, but by the time of the midday attack, they were back on the ground with their fighter escorts. Forty-eight hours of bombing against the airfields accounted for the vast majority of US warplanes and cleared the way for Japanese landings north of Luzon to seize the bases at Vigan, Laoag and Tuguegarao. In the south, Legaspi was seized as a base from which to interdict seaborne US reinforcements.

The main Japanese landings were at Lingayen Bay on 22 December, whence the invaders broke out of their beachhead to advance against Manila. On 23 December MacArthur announced his plan to withdraw to Bataan; five days later, he declared Manila an open city. By early January, the Japanese were gaining ground on the Bataan Peninsula, but their troops were overtaken by disease there and gained little ground for the next two months.

On 12 March 1942, MacArthur was flown out and replaced by Lieutenant General Jonathan Wainwright, who frustrated several Japanese attempts to establish beachheads behind US lines. Not until 3 April, after reinforcement by a fresh division, were the Japanese able to launch their final offensive. Within a week's time, they had penetrated so deeply that US forces were compelled to surrender (7 April). The last American troops held out on Corregidor Island in a siege that ran from January until 5 May, when their artillery was almost entirely knocked out by unceasing bombardments. On that day, Japanese troops landed at Cavalry Point and established their beachhead. It was all over for the time being in the Philippines.

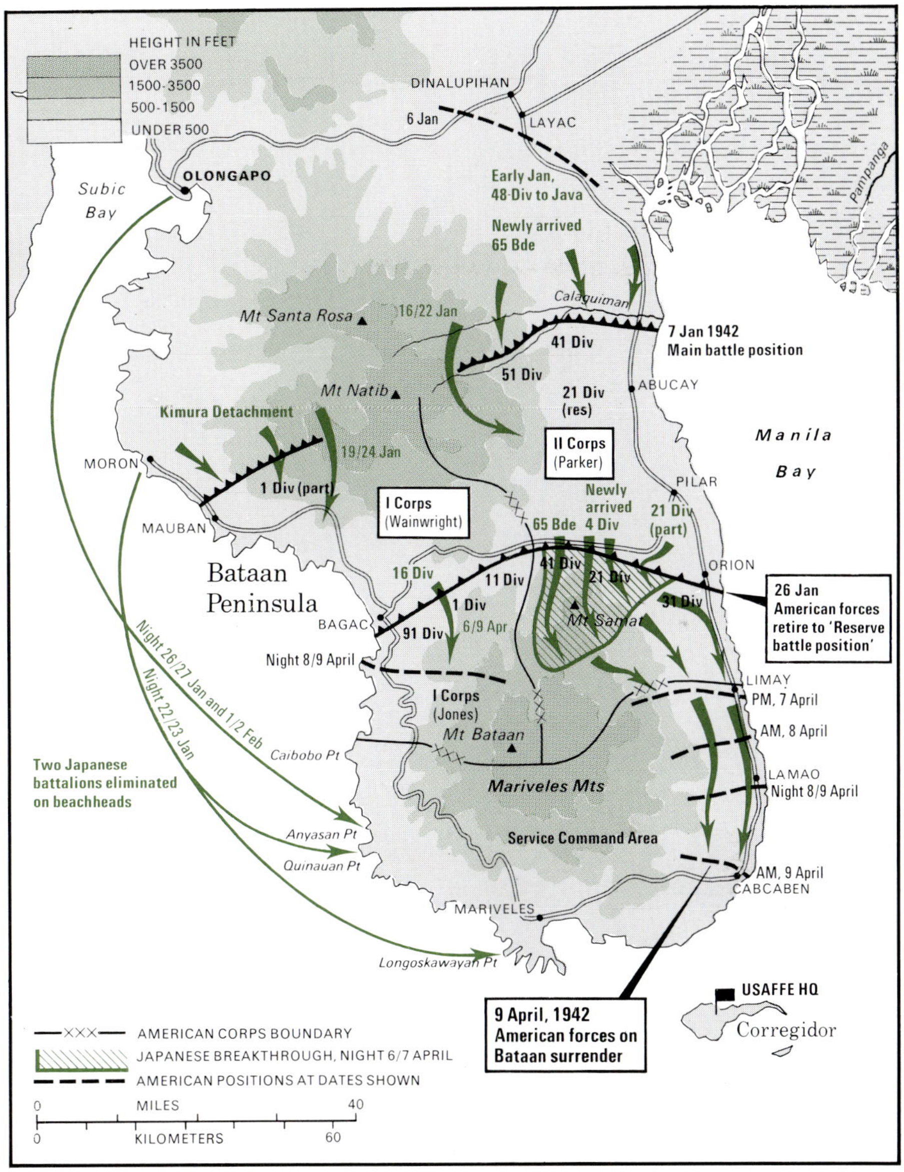

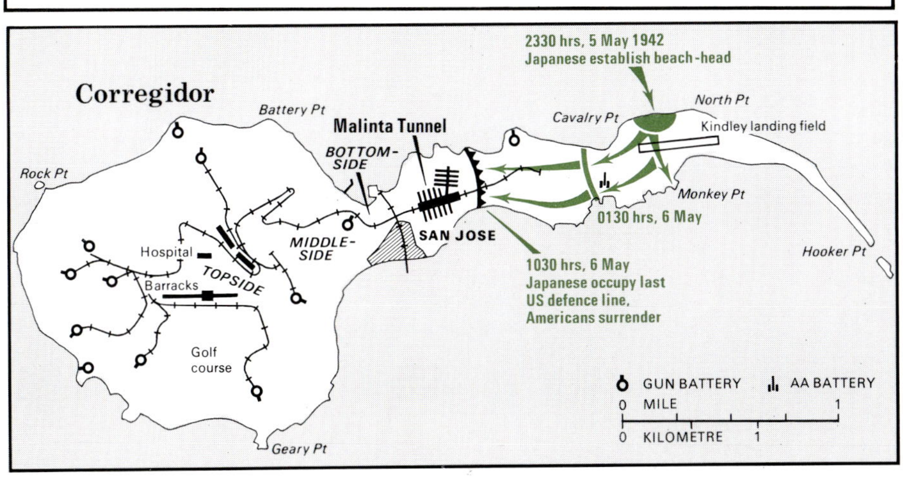

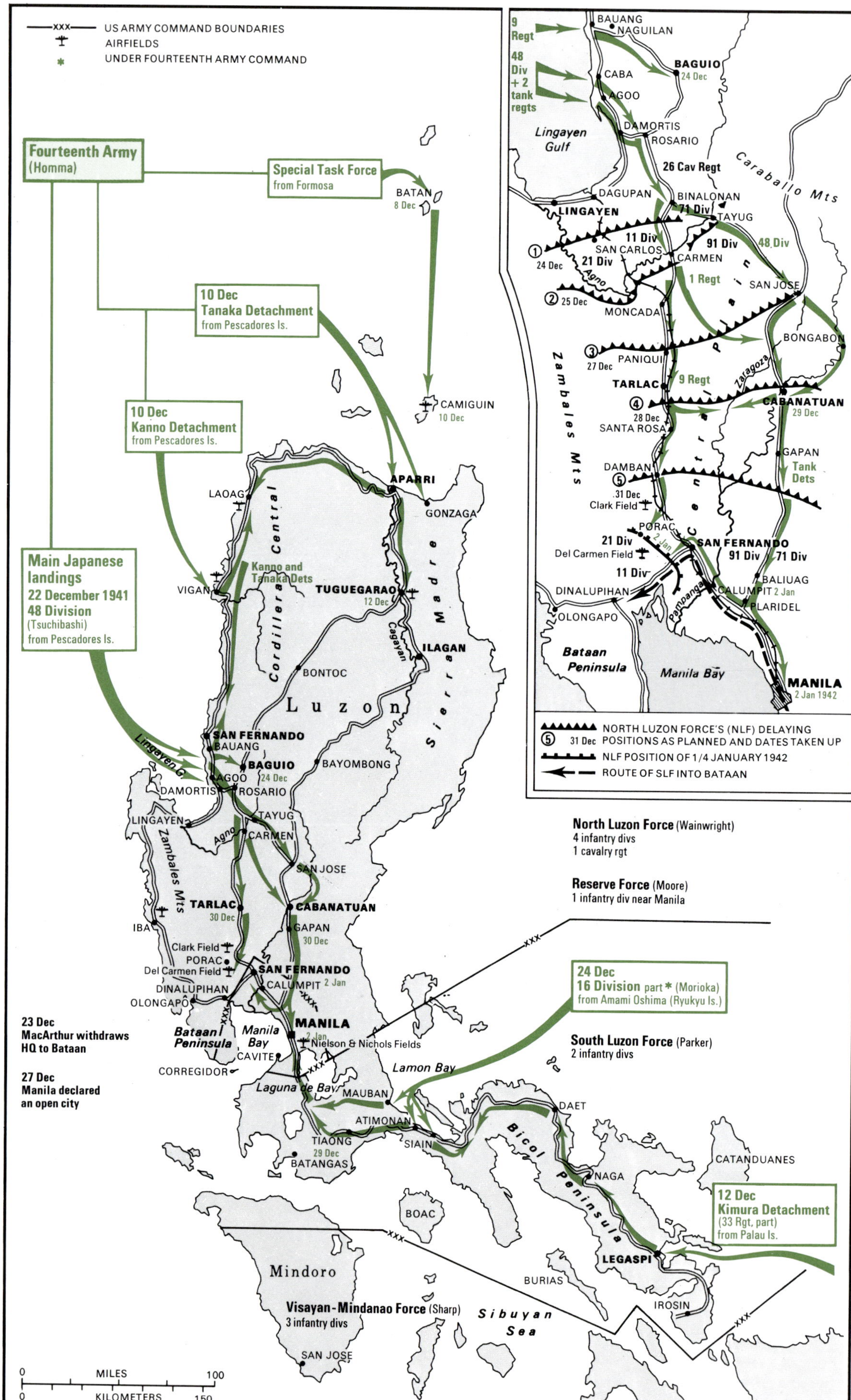
US ARMY COMMAND BOUNDARIES
AIRFIELDS
UNDER FOURTEENTH ARMY COMMAND
Fourteenth Army (Homma)
Special Task Force from Formosa
BATAN 8 Dec
10 Dec Tanaka Detachment from Pescadores Is.
CAMIGUIN 10 Dec
10 Dec Kanno Detachment from Pescadores Is.
APARRI
GONZAGA
LAOAG
Main Japanese landings 22 December 1941 48 Division (Tsuchibashi) from Pescadores Is.
VIGAN
Kanno and Tanaka Dets
Cordillera Central
TUGUEGARAO 12 Dec
Sierra Madre
Cagayan
ILAGAN
BONTOC
Luzon
BAYOMBONG
SAN FERNANDO
BAUANG
BAGUIO 24 Dec
Lingayen G.
AGOO
DAMORTIS
ROSARIO
TAYUG
LINGAYEN
Agno
CARMEN
SAN JOSE
Zambales Mts
TARLAC 30 Dec
CABANATUAN
GAPAN 30 Dec
IBA
Clark Field
PORAC
Del Carmen Field
SAN FERNANDO
DINALUPIHAN
CALUMPIT 2 Jan
OLONGAPO
MANILA 2 Jan
Bataan Peninsula
Manila Bay
Nielson & Nichols Fields
CAVITE
CORREGIDOR
23 Dec MacArthur withdraws HQ to Bataan
27 Dec Manila declared an open city
Lamon Bay
Laguna de Bay
MAUBAN
ATIMONAN
TIAONG 29 Dec
SIAIN
BATANGAS
DAET
Bicol Peninsula
NAGA
CATANDUANES
BOAC
LEGASPI
BURIAS
IROSIN
Mindoro
Sibuyan Sea
SAN JOSE
Visayan-Mindanao Force (Sharp) 3 infantry divs
North Luzon Force (Wainwright) 4 infantry divs 1 cavalry rgt
Reserve Force (Moore) 1 infantry div near Manila
24 Dec 16 Division part * (Morioka) from Amami Oshima (Ryukyu Is.)
South Luzon Force (Parker) 2 infantry divs
12 Dec Kimura Detachment (33 Rgt, part) from Palau Is.
MILES 0 100
KILOMETERS 0 150
9 Regt
48 Div + 2 tank regts
BAUANG
NAGUILAN
BAGUIO 24 Dec
CABA
AGOO
DAMORTIS
ROSARIO
Lingayen Gulf
26 Cav Regt
Caraballo Mts
DAGUPAN
BINALONAN
71 Div
TAYUG
LINGAYEN
11 Div
91 Div
48 Div
SAN CARLOS
24 Dec
21 Div
CARMEN
1 Regt
SAN JOSE
25 Dec
MONCADA
Central Plain
BONGABON
27 Dec
PANIQUI
Zaragoza
TARLAC
9 Regt
CABANATUAN 29 Dec
28 Dec
SANTA ROSA
Zambales Mts
GAPAN
Tank Dets
DAMBAN
31 Dec
Clark Field
PORAC
21 Div
2 Jan
SAN FERNANDO
91 Div
71 Div
Del Carmen Field
11 Div
BALIUAG
DINALUPIHAN
CALUMPIT 2 Jan
PLARIDEL
Pampanga
OLONGAPO
Bataan Peninsula
Manila Bay
MANILA 2 Jan 1942
NORTH LUZON FORCE'S (NLF) DELAYING POSITIONS AS PLANNED AND DATES TAKEN UP
NLF POSITION OF 1/4 JANUARY 1942
ROUTE OF SLF INTO BATAAN

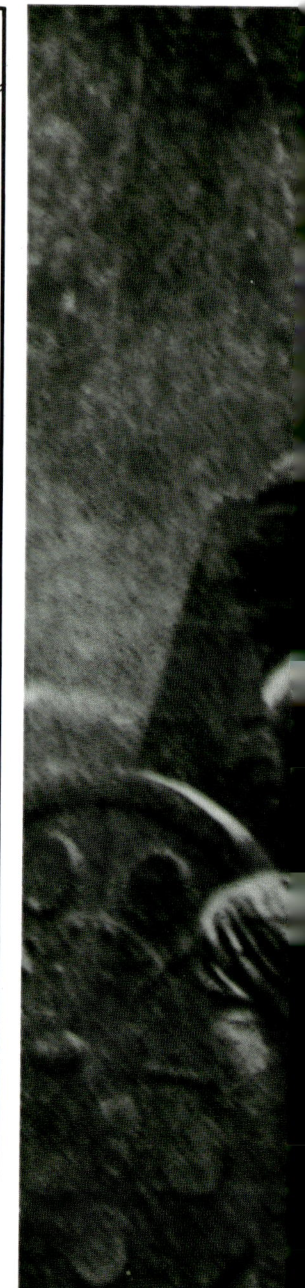

Left: Japanese landings on Luzon, December 1941.
Above: Small Japanese field gun in action during the Bataan campaign, April 1942.
Right: American prisoners of war under guard by Japanese troops after the surrender of Bataan.

The Dutch East Indies

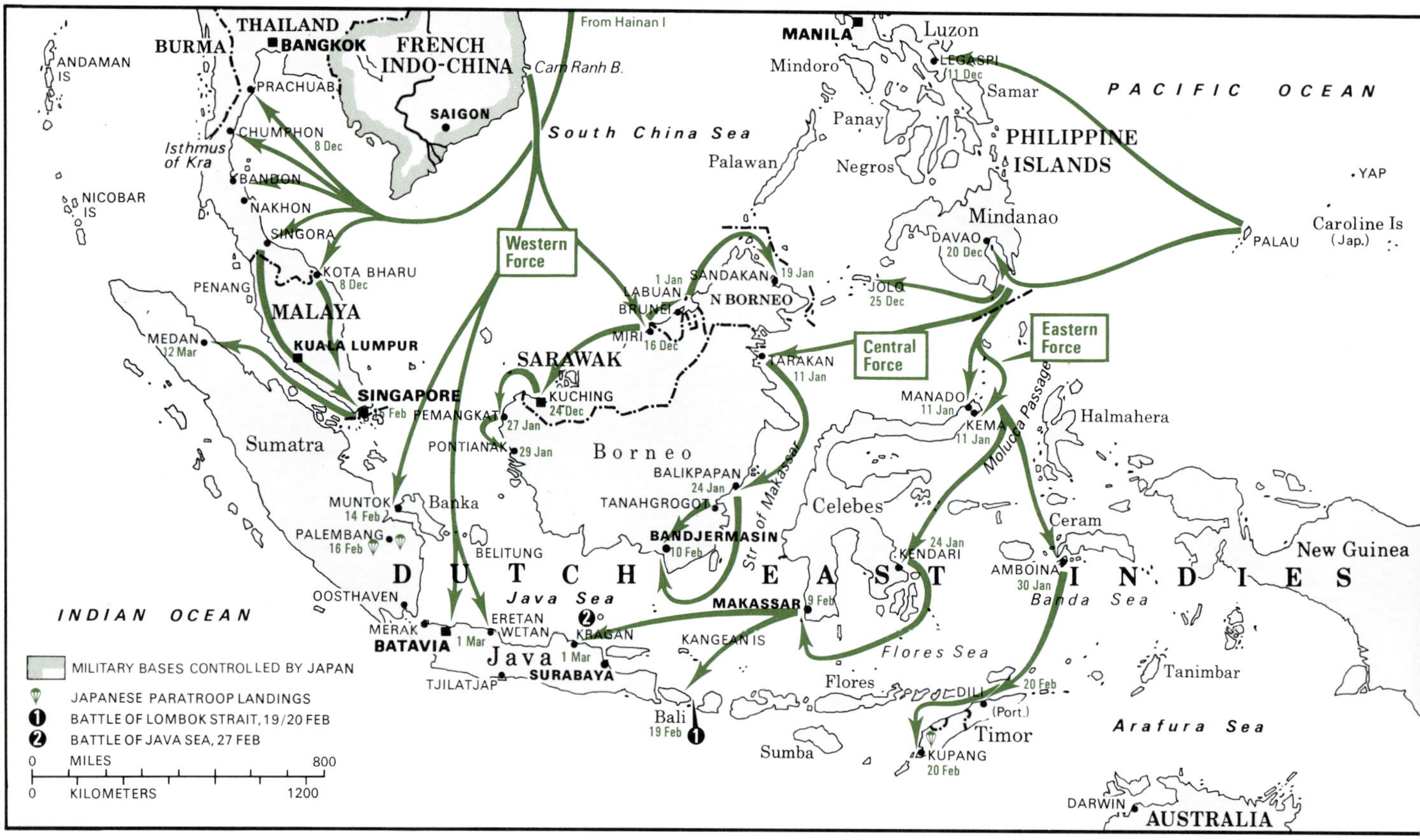

The oil and other resources of the Dutch East Indies made them a prime target for occupation by Japan, which planned a three-part attack on the islands early in 1942. Western Force, from Indochina and newly captured Sarawak, would attack southern Sumatra, Western Java, and North Borneo; Central Force would attack Borneo from Davao; and Eastern Force would jump off from the same point against the Celebes, Amboina, Timor, Bali and eastern Java.

Defense of the islands was undertaken by a combined force of Allies in the Southwest Pacific: American, British, Dutch and Australian (ABDA). General Archibald Wavell and his forces had more courage than support, which consisted largely of a six-cruiser naval flotilla under Dutch Rear Admiral Karel Doorman. The attacks began on 11 January 1942, and proceeded relentlessly from one objective to another in the weeks that followed. Naval engagements off Balikpapan (24 January) and in the Lombok Straits (19-20 February) provided only a slight check to the Japanese advance. On 27 February Admiral Doorman attacked the Eastern Force convoy in the Java Sea, where both Dutch cruisers were sunk before they could inflict any damage. In the aftermath, HMS *Exeter* was also destroyed, as were HMAS *Perth* and USS *Houston* when they resisted the Western Force on the following day – to some effect in terms of damage done. But on 1 March, the Japanese made their inevitable landing on Java, whose Allied defenders succumbed a week later.

Above: Japan captures the East Indies piecemeal, 1942.
Right: A Japanese column in Burma crosses a footbridge south of Moulmein.
Far right: The invasion of Burma was accomplished with little Allied resistance.

Burma Bows to Japan

The Japanese invasion of Burma began on 15 January 1942 with the occupation of Victoria Point by a detachment of Fifteenth Army, which moved north to take Tavoy four days later. British defenses in Burma were pathetically unprepared to resist the Japanese invaders; only two brigades, one Indian and one Burmese, were able to counter the push toward Moulmein that began on 20 January. The British were then forced back from the town under constant threat of being outflanked, and from this point on fought a series of delaying actions all the way to Rangoon – the conduit for all British supplies and reinforcements. Air support from a single RAF squadron and a squadron of Major Claire Chennault's 'Flying Tigers' was insufficient to prevent the capture of Rangoon on 8 March. The British garrison there was very nearly cut off before it could pull out. Meanwhile, Lieutenant General William Slim had taken command of British ground forces, while General Harold Alexander had assumed overall command of the deteriorating British defense. The Chinese Fifth and Sixth Armies arrived to reinforce the Allies, but they fought erratically despite the best efforts of American commander General Joseph Stilwell. Throughout the month of April, Allied forces were in continuous retreat from the Japanese, who were now bringing in reinforcements and air support from conquered Malaya. By mid May they were in control of Burma.

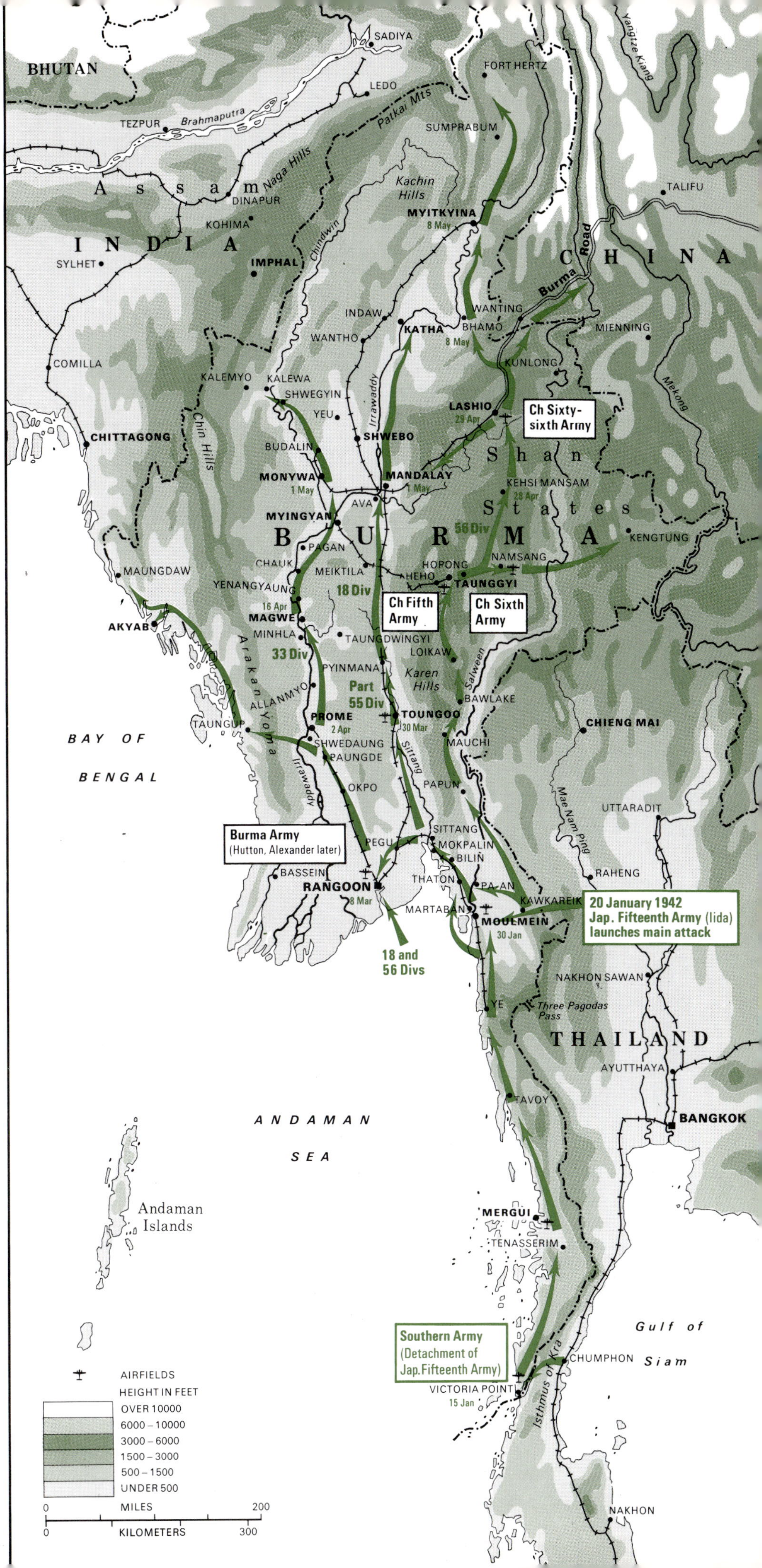

T/5 COX

The Italian Campaign

The Conquest of Sicily

When the Tunisian bridgehead collapsed on 12 May 1943, a demoralized Italy found herself in imminent danger of invasion. Serious strikes in industrial northern Italy had already warned both Mussolini and Hitler of the depth of national discontent. In a meeting with Hitler on 7 April, Mussolini tried – and failed – to persuade his ally to forget about Russia and concentrate on Mediterranean defense. On 5 May General von Rintelin reported to Hitler that an Allied landing in Italy would probably have 'most unpleasant consequences, in view of the prevailing atmosphere of fatalism.' Hitler remained adamant about his doomed adventure on the Eastern Front, which would finally collapse in July at the Battle of Kursk.

Even as Russian and German tanks battered each other in the Kursk Salient, the Allies launched their invasion of Italy, which Churchill had described as 'the soft underbelly of the Axis.' Aerial bombardment from North Africa struck Axis airfields and communications centers in Sicily, Sardinia and southern Italy, beginning in early June. Land forces for the invasion comprised General George S Patton's US Seventh Army and General Bernard Montgomery's British Eighth Army; they were transported to Sicily in a fleet of 3000 vessels. Axis defense of Sicily was entrusted to the Italian Sixth Army under General Alfredo Guzzoni, with strong German support.

On 10 July the Americans landed in Sicily's Gulf of Gela, the British in the Gulf of Syracuse. The landings were a surprise to the Italians, coming as they did in poor weather that seemed to preclude air- or seaborne operations. Vigorous German counterattacks against the Americans came from German divisions on 11-12 July, but Patton's force pressed on toward the north coast, clearing western Sicily by 23 July. Montgomery suffered a check at Catania, but small amphibious operations allowed him to continue his advance to Messina, which he reached on 17 August. Meanwhile, the Italians, who had offered minimal resistance from the first, evacuated the island. The Germans were left to fight a rearguard campaign until the Allied victory of mid August.

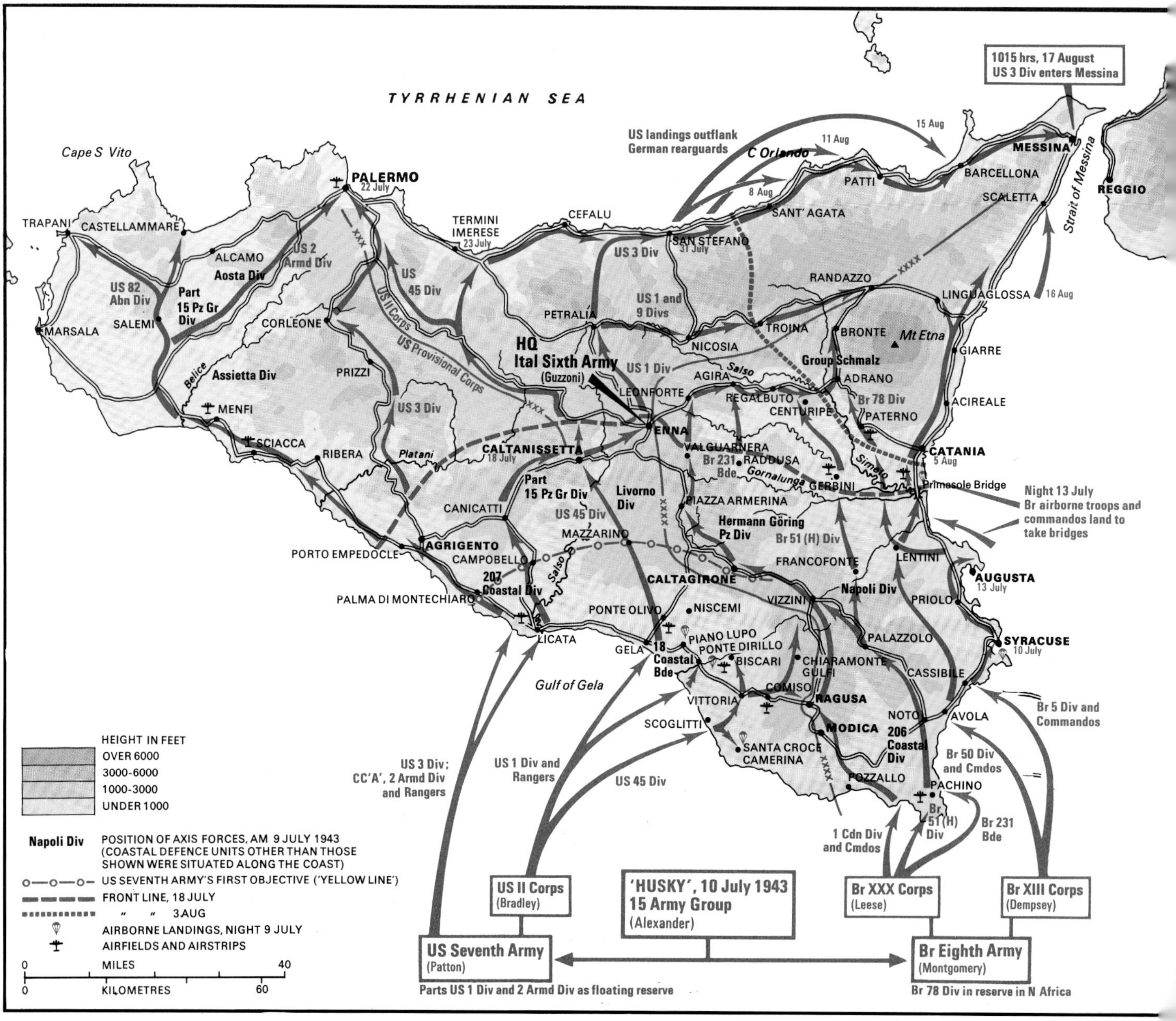

The Peninsular Landings

On 24 July 1943, Mussolini was overthrown. His replacement, Marshal Ugo Cavallero, began secret armistice talks with the Allies. Hitler suspected that the Italians were trying to take themselves out of the war and sent German reinforcements into northern Italy to safeguard communications. Field Marshal Albert Kesselring advised him that an Allied landing in Italy could be expected soon after the conquest of Sicily – probably on the Gulf of Salerno near Naples.

On 3 September, the day that the armistice with Italy was signed, British Eighth Army made a landing on the toe of Italy, at Reggio di Calabria – largely as a diversion. The main landing did take place at Salerno, on 9 September, after the secret armistice with Italy was made public. General Mark Clark's US Fifth Army, with British X Corps, secured only four small beachheads in the face of a well-prepared German defense. Farther south, Montgomery was advancing through Calabria, and there had been a second British landing at Taranto.

From 9 through 14 September, the Fifth Army was in serious trouble at Salerno. German shells from the surrounding hills, followed by a powerful attack on the 12th, almost cut the Allies in half. Reinforcements arrived two days later, barely in time to salvage the operation, and by 18 September Clark's forces had consolidated the beachhead. When Montgomery's advance units arrived on 16 September, Kesselring began to withdraw north to the Gustav Line, which ran along the Rivers Garigliano and Sangro. The Allies pursued from both east and west until 8 October, when a rest halt was called on the Volturno/Termoli Line. The terrain grew increasingly rougher and the weather more severe as the Allied advance resumed in mid October.

Previous page: US troops liberate Rome, June 1944.
Left: Sicily falls to the Allies, 1943.
Above right: The main Allied landing in Italy was undertaken at Salerno by Clark's US Fifth Army.
Right: A diversionary attack at Reggio di Calabria by the British Eighth Army preceded the main attack, while a third landing was made at Taranto in the east.

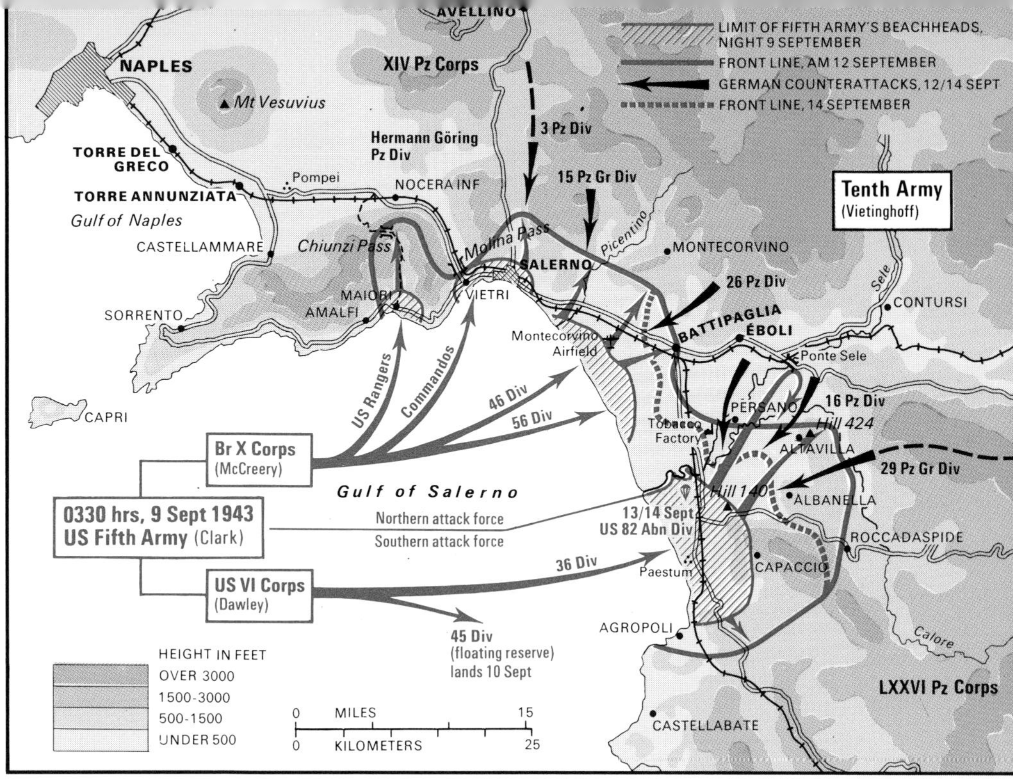

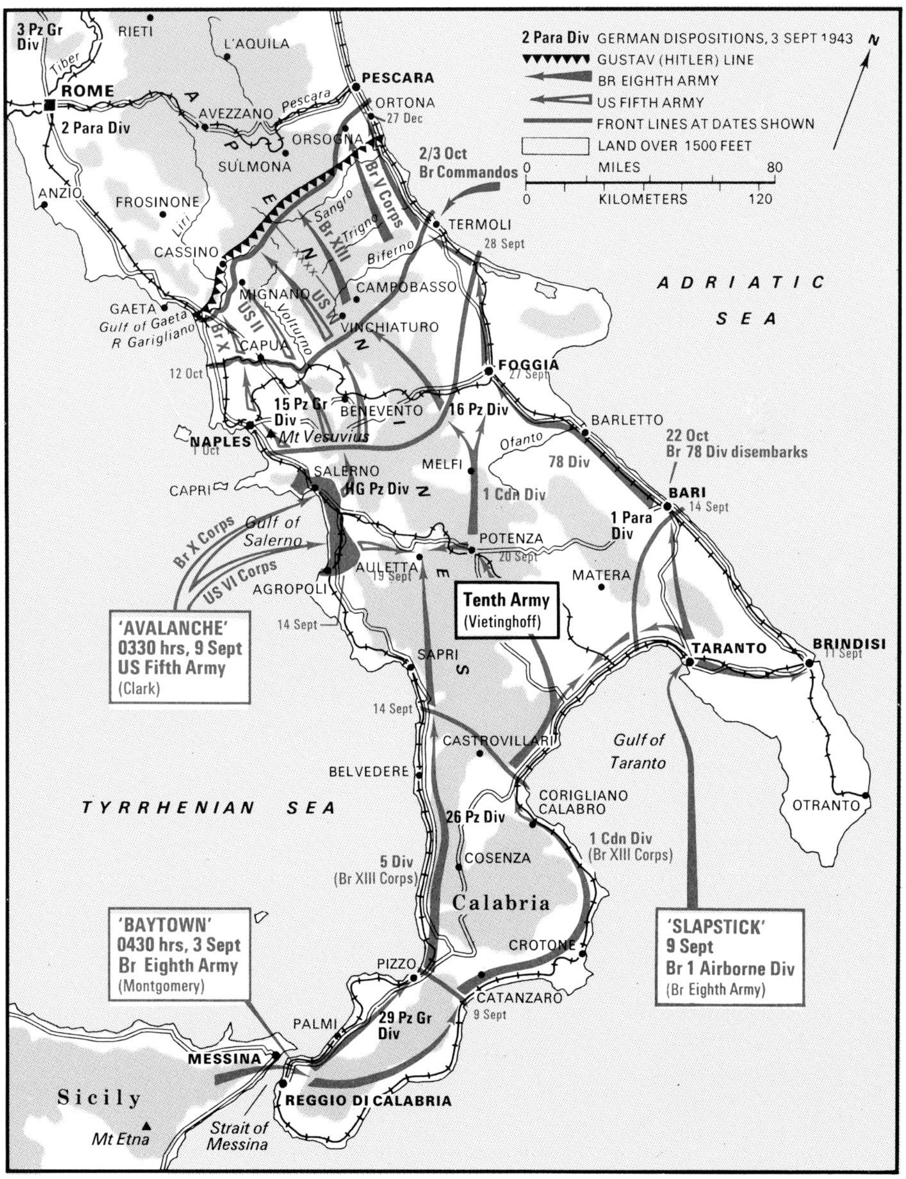

Allied Drive on the Gustav Line

Below: Mussolini (left) and Hitler confer. The former's displacement by Marshal Ugo Cavallero on 24 July 1943 led to Anglo-Italian armistice talks.
Right: The Germans were less prepared to yield than their former allies, finally establishing the Gustav Line as 1943 ended.

Fifth Army made a difficult crossing of the Volturno, swollen by autumn rains, beginning on 12 October 1943. The roadless mountains north of the river posed even greater obstacles. On the east coast, Eighth Army forced a passage over the Trigno River, but their progress on both sides of the central mountains was slowed by skillful German delaying tactics. Kesselring used the time gained to complete the impressive Gustav Line, which ran along the line of the Garigliano and Rapido Rivers, over the central mountains and north of the Sangro River to the Adriatic. German Tenth Army held the line under General Heinrich von Vietinghoff. The western end was especially strong, as it was backed by the mountains on either side of the Liri and by Cassino.

On 20 November US Fifth Army attacked this strong sector, at a very high cost in casualties. Painful progress brought Fifth Army almost as far as the Rapido, but there it was halted at year's end by arctic weather conditions. Montgomery had forced the Sangro on 15 November and broken through the line east of Lanciano. The British took Ortona on 27 December.

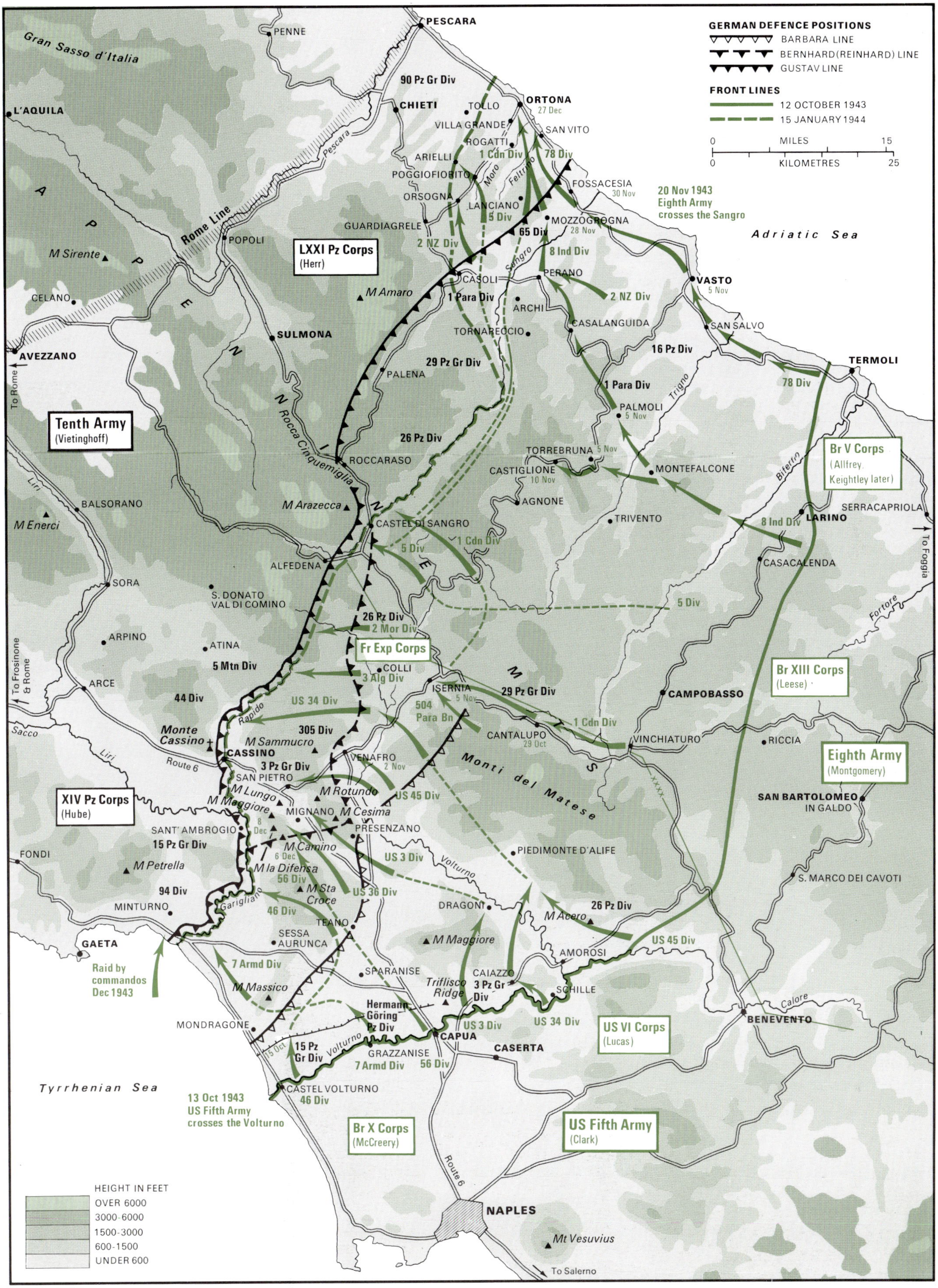
GERMAN DEFENCE POSITIONS
BARBARA LINE
BERNHARD (REINHARD) LINE
GUSTAV LINE
FRONT LINES
12 OCTOBER 1943
15 JANUARY 1944
MILES
0
15
0
KILOMETRES
25
HEIGHT IN FEET
OVER 6000
3000-6000
1500-3000
600-1500
UNDER 600
PESCARA
PENNE
Gran Sasso d'Italia
L'AQUILA
90 Pz Gr Div
CHIETI
TOLLO
ORTONA
27 Dec
VILLA GRANDE
SAN VITO
ROGATTI
1 Cdn Div
78 Div
ARIELLI
POGGIOFIORITO
Moro
Feltrino
FOSSACESIA
30 Nov
20 Nov 1943
Eighth Army
crosses the Sangro
ORSOGNA
LANCIANO
5 Div
MOZZOGROGNA
28 Nov
Adriatic Sea
GUARDIAGRELE
2 NZ Div
65 Div
Sangro
8 Ind Div
Pescara
Rome Line
POPOLI
M Sirente
A P P E N N I N E S
LXXI Pz Corps
(Herr)
PERANO
VASTO
5 Nov
CASOLI
M Amaro
1 Para Div
2 NZ Div
ARCHI
CELANO
SULMONA
TORNARECCIO
CASALANGUIDA
SAN SALVO
16 Pz Div
AVEZZANO
To Rome
29 Pz Gr Div
PALENA
TERMOLI
78 Div
1 Para Div
PALMOLI
5 Nov
Trigno
Tenth Army
(Vietinghoff)
Rocca Cinquemiglia
26 Pz Div
TORREBRUNA
5 Nov
ROCCARASO
CASTIGLIONE
10 Nov
MONTEFALCONE
Br V Corps
(Allfrey,
Keightley later)
Biferno
Liri
BALSORANO
AGNONE
M Arazecca
M Enerci
TRIVENTO
SERRACAPRIOLA
CASTEL DI SANGRO
8 Ind Div
LARINO
1 Cdn Div
5 Div
To Foggia
ALFEDENA
CASACALENDA
SORA
S. DONATO
VAL DI COMINO
5 Div
Fortore
26 Pz Div
2 Mor Div
ARPINO
ATINA
Fr Exp Corps
To Frosinone & Rome
5 Mtn Div
COLLI
3 Alg Div
Br XIII Corps
(Leese)
ARCE
44 Div
ISERNIA
5 Nov
29 Pz Gr Div
CAMPOBASSO
US 34 Div
Rapido
504
Para Bn
1 Cdn Div
Sacco
Monte Cassino
305 Div
M Sammucro
CANTALUPO
29 Oct
VINCHIATURO
RICCIA
CASSINO
Liri
Route 6
3 Pz Gr Div
VENAFRO
2 Nov
Eighth Army
(Montgomery)
SAN PIETRO
Monti del Matese
M Lungo
M Rotundo
US 45 Div
XIV Pz Corps
(Hube)
M Maggiore
SAN BARTOLOMEO
IN GALDO
MIGNANO
M Cesima
SANT' AMBROGIO
8 Dec
PRESENZANO
15 Pz Gr Div
M Camino
FONDI
6 Dec
US 3 Div
Volturno
PIEDIMONTE D'ALIFE
M Petrella
M la Difensa
56 Div
M Sta Croce
US 36 Div
S. MARCO DEI CAVOTI
94 Div
MINTURNO
Garigliano
46 Div
DRAGONI
26 Pz Div
M Acero
TEANO
GAETA
SESSA AURUNCA
M Maggiore
US 45 Div
AMOROSI
Raid by
commandos
Dec 1943
7 Armd Div
SPARANISE
CAIAZZO
3 Pz Gr Div
M Massico
Triflisco Ridge
SCHILLE
Hermann Göring Pz Div
US 3 Div
US 34 Div
US VI Corps
(Lucas)
Calore
BENEVENTO
MONDRAGONE
CAPUA
15 Pz Gr Div
15 Oct
Volturno
CASERTA
GRAZZANISE
7 Armd Div
56 Div
Tyrrhenian Sea
CASTEL VOLTURNO
13 Oct 1943
US Fifth Army
crosses the Volturno
46 Div
Br X Corps
(McCreery)
US Fifth Army
(Clark)
Route 6
NAPLES
Mt Vesuvius
To Salerno

The Fight for Monte Cassino

The ancient abbey of Monte Cassino astride the Gustav Line was the object of heavy fighting in the early months of 1944. The Allies made a frontal assault on the almost impregnable position on 17 January, but a whole series of attacks failed to take it by storm. The French Expeditionary Corps had joined the Allied forces in Italy, but they made only limited advances with very heavy casualties. The New Zealand Corps suffered similar repulses between 15 and 18 February.

A long hiatus followed the first offensive, during which the Allies regrouped and reinforced for a new effort, launched 11 May along a 20-mile front between the area east of Cassino and the sea. The British pushed over the Rapido but were then contained by the Germans. The Americans broke through the Gustav Line along the coast, only to be stopped at Santa Maria Infante. It was the French Expeditionary Force that crossed the Garigliano and cut the German lines of communication; interdiction of German supplies to the point of starvation was also a factor. On 17 May Kesselring conceded the loss of this key position by a withdrawal. The historic abbey had been riddled with tunnels and redoubts to protect its defenders from heavy bombardment; it was reduced to rubble by the time the Allies claimed it on 18 May, at the cost of many lives.

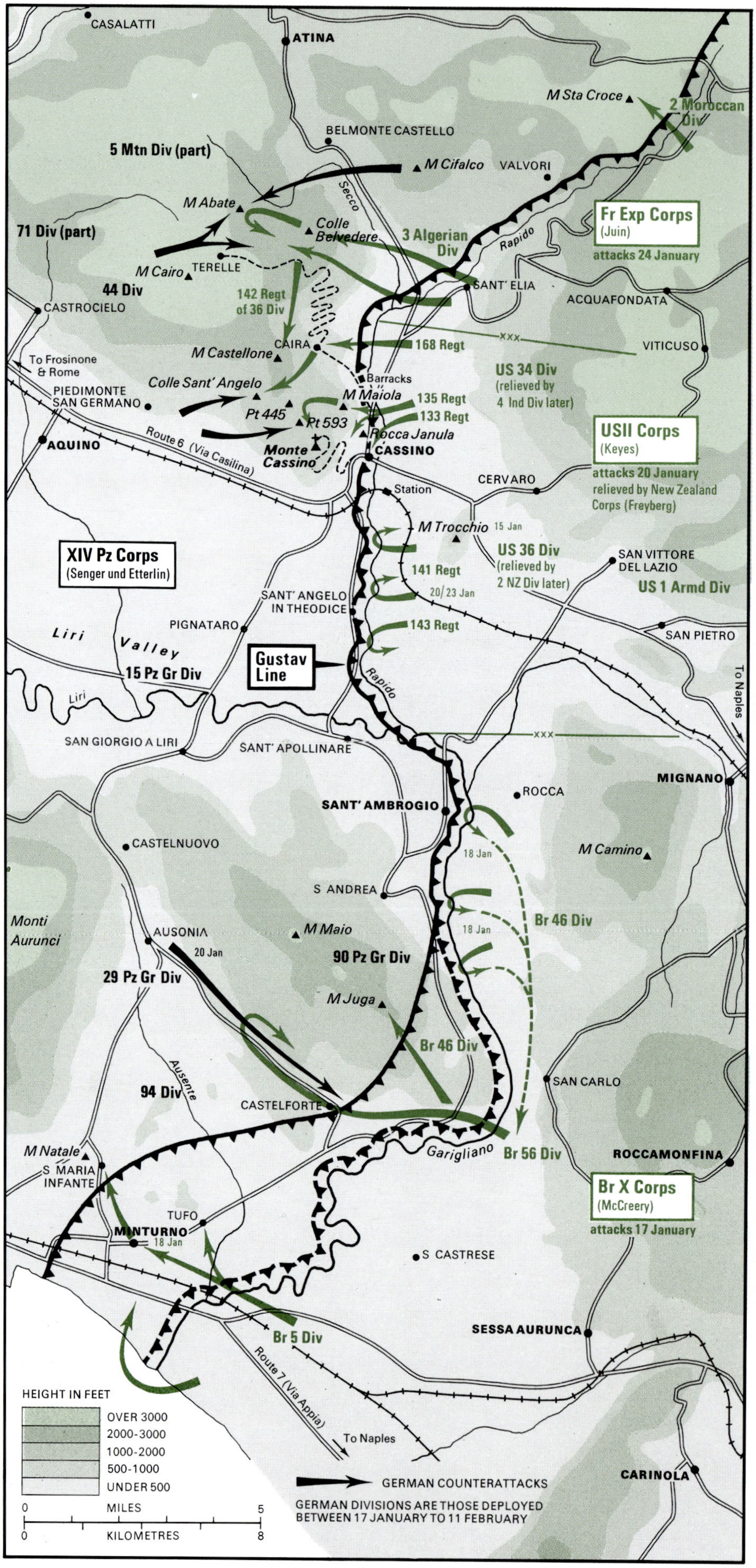

Right: Initial Allied attempts to break the Gustav Line at Cassino in early 1944 met with failure.

Right: Little remained intact after the abbey at Monte Cassino was finally overrun by the Allies on 18 May.
Below: The second Allied offensive on the Gustav Line was somewhat more successful than its predecessor, pushing the Germans to the Führer-Senger line.

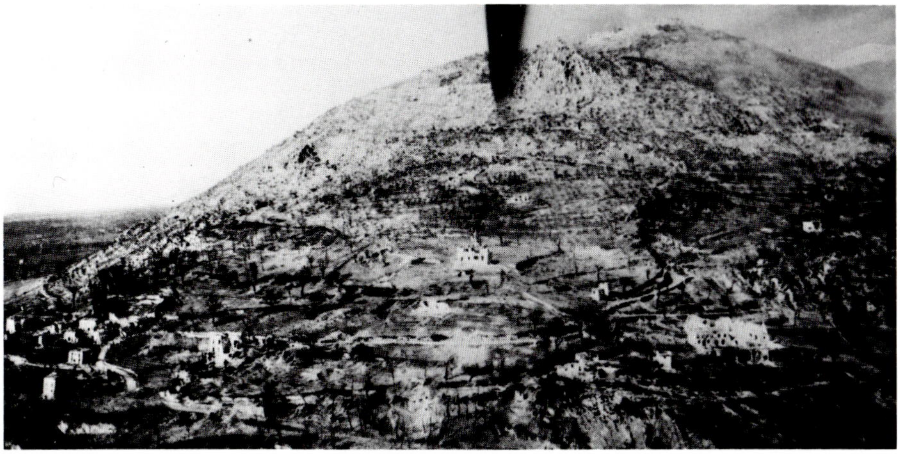

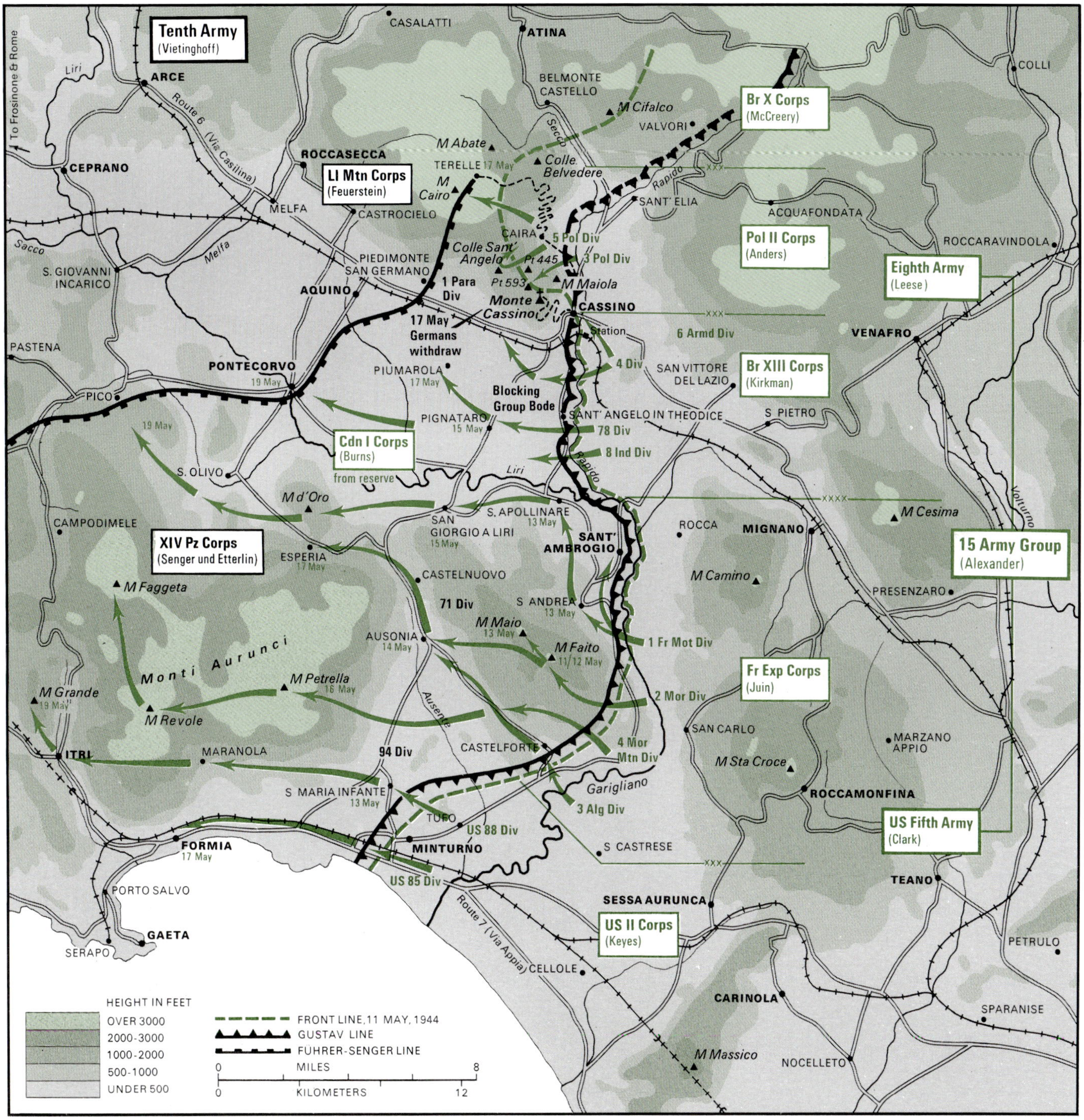

Anzio and the Road to Rome

The Allied landings at Anzio on 22 January 1944 were designed to relieve pressure on Cassino, but the results were just the reverse: only the Allied success at Cassino allowed the US VI Corps to break out of its bungled position on the coast. Fifty thousand troops came ashore under Major General John Lucas, who made the fatal error of establishing a beachhead rather than pressing inland so as to wait for his heavy artillery and tanks. The Germans, under Mackensen, seized this welcome opportunity to pin down VI Corps at Anzio and mass forces for a major counterattack on 16 February. Not until the 19th was this halted, to be followed by a state of siege that would last until late May. Lucas was soon replaced by Major General Lucius Truscott, but it was too late to retrieve the situation.

When the Allies finally broke the Gustav Line at Cassino, Clark's Fifth Army could resume its advance northward. Instead of swinging east in an effort to trap the German Tenth Army, Clark opted for capturing Rome – an important moral victory, though hardly necessary strategically. The Germans were able to delay his troops at Velletri and Valmontone long enough to ensure the escape of virtually all their forces in the area. The Allies finally entered Rome on 4 June 1944, just two days before the invasion of France.

Right: The intention of the Anzio operation was to cut German communications by landing behind their front line.
Below: The Allies on the road to Rome.

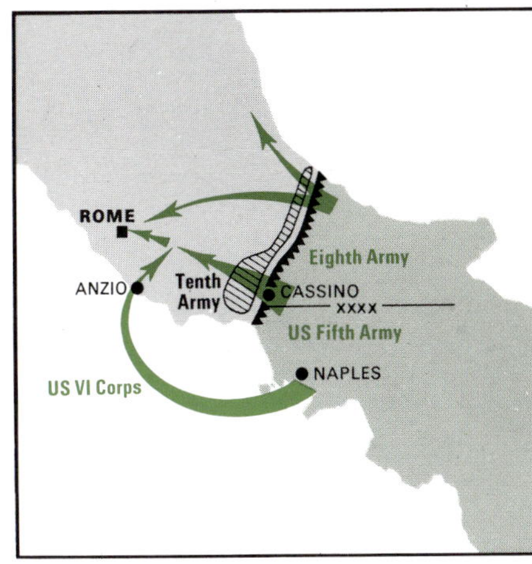

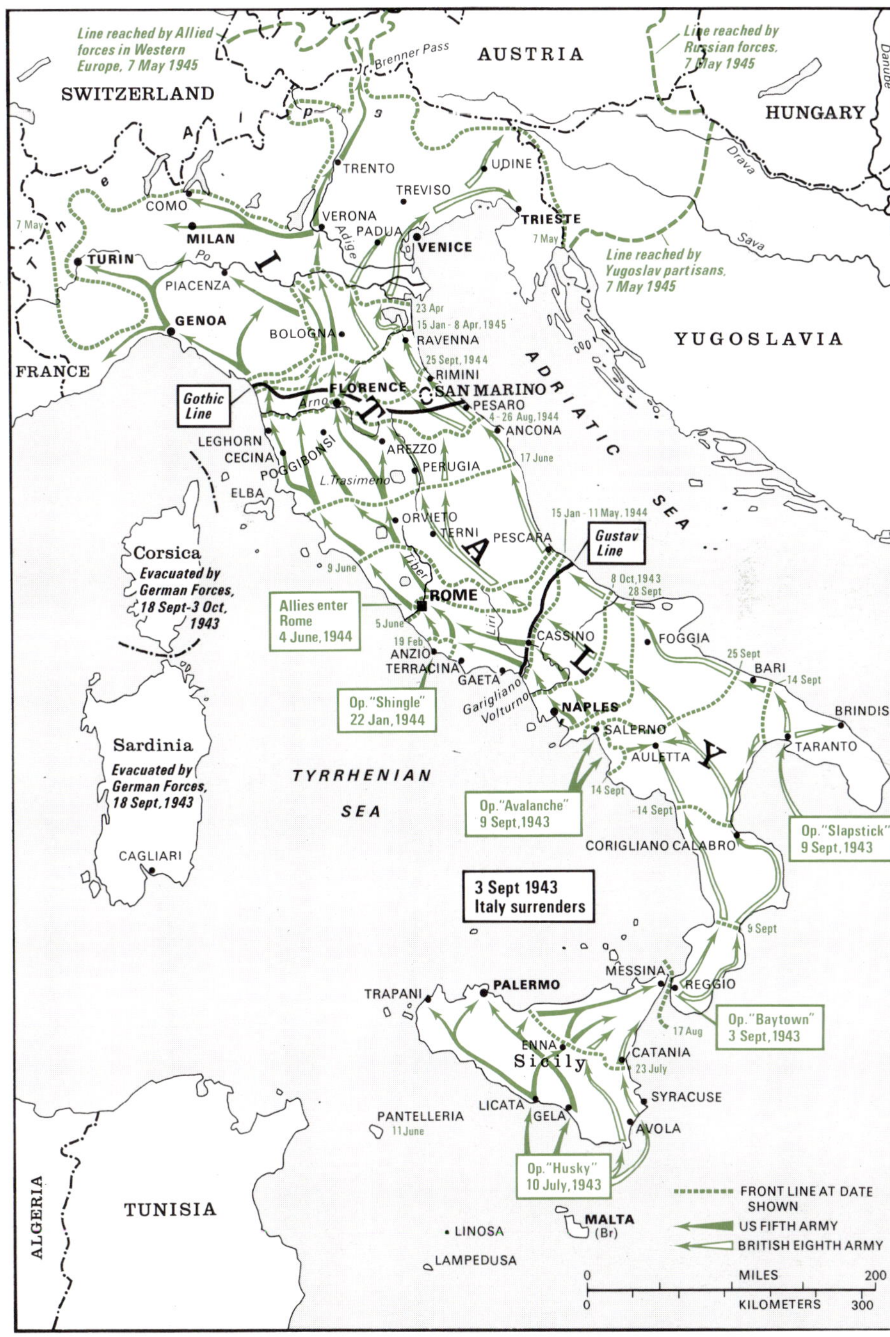

Above left: Mount Vesuvius' symbolic eruption failed to deter B-25 bombers of the US 12th Air Force en route to Cassino.
Left: A second pall of smoke hangs over the city and monastery as the bombs burst.

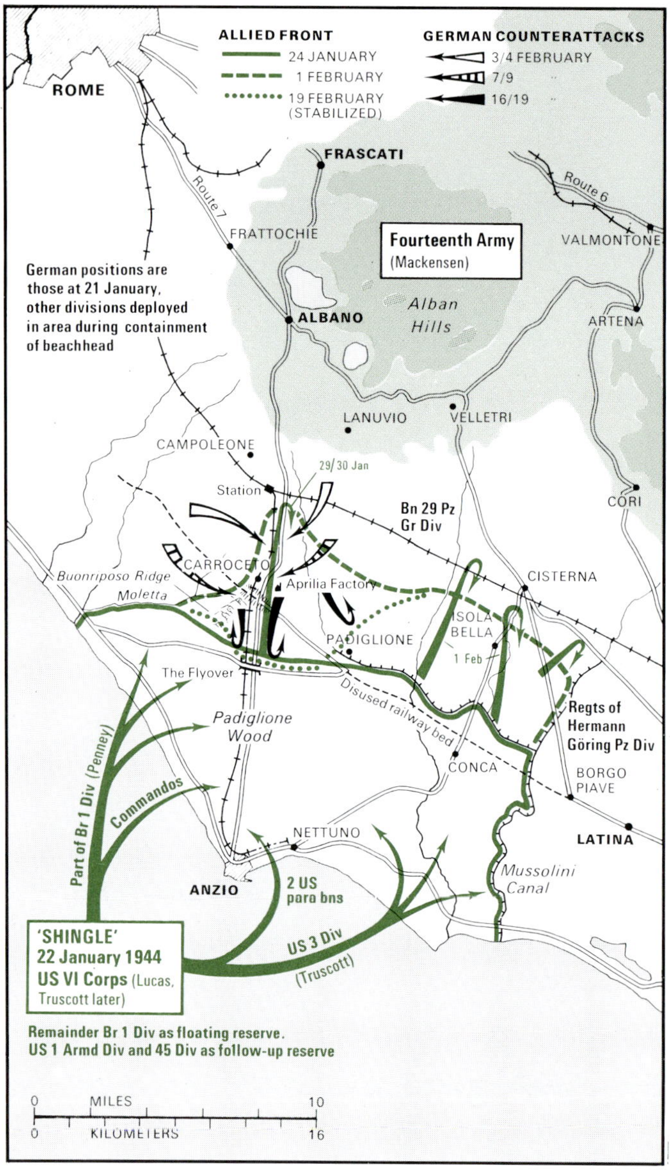
ALLIED FRONT
24 JANUARY
1 FEBRUARY
19 FEBRUARY (STABILIZED)
GERMAN COUNTERATTACKS
3/4 FEBRUARY
7/9
16/19
ROME
FRASCATI
Route 7
Route 6
FRATTOCHIE
Fourteenth Army
(Mackensen)
VALMONTONE
German positions are those at 21 January, other divisions deployed in area during containment of beachhead
ALBANO
Alban Hills
ARTENA
LANUVIO
VELLETRI
CAMPOLEONE
29/30 Jan
Station
Bn 29 Pz Gr Div
CORI
CARROCETO
Buonriposo Ridge
Moletta
Aprilia Factory
CISTERNA
ISOLA BELLA
PADIGLIONE
1 Feb
The Flyover
Padiglione Wood
Disused railway bed
Regts of Hermann Göring Pz Div
CONCA
BORGO PIAVE
Part of Br 1 Div (Penney)
Commandos
NETTUNO
LATINA
Mussolini Canal
ANZIO
2 US para bns
'SHINGLE'
22 January 1944
US VI Corps (Lucas, Truscott later)
US 3 Div (Truscott)
Remainder Br 1 Div as floating reserve.
US 1 Armd Div and 45 Div as follow-up reserve
0 MILES 10
0 KILOMETERS 16

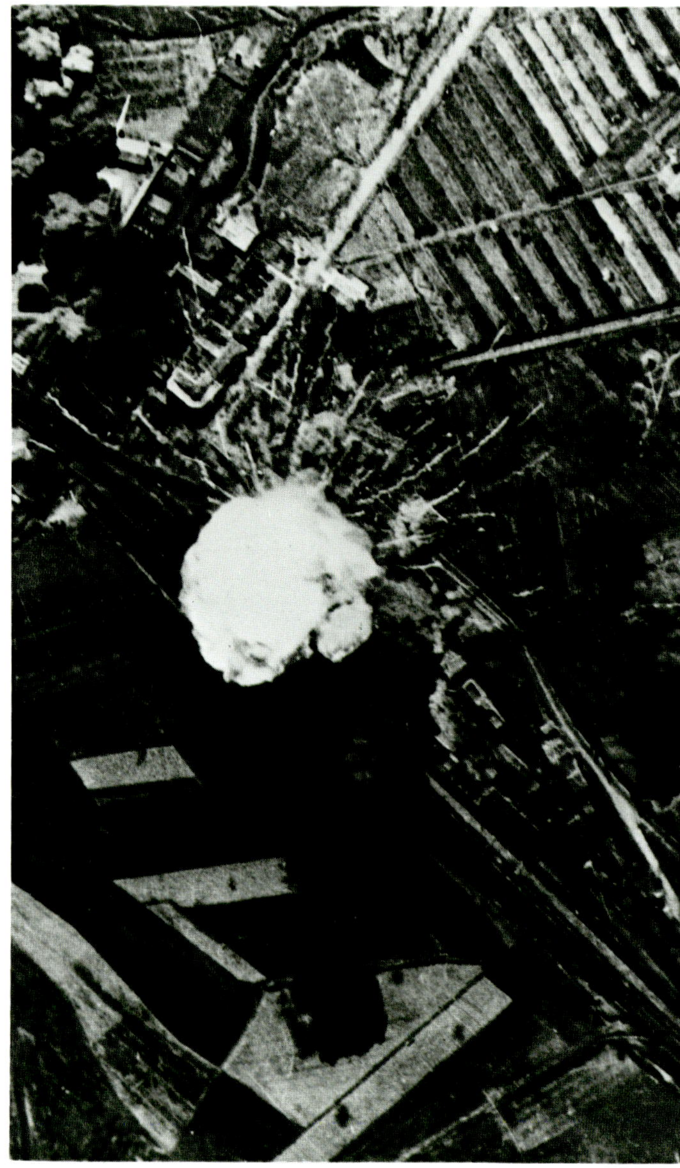

The End in Italy

After Rome fell, the Allies forced the Germans back to their last defense – the Gothic Line. The Germans were now being reinforced from the Balkans and Germany, while Allied troops, aircraft and landing craft had been drawn off to France. British Eighth Army reached the Gothic Line on 30 August 1944 and attacked with considerable success, but the Germans held commanding positions on the Gemmano and Coriano Ridges that slowed the advance to Rimini until late September.

US Fifth Army had also broken through, but the approach of winter found Clark's exhausted forces short of their objective of Bologna. The Allied advance did not resume until April 1945, by which time Clark had become commander of 15 Army Group. Reinforcements and new equipment had reached him during the winter, and he planned a two-pronged offensive against Ferrara (Eighth Army) and Bologna (Fifth Army).

The German Tenth Army, now under General Herr, was surprised by the British attack across Lake Comocchio, which had been covered by a major artillery bombardment beginning on 9 April. The British moved into the Argenta Gap and Fifth Army, now led by Major General Lucius Truscott, broke through Lemelsen's German Fourteenth Army into the Po Valley (20 April). General von Vietinghoff, who had replaced Kesselring as overall commander in Italy, was forced back to the left bank of the Po, leaving behind all his heavy weapons and armor. The Fascist Ligurian Army had disappeared without a trace, and Axis forces in Italy were out of the fight when Bologna fell on 21 April. Vietinghoff signed the surrender of German forces in Italy on 29 April 1945.

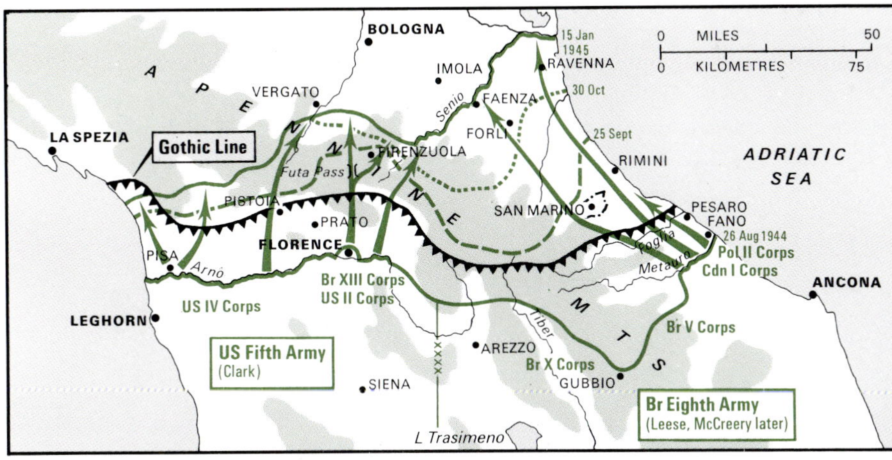

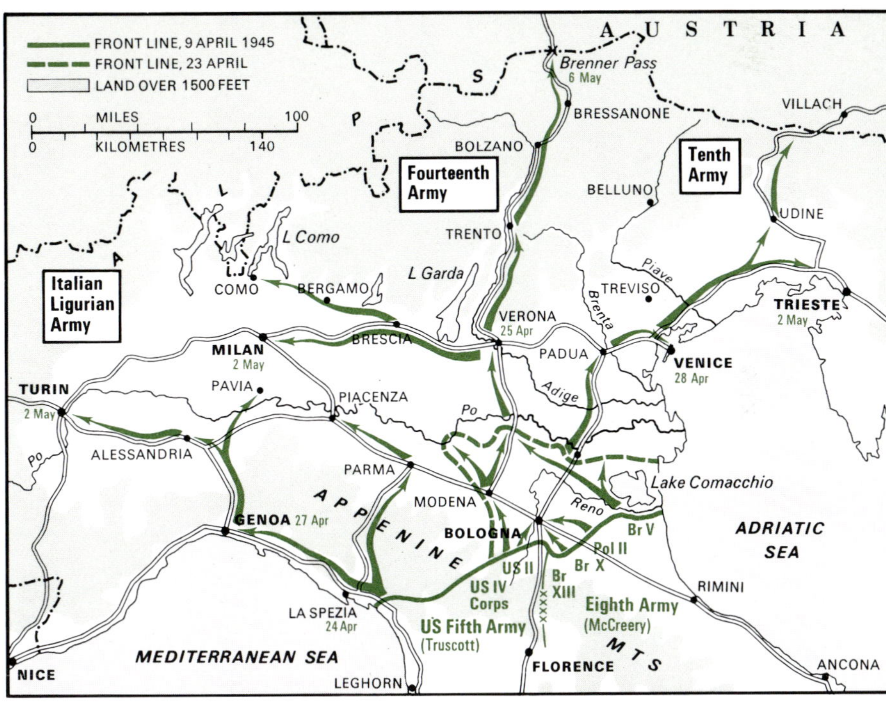

Opposite top left: The unsuccessful Anzio landing on 22 January 1944 which left both sides in a siege position.
Above left: An Axis ammunition train receives a direct hit, March 1944.
Left: Wehrmacht soldiers are marched into captivity north of Anzio.
Top right: Breaking the Gothic Line, the final German defense in Italy.
Above right: The Allies advance into Northern Italy.
Right: US 105mm howitzers fire across the Arno, August 1944.

Ebb Tide in the Pacific

Battle of the Coral Sea

After the Doolittle bombing raid on Tokyo (18 April 1942), Japanese strategists sought ways to extend their defense perimeter in Greater East Asia. One of their options was to strike from Rabaul against Port Moresby, New Guinea; extend their hold on the Solomon Islands; and isolate Australia from the United States. This task was assigned to a five-part force designated MO, under command of Admiral Shigeyoshi Inouye. It comprised a Port Moresby Invasion Group of eleven transports and attendant destroyers; a smaller Tulagi Invasion Group charged with setting up a seaplane base on Tulagi in the southern Solomons; a Covering Group under Rear Admiral Goto that included the carrier *Shoho*; a smaller support group; and Vice Admiral Takagi's Carrier Striking Force, including *Shokaku* and *Zuikaku*. The operation's complexity suggests that no serious opposition was expected from the Allies, but Admiral Nimitz, Commander in Chief of the Pacific Fleet, moved quickly to counter it. A hastily improvised Task Force of three components, including the carriers *Yorktown* and *Lexington*, prepared to rendezvous in the Coral Sea on 4 May. The Japanese attack came one day earlier.

Tulagi was occupied without opposition, after which the opponents lost several days seeking one another in vain. Then Vice-Admiral Frank Fletcher dispatched British Rear-Admiral John Crace and his Task Force 44 to attack the Port Moresby Invasion Group (7 May). The Japanese mistook this group for the main Allied force and bombed it continuously until Crace made his escape by skillful maneuvering at the end of the day – not without inflicting some damage in return. Another Japanese error led to an attack on the tanker *Neosho* and the destroyer *Sims* at the same time that the main Allied force, still undetected, converged on Goto's Covering Group and sank *Shoho*.

The Japanese had already ordered the invasion transports to turn back, but now that Fletcher's position was known an air strike was launched against his group on the night of 7-8 May. Twenty-seven Japanese planes took off, of which only six returned. Then *Shokaku* was attacked and disabled; a reciprocal Japanese strike fatally damaged *Lexington* and put *Yorktown* out of action. At no time in the battle did opposing surface ships sight one another – a circumstance new to naval warfare, but soon to become familiar in the Pacific Theater.

Tactically, the Battle of the Coral Sea was a draw: the Japanese lost more planes, the US more ships. Strategically – and morally – it was a major US victory that came when one was needed most.

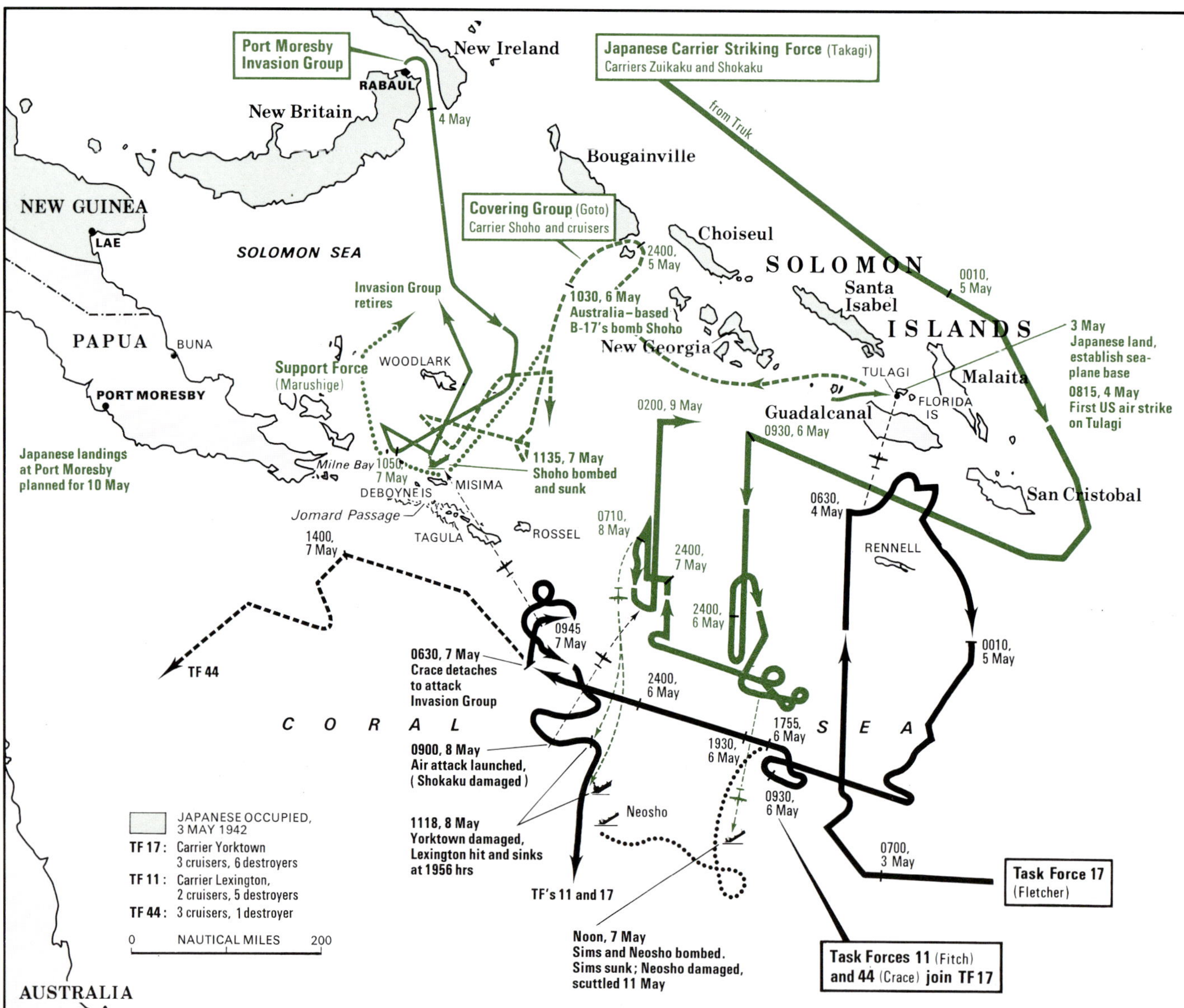

Battle of Midway

Previous page: The final dive of a stricken Japanese bomber west of the Marianas Islands, June 1944.
Opposite below: Coral Sea was the first naval battle fought without surface vessels sighting each other.

Below: The complex Japanese plan of attack at Midway involved no less than eight task forces.
Bottom: The battle took place north of Midway and ended in decisive defeat for the Japanese.

Midway was the turning point in the Pacific War and a watershed in modern history. Having failed to gain their objectives in the Coral Sea operations of early May 1942, the Japanese were determined to capture Midway as a base within striking distance of Hawaii. The destruction of the Pacific Fleet before US industry could build it up again was recognized as a matter of supreme urgency, besides which the occupation of Midway would eliminate the bombing threat to the home islands. Thc operation was scheduled for 4 June 1942.

Fleet Admiral Isoroku Yamamoto, architect of the Pearl Harbor attack, formed a complex plan involving eight separate task forces, one of which was to make a diversionary attack on the Aleutian Islands. Almost all of the Japanese surface fleet would be involved – 162 warships and auxiliaries, including four fleet carriers and three light carriers commanded by Admiral Nagumo.

Information – and the lack of it – played a crucial role in the battle's outcome. Yamamoto believed that the carrier *Yorktown* had been destroyed in the Coral Sea along with *Lexington*. In fact, the damaged ship had been refitted for battle at Pearl Harbor in the incredibly short time of 48 hours. Nor did the Japanese realize that the Americans had broken their fleet code: Nimitz was fully aware of their plans. Although he had only 76 ships, three of them were fleet carriers – *Yorktown*, *Enterprise* and *Hornet*, with a total of 250 planes – whose presence was wholly unsuspected by the Japanese. As a result, Nagumo sent out few reconnaissance flights, which could have warned him of their presence.

Before dawn on 4 June, the Japanese dispatched 108 bombers to Midway, reserving 93 on deck armed for naval contingencies only with armor-piercing bombs and torpedoes. Many US planes were destroyed on the ground in the first attack, but those that survived took off to intercept the incoming bombers. They were largely destroyed by enemy Zeros, but they made a second strike imperative and thereby gave their carriers the chance to attack Nagumo's fleet while it was rearming with high-explosive and fragmentation bombs. When a Japanese reconnaissance plane finally reported detection of enemy carriers, Nagumo's planes were unready to mount a defense. The first few US carrier strikes inflicted little damage, but the decisive blow caught all the newly armed Japanese planes on their flight decks waiting to take off. Five minutes later, three of the four Japanese carriers were sinking. *Hiryu* escaped immediate destruction and disabled *Yorktown*, but damage inflicted on her by *Enterprise* was so severe that she had to be scuttled the following day. It was the end of Japanese naval supremacy in the Pacific.

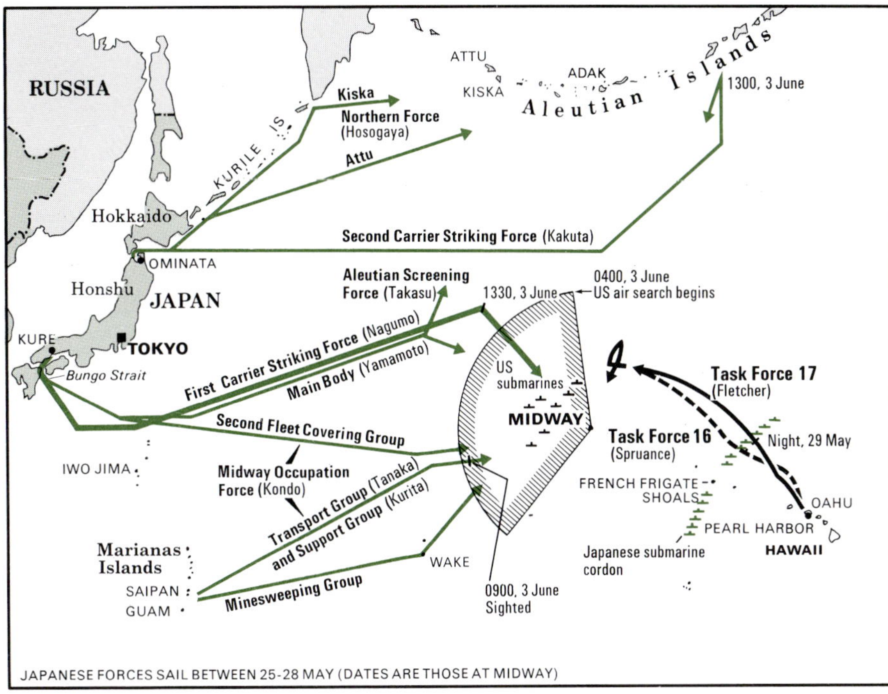

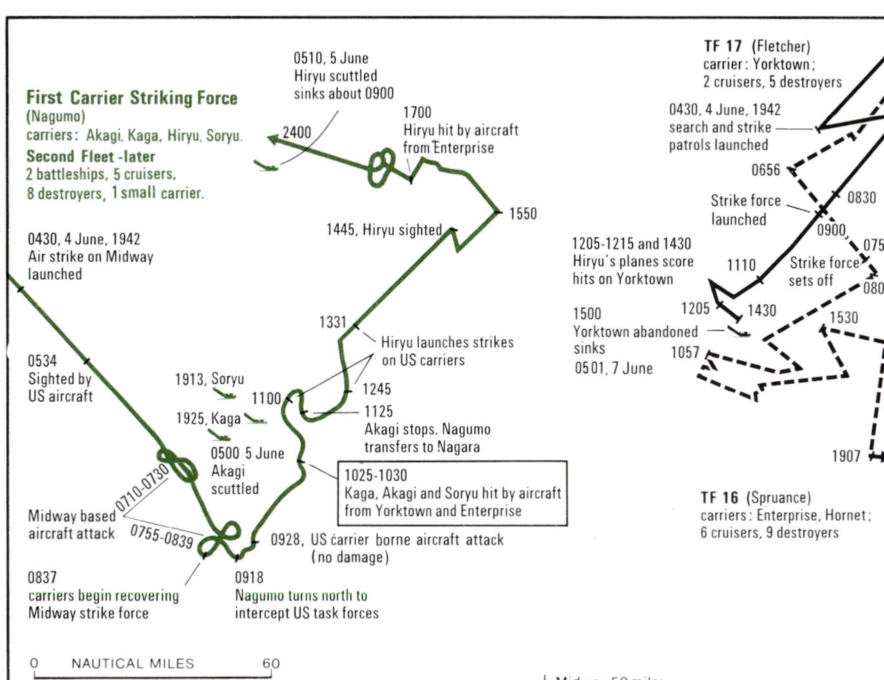

Guadalcanal and the Solomon Islands

Prior to 1942, few Americans had ever heard of those far-flung islands whose names would become so familiar during the war years – names like Okinawa, Iwo Jima and Guadalcanal. Japanese forces waged a six-month battle for this island in the southern Solomons with US Marines who landed there on 7-8 August 1942. Their objective was a Japanese airbase still under construction to offset the loss of carrier air cover at Midway.

Admiral Fletcher, who had distinguished himself at Midway, was in overall command of operations in the southern Solomons. Rear Admiral R Kelly Turner led an amphibious task force responsible for landing the 19,000-man 1st Marine Division and its equipment. The Marines reached the airbase – renamed Henderson Field – soon after landing and found it deserted, but they came under heavy attack from the Japanese Navy, which dominated surrounding waters by night and soon sent reinforcements ashore to retake the island. The Marines strengthened the airfield's perimeter and used it to gain control of the sea lanes by day.

Two costly but inconclusive carrier battles were fought, one in August (Battle of the Eastern Solomons), the other in October (Battle of Santa Cruz), as the Japanese landed additional troops and supplies on Guadalcanal. On land, there were three major attacks on the Marine

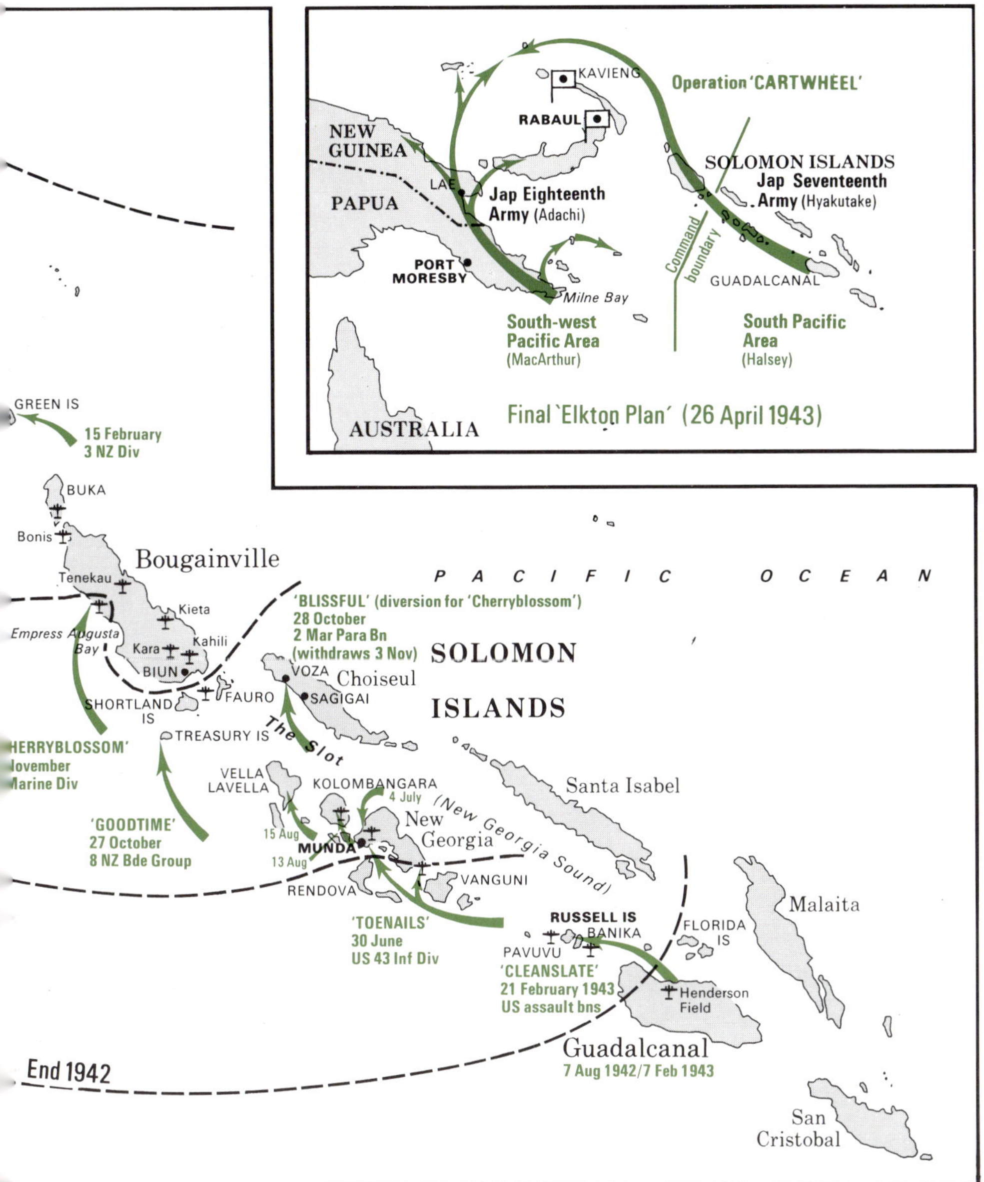

garrison, all of which were thrown back at considerable cost to the Japanese. Despite reinforcement, the Marines were exhausted by December, but the XIV Army Corps relieved them and the Japanese had to withdraw their own depleted forces.

Guadalcanal provided a jumping-off place for successive conquests in the Solomons, culminating with Bougainville in October 1943. The campaign was characterized by surprise landings, followed by hasty construction or repair of airstrips for local defense and as bases for the next attack. Even strongly garrisoned islands like Bougainville, which had 60,000 widely scattered defenders, were seized and isolated, while Japanese strongpoints at Rabaul and Kavieng were bypassed. The Solomons Campaign wound down in mid 1944, after successful Allied landings on New Britain and the Admiralty and St Matthias groups.

Left and inset: Occupying the Solomons was a lengthy process that took the Allies over a year to complete.
Opposite below: An attack by US aircraft at the beginning of the battle for Guadalcanal.
Below: US Marines landing on the island head immediately for cover.

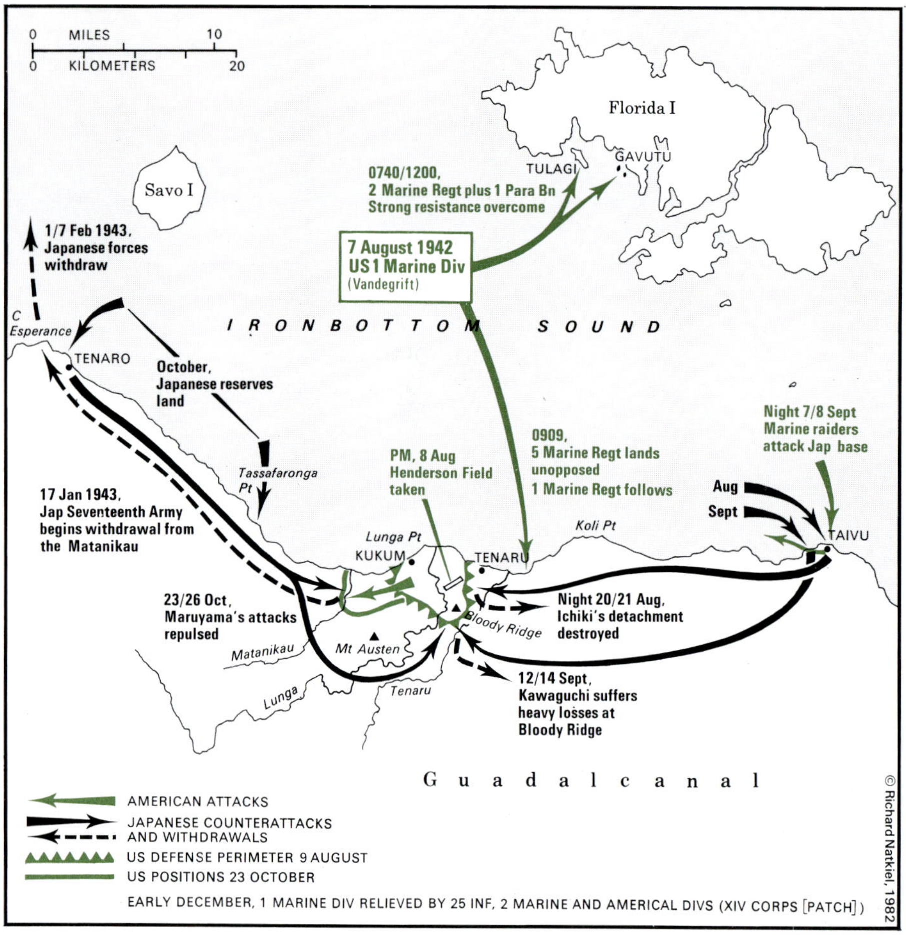

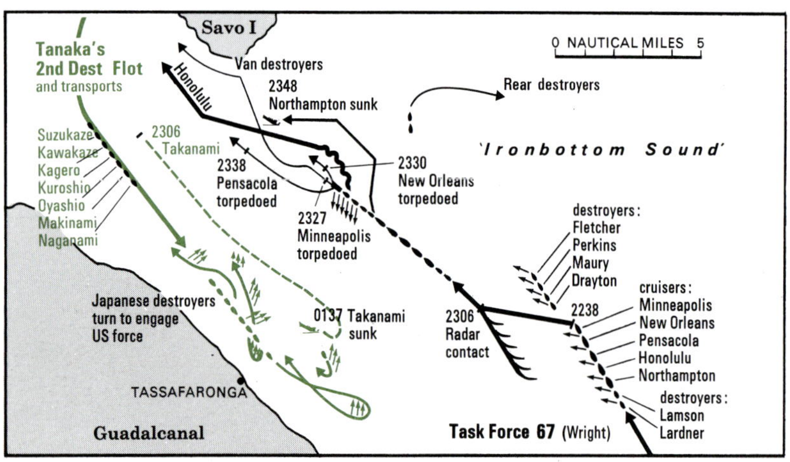

Left: US landings on Guadalcanal and the resistance encountered.
Below left: Japanese supply ships and their escorts met US Task Force 67 near Tassafaronga on 30 November 1942 in one of the many naval actions off Guadalcanal. On this occasion, the Japanese emerged on top.
Bottom left: Marine reinforcements disembark.
Below: US Navy vessels weave to counter air attack off the Solomons.
Right: US landings on New Guinea.
Below right: General MacArthur (right) passes an encouraging word with a paratrooper at Port Moresby.

New Guinea

The Japanese made a second attempt against Port Moresby in July 1942 – an overland advance from Buna – but it was stopped by Australian formations in September. Allied forces built an airstrip at Milne Bay, then proceeded over the Owen Stanley Range against totally adverse ground and weather conditions to capture Buna and Sananenda at year's end. Australian coast-watchers were instrumental in Allied success by providing early warning of Japanese moves, but all combatants were plagued by tropical disease, grueling terrain and a lack of accurate maps of the area.

After Buna fell, Lae and the Markham Valley were captured with the assistance of Allied air forces (excellent co-ordination of all the services involved was a feature of this campaign). A series of operations around the Huon Peninsula was followed by major landings at Hollandia and Aitape in April 1944. These cut off some 200,000 Japanese troops and numerous civilian workers centered around Wewak. The final New Guinea landings, at and near the northern tip of the island, secured airfields to be used in support of operations in the Marianas and the Philippines. By July 1944, an entire Japanese Army had been neutralized in New Guinea, and the Solomons Campaign had nullified the threat to Australia and New Zealand.

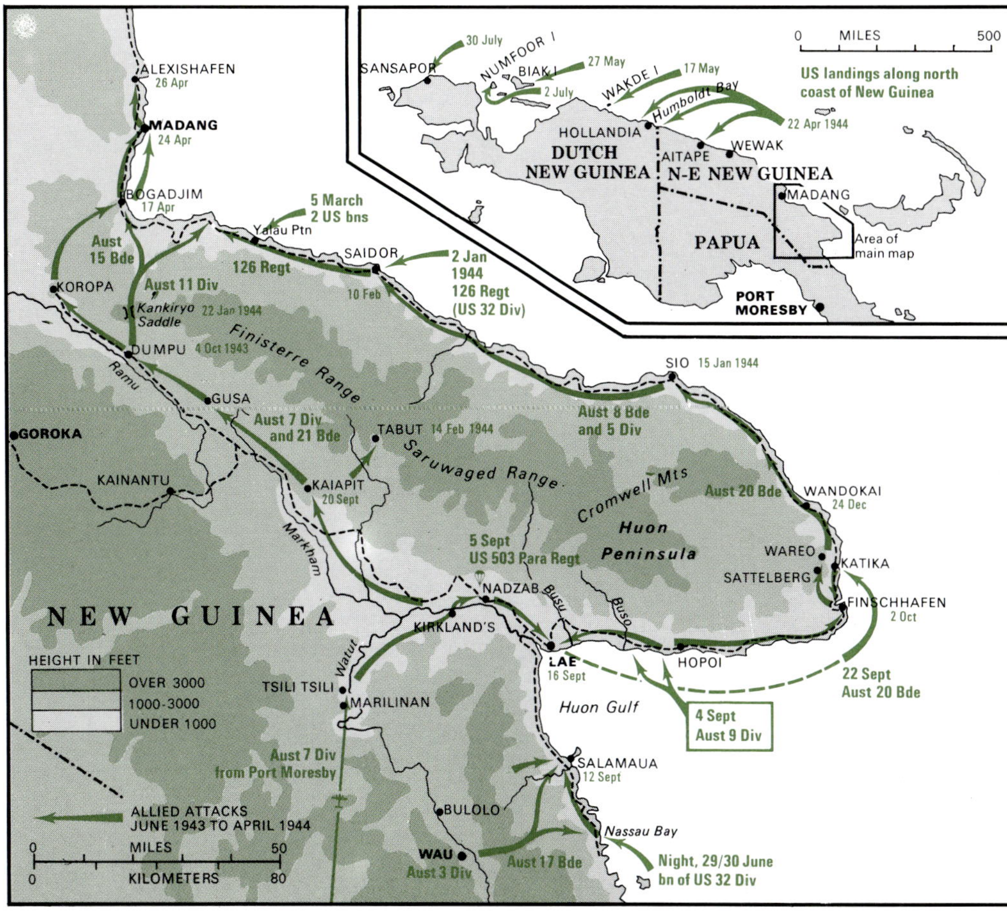

The Battle of the Philippine Sea

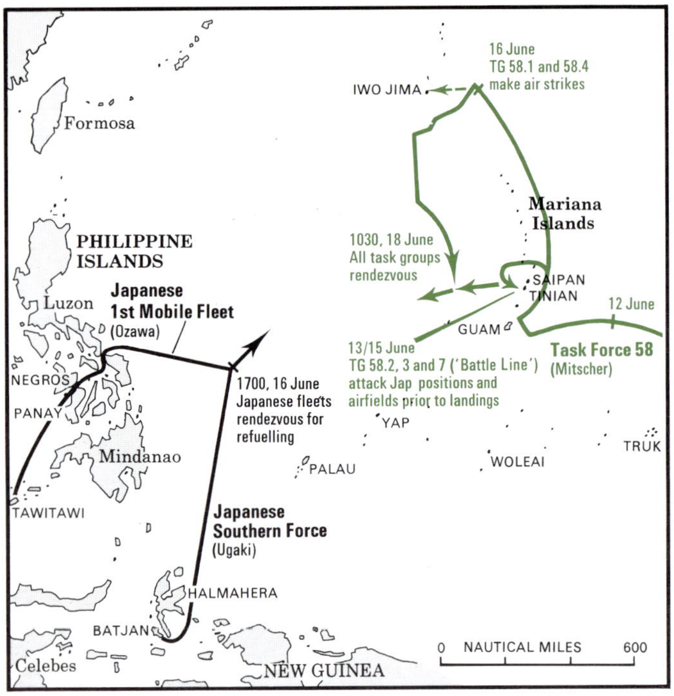

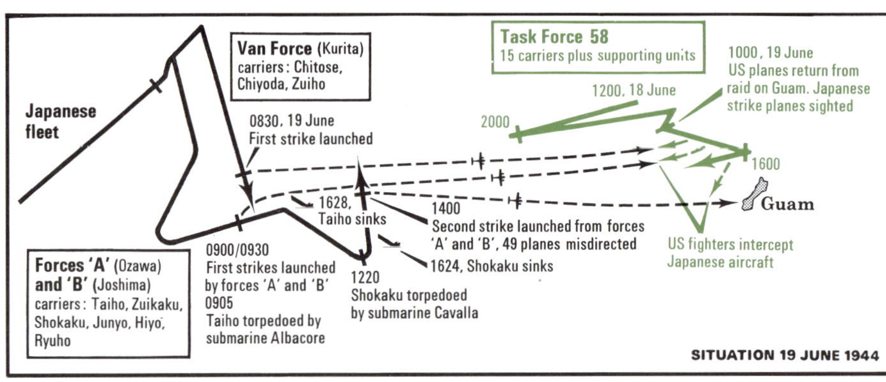

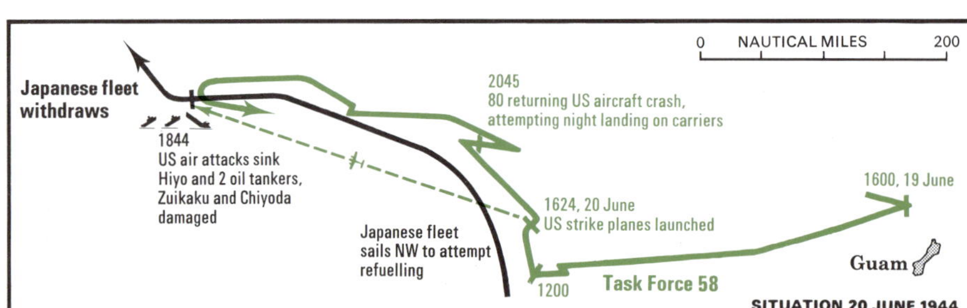

After clearing the Marshall Islands, the US trans-Pacific drive converged on the Mariana group, whose conquest would cut off the Japanese homeland from the Philippines and Southeast Asia. When the US assault fell on the main Japanese defenses at Saipan, Tinian and Guam, the Japanese Navy was there to counter it (June-July 1944).

The Japanese First Mobile Fleet, under Vice-Admiral Jisaburo Ozawa, rendezvoused with Vice-Admiral Matome Ugaki's Southern Force on 16 June. Three days later, Ozawa's scouting planes spotted Vice-Admiral Marc Mitscher's US Task Force 58 underway to give battle; strike aircraft were launched immediately. Meanwhile, US submarines had located Ozawa's force and torpedoed his flagship, the carrier *Taiho*. The veteran *Shokaku* was also sunk. An abortive second strike by Ozawa was misdirected, and US fighters intercepted it on its way to Guam. Japanese losses by nightfall of 19 June included 340 irreplaceable veteran pilots and two carriers. US crewmen dubbed the battle 'The Great Marianas Turkey Shoot.'

Ozawa compounded his errors by lingering in the vicinity, with the result that he lost three more ships the following day. The US had lost only 50 planes and suffered slight damage to a single battleship. Ozawa's reputation as an outstanding commander was impaired by this disaster, but his resignation was refused by his superiors and he fought again at the Battle of Leyte Gulf with skill and tenacity. By that time, however, the Japanese defeat was inevitable.

Top left: The opposing fleets rendezvous.
Center and above: The course of the battle on 19-20 June.
Top: A Japanese divebomber narrowly misses USS Bunker Hill *of Task Force 58.*
Right: Return of an F6F-3 Hellcat fighter to Lexington *during 'The Great Marianas Turkey Shoot'.*

The Struggle for Leyte and Luzon

General Douglas MacArthur's overriding desire to liberate the Philippines played a major part in the Allied High Command decision to make landings on Leyte in October 1944. MacArthur's forces joined Nimitz's for this operation, in a rare display of cooperation between these two competitive leaders. Only 20,000 Japanese held the island against 130,000 men of General Walter Krueger's Sixth Army, who landed on 20 October. Japanese reinforcements could not keep pace with this kind of manpower. By Christmas 1944, major engagements were almost over, with Japanese casualties estimated between 50 and 80,000. The Americans had lost only 3600 men.

At sea, four major actions comprised the Battle of Leyte Gulf (21-25 October), in which Japan sought to prevent the Americans from regaining a foothold in the Philippines. Admiral Ozawa's depleted carrier force was to serve largely as a decoy, luring Admiral Halsey's powerful Third Fleet away from the main action. The real fighting was assigned to four task forces of Japanese battleships and cruisers, which were still plentiful. On the US side, Halsey's force was augmented by Admiral Kincaid's Seventh Fleet, backed by carrier formation TF.38.

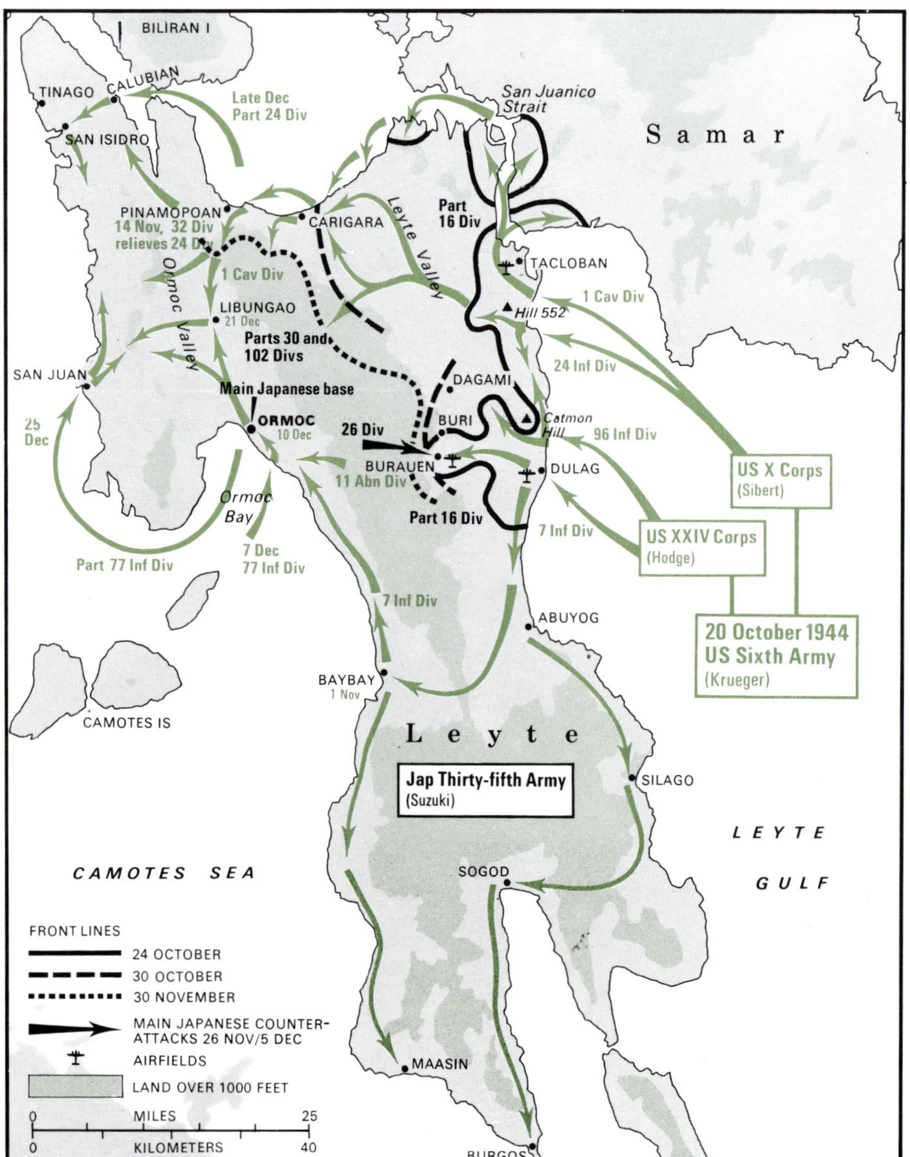

Left: The land battles for Leyte saw superior US forces emerge triumphant. Above: A Japanese fuel dump on Leyte blazes as a result of naval shelling.

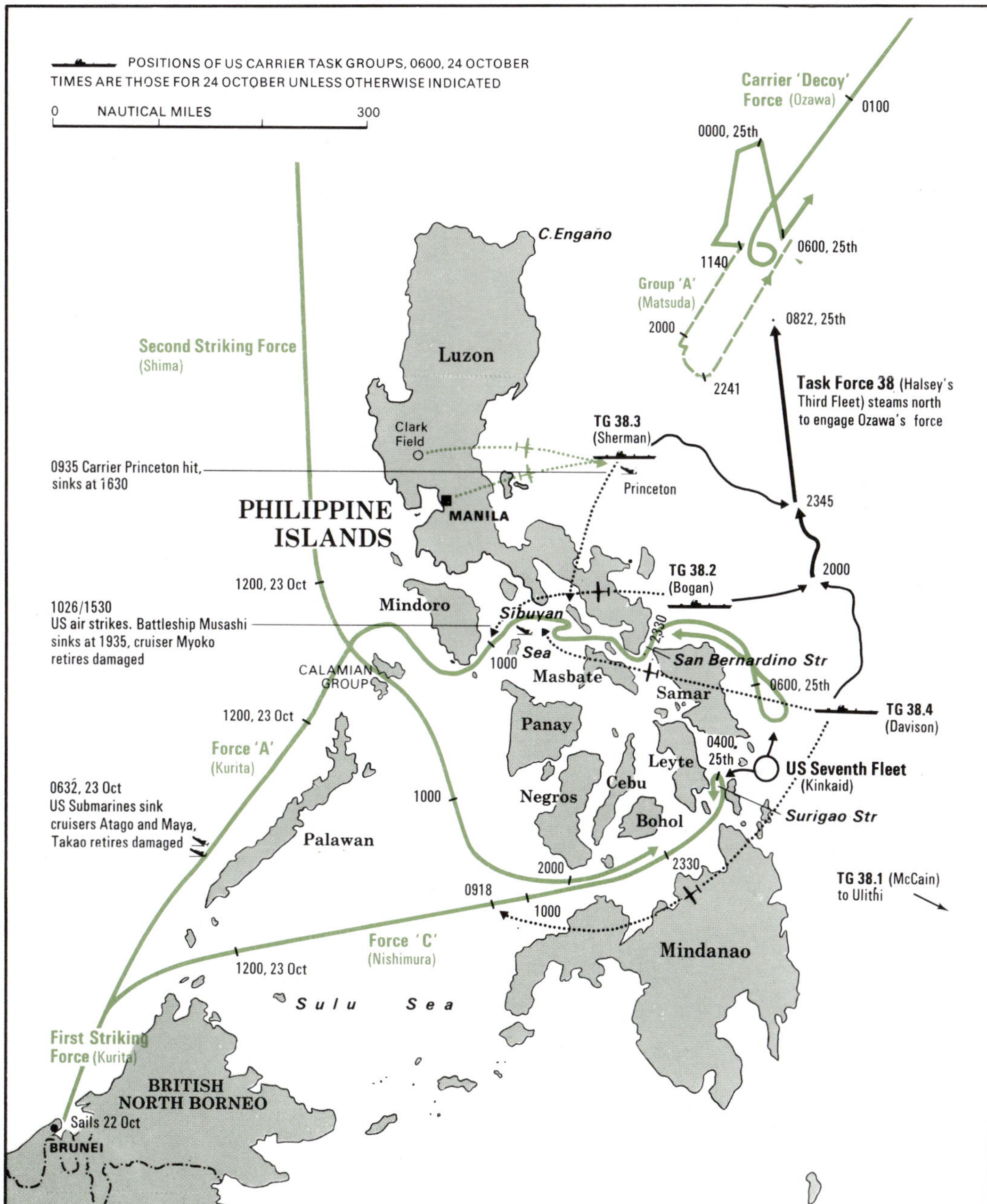

Above right: The sea actions comprising the Battle of Leyte Gulf resulted in a US victory despite the involvement of three separate Japanese forces.

Japanese Force A was turned back by US submarines and carrier aircraft, which then turned north in pursuit of Ozawa's force. Vice-Admiral Nishimura's Force C was almost entirely destroyed in a night battle, and Vice-Admiral Shima's Second Striking Force was turned back. Only Kurita's First Striking Force was still a factor, but it failed to capitalize on its opportunity to wreak havoc on the Seventh Fleet, and withdrew after limited success on 25 October. Meanwhile, many of Ozawa's ships, including the valuable carrier *Zuikaku*, last veteran of Pearl Harbor, had been sunk. Japanese desperation was manifested in the first of the suicidal Kamikaze missions, which struck an Australian cruiser on 21 October.

Lieutenant General Tomoyuki Yamashita, the 'Tiger of Malaya,' had assumed command of Philippine defense just as Leyte was being attacked. When US forces moved to invade Luzon, the

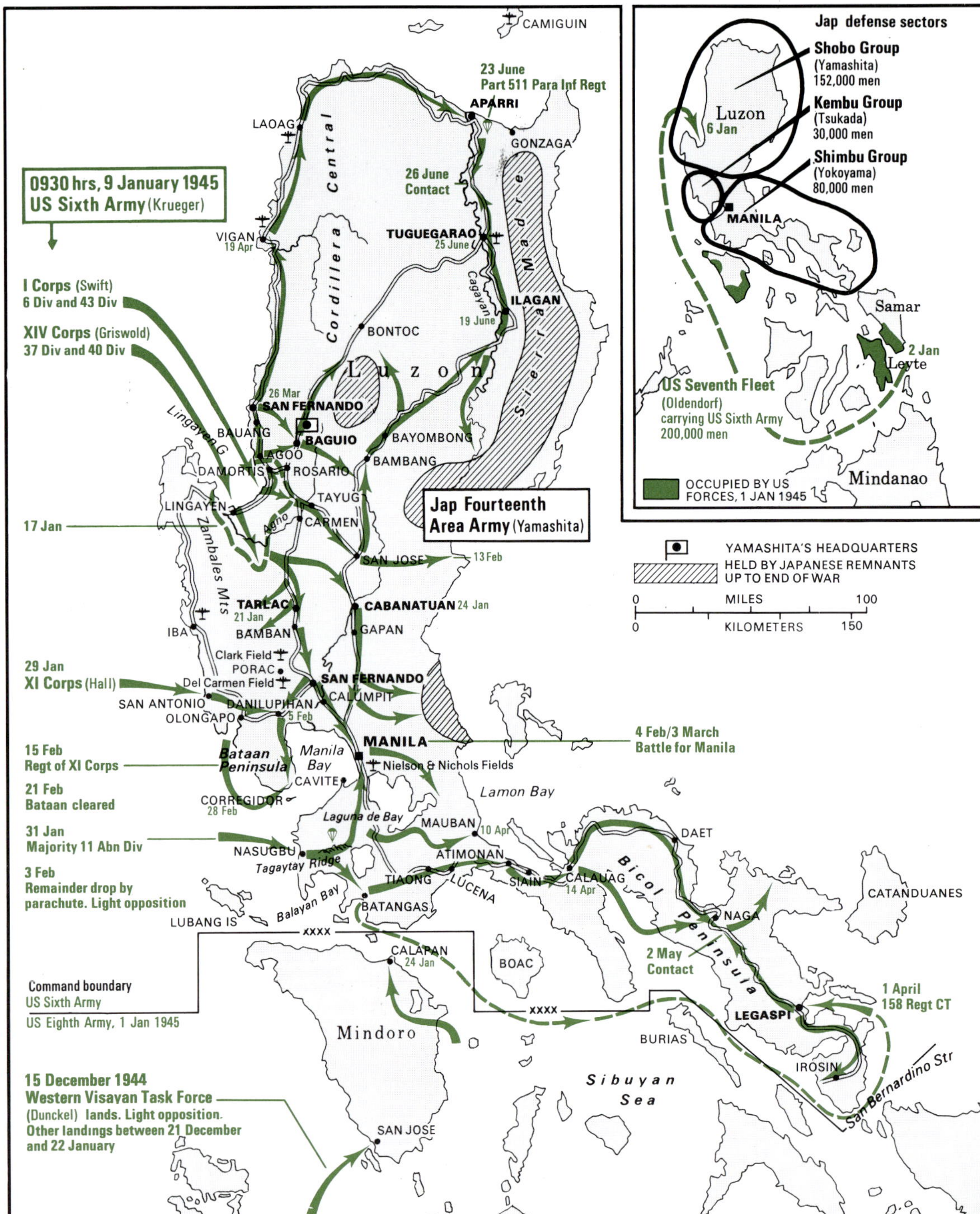

Above and inset: The capture of Luzon. Right: The US make landfall on Leyte.

principal island, in January 1945, his troops were ill prepared and poorly armed, and most of his air support had been destroyed or withdrawn to Formosa. Doubting that he could hold the beaches, Yamashita made his stand in the inland mountain areas with the object of tying up numerous American forces for as long as possible. In the event, he did not surrender until the war's end, when he still had 50,000 fighting men. By that time, most of Luzon and the other islands had been recaptured in fighting that reached its crescendo at Manila in February-March 1945.

Iwo Jima

The rocky island of Iwo Jima, although far from Japan, was part of the Japanese homeland; it offered the dual advantage to the Allies of demoralizing the enemy and providing a fighter airbase in range of Tokyo – if it could be captured. On the minus side, Iwo Jima was devoid of cover and strongly garrisoned by 22,000 troops under Major General Tadamichi Kuribayashi, who had made the eight-square-mile island impervious to aerial bombardment with a network of pillboxes, caves and tunnels.

The most prolonged and intense bombardment of the Pacific War preceded the US Marine landings of 19 February 1945. The Japanese held their fire just minutes too long, hoping to dupe the invaders into believing they would offer no resistance. By the time their weapons opened up against the beachhead, two Marine divisions and all their equipment had landed, with more to come throughout the day.

The Marines broke out and made straight for Mt Suribachi, the sugar-loaf massif at the island's tip. There they succeeded in raising the US flag after three days of combat so costly that it eclipsed even Tarawa, but the northeast of the island remained unconquered. The maze of underground defenses and lack of room to maneuver made for hand-to-hand combat of savage ferocity. Nearly 7000 US Marines and sailors lost their lives in the fighting that raged until 26 March, and the Japanese died almost to a man. Their exemplar in courage was Kuribayashi, who contacted Tokyo days after their food and water ran out with the message: 'Fighting spirit is running high. We are going to fight bravely to the last moment.'

Right: Iwo Jima, a small island with immense strategic significance.
Below: US Marines advance with flamethrowers toward Mt Suribachi.

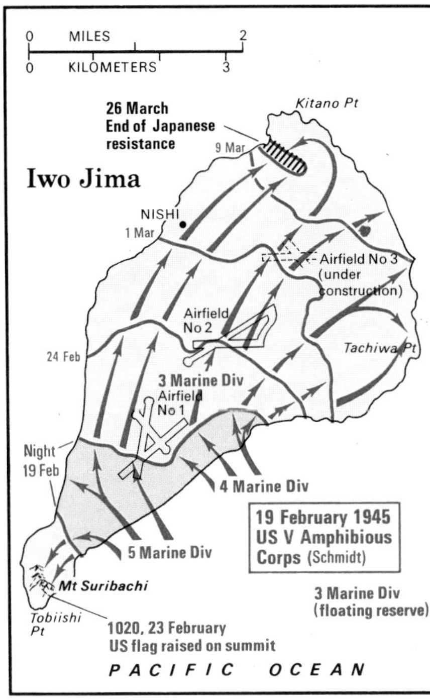

Okinawa

The inexorable Allied advance toward the Japanese home islands reached Okinawa, the main island of the Ryukyu group, in March of 1945. Okinawa's capture was necessary to provide harbor and air-base facilities for the invasion of Japan. The island was defended by the Japanese Thirty-second Army – some 130,000 men – under General Mitsuru Ushijima.

Preliminary air operations were aimed at Japanese air bases on Formosa and the islands surrounding densely populated Okinawa. US and British carrier forces suffered losses to waves of Kamikaze attacks, but the Japanese paid a higher price – 90 percent of their planes were shot down before they could sacrifice themselves on the enemy's ships. From 23 March, Okinawa itself was the target of continuous air and artillery strafing.

Allied forces began to land on 1 April, when General Simon Bolivar Buckner's Tenth Army and associated forces gained a beachhead at the southern end of the island. The Japanese had established themselves behind the formidable Shuri Line, which remained almost impervious to attack until early May, when suicidal counterattacks disclosed the locations of many Japanese defensive positions. From this point on, both of the US corps involved gradually pushed forward, as Ushijima's forces retreated into the hill masses of the island's southern tip. Final resistance was overwhelmed by a massive two-pronged attack on 21 June.

Throughout the operation, code-named Iceberg, supporting naval forces were under constant attack by Kamikaze pilots, who accounted for 36 US and British ships and damaged hundreds of others. The Japanese lost a staggering 4000 aircraft in these suicide missions, and even sacrificed the giant battleship *Yamato*, which was dispatched to Okinawa with insufficient fuel for a return trip to do as much damage as possible before she was destroyed. This happened on 7 April, long before the battleship could reach the target area.

On land, known Japanese dead totaled almost 108,000, and for the first time a significant number of prisoners was taken – over 7000. General Buckner was killed, with over 7000 of his men; almost 32,000 were wounded. US Navy casualties were almost 10,000, of whom roughly half were killed and half wounded. Since Okinawa was considered a 'dress rehearsal' for the invasion of Japan, these figures were sobering to American strategists; General MacArthur estimated that it would take five million men to capture the home islands, of whom perhaps one million would become casualties. Thus Okinawa strengthened the Allied case for ending the war by other means.

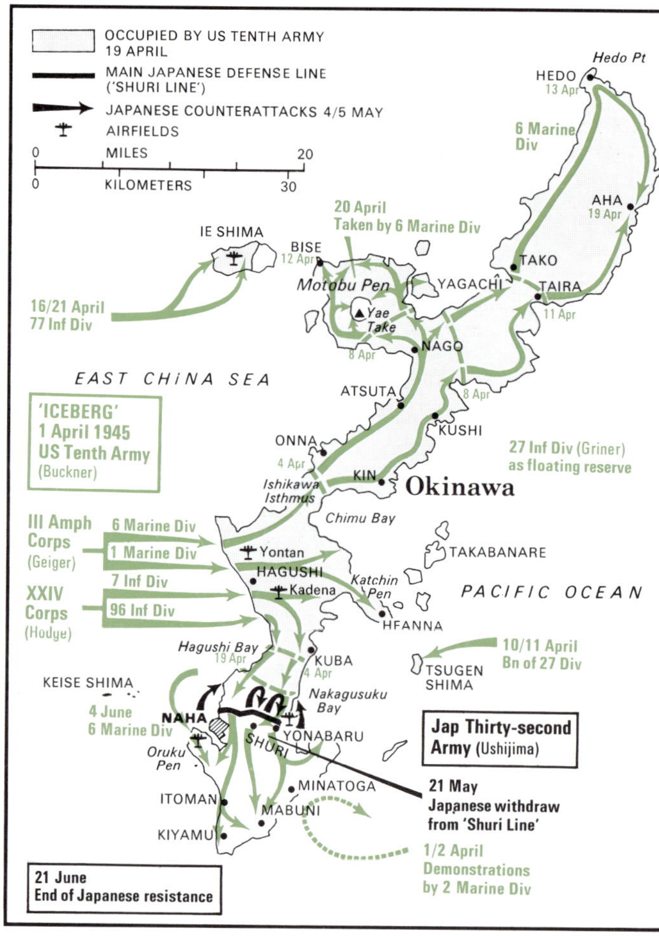

Above: The invasion of Okinawa was seen as the dress rehearsal for a similar action against the Japanese home islands.
Above right: Marines await survivors of an explosive attack on a Japanese hideout on Okinawa.
Right: The Japanese battleship Yamato *was sacrificed in a vain attempt to stem the invasion.*

Air Strikes on the Home Islands

The bomber offensive against Japan could not begin until 1944, for lack of a very-long-range (VLR) bomber capable of carrying heavy loads for over 3000 miles. Such a plane was finally acquired from Boeing by the US Army Air Force (the B-29 Superfortress), but it was so newly developed that operational problems plagued its early operations. The B-29's bombing altitude of 30,000 feet created difficulties with high winds and the effect of ice on instruments and engines. Losses were running high for several months after the first raid, from eastern China, in June of 1944. Additionally, Japanese anti-aircraft defenses proved much more effective than had been anticipated.

Modified tactics resulted in operating the planes at much lower altitudes with heavier bomb loads, which paid off in improved performance. New bases were established in the Marianas Islands of the Central Pacific in November, after which up to 20 Bombardment Groups flew regularly over Japanese cities by day and night. They dropped a total of 9365 tons of incendiaries, which gutted 32 square miles of urban areas. Then escort fighters began to arrive from newly captured Iwo Jima (early April) and American losses reached a new low. As more B-29s became available, mortal blows were dealt to Japanese industry. On 6 and 9 August 1945, the war with Japan was ended – and a new era in human history begun – by the atomic bombing of Hiroshima and Nagasaki.

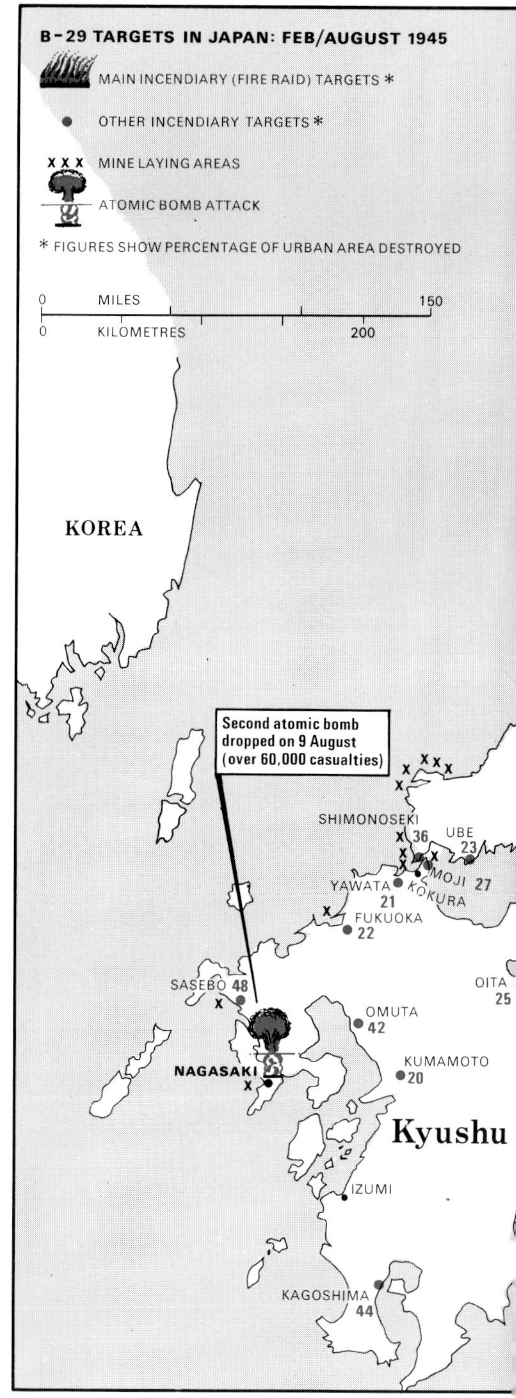

Left: The now-familiar atomic mushroom cloud rises over Nagasaki.
Above: The Japanese homeland and (inset) the radius of US bomber operations over it.
Right: Doolittle's daring one-off raid in April 1942 from the USS Hornet *had been as much a propaganda exercise as an attack. The firebomb raids of 1945 were on a different scale altogether.*
Far right: Tokyo in ruins.

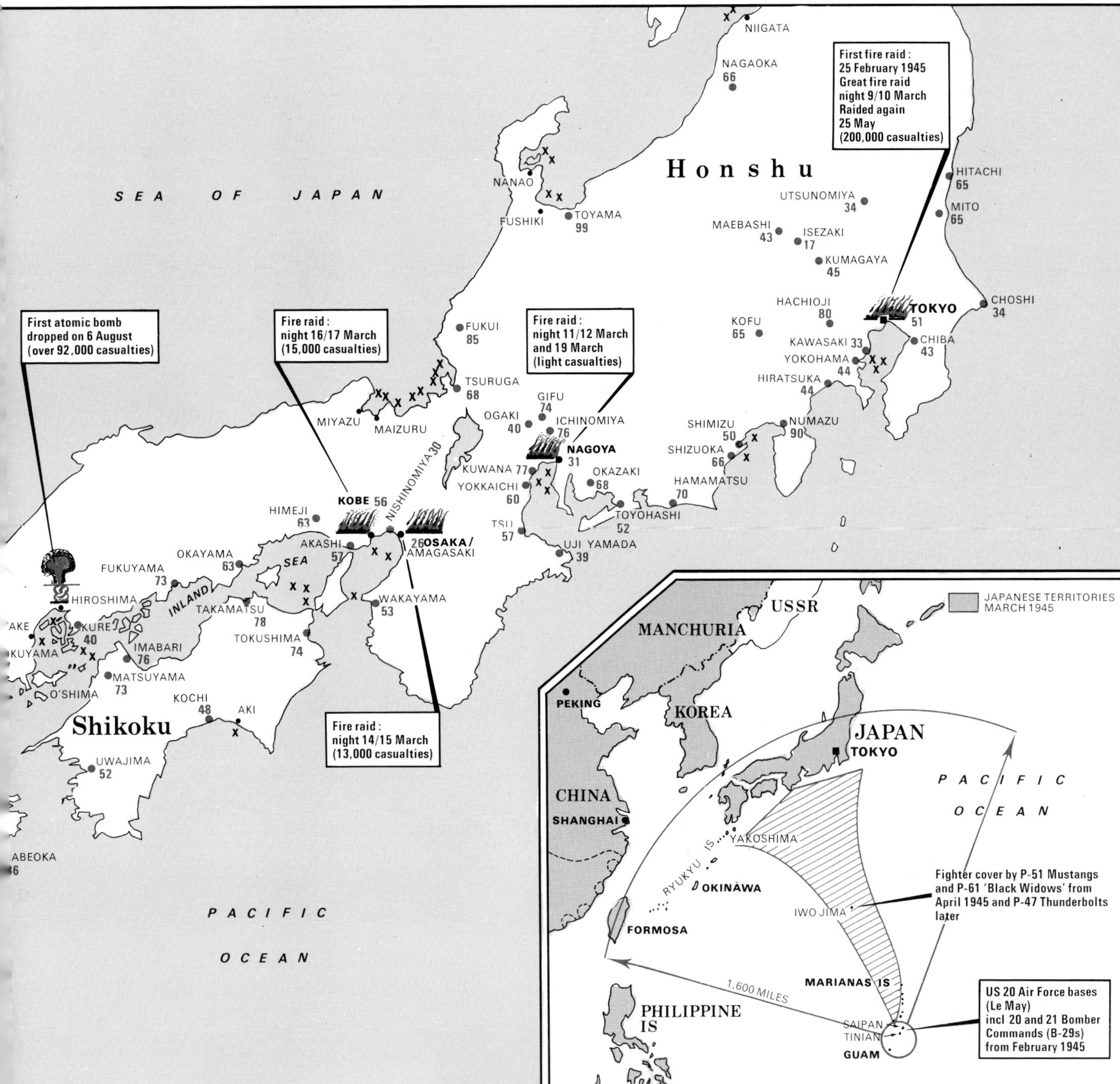
SEA OF JAPAN
Honshu
Shikoku
PACIFIC OCEAN
INLAND SEA
First fire raid : 25 February 1945 Great fire raid night 9/10 March Raided again 25 May (200,000 casualties)
First atomic bomb dropped on 6 August (over 92,000 casualties)
Fire raid : night 16/17 March (15,000 casualties)
Fire raid : night 11/12 March and 19 March (light casualties)
Fire raid : night 14/15 March (13,000 casualties)
NIIGATA
NAGAOKA 66
NANAO
FUSHIKI
TOYAMA 99
UTSUNOMIYA 34
HITACHI 65
MITO 65
MAEBASHI 43
ISEZAKI 17
KUMAGAYA 45
HACHIOJI 80
TOKYO 51
CHOSHI 34
KOFU 65
KAWASAKI 33
CHIBA 43
YOKOHAMA 44
HIRATSUKA 44
FUKUI 85
TSURUGA 68
GIFU 74
OGAKI 40
ICHINOMIYA 76
NAGOYA 31
SHIMIZU 50
NUMAZU 90
SHIZUOKA 66
KUWANA 77
YOKKAICHI 60
OKAZAKI 68
HAMAMATSU 70
TOYOHASHI 52
TSU 57
UJI YAMADA 39
MIYAZU
MAIZURU
NISHINOMIYA 30
KOBE 56
HIMEJI 63
OSAKA/AMAGASAKI 26
AKASHI 57
OKAYAMA 63
FUKUYAMA 73
HIROSHIMA
KURE 40
TAKAMATSU 78
WAKAYAMA 53
TOKUSHIMA 74
IMABARI 76
MATSUYAMA 73
O'SHIMA
KOCHI 48
AKI
UWAJIMA 52
USSR
MANCHURIA
JAPANESE TERRITORIES MARCH 1945
PEKING
KOREA
JAPAN
TOKYO
CHINA
SHANGHAI
PACIFIC OCEAN
RYUKYU IS
YAKOSHIMA
OKINAWA
IWO JIMA
FORMOSA
Fighter cover by P-51 Mustangs and P-61 'Black Widows' from April 1945 and P-47 Thunderbolts later
1,600 MILES
MARIANAS IS
PHILIPPINE IS
SAIPAN
TINIAN
GUAM
US 20 Air Force bases (Le May) incl 20 and 21 Bomber Commands (B-29s) from February 1945

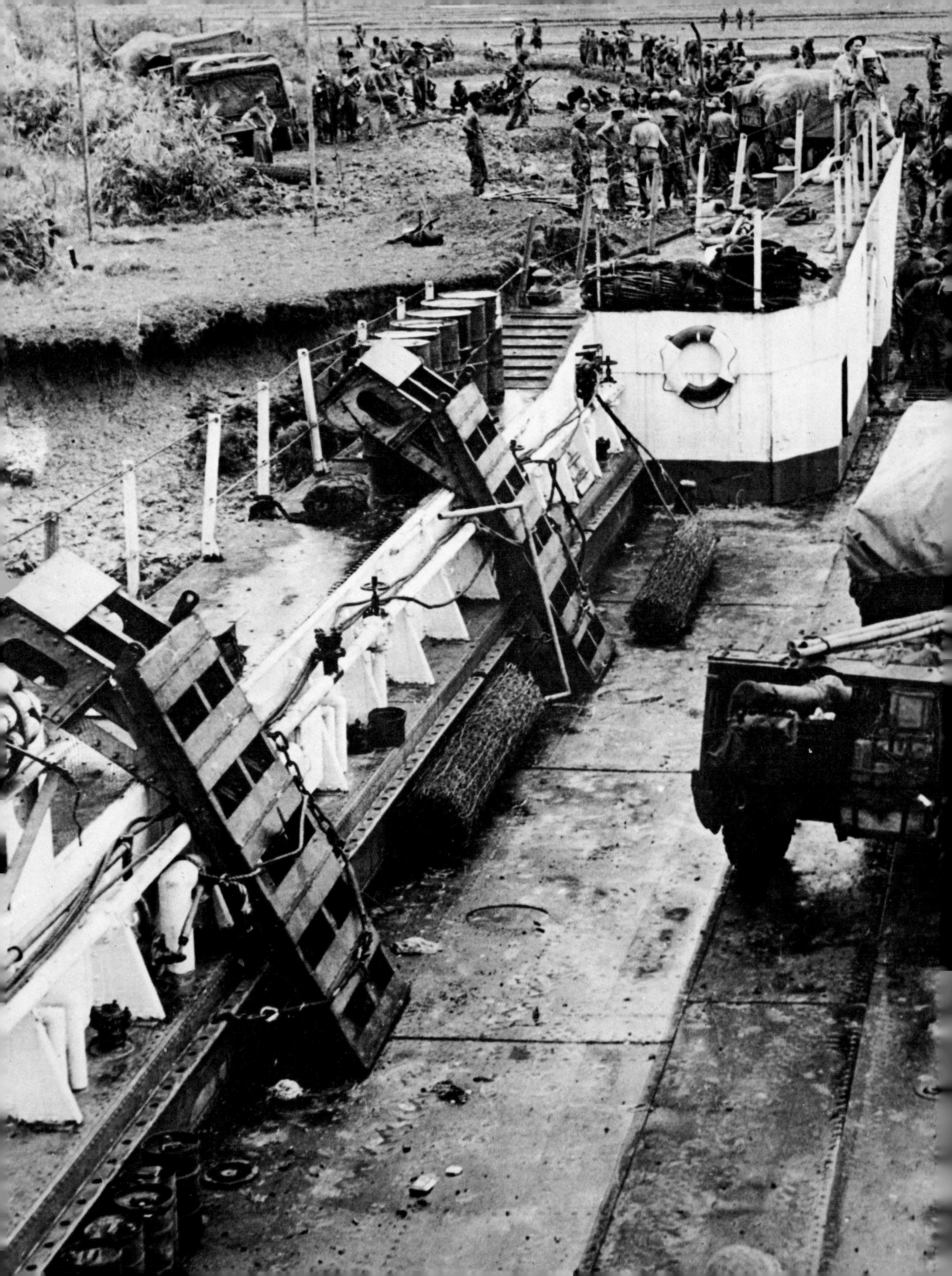

Retaking Burma: The Forgotten War

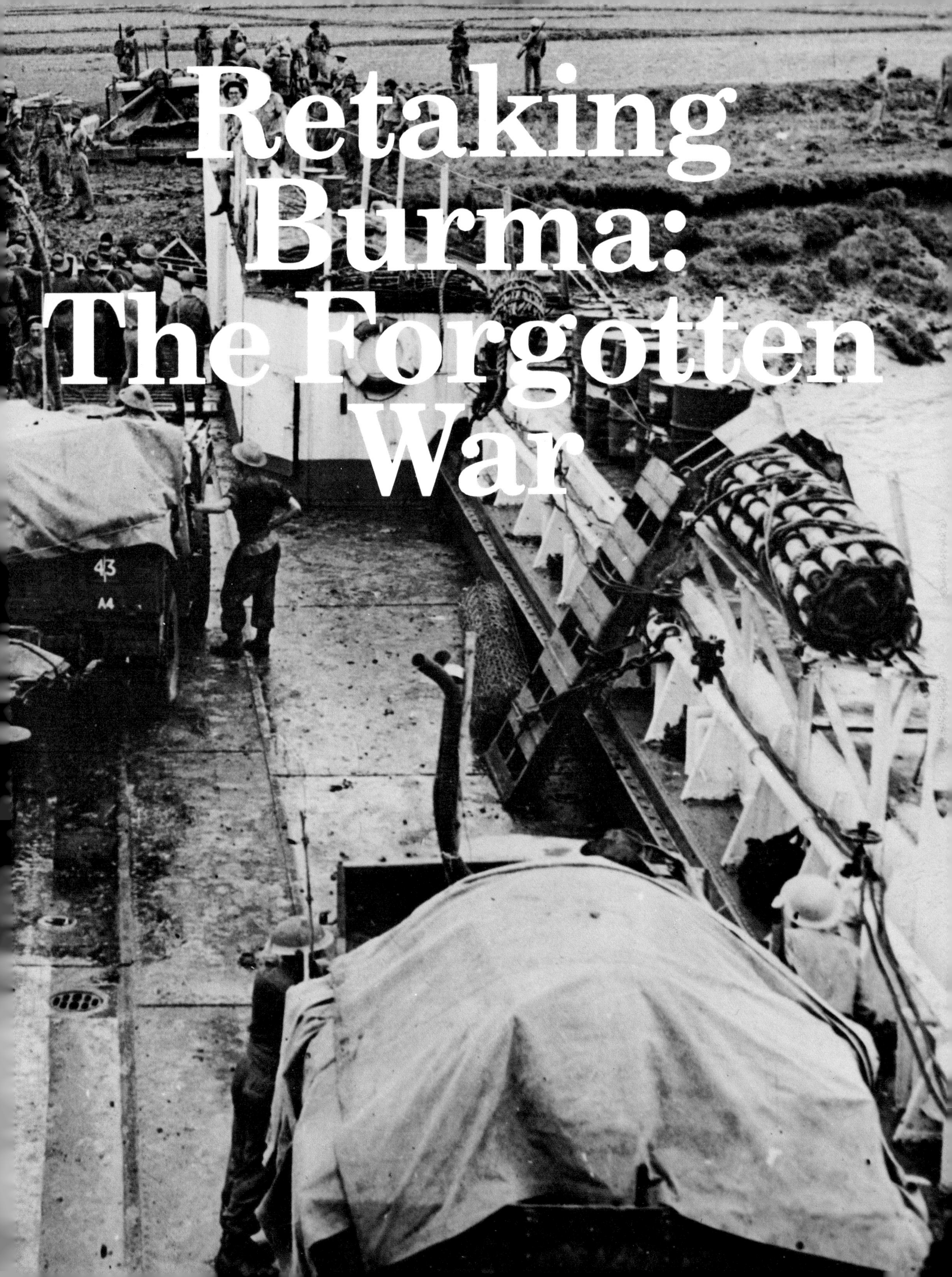

The Arakan Battles

British and US leaders disagreed on strategy in the Burma Theater after the British had been driven into India in May of 1942. The Americans believed that Burmese operations should focus on reopening land communications with the Chinese Nationalists, who were trying to contain large Japanese forces on their home ground. The British had little faith in Chiang Kai-shek's Nationalist movement and maintained their hope of winning back the imperial territories lost to Japan in the 1942 débâcle.

General Archibald Wavell, commanding Allied forces in India, knew that a large-scale invasion was out of the question for the time, but he sought to employ his men and build up morale via small-scale operations near the Indian border. The first of these centered on the Arakan, where the island post of Akyab provided Japan with a position from which to bomb Chittagong and Calcutta. On 21 September Wavell's 14 Indian Division began to advance cautiously into Burma by way of Cox's Bazar. General Iida, the Japanese commander, countered with a series of delaying tactics that created a stalemate lasting until March 1943 when his counterattack on two fronts forced a retreat.

In December 1943, the British sent Christison's XV Corps on a second expedition against Akyab. Lieutenant General Renya Mutaguchi barred the way through the Mayu Peninsula and sent his Sakurai Column through mountainous jungle that was believed impassable to cut off 5 and 7 Indian Divisions. Lieutenant General William Slim, who had led the 900-mile fighting retreat from Rangoon, airlifted supplies to his isolated troops until they had fought their way through to one another in late February 1944. (Slim's use of air supply would ultimately be the key to British success in Burma.) In March XV Corps finally renewed its advance on Akyab, but was stopped short again by the need to send reinforcements back to India for the defense of Imphal.

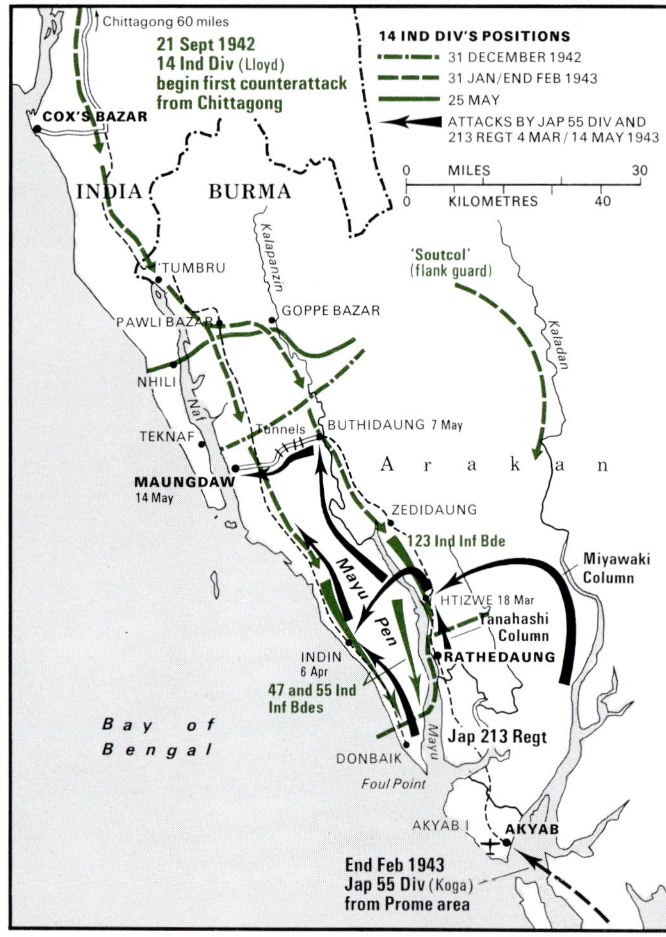

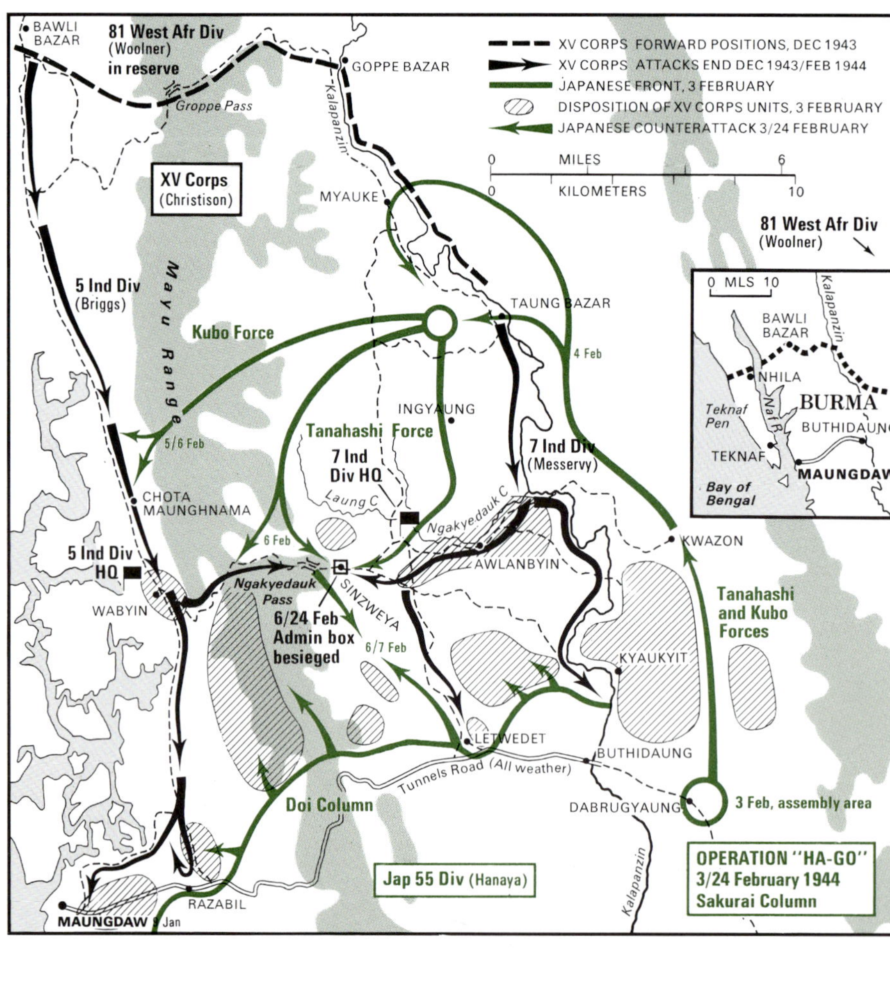

Previous pages: A 25-pounder gun is brought ashore in Rangoon.
Above right: The Allied route southwards along fair-weather tracks was hampered by enemy action.
Right: 5 and 7 Indian Divisions reunite after being isolated by a Japanese thrust.
Opposite: Japanese troops used elephants as a means of transporting supplies across Burma's rugged terrain.

The Chindit Operations

Morale had been a problem in Burma even before the Allies took what Stilwell described as 'a hell of a beating.' During the disastrous campaign of 1942, fighting spirit reached a new low. The Japanese were perceived as unbeatable in jungle warfare, and the Allied forces' sick rate reflected the prevailing malaise: thousands succumbed to dysentery, malaria, skin diseases and other complaints. The heterogeneous assortment of troops involved in Burma – Indian, British and Gurkha – comprised an army beset by problems of discipline and discrimination.

Brigadier Orde Wingate arrived in the Far East early in 1943 with guerrilla-warfare experience gained in Palestine and Abyssinia. Backed by Winston Churchill and General Wavell, he created a 'private army' to penetrate behind enemy lines and disrupt Japanese communications and supplies. In so doing, he would also prove that the Japanese could be defeated in the jungle.

The Chindits (so called after *Chinthe*, a mythical beast) crossed the River Chindwin into Burma in February 1943 and spent four months raiding Japanese territory. They cut the Mandalay-Myitkyina Railway in 75 places before the Japanese counterattacked in force and drove them back into India. The press lionized Wingate, and the mystique of Japanese invincibility began to lose its power. Wingate's superiors then authorized a far more ambitious operation – involving six brigades – to complement Stilwell's advance on Myitkyina.

The main Chindit force was airlifted into Burma in February 1944 to establish blocking points against supplies moving up against Stilwell. They encountered immediate difficulties that grew steadily worse until midsummer, when they had to be withdrawn. Wingate himself was killed in a plane crash soon after the abortive operation began.

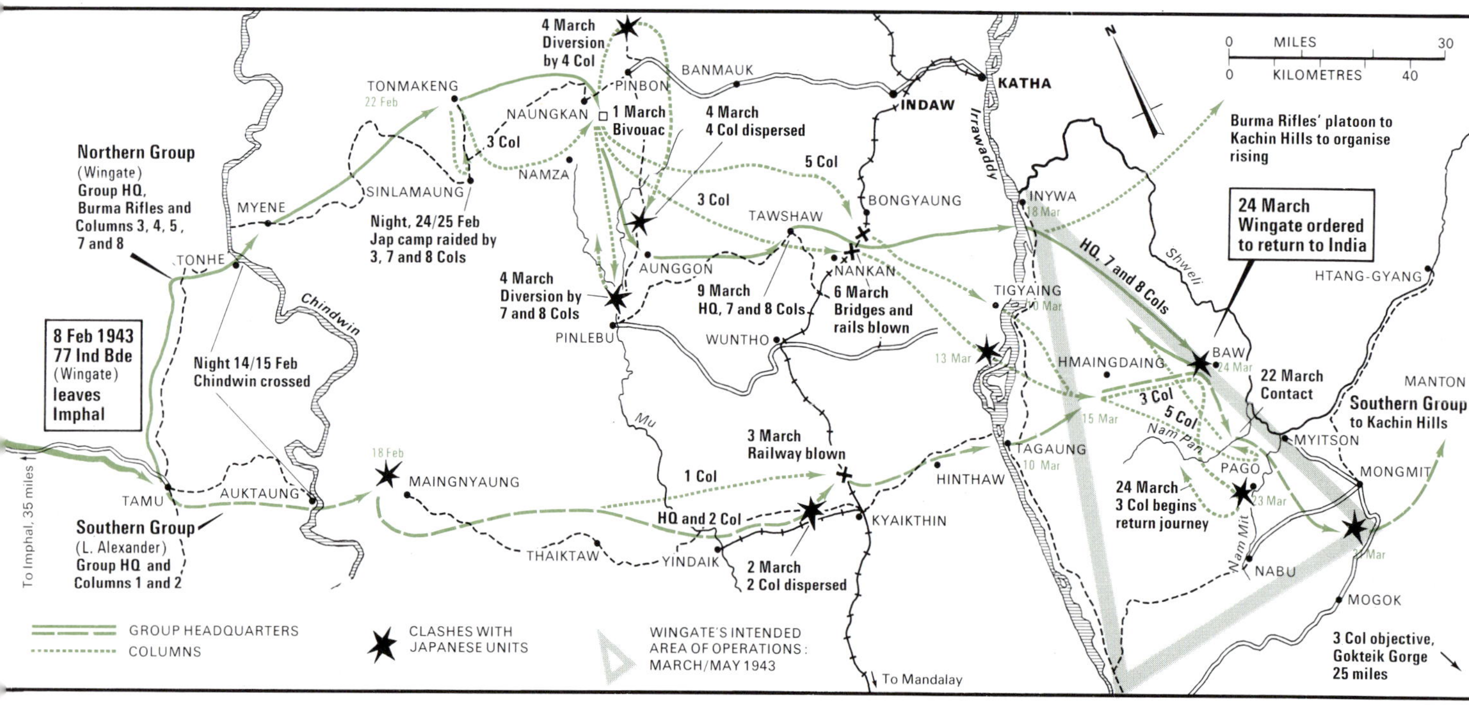

Japanese Defeat at Kohima and Imphal

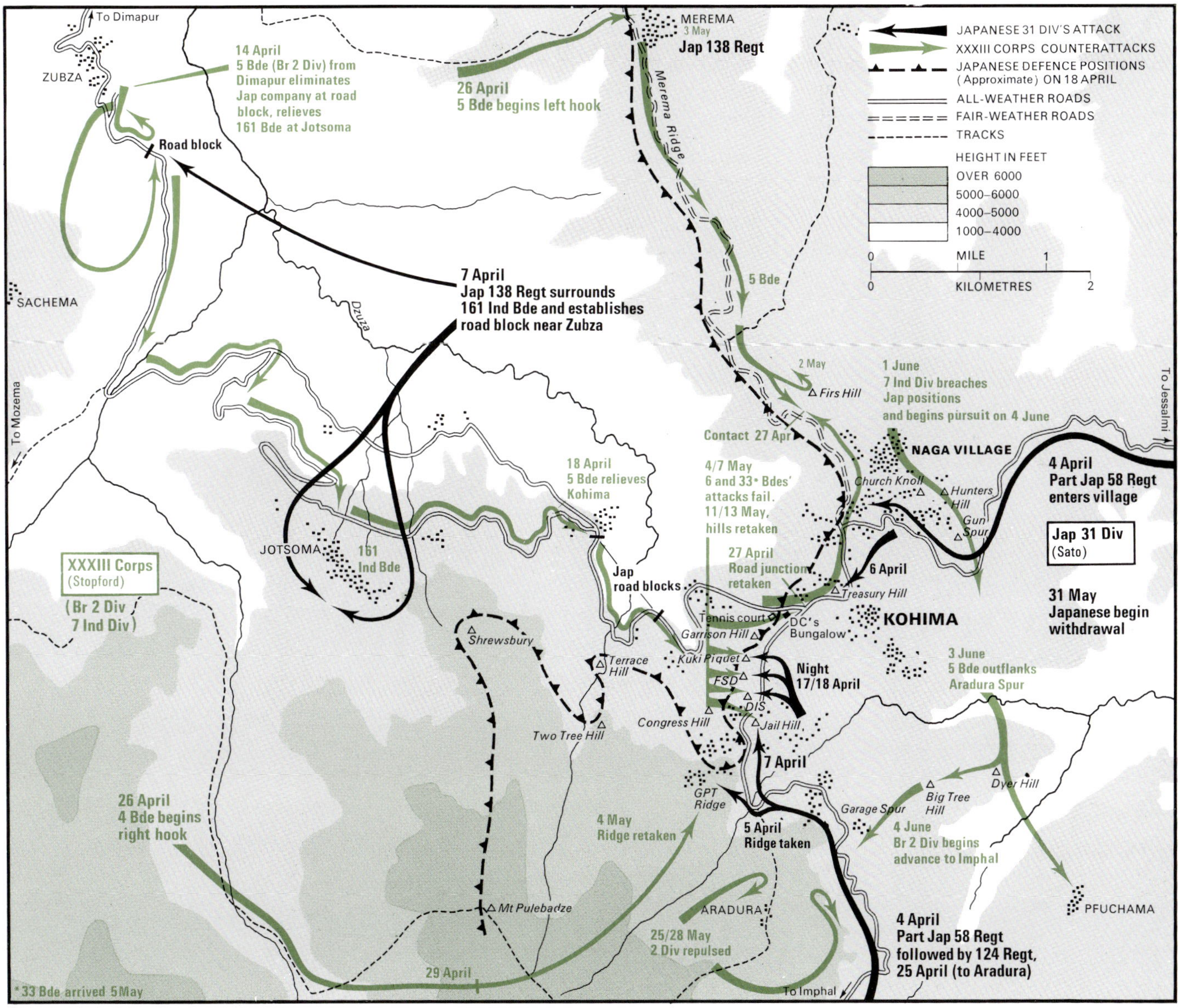

Above left: The Chindit operations in Burma in 1943.
Left: Wingate (center) briefs pilots on invasion plans with the assistance of the USAAF's Colonel Cochran (left).
Above: Troop movements around Kohima.

Three Japanese divisions were ordered to prepare for the invasion of India (Operation U-GO) in early March 1944. It was clear that an Allied offensive was being prepared, and the only practical place from which it could be launched was the plain at Manipur, where Imphal and Kohima were located. Lieutenant General Mutaguchi's Fifteenth Army was to spoil the planned offensive and cut the single railway to Assam, north India.

General William Slim, commanding Fourteenth Army, expected a Japanese advance, but its speed was such that he and his men were taken by surprise. Scoones's XV Corps was cut off at Kohima on 4 April, and the garrison at Imphal a day later. Both forces prepared to hold out with the help of air supply until relief arrived from XXXIII Corps, which was assembling at Dimapur. The quality of Slim's leadership would be reflected in the tenacity of his hard-pressed troops until that help arrived.

Relentless Japanese attacks rolled over the small garrison at Kohima between 7 and 18 April, when British 2 Division's 5 Brigade pushed through the roadblock at Zubza to reinforce the defenders. Then 5 and 4 Brigades undertook a sweeping pincer movement designed to trap the Japanese; this was not achieved until 3 June. Meanwhile, IV Corps was struggling desperately around Imphal, where air supply proved far more difficult than foreseen. Slim reinforced the garrison to some 100,000 men during the siege, which lasted for 88 days. British 2 Division advanced from Kohima to meet IV Corps at Milestone 107, halfway between the two cities, on 22 June. Japanese Fifteenth Army had fought with distinction against increasing odds, but its remnants now had to pull back toward the Chindwin, with British forces in hot pursuit. Mutaguchi had lost some 65,000 men in the heaviest defeat suffered by the Japanese Army in World War II.

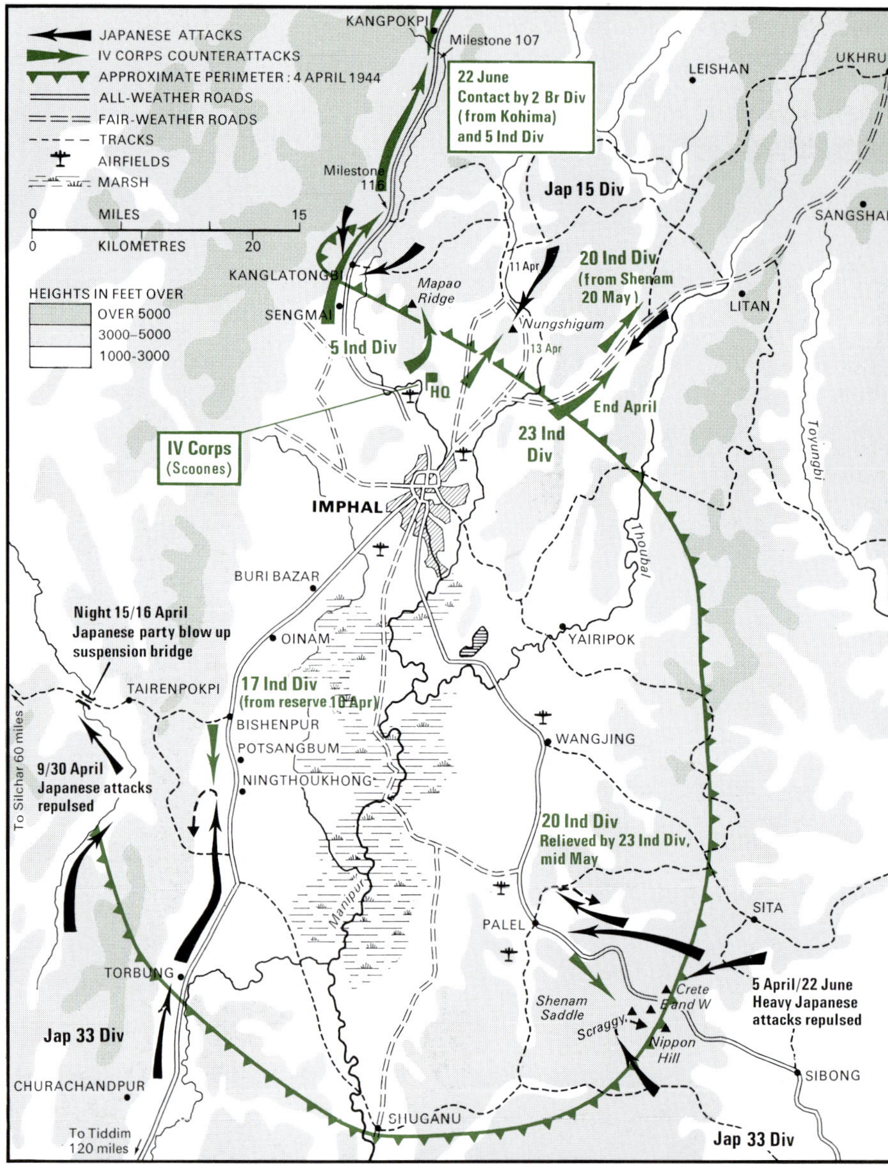

Right: The unsuccessful Japanese siege of Imphal that ended in June.
Below: Merrill's Marauders, the US jungle fighters renowned for their expertise in combating the Japanese in unfriendly terrain.

To Mandalay and Meiktila

Lieutenant General Shihachi Katamura took command of Japanese Fifteenth Army after the disastrous losses at Kohima and Imphal, for which his predecessor was unjustly blamed. During the summer of 1944, he rebuilt his force of 10 divisions and then awaited the expected Allied push into central Burma. This operation, codenamed Extended Capital, began on 19 November and included Stilwell's Northern Combat Area Command, British Fourteenth Army and the XV Corps. On 4 December bridgeheads were secured across the Chindwin, and the British advanced to meet elements of Stilwell's force for the drive across the Irrawaddy into Mandalay. Only General Slim, of all the Allied leaders in Burma, correctly surmised that Katamura would attempt to destroy the Fourteenth Army at the river crossing.

On 3 March 1945, Slim struck at Japanese communication lines to Rangoon located at Meiktila, achieving total surprise. The capture of this vital rail center opened the door to the larger city of Mandalay. Kimura pulled so many troops away from Mandalay to assault Meiktila that he lost both cities to the Allies. Slim raced on to reach Rangoon before the monsoon, but when he arrived the Japanese had already evacuated. Slim's outstanding leadership in the Burma Theater led to his appointment as Commander in Chief of Allied Land Forces in Southeast Asia.

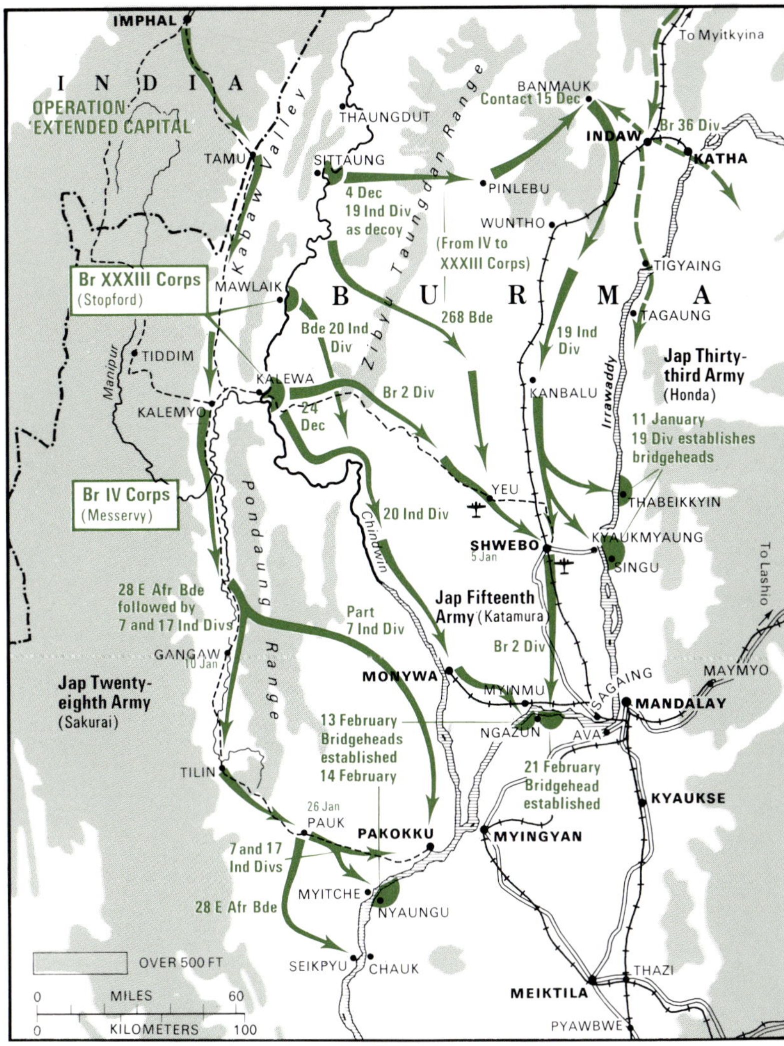

Above right: Operation Extended Capital took the Allies across the Chindwin and on to Mandalay.
Right: Flamethrower and rifle-equipped infantry of the United States Army prepare for action.

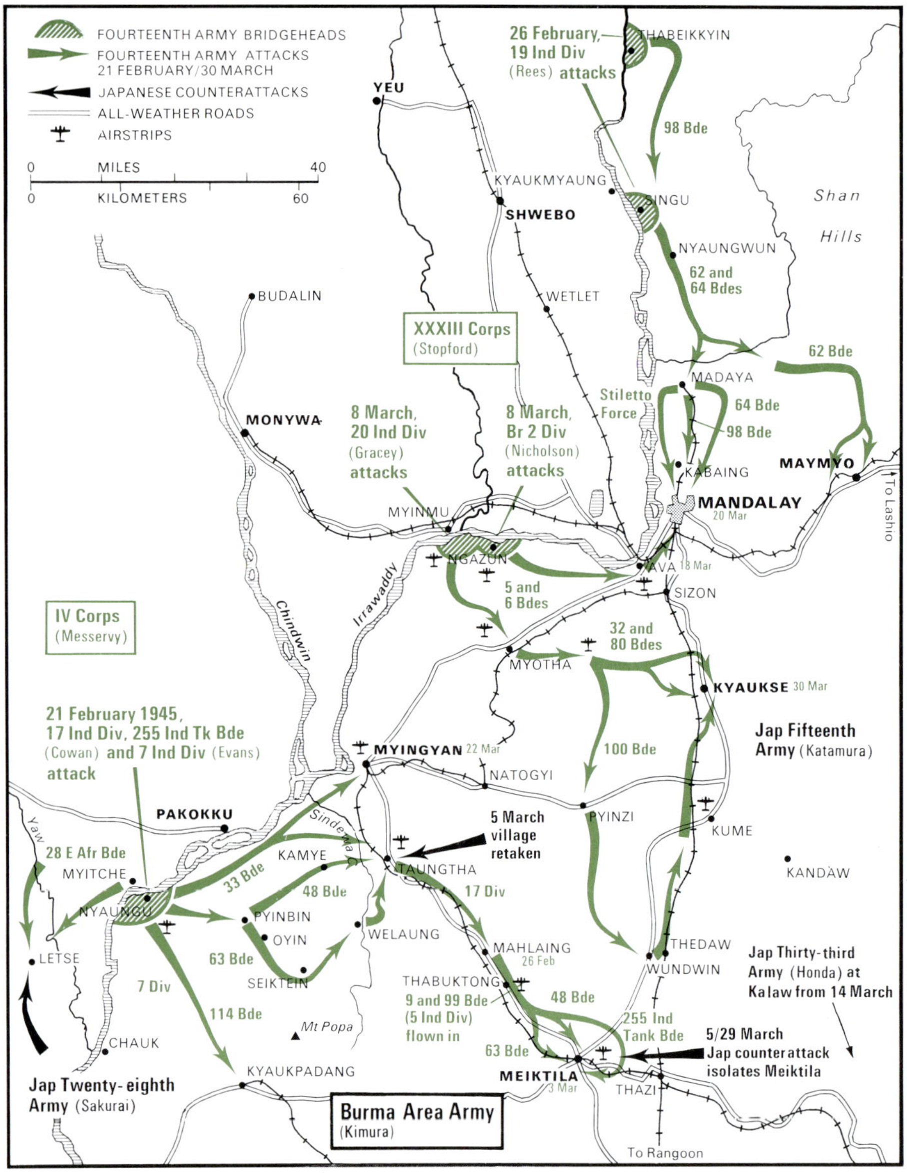

Left: Control of Meiktila was to prove of crucial importance in the battle for Mandalay.
Below: US troops pause on a Burmese jungle trail.
Below right: General Claire Chennault, whose 'Flying Tigers' struck at Japanese ground troops in China and Formosa.
Far right: China's struggle to repel the Japanese invaders.

China – An Erratic Ally

Japan's war on China predated World War II by several years, and by 1939 the aggressive island empire had seized control of China's richest areas. The 'sleeping giant' was especially vulnerable on account of the internal strife between the Nationalists (or Kuomintang) led by Generalissimo Chiang Kai-shek and Mao Tse-tung's Communists.

US General George C Marshall warned the Allies that Nationalist China must be propped up; otherwise, the Japanese Government could flee to China when the home islands were invaded – as was then planned – 'and continue the war on a great and rich land mass.' Throughout the war, the US shipped enormous quantities of supplies to China, first by the Burma Road, and after 1942 by air over the Himalayas – a dangerous route known as 'the Hump.' Chiang's position was strengthened by the creation of the US 14th Air Force, impressively commanded by Brigadier General Claire Chennault, which inflicted heavy damage on Japanese troops both in China and Formosa. General Joseph 'Vinegar Joe' Stilwell was sent in to help retrain the Chinese Army. However, many of the supplies destined for use against the Japanese were diverted into Chiang's war on the Communists; corruption flourished in his Nationalist Party.

US air strikes by Chennault's 'Flying Tigers' provoked a Japanese offensive against the airfields at Liuchow, Kweilin, Lingling and other sites in the spring of 1944. Chinese resistance did not hold up, as was often the case, and the loss of these bases hampered Allied operations until December. Meanwhile, a truce was patched up between the Communists and Nationalists, allowing greater activity against the Japanese, who renewed their offensive in 1945.

In the war's final year, Japanese General Okamura overextended the deployment of his China Expeditionary Army, and the Chinese were able to cut off the corridor to Indochina. They held this position for the duration, after which the Nationalists and the Communists promptly resumed their civil war.

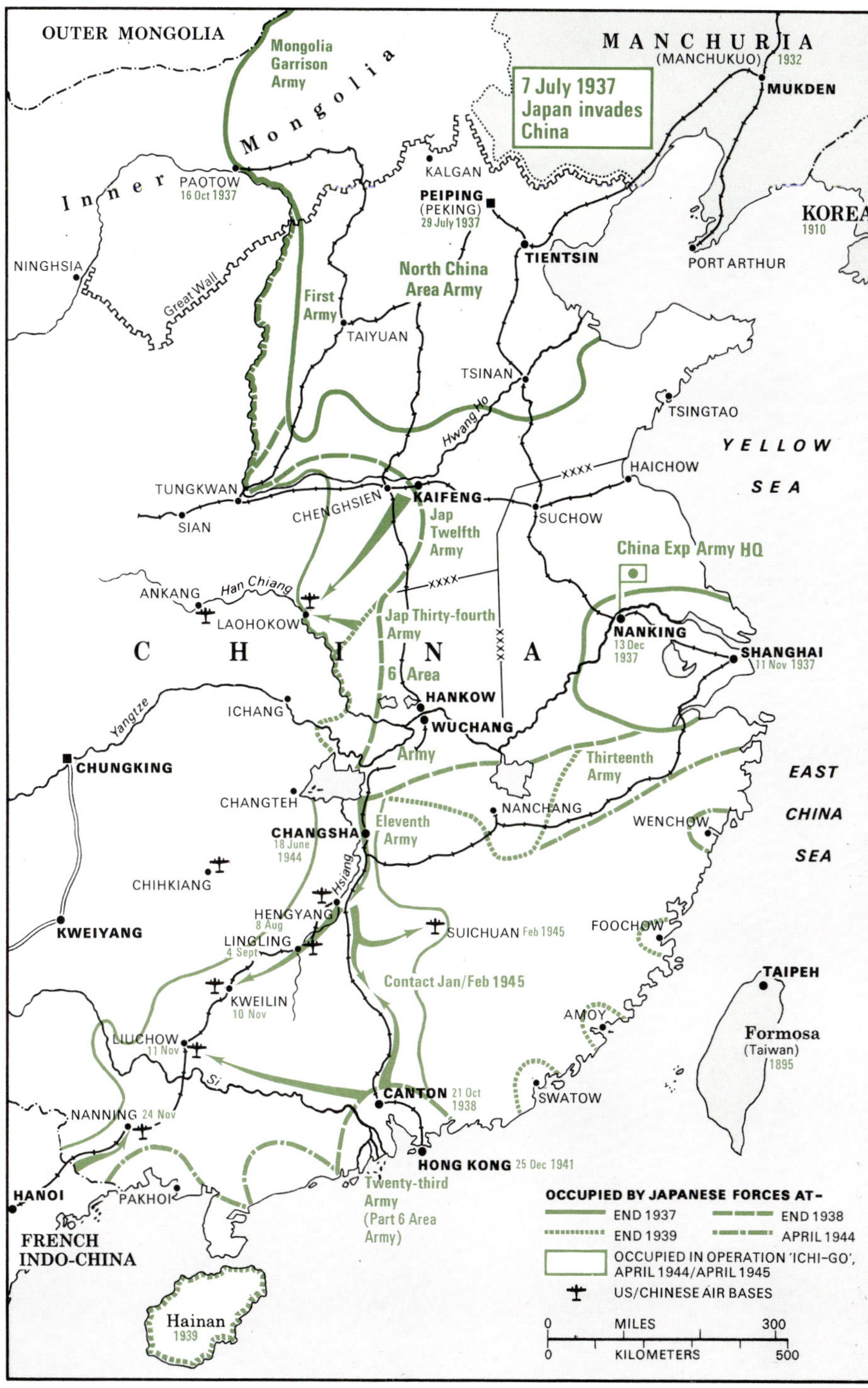

Russia Finds Its Strength

The German Drive to the Volga

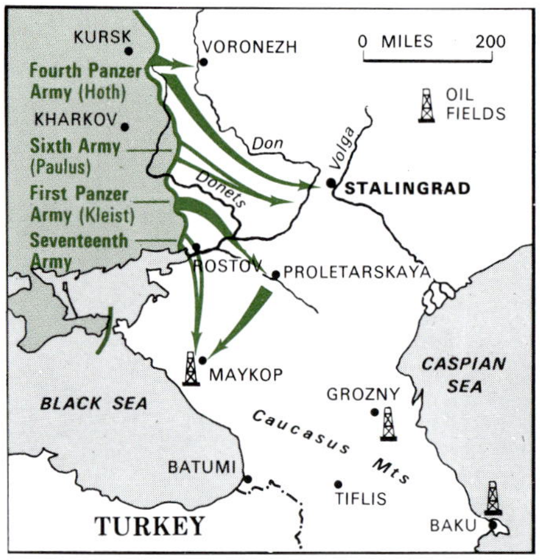

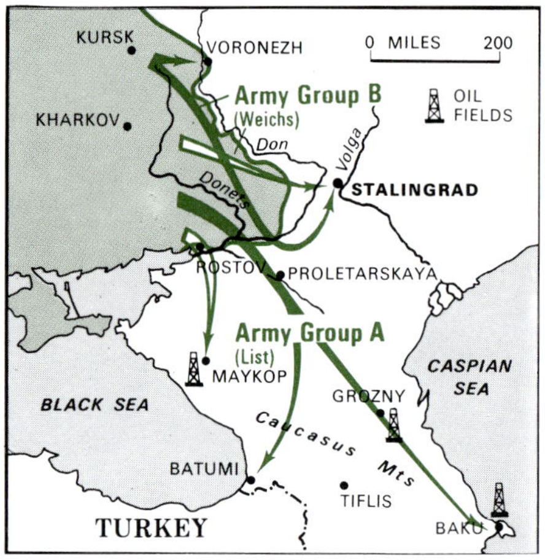

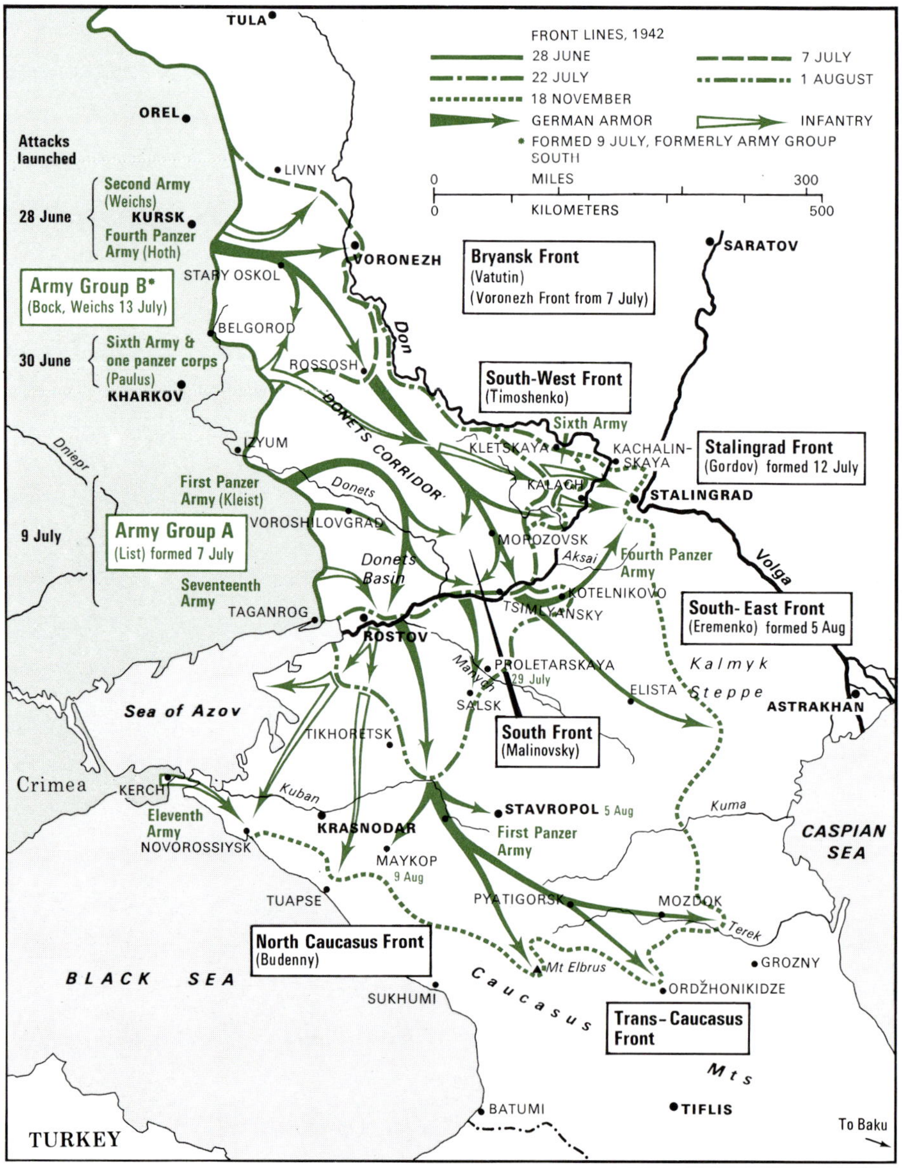

Germany's critical oil shortage was decisive in Hitler's first 1942 campaign plan for the Eastern Front. In April he instructed that the main effort was to be in southern Russia, where German forces must defeat the Red Army on the River Don and advance to the coveted Caucasian oil fields. For this campaign, Bock's Army Group South was reorganized into Army Groups A and B, A to undertake the Caucasus offensive and B to establish a protective front along the Don and go on to Stalingrad. The neutralization of 'Stalin's City' soon gained a compelling hold on Hitler's mind, despite his staff's objections to dividing the German effort before the Red Army had been shattered. Stalingrad was a major rail and river center, whose tank and armaments factories offered additional inducements to attack it.

The obsession with Stalingrad was a disastrous mistake on Hitler's part, compounded by his seizure of control from his dissenting officers. Army Group A made a rapid advance from 28 June to 29 July, capturing Novorossiysk and threatening the Russian Trans-Caucasus Front. But the diversion of 300,000 German troops to the Stalingrad offensive prevented them from achieving their original objective – the Batumi-Baku Line. They were left to hold a 500-mile Caucasian front against strong Russian opposition – leaderless, except for the erratic and contradictory orders of Hitler himself.

The Russians had made good their 1941 manpower losses from the subject peoples of Asia, and they threw the T-34 tank into the field at this point to complete the German fiasco in the Caucasus. The vital oil fields were lost to Germany. Army Group B raced toward Stalingrad to attempt what had now become the only possible success of the campaign. The city could not be encircled without crossing the Volga, which General Weichs lacked the resources to attempt, so a frontal assault was launched on 31 August.

Previous pages: Red Army sappers clear German barbed wire defenses.
Above right: The original German battle plan, with oilfields the main objective.
Above far right: Splitting the forces to strengthen the attack on Stalingrad proved a major error.
Right: The German advance southeastwards with armor and artillery.
Opposite: Commander Chuikov of the Russian 62nd Army at the Volga.

Stalin's City Holds Out

Below: The German forces attack.
Below left: Stalingrad's position on the banks of the Volga enhanced its defensive capabilities.
Bottom: Manstein's forces are repulsed.

The slow pace of the German summer offensive of 1942 allowed Stalingrad's defenders to strengthen their position considerably. The city was home to half a million Russians, who were united in their determination to repel the German assault. Most of the Soviet soldiers were assigned to the defense perimeter, the city itself being entrusted largely to armed civilians, whose high morale promised fierce resistance.

The Volga wound through many channels around the city, posing serious obstacles to any attempt at bridging it. The Germans made no effort to establish a bridgehead north of the city so as to block river traffic and reinforcement.

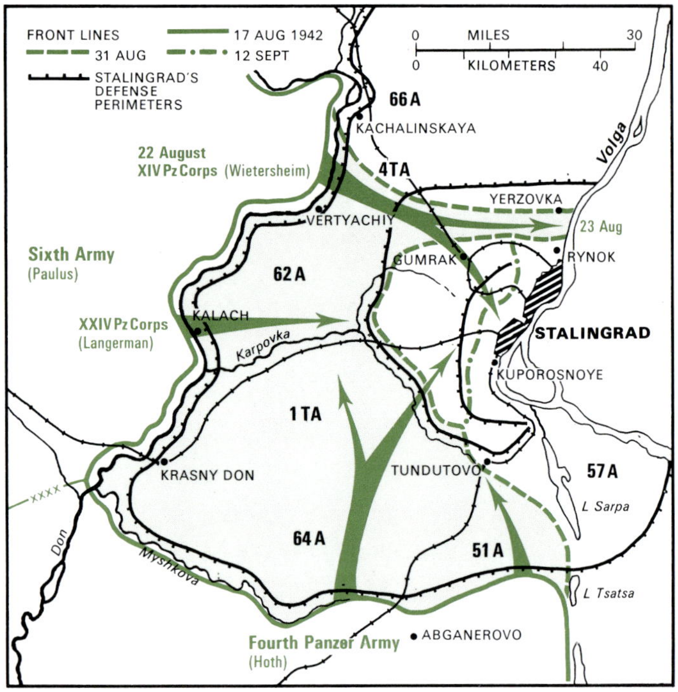

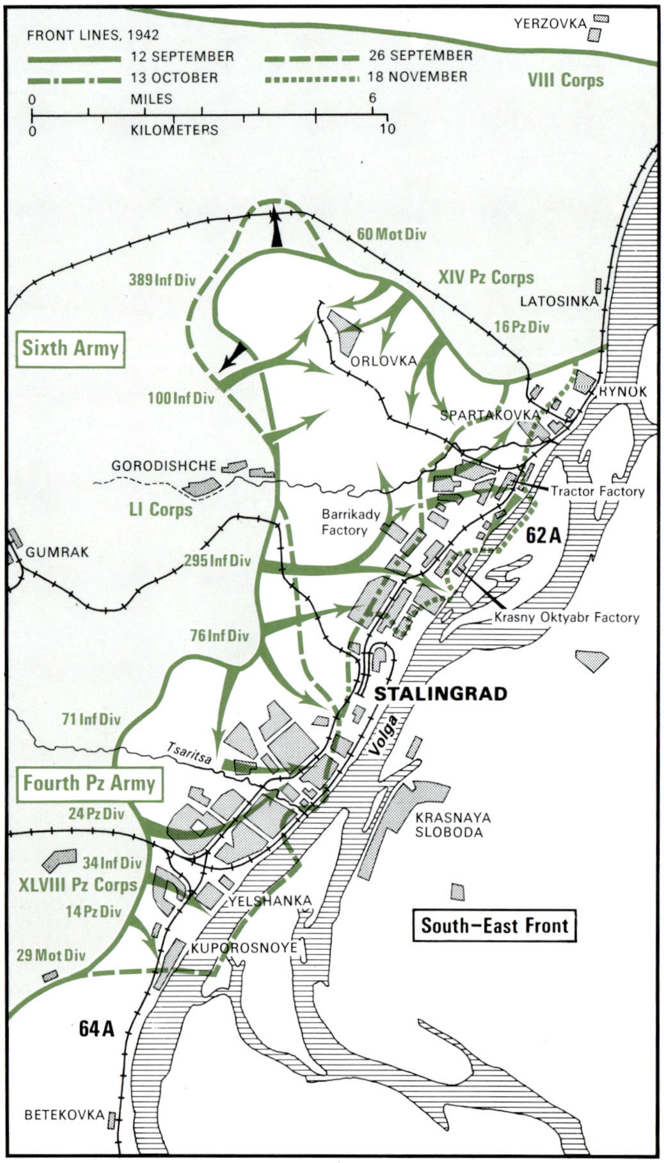

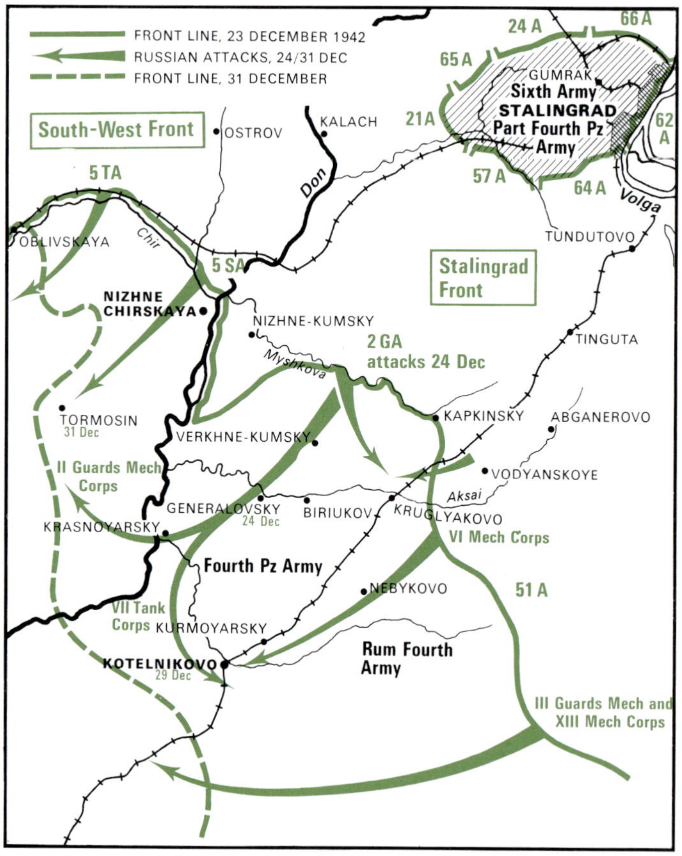

Right: A German soldier shows the strain of fighting an unwinnable battle.
Bottom: The red flag flies victorious over Stalingrad in February 1943 as the Germans finally surrender.

This was only one of many mistakes, the worst of which was the decision to carry the city by direct attack. The resultant battle would become the Verdun of World War II.

By the end of August, the Russian defenders had been squeezed into a small perimeter, and twelve days later the Germans were in the city, striving to fight their way to the western bank of the Volga. Soviet civilians and soldiers struggled side by side in a constant barrage of bombs and artillery fire, falling back a foot at a time. House-to-house fighting raged until 13 October, when the exhausted German infantry reached the river in the south city. But the northern industrial sector remained unconquered. Hitler ordered intensified bombardments that served only to make the infantry's task more difficult. Stalingrad's defenders continued to fight regardless.

By 18 November, when the winter freeze was imminent, Hitler's armies around Stalingrad were undersupplied, overextended and vulnerable to the Russian counterattack that was forming. Before the Germans were forced to surrender (February 1943), they had lost 100,000 of the 200,000 men involved. Five hundred Luftwaffe transport planes had been destroyed in impotent efforts to supply them, and six months' worth of German war production had been thrown away. Wehrmacht morale was shattered, not only by the great defeat itself, but by the wanton intrusions into military planning that had wrecked the campaign from Berlin.

The Battle of Kursk

The success of the 1942 Russian winter offensive left a large salient around Kursk that tempted the German High Command into mounting a major attack. The fact that US and British aid was now flowing freely into Russia lent urgency to this plan of attack, as Germany's resources were steadily draining away.

The armored pincer movement against the Kursk Salient – codenamed Operation Citadel – was scheduled for July of 1943. Early intelligence of it enabled the Russians to prepare by moving in two armies and setting up eight concentric circles of defense. When the Germans launched their attack on 5 July, it was in the belief that they would achieve surprise. On the contrary, Russian defenses at Kursk were the most formidable they had ever assaulted. The Soviet T-34 tank was superior to anything the German Panzer groups could field, and air command was seized at the outset by multitudes of Russian planes. They were not equal to the Luftwaffe in technology, but they were far superior in numbers.

In the north, German Ninth Army advanced only six miles in the first few days, at a cost of 25,000 killed and 400 tanks and aircraft. In the south, Manstein's Fourth Panzer Army drove through the Russian Sixth Army – again at high cost – only to face fresh Soviet

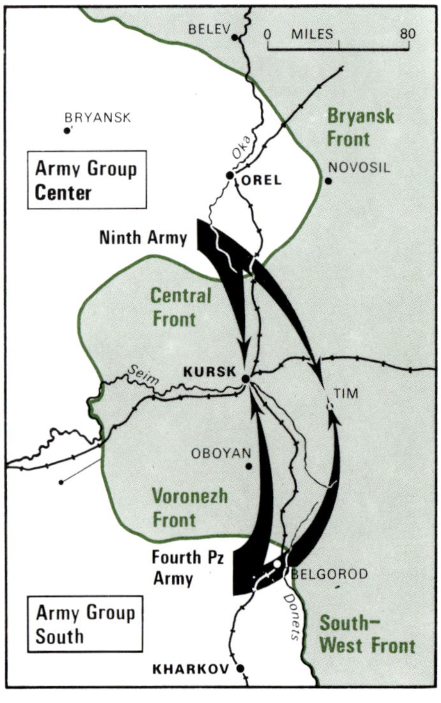

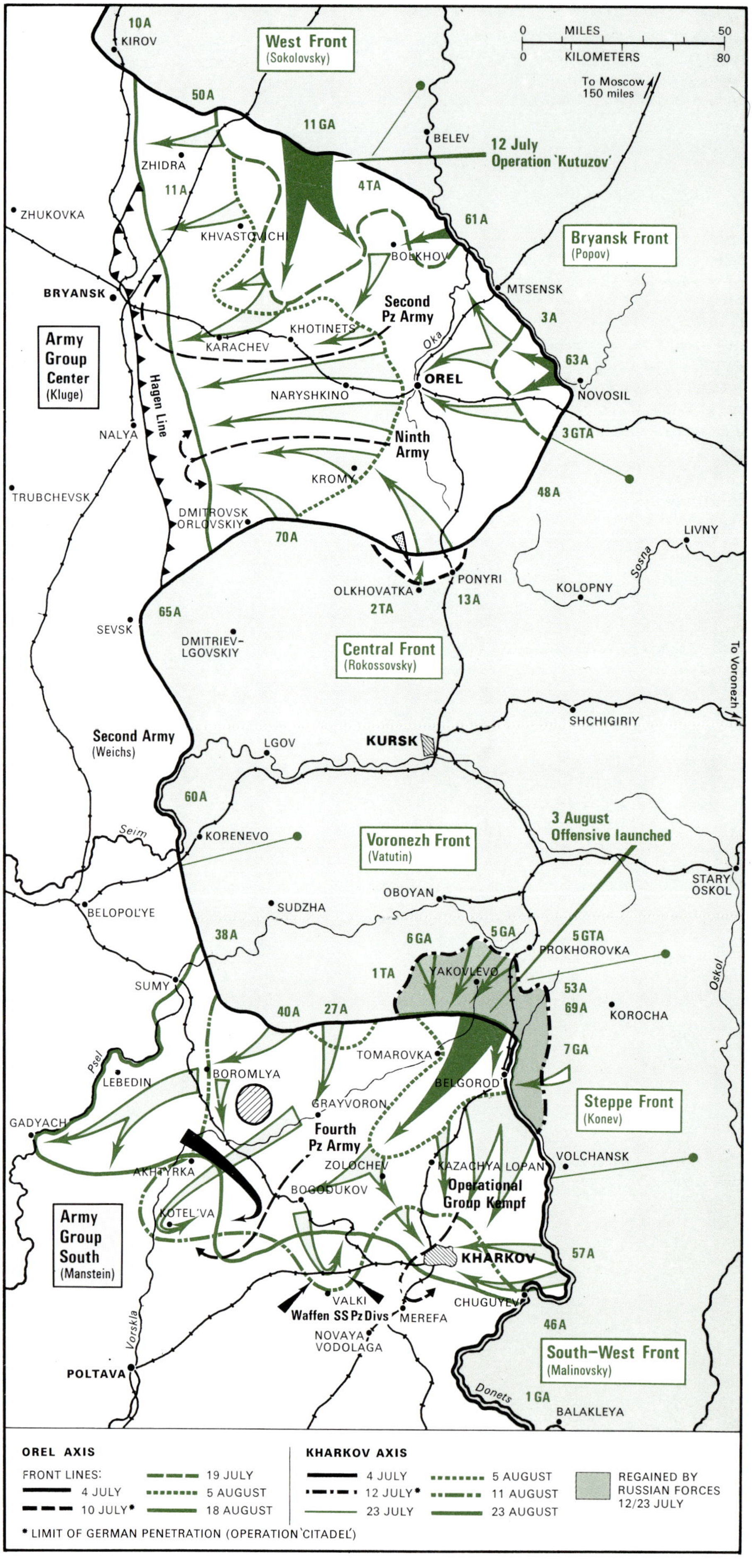

Opposite far left: The German offensive against Kursk, launched on 5 July.
Left: By 20 July German forces were in full retreat.
Right: The heavily armored KV-1 tanks gave the Germans many problems.
Below: Soviet T-34s take part in the biggest tank battle of the war near Prokhorovka in the south.

tank units from the Russian Steppe Front reserve. The largest tank armies in history clashed near Prokhorovka on 12 July and fought for seven days. Initial German success was followed by increasing Soviet ascendancy, and by 20 July all German forces were in full retreat. Two million men had been involved, with 6000 tanks and 4000 aircraft. Many of the surviving German tanks were dispatched immediately to Italy to counter the Allied offensive that had begun with landings in Sicily. The Russians maintained their momentum in successful advances south of Moscow.

The Dniepr and Smolensk

By fall of 1943, the Soviets had pushed their front line far to the west against diminishing German forces that managed to stay intact and resist, although they could not prevail. In mid September the Russians threatened Smolensk in the north and Kiev in the center. They crossed the Donets in the south and by 30 September had captured Smolensk and established themselves along most of the Dniepr.

German Army Group A, virtually abandoned at its bridgehead in the Caucasus since the previous summer, was pulled out to operate on the right of Manstein's Army Group South, its parent formation. Manstein had recaptured Kharkov in February – against numerical odds of seven to one – but his losses had been staggering. When the Russians took Kiev (6 November) and penetrated his sector, he called for evacuation of the Seventeenth Army from the Crimea. Hitler's characteristic 'No retreat' order was Manstein's reward for months of superhuman effort. Seventeenth Army was cut off in the Crimean Peninsula, just as he had foreseen, and by year's end the Russians had effectively regained all the territory lost in 1942 and more.

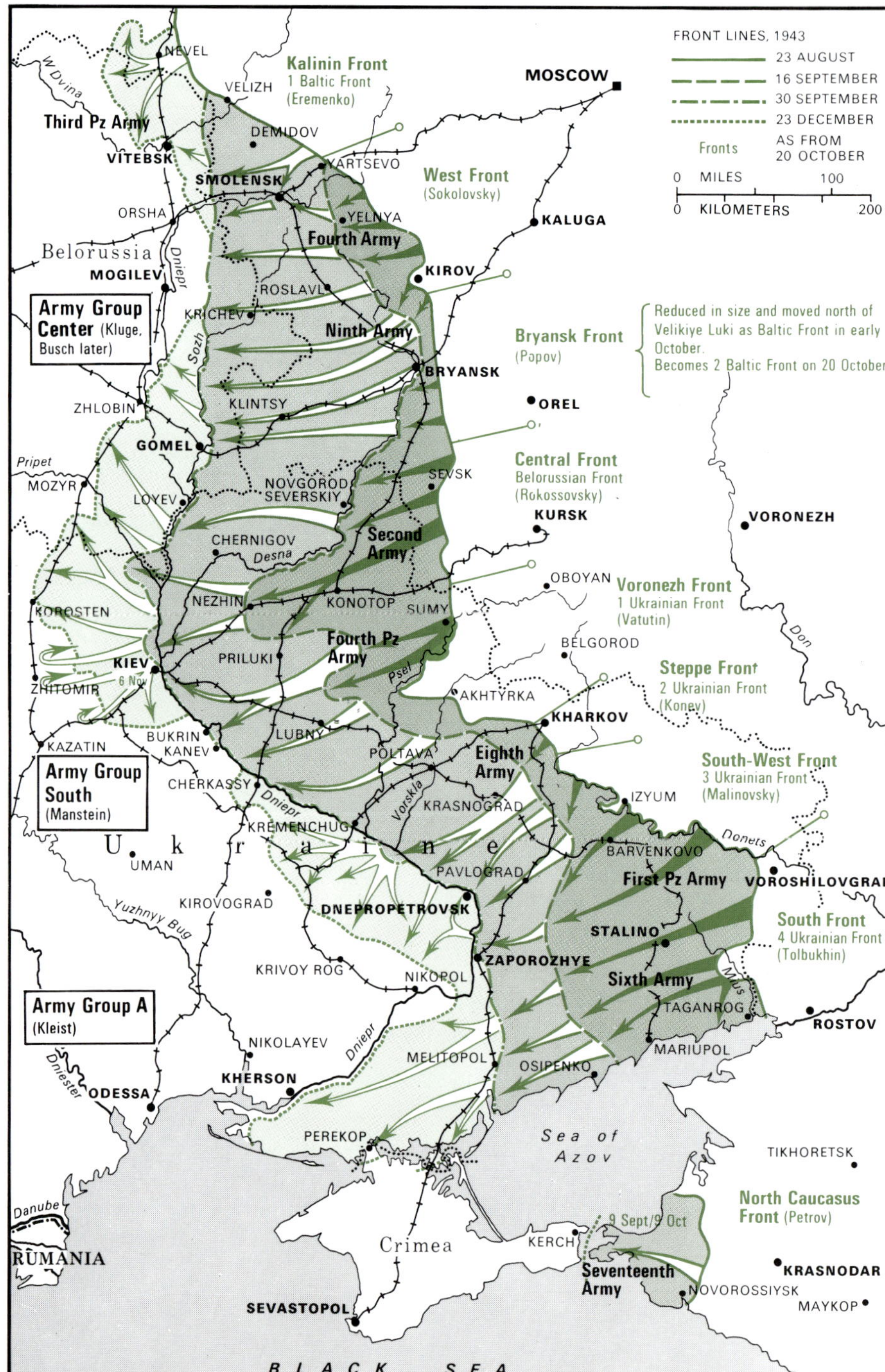

Left: The scope of Soviet reoccupation at their western border.
Above: The eventual German withdrawal was made all the more inevitable by the removal of armor and personnel to the Italian Front.
Opposite: A German NCO leads his infantry section at the front line.

The Relief of Leningrad

Leningrad had been isolated from the rest of Russia since 1941 by the German-held corridor between Tosno and Lake Ladoga. For 900 days its people were deprived of food, fuel and arms; by the end of the siege, they were dying of hunger and cold at the rate of 20,000 a day. Throughout this ordeal, Leningrad's citizens continued to produce goods in their factories, even at greatly reduced levels, and to provide for civil defense. A trickle of supplies began to arrive in January 1943, thanks to a concerted effort by the Leningrad and Volkhov Fronts to secure a supply line south of Lake Ladoga. It was little enough, but it prevented total starvation. Not until a year later did real relief reach Leningrad.

In mid-January 1944, three Russian Fronts – Leningrad, Volkhov and 2 Baltic – launched attacks against German Army Group North, commanded first by Küchler and after 29 January by Field Marshal Walther Model. By that time the Russians had cleared the Moscow-Leningrad Railway and recaptured Novgorod. Now threatened by encirclement, Model withdrew Army Group North east of Lake Chudskoye and subsequently stopped the Soviet advance into the Baltic States. Beleaguered Leningrad was restored to the Soviet Union.

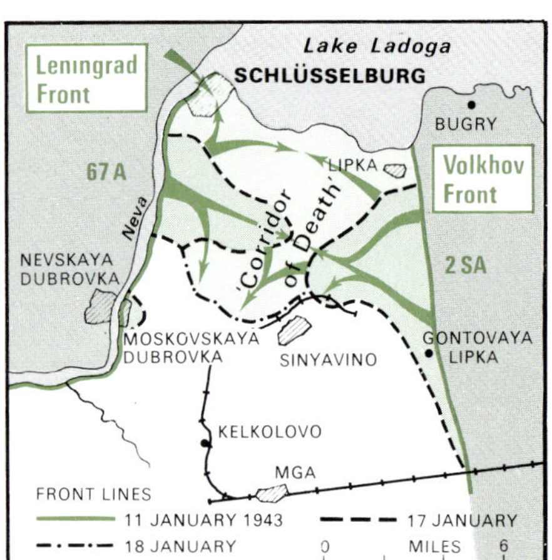

Above: Supplies reached Leningrad in limited quantities through the so-called 'Corridor of Death'.
Above right: The earlier division of the Leningrad and Volkhov Fronts.
Right: Final relief of the siege was achieved early in 1944.
Opposite: Defenders dig in at Leningrad's perimeter.

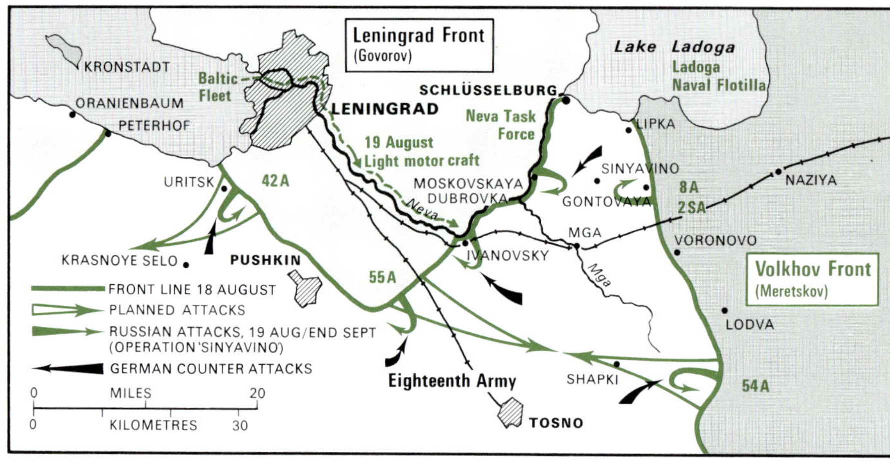

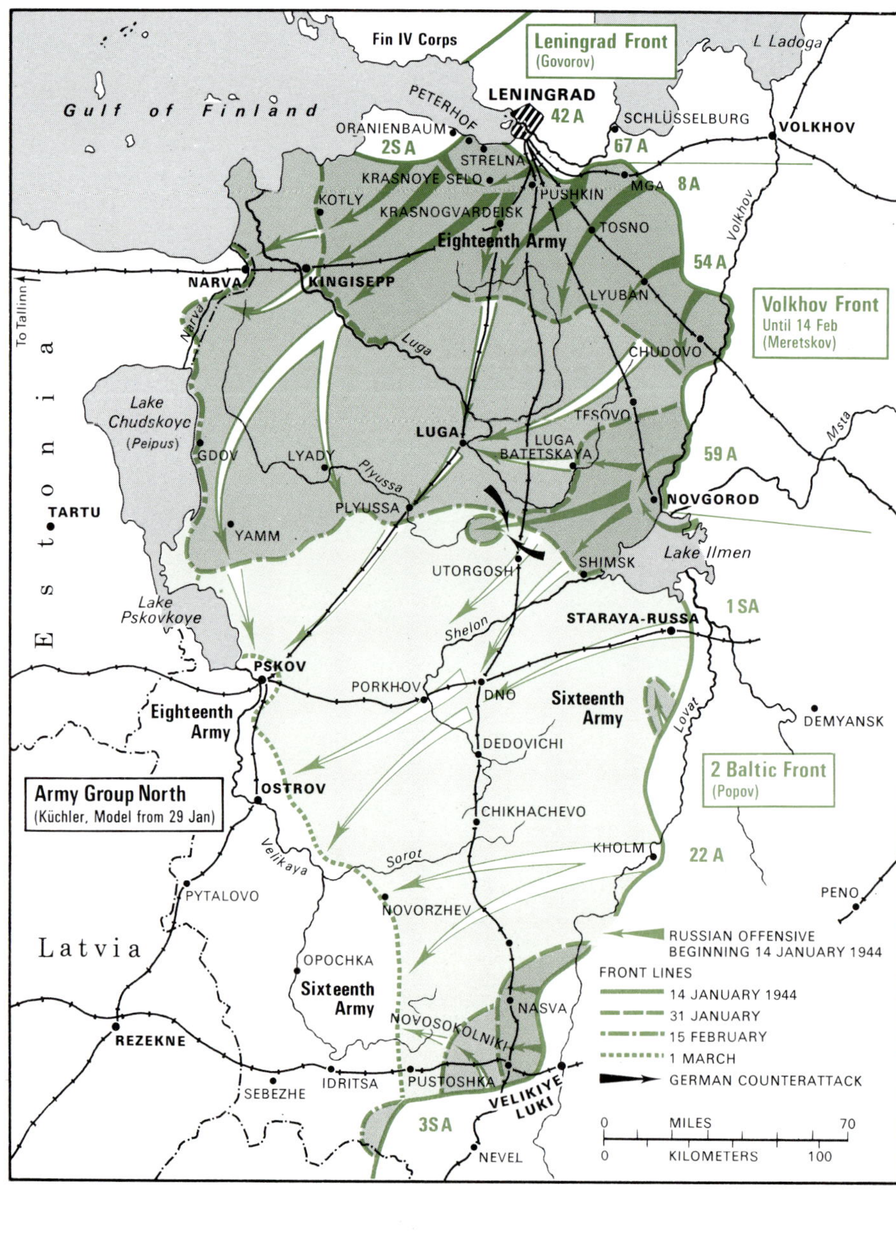

Regaining the Ukraine

During the drive to relieve Leningrad, Russian forces in the south were equally active. The 1 and 2 Ukrainian Fronts launched attacks on all German forces in the Ukraine between 24 December 1943 and 5 January 1944. German First Panzer Army was trapped, and both Manstein's Army Group North Ukraine and Kleist's Army Group A were hard pressed. Manstein tried to counterattack under blizzard conditions, but could do little to slow the Russian advance to the Rivers Bug and Dniestr.

An improvised airlift kept First Panzer Army supplied until it could fight its way out behind Russian lines. German tenacity in south Russia at this time was almost unbelievable, but it was a losing fight. Kleist had to fall back to Odessa, leaving elements of Sixth and Eighth Armies surrounded. On 10 April he was forced out of Odessa, and the Russian front was extended almost as far as Brest Litovsk.

The last rail link between the Germans in Poland and those in southern Russia had been severed in March with the capture of Chernovtsy by First Ukraine Front. The abandoned German Seventeenth Army was driven from the Crimea, and Sevastopol fell to the Soviets on 12 May.

Hitler was enraged by the losses in the Ukraine, whose rich mineral resources were desperately needed by the Reich. Instead of rewarding Manstein's heroic role there, he relieved him of his command and put the trouble-shooting Model in his place. Kleist was ousted in favor of the ambitious Field Marshal Friedrich Schörner.

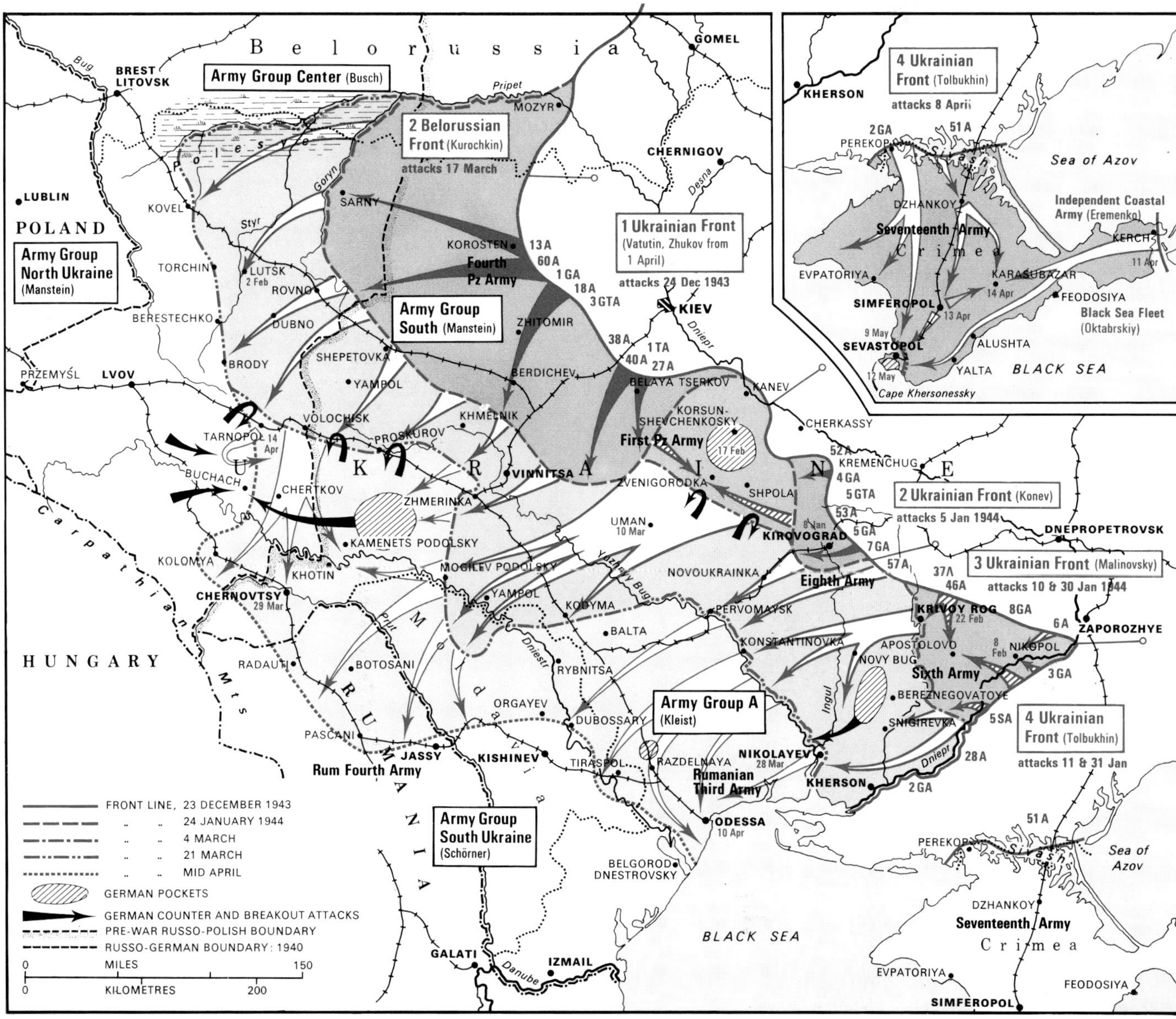

Left: A column of Germans captured near the pocket of resistance at Korsun-Shevchenkosky.
Above: Soviet advances on a grand scale.
Right: German soldiers advance through the maize fields of the Ukraine.

From Warsaw to the Oder

Below: The frontiers of German occupation are pushed back.
Bottom: Marshal Ivan Konev, Commander of 1 Ukrainian Front, 1944.
Right: Russian forces halt at the Oder prior to the final push to Berlin.
Below right: Troops of 4 Ukrainian Front plod over the Polish Carpathians in the winter of 1944-45.

Early summer of 1944 found widely scattered German forces trying to hold a 1400-mile Eastern Front with very few reserves. On 23 June the Soviets struck along the central sector with three fronts under overall command of Marshal Georgi Zhukov, now deputy supreme commander in the USSR. With a density of almost 400 guns per mile, these troops assaulted General Busch's Army Group Centre just as partisan activity in its rear disrupted communications entirely. There was no contest in the air, as many Luftwaffe units had already been taken west. Busch lost half a million men, killed or captured, from his 33 divisions and was replaced by Model immediately. By the end of August, Zhukov's offensive was at the gates of Warsaw – in the the north, at Riga. Model barely succeeded in preventing the Russians from entering Warsaw; their own pause to resupply outside the city was providential for him. Farther south, Soviet troops had crossed the Vistula for a combined advance of 450 miles in two months. Operations had to be suspended until supply lines could catch up.

By January 1945 the Russians were poised to invade Germany for the first time since 1914. Rokossovsky's 2 Belorussian Front of nine armies assaulted the German Second Army north of Warsaw, while the Russian Forty-seventh Army encircled the city, which fell on 17 January. Army Group Centre was driven back into a few pockets along the Bay of Danzig, from which the German Navy extricated some half a million men in March and April. On 9 May the last German beachheads surrendered.

As Rokossovsky attacked north of the Vistula, the 1 Belorussian and 1 Ukrainian Fronts advanced at top speed on a wide front from Warsaw to Jasto. They had reached the Oder by 31 January, bypassing pockets of German resistance. Russian armies of over 1,500,000 men confronted German forces of 596,000, with still greater inequalities in armaments and aircraft. By 24 February Pomerania and Silesia had fallen, giving Soviet forces a solid front along the Oder less than 40 miles from Berlin. Only one sizeable German force would be left in Europe after the fall of Berlin: Schörner's Army Group Centre, which had moved into Czechoslovakia. The Russian 'liberation' of that country would be a microcosm of what transpired in Eastern Europe after the German defeat.

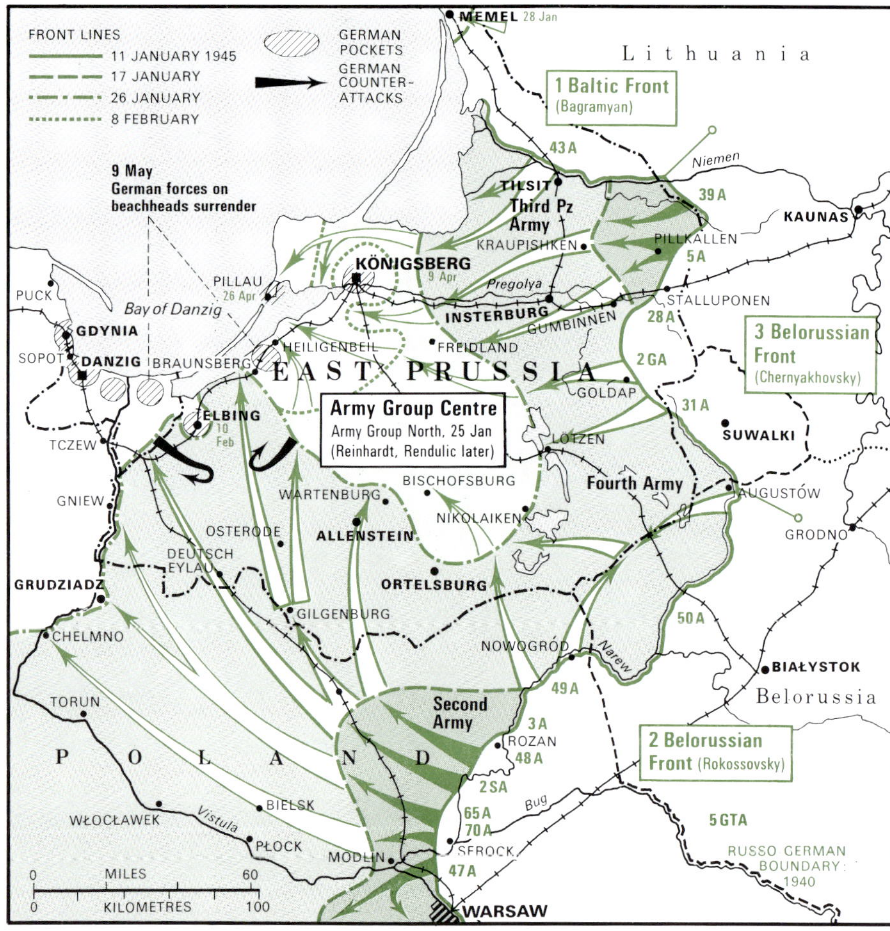

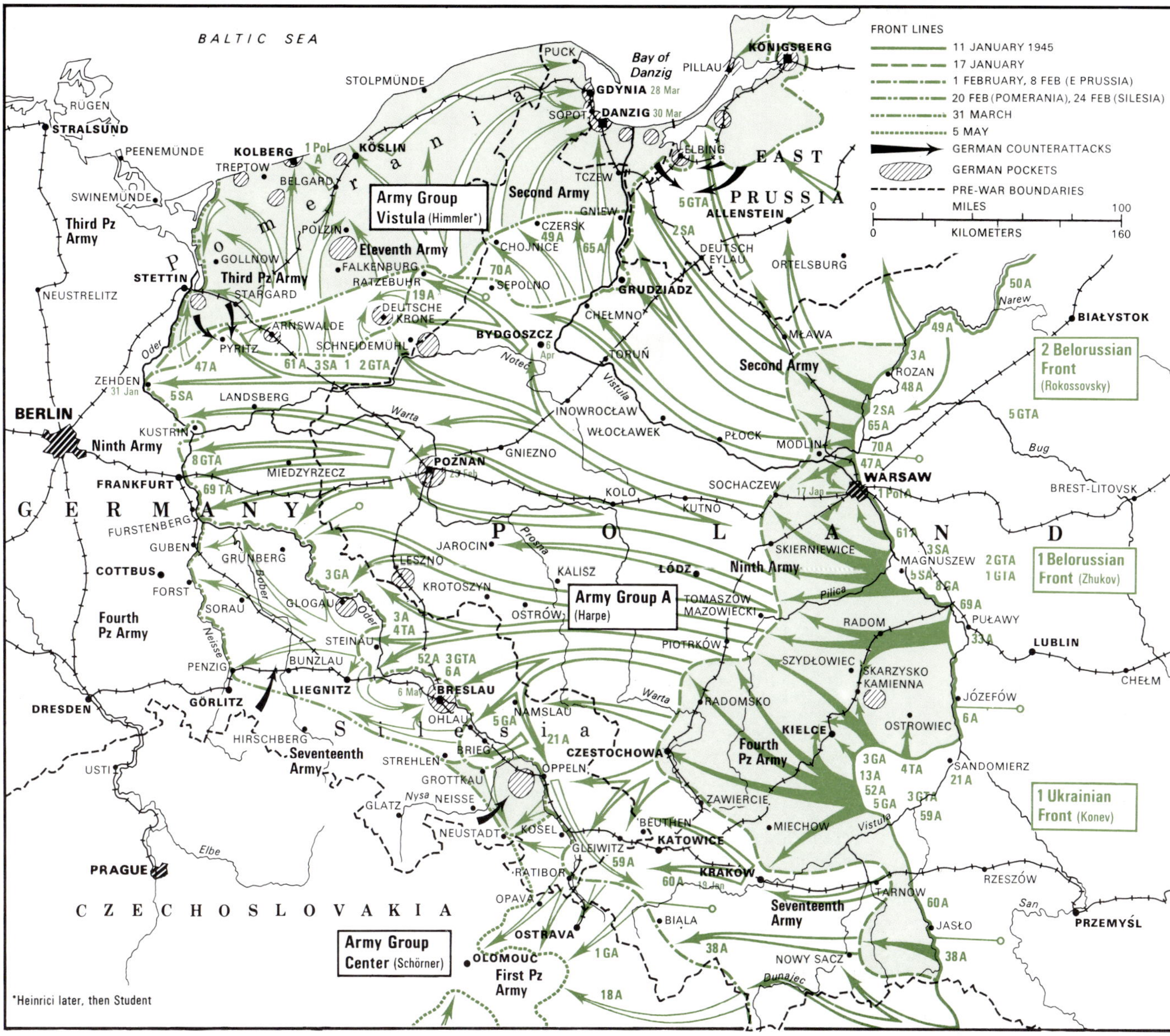
BALTIC SEA
FRONT LINES
11 JANUARY 1945
17 JANUARY
1 FEBRUARY, 8 FEB (E PRUSSIA)
20 FEB (POMERANIA), 24 FEB (SILESIA)
31 MARCH
5 MAY
GERMAN COUNTERATTACKS
GERMAN POCKETS
PRE-WAR BOUNDARIES
MILES
KILOMETERS
0
100
0
160
Bay of Danzig
PUCK
STOLPMÜNDE
GDYNIA 28 Mar
SOPOT
DANZIG 30 Mar
PILLAU
KÖNIGSBERG
RÜGEN
STRALSUND
PEENEMÜNDE
KOLBERG
1 Pol A
KÖSLIN
TREPTOW
BELGARD
SWINEMÜNDE
Third Pz Army
Army Group Vistula (Himmler*)
Second Army
ELBING
EAST PRUSSIA
TCZEW
GNIEW
5 GTA
ALLENSTEIN
2 SA
CZERSK
49 A
65 A
POLZIN
GOLLNOW
Eleventh Army
CHOJNICE
DEUTSCH EYLAU
ORTELSBURG
STETTIN
Third Pz Army
FALKENBURG
RATZEBUHR
70 A
SEPOLNO
GRUDZIADZ
NEUSTRELITZ
STARGARD
19 A
DEUTSCHE KRONE
CHEŁMNO
ARNSWALDE
PYRITZ
SCHNEIDEMÜHL
BYDGOSZCZ 6 Apr
MŁAWA
50 A
Narew
49 A
BIAŁYSTOK
Oder
47 A
61 A
3 SA
1
2 GTA
Noteć
TORUŃ
Second Army
3 A
ROZAN
48 A
2 Belorussian Front (Rokossovsky)
ZEHDEN 31 Jan
5 SA
LANDSBERG
Vistula
2 SA
65 A
5 GTA
Warta
INOWROCŁAW
BERLIN
KUSTRIN
WŁOCŁAWEK
PŁOCK
MODLIN
70 A
Bug
Ninth Army
8 GTA
POZNAŃ 23 Feb
GNIEZNO
47 A
FRANKFURT
MIEDZYRZECZ
69 TA
SOCHACZEW
WARSAW
BREST-LITOVSK
17 Jan
1 Pol A
KOLO
KUTNO
GERMANY
POLAND
FURSTENBERG
GUBEN
JAROCIN
Prosna
61 A
3 SA
MAGNUSZEW
2 GTA
1 GTA
5 SA
8 GA
1 Belorussian Front (Zhukov)
SKIERNIEWICE
COTTBUS
GRÜNBERG
3 GA
LESZNO
KALISZ
ŁÓDŹ
Ninth Army
FORST
Bober
KROTOSZYN
Army Group A (Harpe)
TOMASZÓW MAZOWIECKI
Pilica
69 A
PUŁAWY
SORAU
GLOGAU
3 A
4 TA
OSTRÓW
RADOM
33 A
LUBLIN
Fourth Pz Army
Neisse
STEINAU
PIOTRKÓW
PENZIG
BUNZLAU
52 A
3 GTA
6 A
SZYDŁOWIEC
SKARZYSKO KAMIENNA
CHEŁM
DRESDEN
GÖRLITZ
LIEGNITZ
6 May
BRESLAU
Warta
RADOMSKO
JÓZEFÓW
NAMSLAU
5 GA
6 A
OHLAU
Silesia
KIELCE
OSTROWIEC
HIRSCHBERG
Seventeenth Army
STREHLEN
BRIEG
21 A
CZESTOCHOWA
Fourth Pz Army
3 GA
4 TA
SANDOMIERZ
USTI
13 A
21 A
GROTTKAU
OPPELN
52 A
Nysa
5 GA
3 GTA
1 Ukrainian Front (Konev)
GLATZ
NEISSE
ZAWIERCIE
59 A
NEUSTADT
KOSEL
BEUTHEN
MIECHOW
Vistula
Elbe
GLEIWITZ
KATOWICE
PRAGUE
59 A
RATIBOR
60 A
KRAKÓW 19 Jan
RZESZÓW
OPAVA
TARNÓW
60 A
CZECHOSLOVAKIA
BIAŁA
Seventeenth Army
San
JASŁO
PRZEMYŚL
OSTRAVA
38 A
Army Group Center (Schörner)
OLOMOUC
1 GA
NOWY SACZ
38 A
First Pz Army
Dunajec
18 A
*Heinrici later, then Student

The Drive into Czechoslovakia

Desperate Nazi plans focused on the formation of a 'national redoubt' on the German/Czechoslovak border after the fall of Berlin. These plans were based on Schörner's armies of almost a million men, which held the Reich's last important industrial area. In reality, however, their situation was hopeless, surrounded as they were by the Russians on three sides and with Patton's US Third Army approaching from the west.

By 6 March 1945 the Russians had already overrun much of Slovakia, and two months later they held over half the country. Czech partisans in Prague and other cities disrupted German communications and harassed German forces in every way they could. On 8 May a concerted Russian offensive attacked from north, south and east, and Prague was liberated the following day. US Army closed the circle on 12 May along a line from Karlovy Vary to Linz. Schörner surrendered with all his forces, five days after the formal surrender of Germany.

Left: The western boundaries of Soviet wartime expansion.
Below: The Allies drive into Czechoslovakia from all directions.
Opposite: Soviet anti-tank gunners.

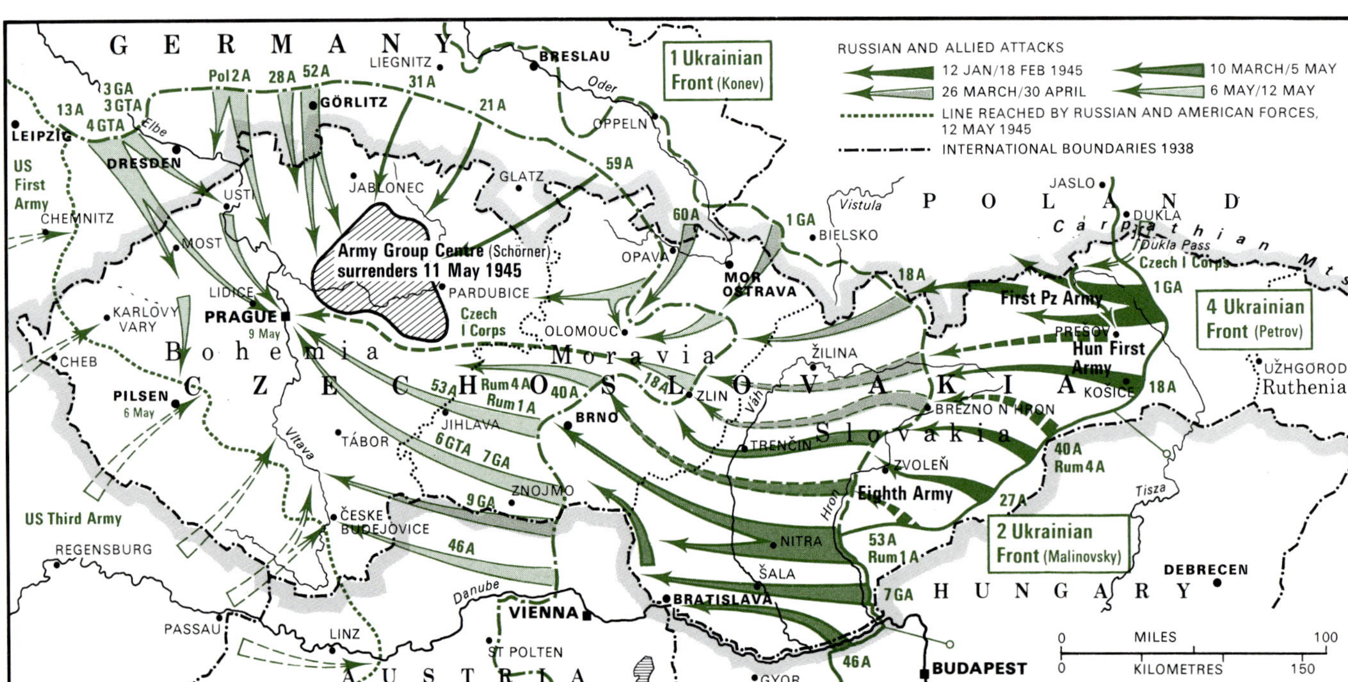

Fortress Europe Overthrown

The Bomber Offensive on Germany

Allied air raids on Germany began as early as 1940, but it was not until late 1943 that the bombing offensive became systematic and widespread. At that time American 8th Air Force units joined the RAF Bomber Command in force, and several months later an increasing range of escort fighters allowed deep penetration raids over the whole of Germany. RAF Bomber Command concentrated on night bombing of German cities, while the US 8th Air Force, with fewer planes, targeted specific military installations by day.

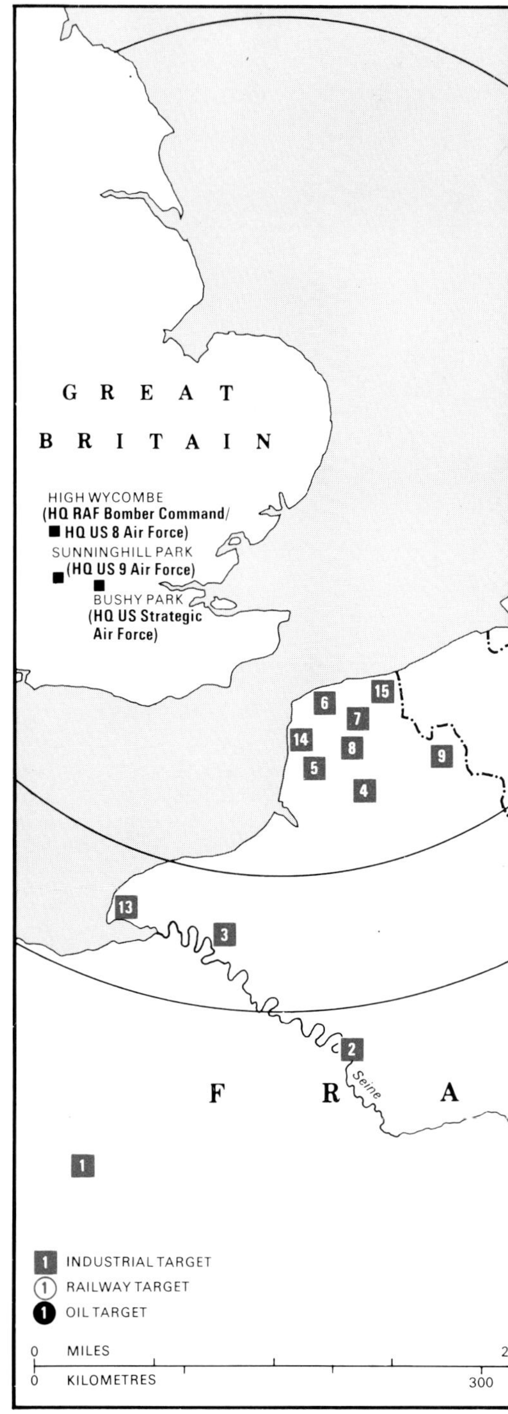

Previous pages: Russian troops in Red Square with captured Nazi banners.
Left: B-24 bombers of the USAAF continue their daylight raids on the Reich.
Above: The ever-expanding operational range of US escort fighters ensured that yet more bombers would hit the target.

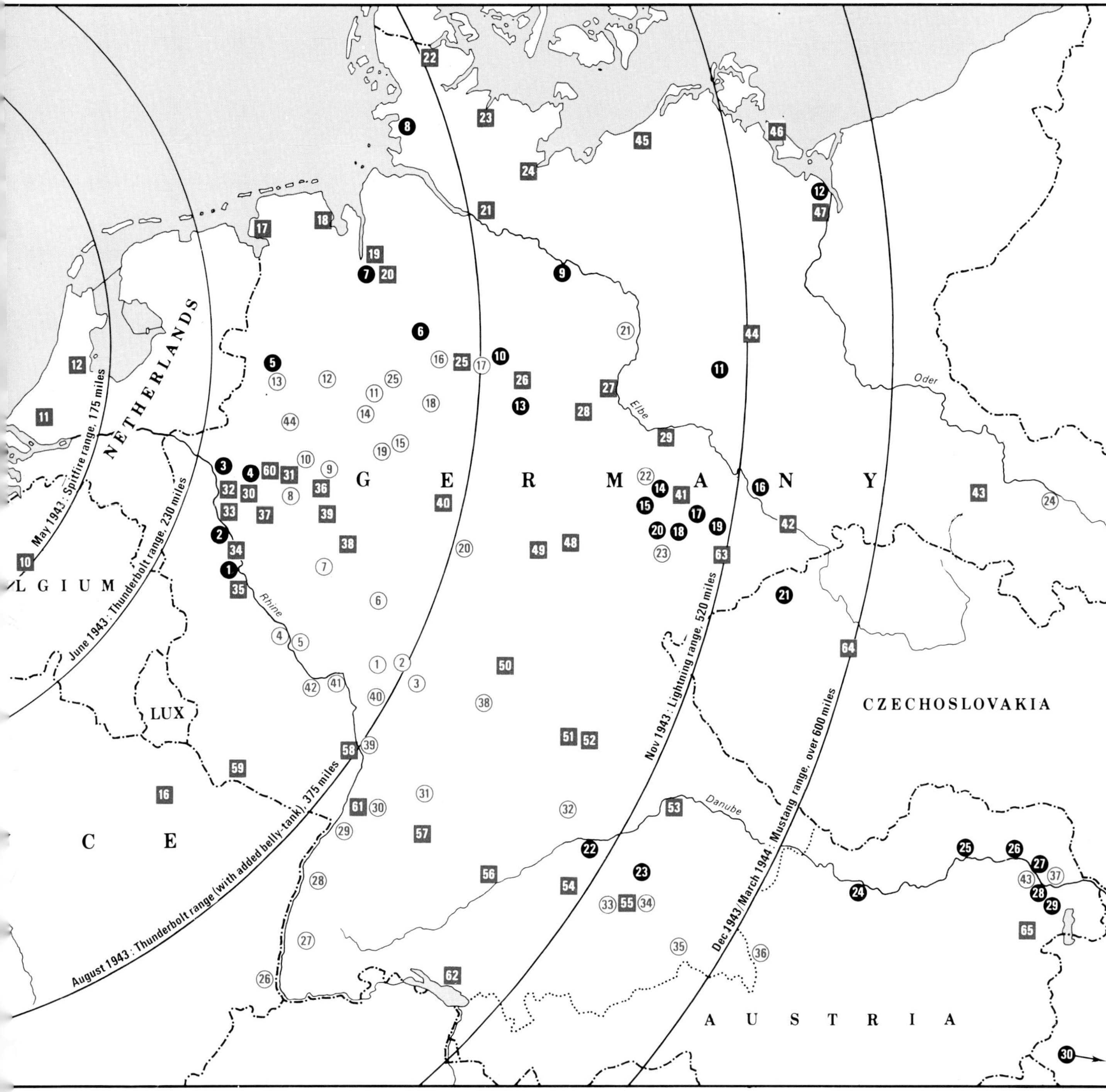

Prior to this, several historic raids had been made, including the first '1000-bomber' raid on Cologne (31 May 1942), which destroyed half the target area. Three months later, US 8th Air Force dispatched 12 Flying Fortresses against the marshalling yards near Rouen. Damage was slight, but no American planes were lost, and this raid set the pattern for US concentration on precision bombing in daylight hours.

The night of 18-19 November 1943 brought the first of sixteen major raids on Berlin, where serious damage was inflicted with loss of only nine RAF aircraft. With the arrival of escort fighters in spring of 1944, the 8th Air Force attacked the Erkner ball-bearing factory in Berlin, disrupting production considerably at a cost of 37 planes. Three weeks later, the RAF struck Nuremberg with almost 800 aircraft, causing some relatively minor damage but losing 95 bombers in the process; 71 others were damaged. The British abandoned area raids on distant objectives after this resounding failure.

The most controversial raid of the war in Europe was that on Dresden (13-14 February 1945). Estimates of civilians killed in this raid ranged from 35,000 to 135,000. Over 1500 acres of the beautiful and historic city – of no military value whatever – were destroyed. The first devastating fire bombing was carried out by 805 Bomber Command aircraft, with the loss of only eight planes. The following day, 8th Air Force bombers overflew the city again.

Strategy: Operation Overlord

At the 1943 Trident Conference in Washington, Allied leaders made their plans for the invasion of Europe – Operation Overlord – during the coming year. France was selected as the target of a cross-Channel assault, with beachheads to be established in Normandy between Cherbourg and Le Havre. This area was within easy reach of fighter bases in southern England and represented the shortest possible route for a massive amphibious operation, excluding the Pas de Calais. Since the Allied invasion was expected in the latter area, the Normandy beaches would be less heavily defended.

The main assault force consisted of the US First and the British Second Armies, with air support from the US 82 and 101 Airborne Divisions and the British 8 Airborne Division. These forces would land right and left of the target beaches to cover the landings. Two artificial ports (called Mulberry Harbors) would be towed across the Channel to permit the landing of tons of supplies before a port could be secured.

Elaborate plans were laid to deceive the Germans into believing that Pas de Calais was the intended target. A dummy headquarters and railroad sidings were built; dozens of sorties were flown over the area; while tons of bombs were dropped west of Le Havre.

German forces guarding the coast of France consisted of Army Group B, commanded by Rommel, and Seventh Army under Dollmann. Hitler had a bad habit of bypassing von Rundstedt, Commander in Chief West, when he issued orders to his Army Group leaders, so the Germans had no effective chain of command in the west. Their position was further jeopardized by topography; destruction of the river crossings on the Loire and the Seine would isolate their forces in Normandy.

Below: Nearly three million men made up the Allied army and supporting forces ready for invasion.
Right: The first landings take place on the Normandy beaches.
Far right: The disposition of opposing German forces.

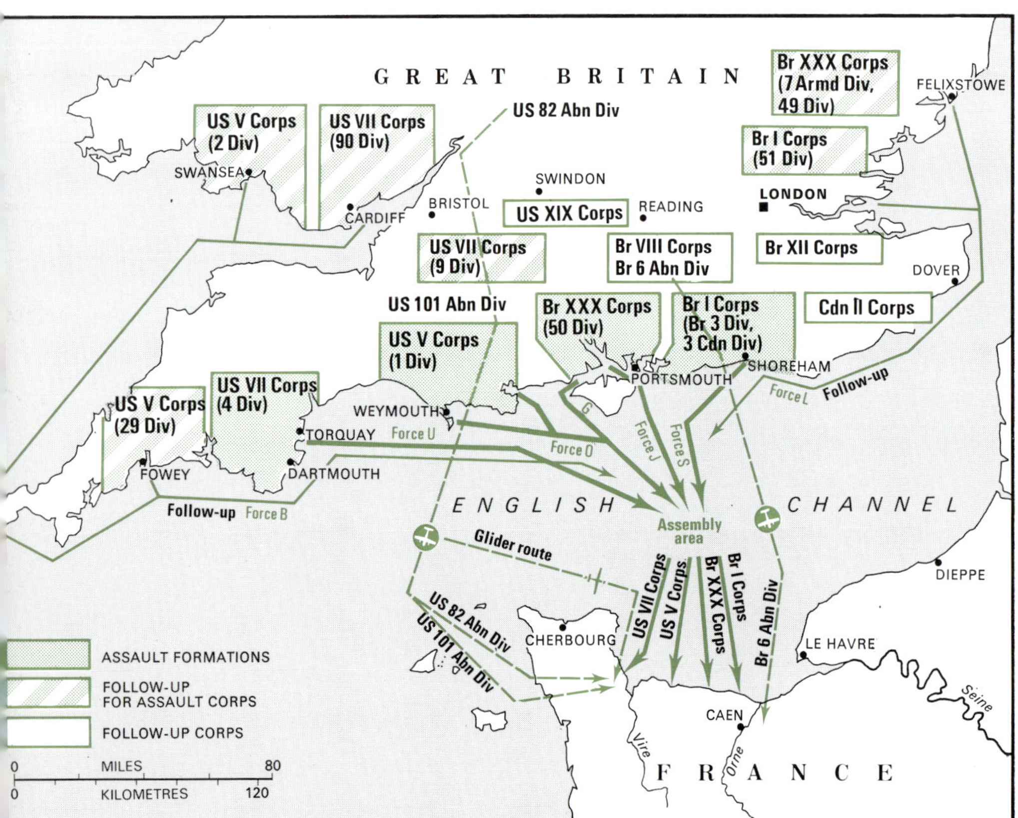

D-Day

All the careful Allied planning that went into the invasion of France was subject to one imponderable – the weather. June of 1944 opened with unseasonable cold and high winds, which posed serious problems for the strategists. Optimum conditions of moon and tide occurred only a few days each month, and the first week of June comprised such a period.

General Dwight D Eisenhower, Supreme Commander of the operation, decided that the landings must go ahead on schedule. Then a fortunate break in the weather allowed the huge force to launch the largest combined operation in military history on D-Day – 6 June 1944. Three million men, 4600 transports and warships, and almost 10,000 aircraft were involved. General Montgomery

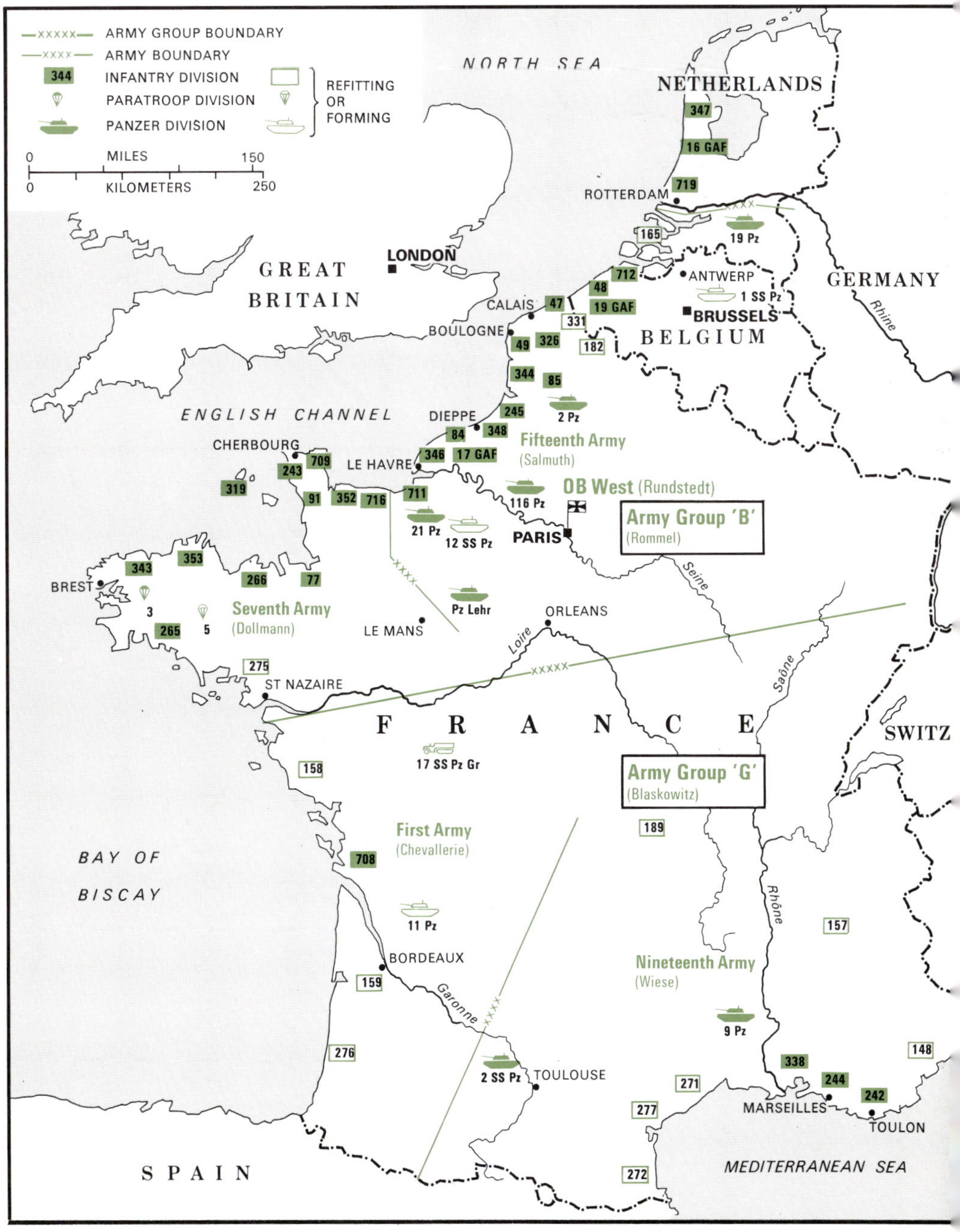

Left: Loading Allied wounded aboard a C-47 Dakota. Note the aircraft's black-and-white invasion stripes, adopted for easy identification.
Below: The invasion beaches.
Right: LCVP landing craft en route to the French coast.

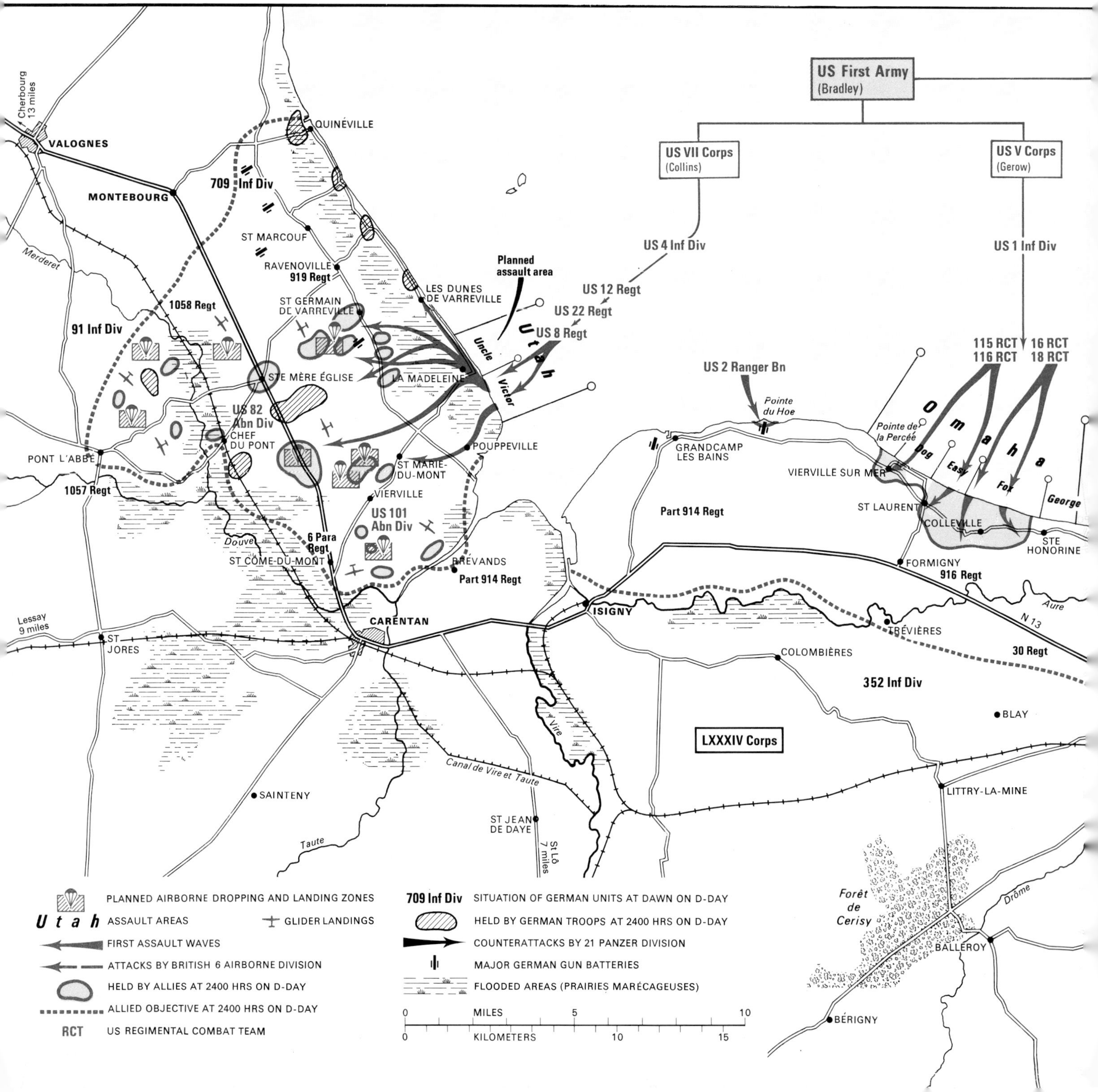

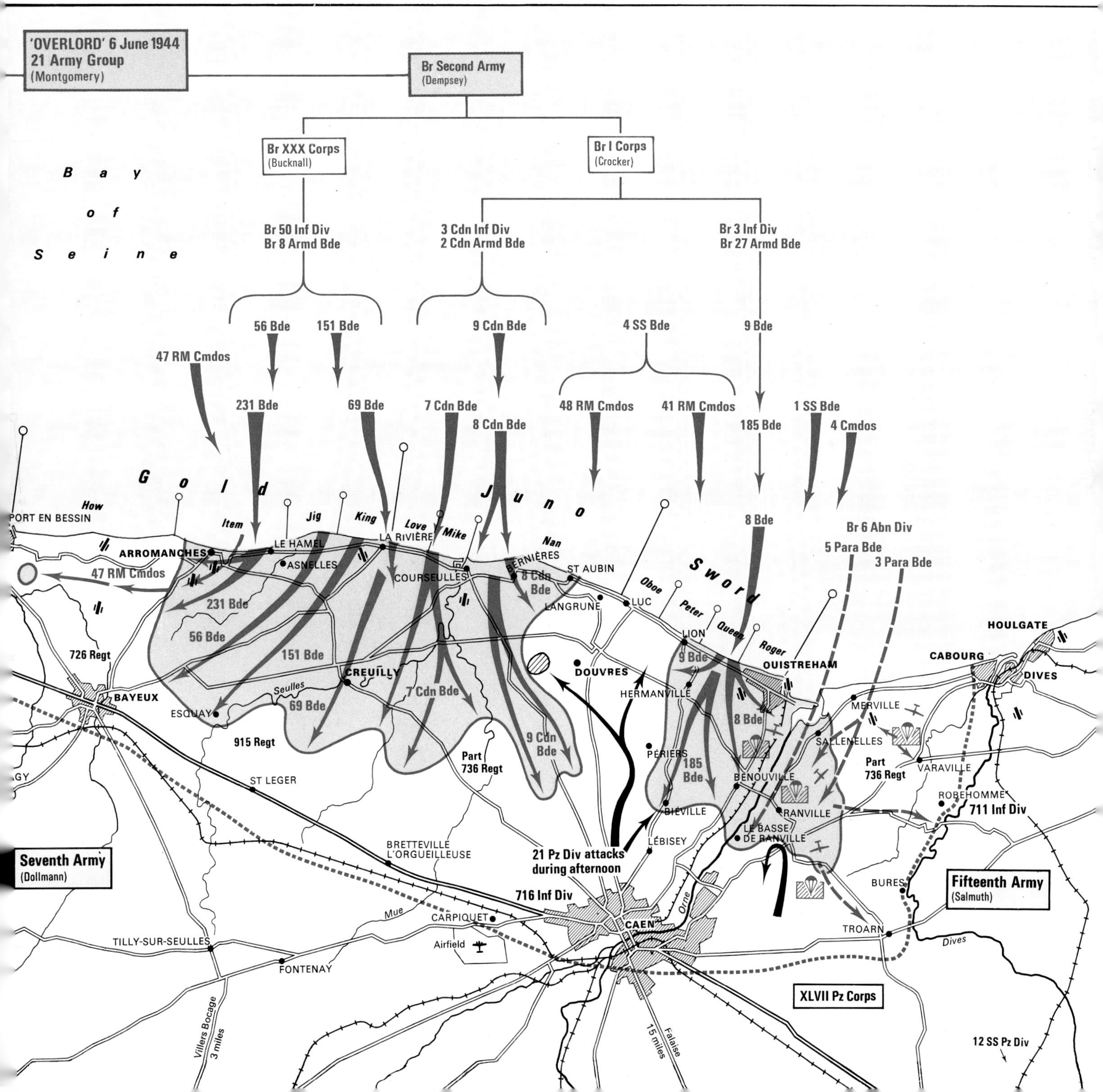

'OVERLORD' 6 June 1944
21 Army Group
(Montgomery)
Br Second Army
(Dempsey)
Br XXX Corps
(Bucknall)
Br I Corps
(Crocker)
Bay of Seine
Br 50 Inf Div
Br 8 Armd Bde
3 Cdn Inf Div
2 Cdn Armd Bde
Br 3 Inf Div
Br 27 Armd Bde
56 Bde
151 Bde
9 Cdn Bde
4 SS Bde
9 Bde
47 RM Cmdos
231 Bde
69 Bde
7 Cdn Bde
8 Cdn Bde
48 RM Cmdos
41 RM Cmdos
185 Bde
1 SS Bde
4 Cmdos
Gold
Juno
Sword
How
Item
Jig
King
Love
Mike
Nan
Oboe
Peter
Queen
Roger
8 Bde
Br 6 Abn Div
5 Para Bde
3 Para Bde
PORT EN BESSIN
ARROMANCHES
LE HAMEL
ASNELLES
LA RIVIÈRE
COURSEULLES
BERNIÈRES
ST AUBIN
LANGRUNE
LUC
LION
OUISTREHAM
HOULGATE
CABOURG
DIVES
MERVILLE
SALLENELLES
VARAVILLE
ROBEHOMME
711 Inf Div
47 RM Cmdos
231 Bde
56 Bde
151 Bde
726 Regt
BAYEUX
CREUILLY
Seulles
69 Bde
7 Cdn Bde
ESQUAY
915 Regt
Part 736 Regt
9 Cdn Bde
8 Cdn Bde
DOUVRES
HERMANVILLE
9 Bde
8 Bde
PÉRIERS
185 Bde
BÉNOUVILLE
RANVILLE
Part 736 Regt
BIÉVILLE
LE BASSE DE RANVILLE
LÉBISEY
ST LEGER
BRETTEVILLE L'ORGUEILLEUSE
21 Pz Div attacks during afternoon
716 Inf Div
Seventh Army
(Dollmann)
Fifteenth Army
(Salmuth)
BURES
Orne
CARPIQUET
Mue
CAEN
TROARN
Dives
TILLY-SUR-SEULLES
Airfield
FONTENAY
XLVII Pz Corps
Villers Bocage 3 miles
15 miles Falaise
12 SS Pz Div

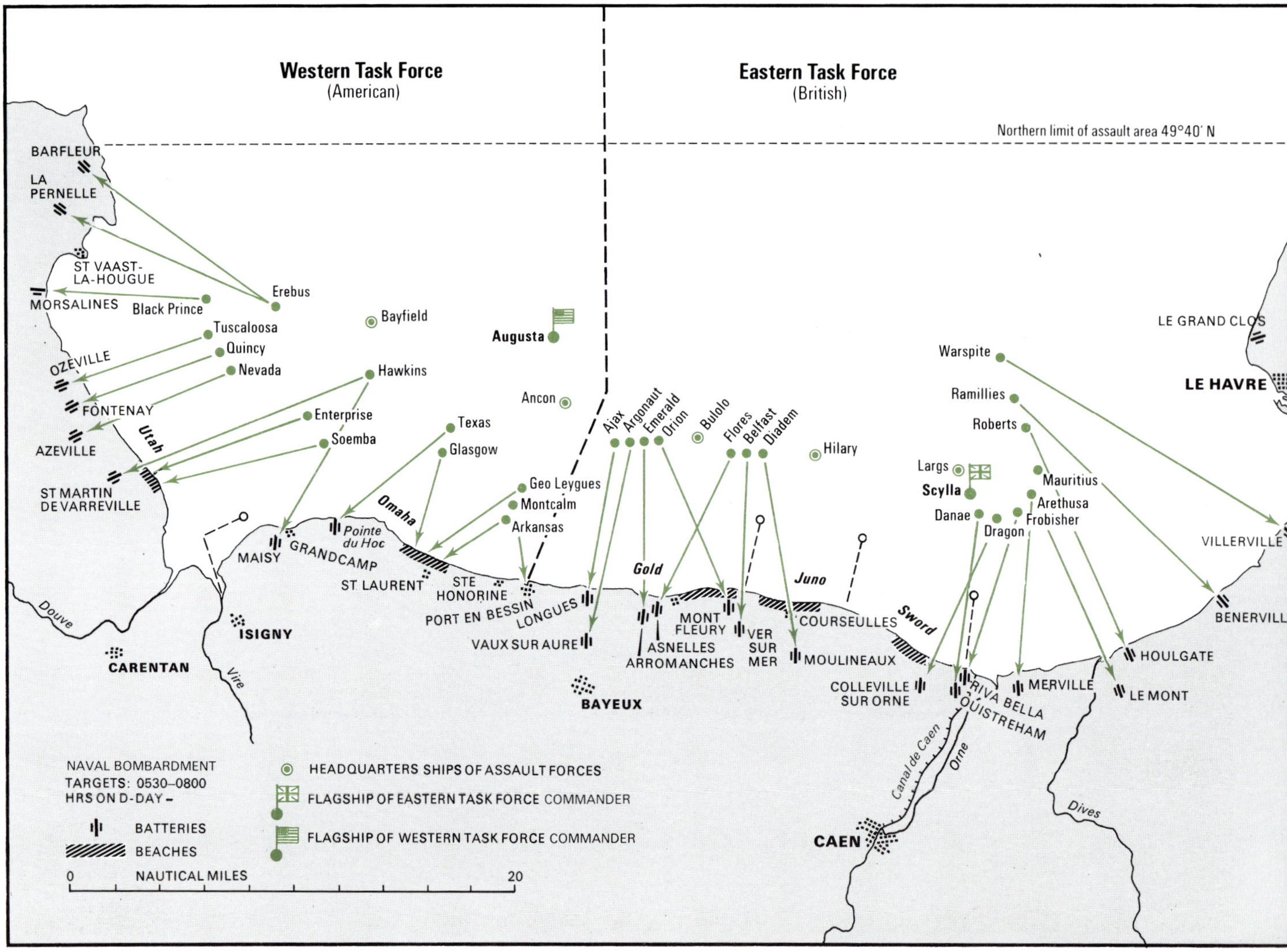

commanded ground forces, Admiral Ramsay co-ordinated naval operations and Air Marshal Leigh-Mallory was charged with air support. Preparatory air attacks were particularly important in view of the shortage of paratroop-transport aircraft and the comparative strength of opposing ground forces – some half a million men of the German Seventh Army.

Hitler himself contributed to Allied success by misusing the advice of two of his ablest generals to produce a compromise scheme that seriously hampered the German defense. Field Marshal von Rundstedt, Commander in Chief West, wanted to form a strong central reserve until the true Allied plan was known and then use it to repel the invasion, keeping beach defenses to a minimum. Rommel, commanding German armies in northern France and the Low Countries, cautioned that Allied air power would prevent Rundstedt's reserve from coming into action and recommended that the Allies should be defeated on the beaches before they could reach full strength. Hitler's compromise – strongly influenced by inflated reports of Allied manpower – neither strengthened the beaches sufficiently nor allowed for the flexible use of Rundstedt's reserve.

Five beaches were targeted for the Allied landings, code-named Utah, Omaha, Gold, Juno and Sword. At 2:00 AM on 6 June, US and British airborne forces descended on their objectives and consolidated a position within the hour. Tactical surprise was complete, thanks to the months of painstaking work by the deception team. An hour later, aerial bombardment of the beaches began, soon followed by fire from the 600 warships that had assembled off the coast. At 6:30 AM the first waves went ashore, US First Army on Utah and Omaha Beaches and British Second Army on Gold, Juno and Sword. Real problems were encountered only on Omaha, where landing forces were deprived of full amphibious tank support by rough seas. They were pinned down on the beach for hours, but managed to fight their way out to the coast road by nightfall. Within 24 hours, the Allies had achieved almost all their objectives for D-Day.

Above: Disposition of Allied bombardment vessels on D-Day.
Top right: LST landing ships disgorge men and matériel.
Right: A convoy of US Coast Guard landing craft (LCI) head for Normandy.

The Anvil Landings in Southern France

US and British leaders disagreed on the necessity of landing forces in southern France to support Operation Overlord on the Normandy coast. The Americans argued that such landings could open the much-needed port of Marseilles and draw off German troops from the north, but this could be done only by transferring troops from Italy. British leaders saw vast untapped potential in the Italian campaign and argued for pouring men and munitions into Italy to facilitate an advance over the Alps toward Vienna and the Danube. Stalin had his own vested interest in an Anglo-American effort as far west of Russia as possible, and he enlisted US President Franklin D Roosevelt's support. It was the American plan that prevailed.

Operation Anvil was postponed from June 1944 – simultaneous with D-Day – to 15 August, due to a shortage of landing craft. On that date US Seventh Army made landings between Toulon and Cannes. Ninety-four thousand men and 11,000 vehicles came ashore with fewer than 200 casualties: all of southern France was defended by only eight German divisions. The French II Corps, under General de Lattre de Tassigny, then advanced toward Toulon and Marseilles, while US elements closed in on the German Nineteenth Army, taking 15,000 prisoners. De Lattre captured both his objectives, and US Lieutenant General Alexander Patch fought his way up the Rhône Valley to make contact with Patton's Third Army on 12 September. The newly formed French First Army then combined with US Seventh to form the US 6 Army Group under Lieutenant General Jacob Devers to drive into Germany on the right of the Allied line.

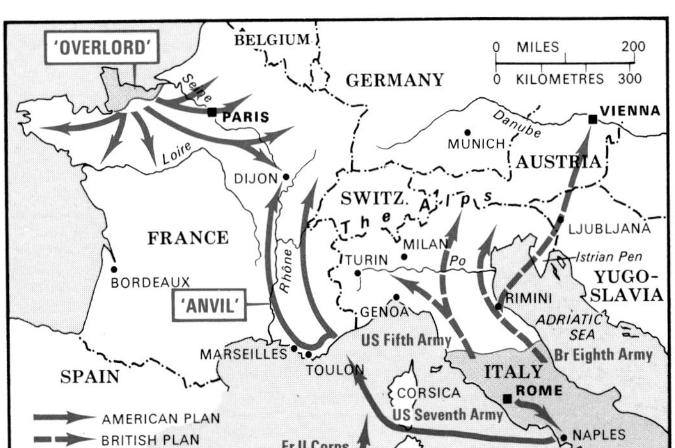

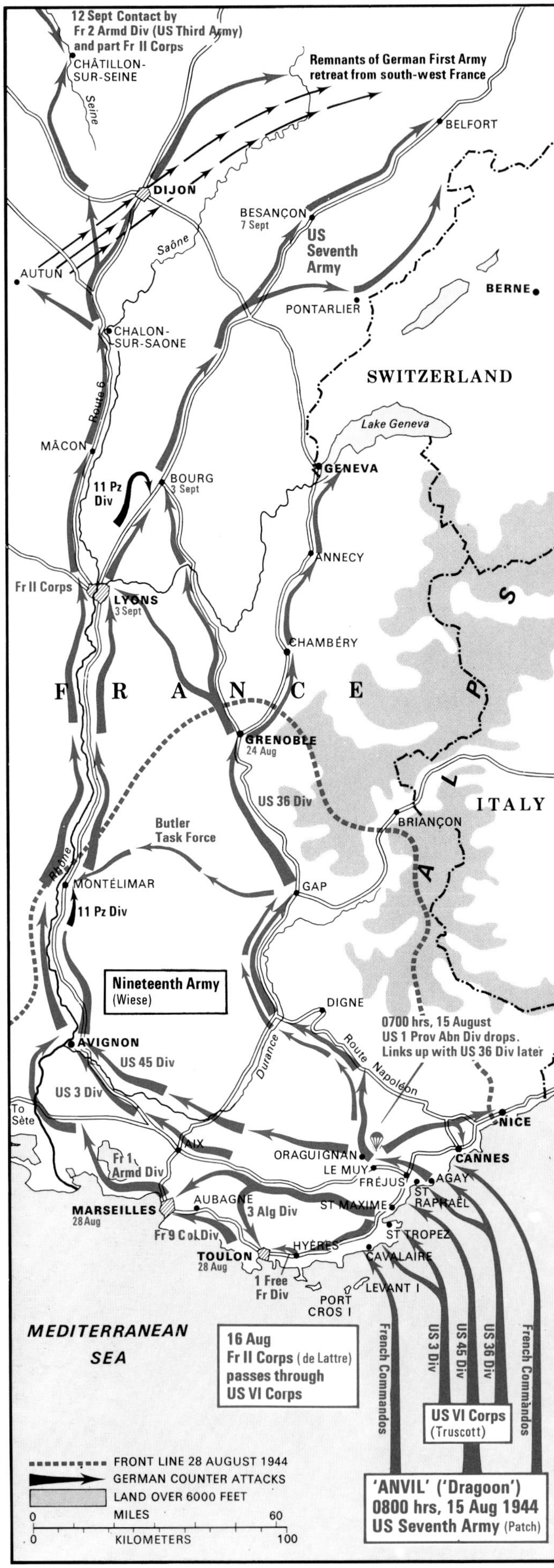

The Allied Breakout from Normandy

It took over half the summer for Allied forces to extend their initial beachheads well into Normandy, where Rommel had been reinforced from the south of France. Montgomery adhered to his original campaign plan and made slow but steady progress (although not enough to satisfy his critics, who were numerous). By 27 July (D+50), the Cotentin Peninsula was in Allied hands. Patton's US Third Army broke through the Avranches gap into Brittany and central France, and US, British and Canadian Forces attacked south and east in early August.

Hitler responded with orders for immediate counterattacks, which failed to contain the Allied advance. Both von Rundstedt and Rommel had been replaced in early July, and their successor, von Kluge, was pulled out on 25 August after four Allied armies pursued him to the Seine crossings. Patton's armor reached the Seine at Fontainbleu on the same day that US and Canadian forces closed the gap at Falaise, cutting off the escape of German Seventh and Fifth Panzer Armies. By this time, 10,000 German soldiers had died and 50,000 more had been taken prisoner.

The US XV Corps established a bridgehead downstream of Paris as soon as it reached the Seine, and five days later, on 25 August, the French capital was liberated. Kluge had succeeded in salvaging much of Army Group B, but his command was turned over to General Model by way of thanks.

Opposite bottom: Anvil, Overlord and the British plan over which they prevailed.
Left: US troops drive the Germans from southern France.
Below: Patton's Third Army pours through the Avranches Gap and sweeps south toward the Loire.
Inset: Pursuit and defeat of German forces at the Atlantic coast.

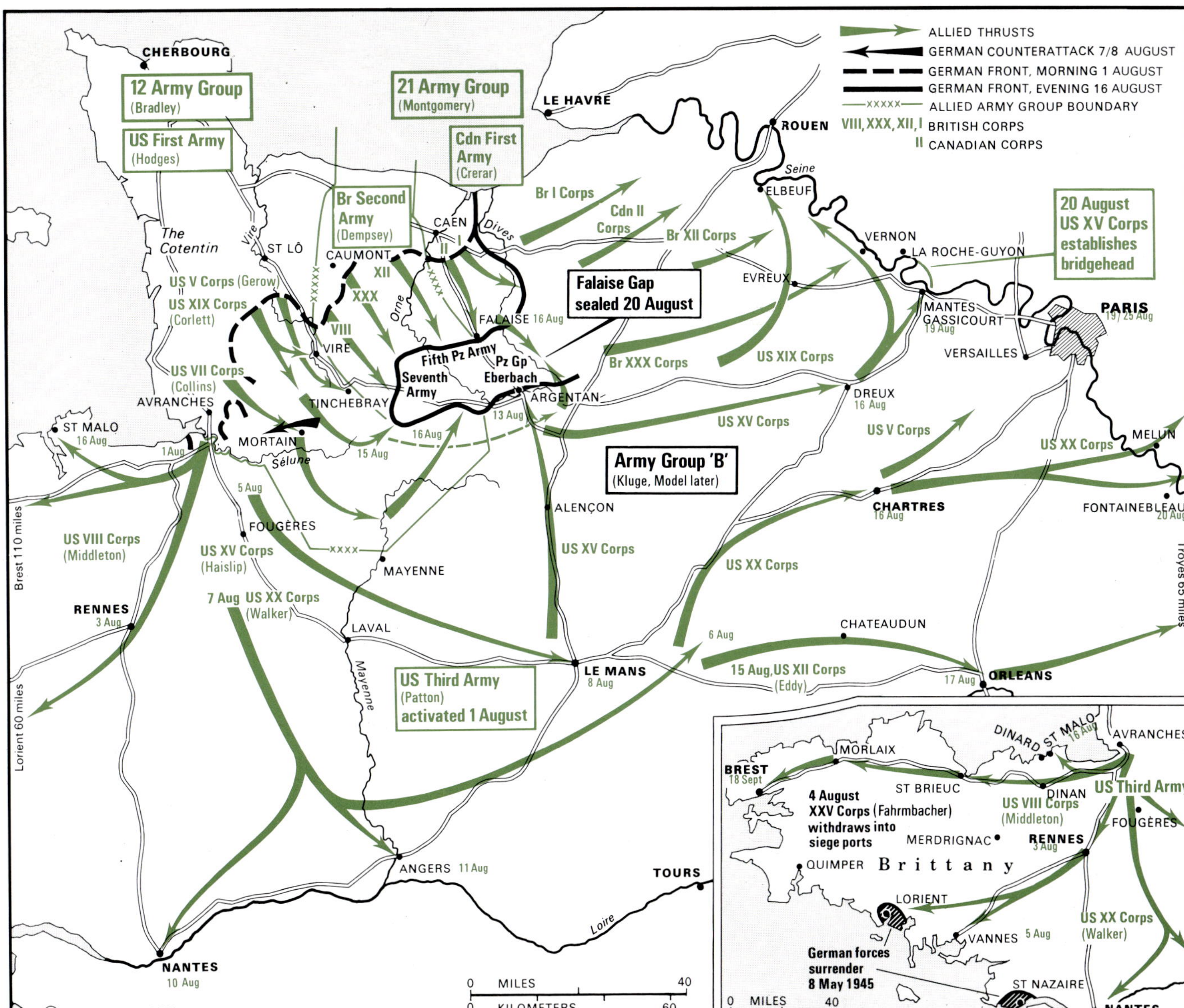

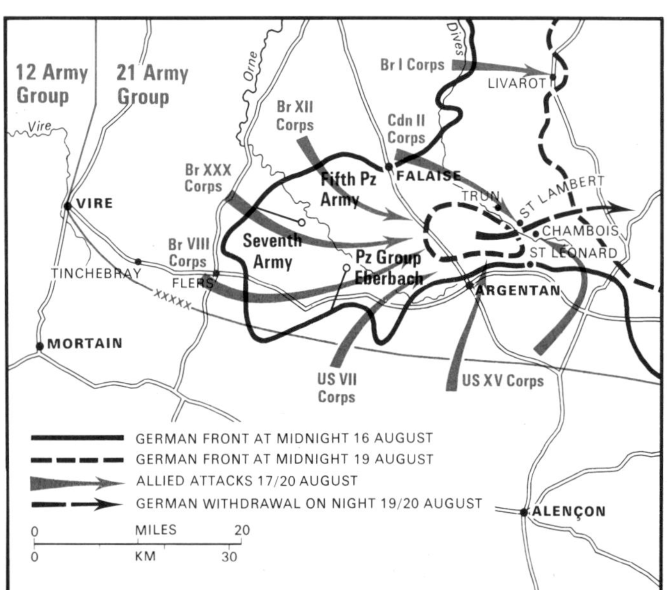

Above: US armor crosses the Siegfried Line en route for Germany.
Left: The escape route for the Fifth and Seventh German armies ended at Falaise.
Above right: Reclaiming France and the Low Countries, summer 1944.
Right: German soldiers pictured on the long march to captivity.

Advance to Antwerp

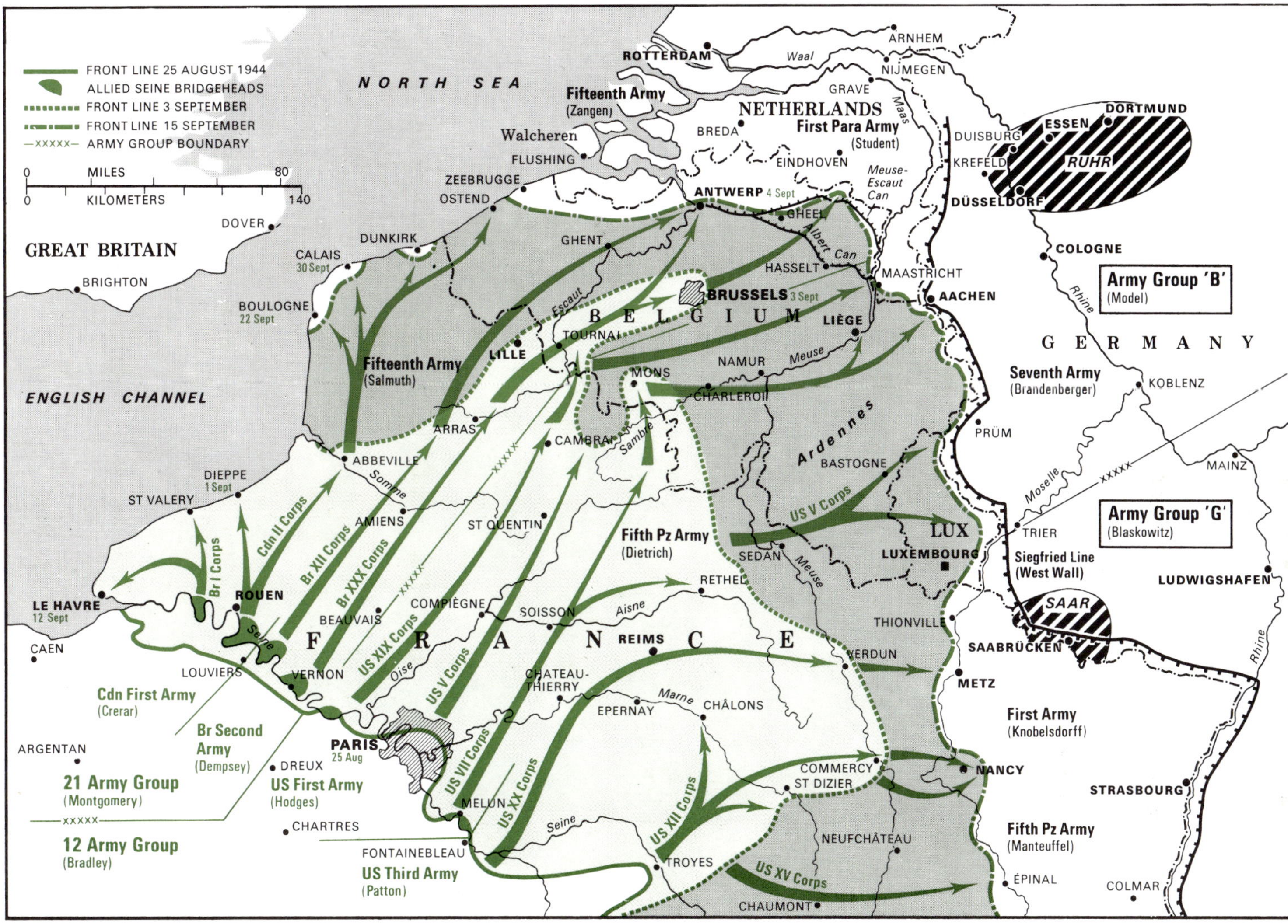

The remarkable achievement of Allied operations in Normandy should have been followed up, according to Montgomery and other strategists, by a narrow-front thrust into Germany to end the war in 1944. Eisenhower, who assumed direct control of ground forces in September as a function of supreme command, favored a slow advance in line by all Allied forces. The critical issue in August 1944 was that of supply: the logistics of providing food, fuel and other necessities to four Allied armies now 300 miles from the Normandy coast had become unworkable. A port was needed desperately.

Montgomery, Bradley and other narrow-front proponents argued for supplying part of the Allied force abundantly and sending it through Belgium to encircle the Ruhr and advance on Berlin at top speed. Eisenhower held out for a more cautious advance that did not underestimate the power of German armies still in the field despite their losses – 700,000 men since D-Day. There was far less risk in this approach, both strategically and politically. The disadvantage was in dragging out the war until 1945, which meant that the Russians would have time to establish their armies far west of their borders.

The Canadian First Army seized several small French Channel ports, and on 4 September the Allies captured the large port of Antwerp with its facilities almost intact. But failure to consolidate their grip on this valuable harbor immediately resulted in loss of control of the Scheldt Estuary, its seaward approach, to the Germans.

Arnhem and the Drive to the Rhine

Below: The Allies advance.
Bottom: The two tactical alternatives – a strong thrust (left) and the more cautious advance actually adopted (right).
Right: Operation Market Garden, mounted against four key river bridges.
Far right: British airborne forces ran into trouble at Arnhem.
Below right: US troops bridge the Rhine.

Once Belgium was liberated, the Allies sought to secure a continuous northernward advance by capturing a series of four bridges at key canal and river crossings. This would create a corridor through the Netherlands for a swing around the northern end of Germany's West Wall defenses (which were by no means as strong as the Allies supposed). Montgomery planned to drop three airborne divisions near the bridges at Veghel, Grave, Nijmegen and Arnhem in an operation that was hastily assembled under the code name of 'Market Garden.'

The 17 September landings at Veghel and Grave by US 101 and 82 Airborne Divisions were successful, and British XXX Corps linked up with these forces the following day. They captured the bridge at Nijmegen on 20 September, but were unable to make further progress. At Arnhem, British 1 Airborne Division was in desperate straits as a result of landing too far from the bridge in a strongly defended area. Only one battalion reached the objective, where it was immediately cut off, and the rest of the division was surrounded. Only 2200 survivors made it back to British lines; 7000 others remained behind to be killed, wounded or captured.

The port of Antwerp was still useless to the Allies on account of German forces in the Scheldt Estuary, which was not cleared until early November. Then Bradley's 12 Army Group was enlarged by the arrival of the US Ninth Army, and 6 Army Group pushed through the Vosges Mountains to the German border. By 15 December 1944, the Allies were poised to cross the Rhine.

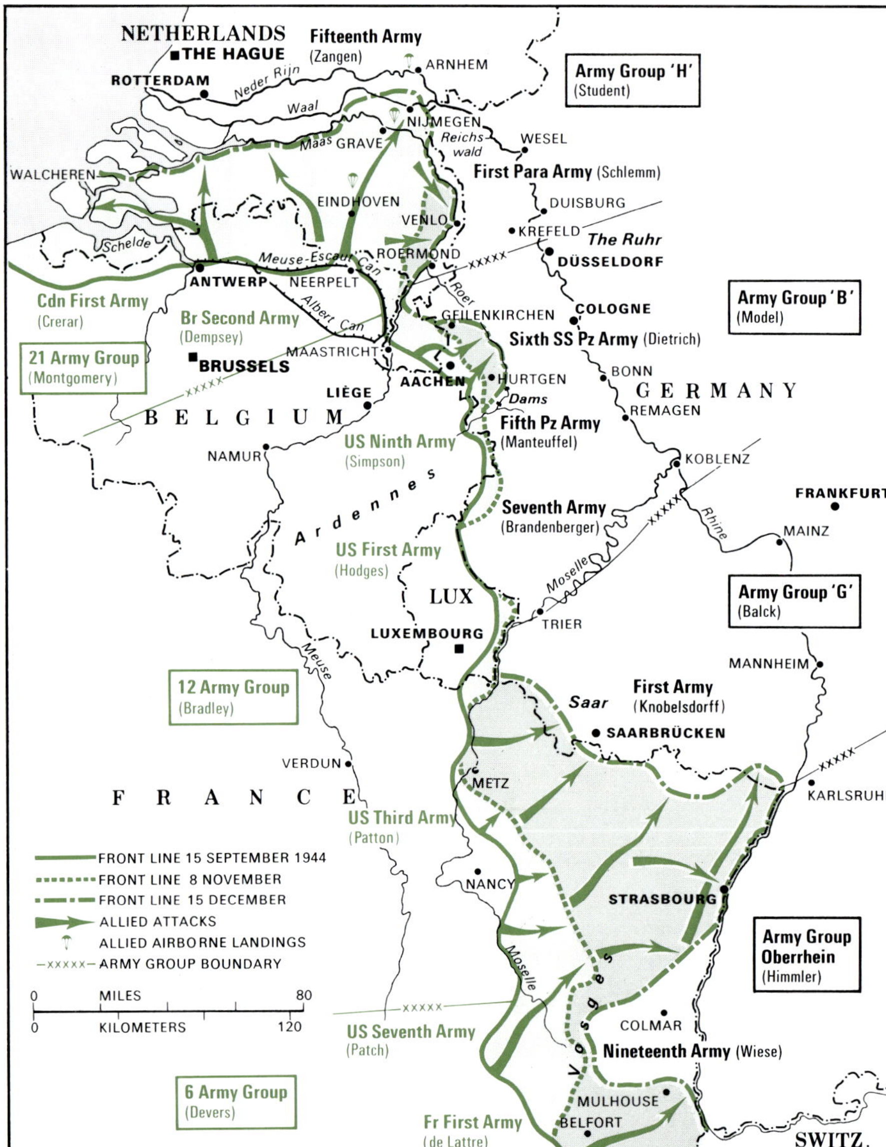

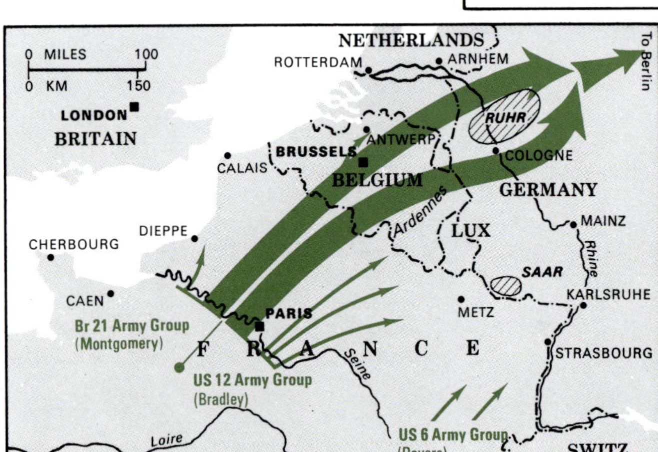

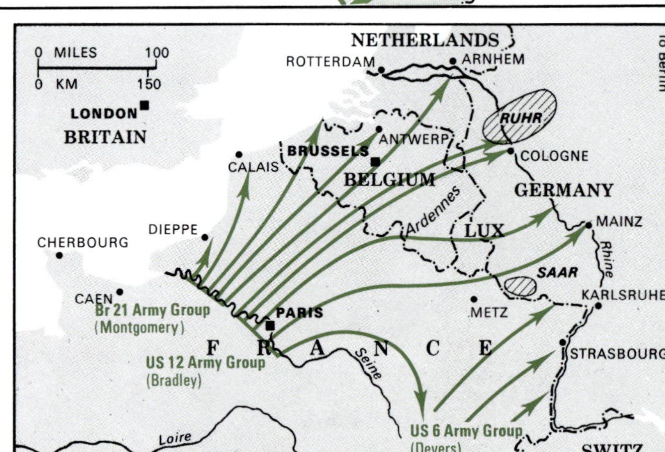

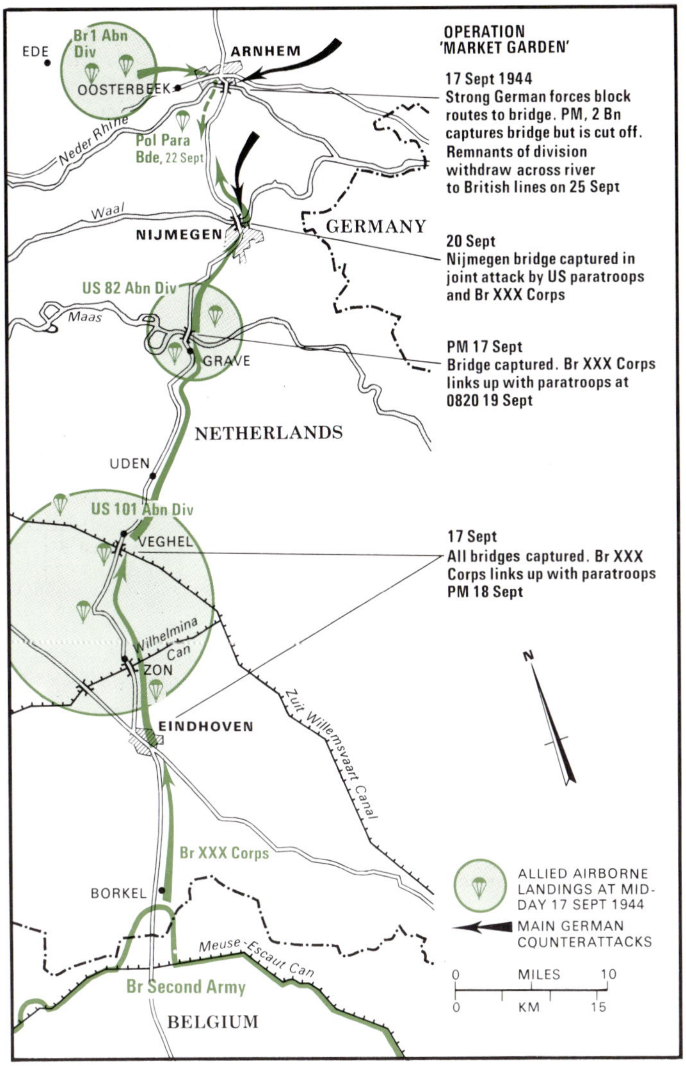
OPERATION
'MARKET GARDEN'
17 Sept 1944
Strong German forces block routes to bridge. PM, 2 Bn captures bridge but is cut off. Remnants of division withdraw across river to British lines on 25 Sept
20 Sept
Nijmegen bridge captured in joint attack by US paratroops and Br XXX Corps
PM 17 Sept
Bridge captured. Br XXX Corps links up with paratroops at 0820 19 Sept
17 Sept
All bridges captured. Br XXX Corps links up with paratroops PM 18 Sept
Br 1 Abn Div
EDE
ARNHEM
OOSTERBEEK
Neder Rhine
Pol Para Bde, 22 Sept
Waal
NIJMEGEN
GERMANY
US 82 Abn Div
Maas
GRAVE
NETHERLANDS
UDEN
US 101 Abn Div
VEGHEL
Wilhelmina Can
ZON
EINDHOVEN
Zuit Willemsvaart Canal
N
Br XXX Corps
BORKEL
Meuse-Escaut Can
Br Second Army
BELGIUM
ALLIED AIRBORNE LANDINGS AT MID-DAY 17 SEPT 1944
MAIN GERMAN COUNTERATTACKS
0 MILES 10
0 KM 15

Germany's Last Throw: The Battle of the Bulge

As they prepared to cross the Rhine into Germany, the Allies discounted any possibility that the Germans would launch a last-ditch offensive. In fact, Hitler had scraped together his last reserves and ordered them to break through the Allied front in the Ardennes, split US and British forces, and drive on to Antwerp to cut off Allied supplies. Twenty-four German divisions, 10 of them armored, were involved in this bold offensive, which came dangerously close to succeeding.

Since they lacked air cover, the Germans were fortunate that low cloud and a heavy snowfall concealed their movements through the Ardennes. On 16 December eight Panzer Divisions appeared seemingly from nowhere to fall upon the US VIII Corps in the first encounter of a six-week struggle. The British would call it the Battle of the Ardennes, the Americans the Battle of the Bulge.

German tactical surprise was complete, and additional confusion spread through the US lines when English-speaking German soldiers in Allied uniforms (carefully coached in American slang) made their presence known. Eisenhower was forced to commit his reserves to the bulge in his line, including airborne divisions that were still resting from Operation Market Garden. The US 101 Airborne Division arrived in Bastogne only to be trapped on 20 December, as German forces prepared to head for the Meuse.

Then the Allies rallied to mount a concerted attack on the German salient by Hodges' US First Army and Patton's Third Army. Montgomery took charge of all Allied units north of the bulge, and Bradley assumed command in the south. By Christmas Eve, the Ardennes Offensive was grinding to a halt for lack of fuel. The Germans were unable to overrun Allied fuel dumps, and stiffening opposition completed their undoing. The last

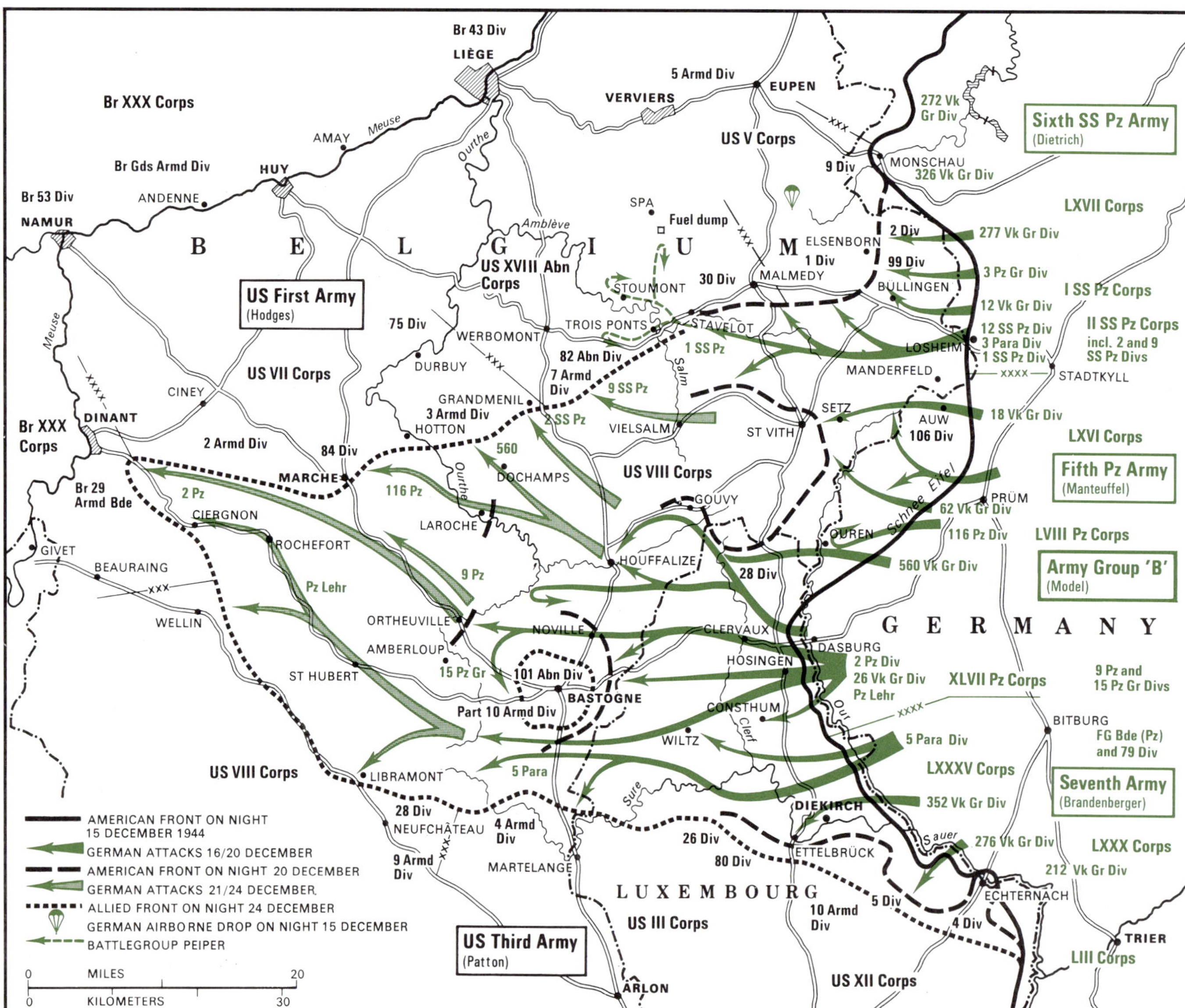

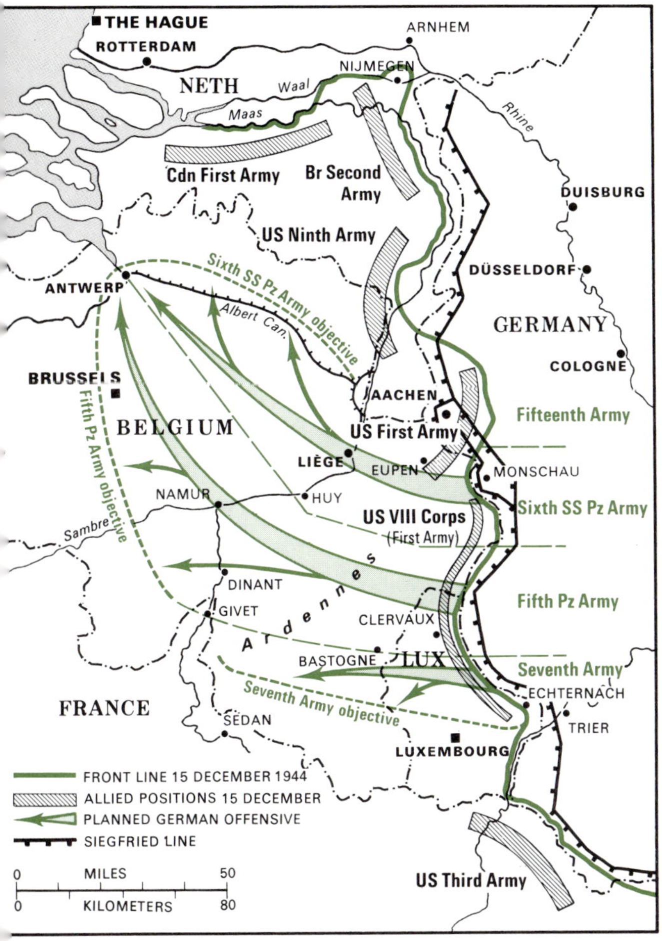

major Luftwaffe effort of the war, against airfields in France, Belgium and Holland, had no effect on the punishing aerial attacks that supported Allied ground forces in the Ardennes.

Hitler's gamble had failed long before 7 February 1945, when the salient was finally eliminated. With it went the last German forces that might have stopped the Russian onslaught now preparing to fall upon the German homeland.

Above: Hitler's plan to split the British and US forces by making for Antwerp.
Left: The Panzers break out into the Ardennes.
Above right: An Allied supply line rolls through Bastogne in January 1945 after its relief.
Right: Bastogne under siege in December 1944; the US 101st Airborne Division defends the perimeter.

Crossing the Rhine

Below: A US Army half-track guards against air attack at Remagen, a key Rhine crossing-point captured on 7 March.
Bottom: German prisoners taken in the drive to the Rhine east of the Roer river, February 1945.
Right: Crossing the Rhine.

The Rhine River was the greatest water obstacle in Western Europe, and no Allied leader expected to cross it with impunity. Not until early March 1945 were sufficient forces in place to attempt the capture of a vital bridge. This was achieved on 7 March in a brilliant stroke by men of Hodges' US First Army, who seized the Ludendorff railroad bridge at Remagen intact, then established a bridgehead with bewildering speed. Valuable as this was, additional crossings had to be secured both up- and downstream of Remagen before it could be exploited.

On 22 March, US Third Army made a second crossing at Nierstein, soon followed by others at points from Nijmegen to Mannheim. Wiesbaden was captured on 27 March; the day before, US Seventh Army had crossed near Worms to link up with Patton's Third Army on the east bank. From 31 March onward, the French First Army began to force crossings south of Mannheim, and within a week's time the Germans had lost all their positions on the Rhine's east bank.

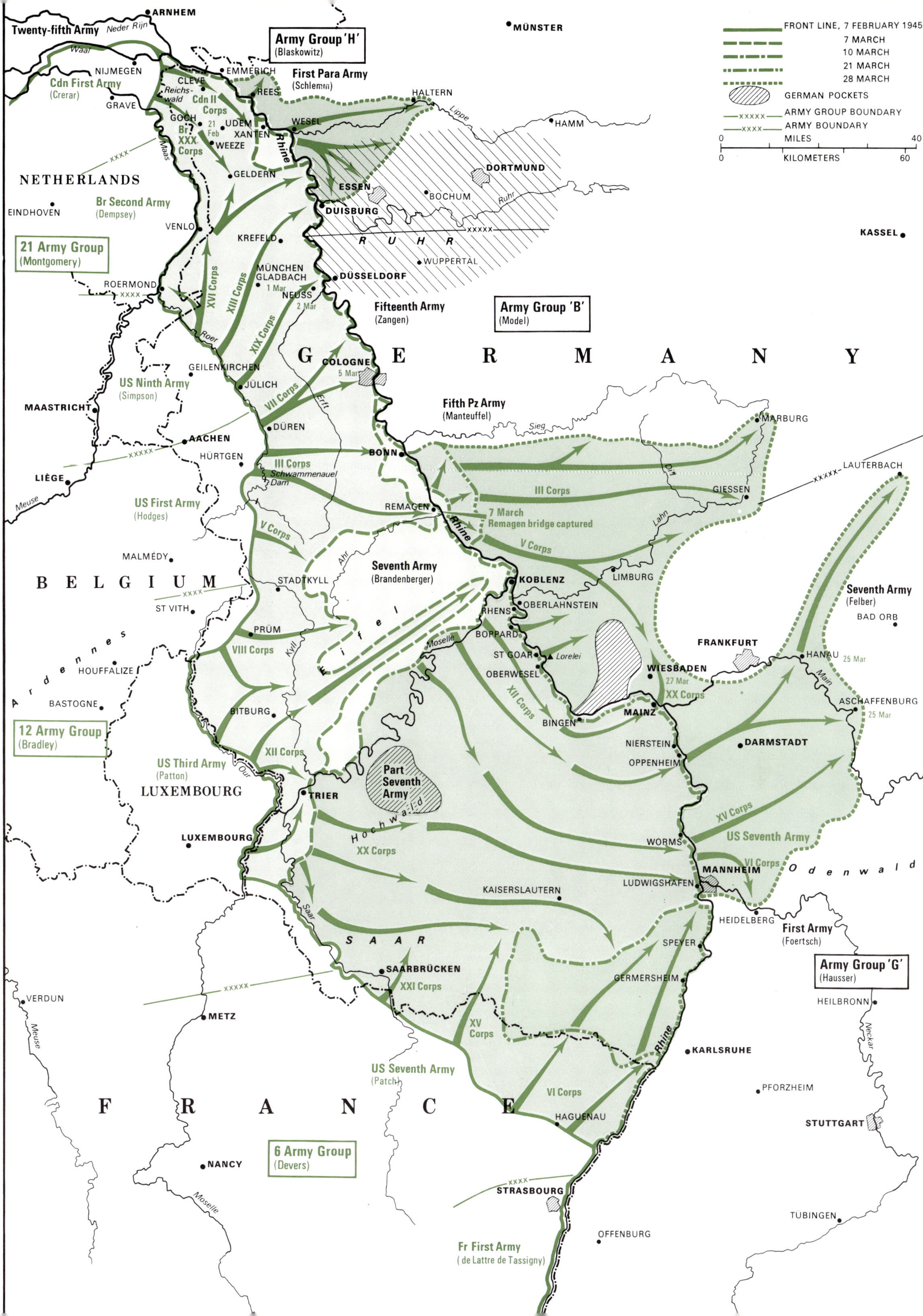

FRONT LINE, 7 FEBRUARY 1945
7 MARCH
10 MARCH
21 MARCH
28 MARCH
GERMAN POCKETS
ARMY GROUP BOUNDARY
ARMY BOUNDARY
MILES
KILOMETERS
Army Group 'H' (Blaskowitz)
Twenty-fifth Army
First Para Army (Schlemm)
Cdn First Army (Crerar)
Cdn II Corps
Br XXX Corps
Br Second Army (Dempsey)
21 Army Group (Montgomery)
XVI Corps
XIII Corps
XIX Corps
VII Corps
US Ninth Army (Simpson)
Fifteenth Army (Zangen)
Army Group 'B' (Model)
Fifth Pz Army (Manteuffel)
III Corps
US First Army (Hodges)
7 March Remagen bridge captured
V Corps
Seventh Army (Brandenberger)
VIII Corps
XII Corps
12 Army Group (Bradley)
US Third Army (Patton)
Part Seventh Army
XX Corps
XII Corps
XX Corps
XV Corps
US Seventh Army
VI Corps
Seventh Army (Felber)
First Army (Foertsch)
Army Group 'G' (Hausser)
XXI Corps
XV Corps
US Seventh Army (Patch)
VI Corps
6 Army Group (Devers)
Fr First Army (de Lattre de Tassigny)
NETHERLANDS
BELGIUM
LUXEMBOURG
FRANCE
GERMANY
RUHR
Eifel
Ardennes
Hochwald
SAAR
Odenwald
Reichswald
Rhine
Maas
Meuse
Roer
Erft
Ahr
Kyll
Moselle
Our
Saar
Lippe
Ruhr
Sieg
Dill
Lahn
Main
Neckar
Waal
Neder Rijn
Lorelei
Schwammenauel Dam
ARNHEM
NIJMEGEN
GRAVE
CLEVE
EMMERICH
REES
GOCH
UDEM
XANTEN
WEEZE
WESEL
HALTERN
MÜNSTER
HAMM
DORTMUND
ESSEN
BOCHUM
DUISBURG
GELDERN
EINDHOVEN
VENLO
KREFELD
WUPPERTAL
KASSEL
ROERMOND
MÜNCHEN GLADBACH
1 Mar
NEUSS
2 Mar
DÜSSELDORF
21 Feb
GEILENKIRCHEN
COLOGNE
5 Mar
JÜLICH
MAASTRICHT
DÜREN
AACHEN
HÜRTGEN
LIÈGE
BONN
MARBURG
LAUTERBACH
GIESSEN
REMAGEN
MALMÉDY
STADTKYLL
KOBLENZ
LIMBURG
ST VITH
RHENS
OBERLAHNSTEIN
BOPPARD
ST GOAR
OBERWESEL
PRÜM
HOUFFALIZE
BASTOGNE
BITBURG
FRANKFURT
BAD ORB
HANAU
25 Mar
WIESBADEN
27 Mar
XX Corps
MAINZ
BINGEN
ASCHAFFENBURG
25 Mar
NIERSTEIN
OPPENHEIM
DARMSTADT
TRIER
LUXEMBOURG
WORMS
MANNHEIM
LUDWIGSHAFEN
KAISERSLAUTERN
HEIDELBERG
SPEYER
SAARBRÜCKEN
GERMERSHEIM
HEILBRONN
VERDUN
METZ
KARLSRUHE
PFORZHEIM
HAGUENAU
STUTTGART
NANCY
STRASBOURG
TUBINGEN
OFFENBURG

The Drive into Germany

Below: German anti-aircraft artillery claims a direct hit on a US B-26 attacking road and rail targets in support of Allied ground troops.
Right: The Allied drive into Germany halted at the Elbe.

The Allied advance through Germany from the Rhine to the Elbe met bitter opposition at several points where determined German leaders still commanded veteran troops. But for the most part, resistance was minimal; German units lacked food, fuel, ammunition and leadership by this time, and many welcomed the opportunity to surrender to the Americans rather than face the Russians.

Eisenhower had focused most of his attacks in the south, due partly to reports that the Germans would retreat to an 'Alpine Redoubt' whose unspecified location was largely in Hitler's mind. First and Third Armies had crossed the Rhine south of Aachen with unexpected ease, and German communications had broken down almost entirely. There is no doubt that the Allies could have reached both Berlin and Prague in April 1945, but US commitments to the Soviet Union mandated a halt on the Elbe. As the Allied armies advanced through Germany to link up with the Russians, they discovered Belsen, Buchenwald and other camps whose infamies had been rumored but not fully known until that time. Anger against the Nazi régime hardened with every appalling discovery, as films and pictures from the camps began to reach the world.

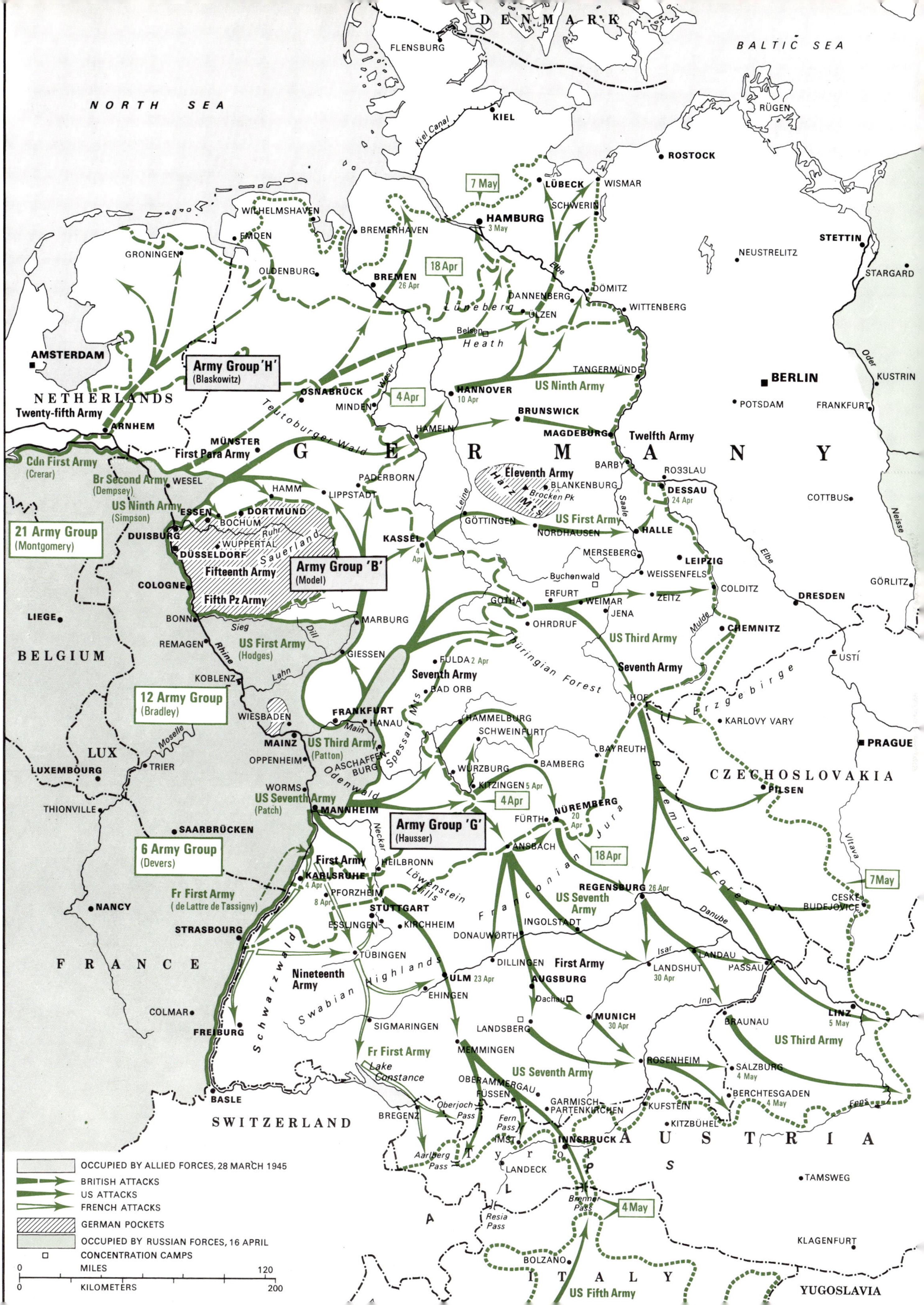
DENMARK
FLENSBURG
BALTIC SEA
NORTH SEA
KIEL
Kiel Canal
RÜGEN
ROSTOCK
7 May
LÜBECK
WISMAR
SCHWERIN
HAMBURG
3 May
WILHELMSHAVEN
BREMERHAVEN
EMDEN
GRONINGEN
OLDENBURG
STETTIN
NEUSTRELITZ
18 Apr
BREMEN
26 Apr
Elbe
STARGARD
DÖMITZ
DANNENBERG
Lüneberg
UELZEN
WITTENBERG
Belsen
Heath
AMSTERDAM
Army Group 'H'
(Blaskowitz)
TANGERMÜNDE
Oder
KUSTRIN
BERLIN
NETHERLANDS
OSNABRÜCK
Weser
4 Apr
HANNOVER
10 Apr
US Ninth Army
Twenty-fifth Army
MINDEN
POTSDAM
FRANKFURT
ARNHEM
Teutoburger Wald
BRUNSWICK
HAMELN
MAGDEBURG
Twelfth Army
MÜNSTER
First Para Army
GERMANY
Cdn First Army
(Crerar)
BARBY
Eleventh Army
ROSSLAU
Br Second Army
(Dempsey)
WESEL
PADERBORN
Harz Mts
BLANKENBURG
Brocken Pk
HAMM
LIPPSTADT
DESSAU
24 Apr
COTTBUS
US Ninth Army
(Simpson)
ESSEN
DORTMUND
Leine
Saale
BOCHUM
GÖTTINGEN
US First Army
Neisse
21 Army Group
(Montgomery)
DUISBURG
Ruhr
NORDHAUSEN
HALLE
WUPPERTAL
Sauerland
KASSEL
4 Apr
DÜSSELDORF
MERSEBERG
LEIPZIG
Elbe
Fifteenth Army
Army Group 'B'
(Model)
Buchenwald
WEISSENFELS
GÖRLITZ
COLOGNE
ERFURT
COLDITZ
Fifth Pz Army
GOTHA
WEIMAR
ZEITZ
DRESDEN
LIEGE
BONN
MARBURG
JENA
Sieg
Dill
OHRDRUF
Mulde
CHEMNITZ
REMAGEN
US First Army
(Hodges)
US Third Army
BELGIUM
Rhine
GIESSEN
FULDA 2 Apr
Thüringian Forest
USTI
Lahn
Seventh Army
KOBLENZ
Seventh Army
BAD ORB
Erzgebirge
12 Army Group
(Bradley)
HOF
WIESBADEN
FRANKFURT
HANAU
Main
HAMMELBURG
KARLOVY VARY
Spessart Mts
LUX
Moselle
MAINZ
US Third Army
(Patton)
SCHWEINFURT
PRAGUE
BAYREUTH
LUXEMBOURG
TRIER
OPPENHEIM
ASCHAFFENBURG
BAMBERG
WÜRZBURG
CZECHOSLOVAKIA
Odenwald
KITZINGEN 5 Apr
WORMS
4 Apr
Bohemian Forest
PILSEN
US Seventh Army
(Patch)
NUREMBERG
THIONVILLE
MANNHEIM
FÜRTH
20 Apr
Jura
Army Group 'G'
(Hausser)
Neckar
SAARBRÜCKEN
ANSBACH
Vltava
6 Army Group
(Devers)
18 Apr
First Army
HEILBRONN
KARLSRUHE
4 Apr
Löwenstein Hills
Franconian
7 May
Fr First Army
(de Lattre de Tassigny)
PFORZHEIM
REGENSBURG 26 Apr
8 Apr
US Seventh Army
NANCY
STUTTGART
CESKE BUDEJOVICE
Danube
KIRCHHEIM
INGOLSTADT
STRASBOURG
ESSLINGEN
DONAUWÖRTH
Isar
TÜBINGEN
LANDAU
FRANCE
Schwarzwald
DILLINGEN
First Army
LANDSHUT
30 Apr
PASSAU
Nineteenth Army
Swabian Highlands
ULM 23 Apr
AUGSBURG
EHINGEN
Dachau
Inn
COLMAR
MUNICH
30 Apr
LINZ
5 May
SIGMARINGEN
BRAUNAU
FREIBURG
LANDSBERG
US Third Army
Fr First Army
MEMMINGEN
Lake Constance
US Seventh Army
ROSENHEIM
SALZBURG
4 May
OBERAMMERGAU
BERCHTESGADEN
4 May
BASLE
FÜSSEN
GARMISCH-PARTENKIRCHEN
KUFSTEIN
Enns
Oberjoch Pass
SWITZERLAND
BREGENZ
KITZBÜHEL
Fern Pass
IMST
INNSBRUCK
AUSTRIA
Aarlberg Pass
Tyrol
LANDECK
ALPS
TAMSWEG
Brenner Pass
4 May
Resia Pass
KLAGENFURT
BOLZANO
ITALY
US Fifth Army
YUGOSLAVIA
OCCUPIED BY ALLIED FORCES, 28 MARCH 1945
BRITISH ATTACKS
US ATTACKS
FRENCH ATTACKS
GERMAN POCKETS
OCCUPIED BY RUSSIAN FORCES, 16 APRIL
CONCENTRATION CAMPS
0
MILES
120
0
KILOMETERS
200

The Fall of Berlin

Below: The victors and the defeated. Soviet troops enter Berlin, May 1945.
Below left: The partition of Berlin.
Bottom: Occupied Germany as it appeared at the war's end.
Right: As Berlin falls, the war in Europe comes to an end.

By mid April 1945, Soviet forces along the Oder were ready to advance on Berlin. Konev's 1 Ukrainian Front and Zhukov's 1 Belorussian Front (some 2,500,000 men) faced a million German defenders in strong positions on the Oder's west bank. The desperate Germans were keenly aware of the consequences should the Russians break through, and they were prepared to fight as never before.

The opening Russian bombardment employed a record-breaking concentration of one gun per 13 feet of front. It was a fitting prelude to one of the most ferocious bouts of the war. Only two small bridgeheads were achieved in the first two days (16-18 April), but deeper penetrations were made in the following 48 hours. By 20 April, German resistance on the Oder was shattered, and five days later the two Russian forces had encircled the city to meet on its west side. It was on the same day, 25 April, that US and Soviet forces made contact on the Elbe at Torgau.

Berlin contained 2,000,000 civilians and a garrison of some 30,000. Its rudimentary defenses were wholly unequal to the forces massed against it, but the city resisted to the last. From 26 April to 2 May, fighting raged in the streets, as the two Russian armies moved in from north and south to meet across the Charlottenberg Chaussee. Before they made contact, the Reichstag fell (30 April), and Hitler died by his own hand, naming Admiral Karl Dönitz as his successor.

On 4 May 1945, General Montgomery accepted Germany's unconditional surrender, and three days later the war in Europe was formally at an end. The victors divided both Germany and Berlin (which was deep in the Soviet sector) into four zones each, to be controlled by the four major Allies. The stage was set for Soviet hegemony in Eastern Europe, the Cold War, emerging nationalism among former subject peoples around the world, and the precarious new balance of power that persists to this day.

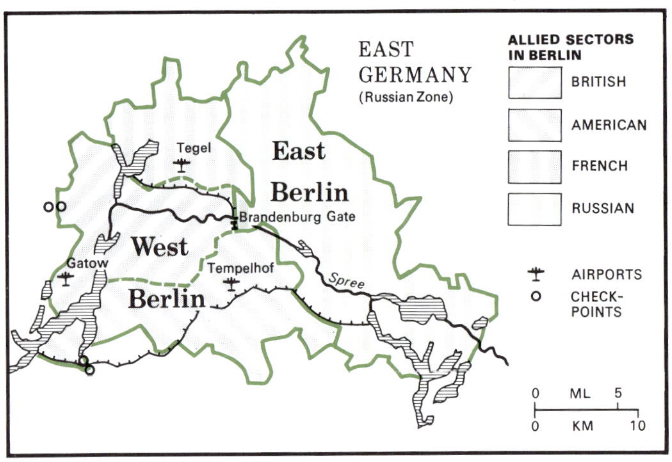

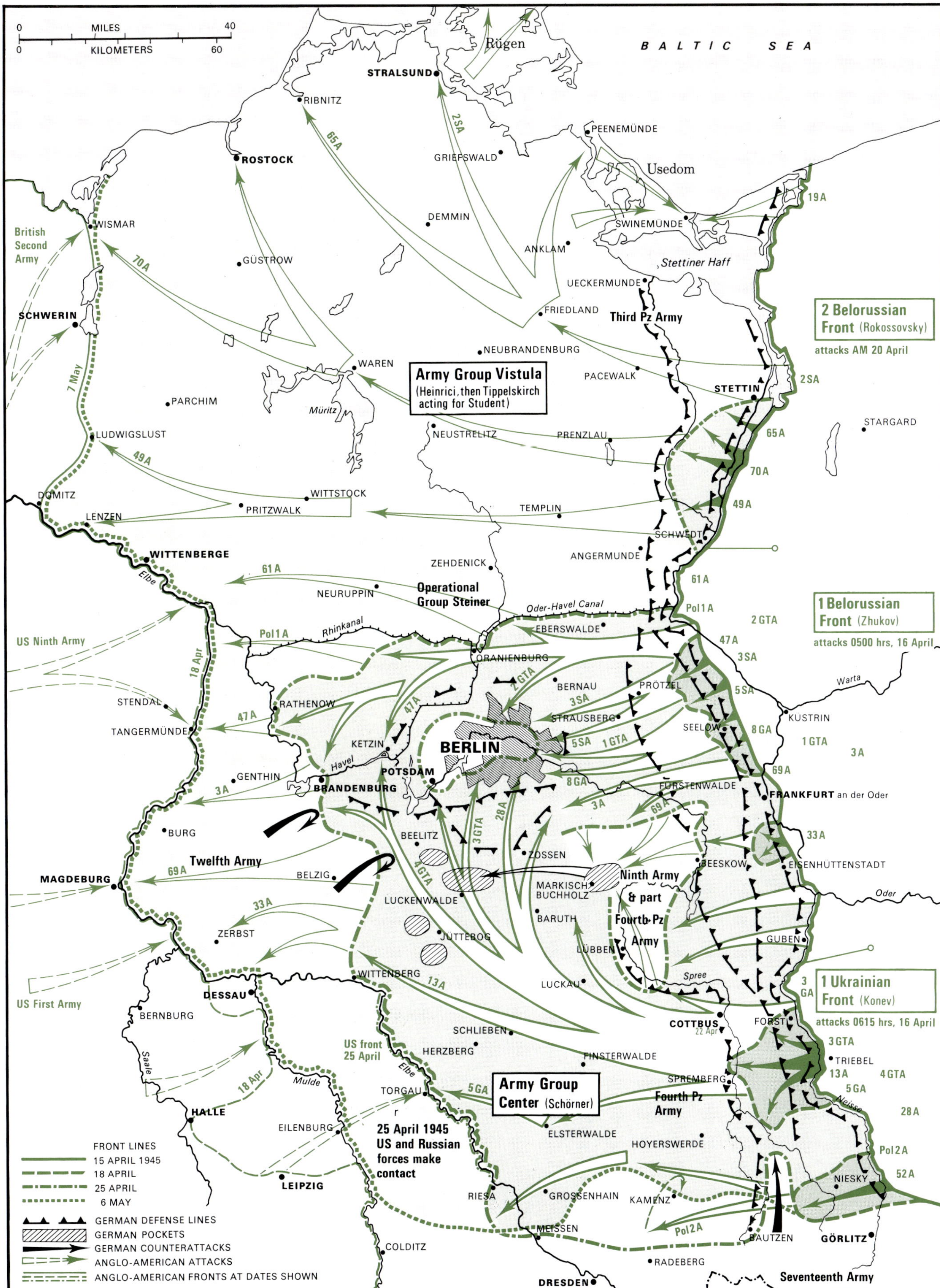

0 MILES 40
0 KILOMETERS 60
BALTIC SEA
Rügen
STRALSUND
RIBNITZ
2SA
65A
PEENEMÜNDE
Usedom
ROSTOCK
GRIEFSWALD
19A
DEMMIN
SWINEMÜNDE
WISMAR
British Second Army
ANKLAM
Stettiner Haff
GÜSTROW
70A
UECKERMÜNDE
2 Belorussian Front (Rokossovsky)
attacks AM 20 April
SCHWERIN
FRIEDLAND
Third Pz Army
NEUBRANDENBURG
WAREN
Army Group Vistula
(Heinrici, then Tippelskirch acting for Student)
PACEWALK
STETTIN
2SA
7 May
PARCHIM
Müritz
STARGARD
LUDWIGSLUST
NEUSTRELITZ
PRENZLAU
65A
49A
70A
DÖMITZ
WITTSTOCK
PRITZWALK
TEMPLIN
49A
LENZEN
SCHWEDT
WITTENBERGE
ANGERMÜNDE
Elbe
61A
ZEHDENICK
61A
NEURUPPIN
Operational Group Steiner
Oder-Havel Canal
Pol 1 A
1 Belorussian Front (Zhukov)
attacks 0500 hrs, 16 April
2 GTA
US Ninth Army
Pol 1 A
Rhinkanal
EBERSWALDE
47A
3SA
ORANIENBURG
18 Apr
2 GTA
BERNAU
Warta
PRÖTZEL
5SA
STENDAL
RATHENOW
3SA
47A
STRAUSBERG
KUSTRIN
47A
TANGERMÜNDE
SEELOW
8GA
KETZIN
BERLIN
5SA
1 GTA
1 GTA
3A
Havel
POTSDAM
69A
GENTHIN
BRANDENBURG
8GA
FÜRSTENWALDE
FRANKFURT an der Oder
3A
3A
69A
28A
3GTA
BURG
BEELITZ
33A
Twelfth Army
ZOSSEN
EISENHÜTTENSTADT
BEESKOW
MAGDEBURG
69A
BELZIG
4GTA
MARKISCH-BUCHHOLZ
Ninth Army
& part
Fourth Pz Army
Oder
LUCKENWALDE
33A
BARUTH
ZERBST
JUTTEBOG
GUBEN
LÜBBEN
Spree
WITTENBERG
13A
1 Ukrainian Front (Konev)
attacks 0615 hrs, 16 April
3 GA
US First Army
LUCKAU
DESSAU
BERNBURG
COTTBUS
22 Apr
FORST
SCHLIEBEN
3GTA
US front 25 April
HERZBERG
TRIEBEL
Saale
FINSTERWALDE
13A
4GTA
Elbe
5GA
18 Apr
Mulde
SPREMBERG
TORGAU
5GA
Army Group Center (Schörner)
Fourth Pz Army
Neisse
28A
HALLE
25 April 1945
US and Russian forces make contact
EILENBURG
ELSTERWALDE
HOYERSWERDE
Pol 2A
52A
LEIPZIG
NIESKY
RIESA
GROSSENHAIN
KAMENZ
MEISSEN
Pol 2A
BAUTZEN
GÖRLITZ
COLDITZ
RADEBERG
DRESDEN
Seventeenth Army
FRONT LINES
15 APRIL 1945
18 APRIL
25 APRIL
6 MAY
GERMAN DEFENSE LINES
GERMAN POCKETS
GERMAN COUNTERATTACKS
ANGLO-AMERICAN ATTACKS
ANGLO-AMERICAN FRONTS AT DATES SHOWN

Index

Index of maps

General Index

Page numbers in italics refer to illustrations

Acknowledgements
The publishers would like to thank Adrian Hodgkins who designed this book and Ron Watson who compiled the index. The following agencies and individuals kindly supplied the photographs.
Bison Picture Library 2-3, 8, 9, 10-11, 17, 20-21, 23, 24 both, 40-41, 42-43, 47, 50-51, 64-65, 72-73, 73, 82, 83, 85 (all), 87, 101, 102, 106-107, 108-109, 112, 116 bottom, 137 right, 141, 153 top, 157, 149, 161, 181 top
Bison/IWM 48
Bundesarchiv 1, 13, 15, 25, 59, 61, 81, 178-179
Crown © 52, 138-139
Imperial War Museum 4-5, 6-7, 26, 28 both, 32-33, 44, 45, 55, 56-57, 57, 58-59, 60, 126 left, 134-135 bottom, 148-149, 155 top, 170-171, 172
Novosti Press Agency 66, 68, 74, 77, 151, 153 bottom, 155 bottom, 160, 162, 163, 165, 166-167, 188
Peter Newark's Historical Pictures 70-71
US Air Force 93, 95, 100 bottom, 115, 116 top, 118, 136, 142, 168, 186
US Army 53, 80, 89, 118, 119, 127, 130-131, 145, 146, 147, 178, 181 bottom, 183 both, 184 both
US Coast Guard 34-35, 132, 175-176, 176
US Marine Corps 125, 133
US National Archives 18, 30, 91, 100 top, 144
US Naval Historical Center 96-97
US Navy 36-37, 78-79, 99, 120-121, 124, 126 right, 128, 129, 134-135 top, 137 left, 173, 175
Dr Diosdado M Yap, Bataan Magazine 104-105, 105